The Conqueror's Tread

The Conqueror's Tread

A Reasoned Approach to Spiritual Warfare

SHANDON L. GUTHRIE

WIPF & STOCK · Eugene, Oregon

THE CONQUEROR'S TREAD
A Reasoned Approach to Spiritual Warfare

Copyright © 2022 Shandon L. Guthrie. All rights reserved. Except for brief quotations in critical publications or reviews, no part of this book may be reproduced in any manner without prior written permission from the publisher. Write: Permissions, Wipf and Stock Publishers, 199 W. 8th Ave., Suite 3, Eugene, OR 97401.

Wipf & Stock
An Imprint of Wipf and Stock Publishers
199 W. 8th Ave., Suite 3
Eugene, OR 97401

www.wipfandstock.com

PAPERBACK ISBN: 978-1-6667-3302-0
HARDCOVER ISBN: 978-1-6667-2726-5
EBOOK ISBN: 978-1-6667-2727-2

01/04/22

Scripture quotations are taken from The Holy Bible, English Standard Version® (ESV®), copyright © 2001 by Crossway, a publishing ministry of Good News Publishers. Used by permission. All rights reserved.

To aspiring conquerors everywhere
"[W]e are more than conquerors through him who loved us"

—Romans 8:37

Contents

Acknowledgments   ix

1. Introduction   1
2. A Prolegomenous Defense of Spiritual Warfare as Conflict   10

PART I | THE THEATER OF WAR

3. The Enemy Triumvirate   19
4. The Satan   25
5. The World   42
6. The Flesh   46
7. The Enemy of My Enemy: God   50
8. Angels: The Good, the Bad, and the Fallen   60

PART II | WARFARE LANGUAGE IN THE BIBLE

9. Biblical Metaphors for Spiritual Warfare   77
10. Metaphors for Attack   83
11. Metaphors for Defense   91
12. Metaphors for Retreat   98
13. Metaphors for Victory   102
14. Miscellaneous Metaphors   106

PART III | SPIRITUAL WARFARE

15. Spiritual Warfare Is Not Mythology   119
16. Spiritual Warfare is not Exorcism   145
17. Spiritual Warfare Is Not Wizardry   172
18. Spiritual Warfare as the Examined Life Worth Defending   193

PART IV | EQUIPPING THE SAINTS

19	Recruit Training: Studying to Show Yourself Approved	221
20	The Warrior Ethos: Holiness in Practical Living	233
21	The Front Line: Apologetics	252
22	Concluding Thoughts	260

Appendix A: Why Does God Allow Spiritual Warfare to Befall Us?	265
Appendix B: Can Satan Read Our Minds?	270
Appendix C: On Territorial Spirits	272
Appendix D: Paranormal Activity and the Occult	281
Bibliography	287
Subject Index	295
Author and Name Index	299

Acknowledgments

THIS BOOK WOULD NOT have been possible if not for the encouragement and support of like-minded colleagues and dear brothers and sisters in the Lord. Based on various conversations I'd had with other philosophers, theologians, and past students of mine, it became apparent to me that a semi-philosophical work on spiritual warfare is needed in today's climate. Combined with the feedback I'd also received from friends, acquaintances, and family members, I was motivated by their expressed interests in my crafting a work that preserves philosophical and theological rigor but is also one suited for the average reader. Everyone with whom I came into contact helped me to realize that this topic is just too important to hide under an academic bushel.

Whatever deficits and inadequacies remain in the book, I must take the blame for those. Indeed, a number of people helped and encouraged me to make this project better than it would have been without their input. A special thanks goes out to Dr. Jonathan King for his thoughtful feedback in reviewing an earlier draft of this manuscript. Unquestionably, this work would have fallen short in terms of composition and content if it had not been for his thoughtful, critical remarks. I have enjoyed our conversations both inside and outside professional conferences, and his own professional pursuit of theological demonology and angelology has helped me to refine and clarify my own views in the process.

I would also like to thank David Tatlock, pastor of The Oasis Church in North Las Vegas, Nevada, for believing in the project at the start. His moral support has been encouraging to me in seeing the importance of such a work for the wider Christian community. In addition, our friend and ministry partner Robert Polk has prayed alongside me in seeing this project to fruition. Both men have helped to keep me grounded as well as focused on the needs of everyday Christians. As close members of the body of Christ, their moral and spiritual support has been invaluable.

And, of course, none of what you hold in your hand would have been possible had it not been for my loving wife, Shelli, and our three children. They provide the best environment in which to write—offering moments of reprieve and laughter when things get too serious. The fact that they celebrate alongside of me the completion of this project encourages me to the core. God has gifted them to me undeservedly as a way to keep me personally grounded and surrounded by the love of God in their mutual love for me.

I count it a privilege to "stand" with my fellow conquerors—my family, friends, and colleagues—"against the schemes of the devil" (Eph 6:11). *Soli Deo Gloria!*

1

Introduction

IN THE LAST BOOK of the Bible, Jesus addresses the church of Laodicea in this offer of hope to those who endure and overcome the end trials that befall them:

> The one who conquers, I will grant him to sit with me on my throne, as I also conquered and sat down with my Father on his throne. He who has an ear, let him hear what the Spirit says to the churches. (Rev 3:12–22)

Being secondarily directed to "[h]e who has an ear" ensures that these words are ultimately intended for a wider audience beyond the named Laodiceans. This includes every believer living today. They reveal that Jesus was a conqueror and that we are to follow in his footsteps—his tread, if you will—as fellow conquerors. While Jesus's conquering is documented for us in the Gospels, what does this conquering look like for the everyday believer?

This language of conquest is undoubtedly linked to the monumental struggle Christians have against adverse forces in a cosmic conflict better known in all quarters as "spiritual warfare." As for what those forces are or what "spiritual warfare" in general means beyond this, the universal church has not been sufficiently clear. Unfortunately, there have arisen too many conflicting voices on the matter ranging from Enlightenment theologians who have closed their eyes to the supernatural to armchair popularizers who wildly pontificate about the extraordinary. Both extremes have the average Christian caught in the middle. It's quite a mess of interpretations today. *How did we get to this point?*

In this introduction, we will explore how this confusion arose in the history of the church and how it became a problem for the modern Christian who wants to understand spiritual warfare. I will then chart out the objectives of this book and how it is set up to resolve the confusions surrounding the nature of spiritual warfare. I'll be sure to offer up a working definition of spiritual warfare before proceeding to the next chapter. So, let us begin at the beginning as to how things got so convoluted when it comes to spiritual warfare.

HOW THE CHURCH GREW TO HAVE CONFLICTING VIEWS ABOUT SPIRITUAL WARFARE

The history of conflicting views about spiritual warfare begins during the early stages of the developing church around the second century. As the church matured past the New Testament, believers saw themselves as conquerors primarily over otherworldly foes—fallen angels and/or demons spearheaded by their chief, Satan. The fact is ancient Jewish and later Christian histories were all filled with audacious supernatural perspectives about the composition of reality. That is, they believed that we are not merely living in a material universe governed by physical laws but that we are also living among real spiritual beings who mean to do us harm. Fortunately, it was also a part of their teachings that we are amidst an aggregate of spiritual beings deployed by God himself to protect and minister to us. It was, for those early Jews and Christians, how they construed spiritual warfare. Their conclusion? That all those oppositional beings need to be countered and overwhelmed by the power of God acting through us and around us. The fact that there is yet no final victor means we are still living in that state of spiritual war. So far, this portrait of spiritual warfare may sound familiar and rather uncontroversial.

In subsequent centuries, orthodox Christians for the most part continued to double-down on this supernatural worldview. Medieval art and literature became filled with various supernatural depictions of spiritual warfare so understood. Their work often telegraphed the plight of the Christian as one who forcefully engages demons directly while allying with God and his angelic forces who aid in the cosmic battle. But things eventually reached critical mass. By the sixteenth century, extraordinary stories about making pacts with the devil and magical ways to combat him and his earthly sorcerers emerged. In the century that followed, demons were considered not only capable of various acts of mischief and sorcery but also capable of extravagant feats, including their materializing as human doppelgängers and casting spells on human victims. The conjunction of the atrocities subsequently committed in the name of expelling Satan along with a burgeoning intellectual movement among the pious soon fomented Christians to rethink the nature and powers of the diabolical. The "more reasonable" Christians felt like it was now time to reassess demonology and spiritual warfare and move past such superstitious imprudence.

Concerns about the supernatural looking like ancient mythologies long dispelled led to the eventual philosophical purge of supernaturalism during the so-called Age of Reason around the eighteenth century. In their minds, they were facilitating a more sensible Christianity—one friendly to an ever-increasing scientific worldview. Nevertheless, the orthodox pushed back against this demythologization at the hands of Enlightenment theologians. For, Enlightenment thinkers not only eliminated unnecessary superstitions, but they also eradicated the entire spiritual world. To the faithful, the demythologizing process went too far. It was, in their eyes, the removing of a splinter in a finger by means of amputating the entire arm. Coincidentally, American transcendentalist thinkers and poets not motivated by religion were rebelling against the kind of dry and meaningless world an unbridled secularism was bringing to our consciences.[1] Human life and behavior were being reduced to nothing but matter in motion. Christians lamenting the shift away from supernaturalism along with its deleterious effects cited the intellectual deliverances of David Hume, Immanuel Kant, and G. W. F. Hegel as those primarily responsible for the burgeoning anti-Christian secularism.[2] And atheists like Jean-Paul Sartre, Friedrich Nietzsche, Arthur Schopenhauer, and Albert Camus agreed that the materialistic world divested of the supernatural left us with a bleak outlook about the ultimate meaning of life.

By the early twentieth century, supernaturalism was about to get its revenge. Pentecostalism was born. The extraordinary was once again becoming the ordinary in Christian circles. The newer literary arts along with new forms of entertainment media (such as movies and television programs) were fast becoming highly influential vehicles for new fanciful stories about spiritual conflict among these supernatural reformers. Christians took it upon themselves to reenchant our perceptions of spiritual warfare through popular media and literary storytelling. Enlightenment thinkers pushed back from their ivory towers while enchantment thinkers continued to resist from the grassroots. Such division of thought was due not only to

---

1. MacKinnon, *American Philosophy*, ch. 3.
2. MacGregor, *Contemporary Theology*.

theological and scriptural differences, but it was also, if not primarily, due to prior philosophical commitments. The perception of these new rebels was that metaphysical naturalism (the view that the physical universe is a closed system and there is no transcendent reality like God) tended to be too prohibitive since it denied the existence of any spiritual realities whatsoever, and metaphysical supernaturalism tended to be too permissive since it lacked any clear boundaries about what spiritual realities can do.

Unless the average reader takes the time to survey and evaluate these philosophical commitments that give rise to the mutually exclusive approaches, there will be no clear winner in their eyes about what to believe regarding spiritual warfare. There is, however, something we can do about it.

WHAT CAN BE DONE

We ought not to limit our information about spiritual warfare to the musings of our favorite teachers on the radio or on the internet. We're going to have to think for ourselves. We're going to have to think about these matters *reasonably* as well as *biblically*. We will thus need both theology *and* philosophy—something that has not really been done in any discussion about spiritual warfare to date. Taking both disciplines into account in discussing spiritual warfare will, I think, provide us a sensible and winning strategy— one that demands neither that we abandon the reality of the supernatural nor avoid the limits of what we are entitled to believe based on the evidence. In attempting to do just that, this book will make a case from both Scripture and reason for a general and practical model of spiritual warfare that I think best accords with the totality of the data—scriptural, theological, and philosophical. And, as I hope to show, one does not need to be a specialist in any of these fields to appreciate how this can be done.

WHY ANOTHER BOOK ON SPIRITUAL WARFARE?

Modern readers will find that most popular-level books devoted to the subject of spiritual warfare are filled with depictions of Christians boldly confronting oppressive forces. But such portraits end up sounding more like the fictional blood-soaked skirmishes in J. R. R. Tolkien's *The Lord of the Rings* than the virtue-building conflicts of John Bunyan's *The Pilgrim's Progress*. Up until the turn of the new millennium, most contemporary Christians had in their memories the works of the Christian novelist Frank Peretti. In his most notable, fictional adventures of the Christian walk—*This Present Darkness* (Kingsway, 1986) and its sequel, *Piercing the*

Darkness (Turtleback, 1989)—readers were brought on a journey to a fictional town where they were treated to a dramatic unveiling of the spiritual realm. Within this realm, combative interactions between angels and demons ensued, being described in rather sensational ways. Audiences were titillated and runaway speculation about spiritual warfare began to take over all teaching and discourse on the subject. Peretti's works, contrary to his intentions, thus became the *de facto* canon for mostly Protestant pastors regarding what spiritual warfare involves (much like how William Blatty's *The Exorcist* became the standard framework for what demonic possessions and exorcisms supposedly look like).

Alas! Christians in all positions of leadership have, by and large, unconsciously adopted the new canons of spiritual warfare. The laity seem to take it as fact that spiritual beings act in the extraordinary ways depicted because metaphysical naturalism is surely false—as if polarizing extremes are the only options on the table. While I am not one to disparage works of Christian fiction for their entertainment value, much of the theology and philosophy that inform popular concepts like spiritual warfare are justifiably open to criticism. As a philosopher and a Christian interested in the subject, and one who has researched and written scholarly works on the subjects of angelology and demonology in academia,[3] I aim to provide a critical but readable approach to the notion of spiritual warfare as taught in Scripture. I want to argue for a more sensible compromise that avoids radical and even semi-radical notions that exceed the bounds of Scripture and reason. But I want to do more than that. I also want to offer some practical tips on how the Christian can enhance her conquering posture in rebuffing those forces that seek to inhibit—indeed destroy—our Christian walk.

Therefore, this book comes at a time when it is crucial for Christians to understand precisely what is at stake, why matters are the way they are, and how we are to engage the conflict in order to achieve victory. Though we will be filling out the details of what spiritual warfare is and contrasting that with what it is not over the course of the book, we should consider an initial summary understanding about it right up front—a sort of working definition that attempts to avoid early controversy. Since not everyone thinks that there even *is* a spiritual warfare, regardless of whether demons exist or not, I will address and critique that in the next chapter. In the chapters that follow that one, we will explore what Scripture has to say on the subject followed by a critical analysis of competing views. I will offer up a systematized framework of my own, not because it is a new one *per se*, but

---

3. E.g., Guthrie, "New Metaphysics for Christian Demonology"; Guthrie, "Warfare Theodicy"; Guthrie, *Gods of This World*; Guthrie, "Angels, Early Theories."

because it is new in how it implements a philosophical approach to what already seems evident in Scripture. I will help myself to the tools of biblical exegesis as well as my training in philosophy in constructing a full-orbed portrait of spiritual warfare.

So, on to the preliminary question: What is spiritual warfare?

DEFINING SPIRITUAL WARFARE

The Christian is often told that she is amidst a war over her very soul. The alleged declarations of Scripture of active warfare suppose that there is a resistive force with the possibility that we could fail to overcome it. Of course, it is also possible that we could be victorious—something that Christ and his apostles have equipped us for. That a vigilant Jesus-follower could lose makes the matter look rather paradoxical in Scripture. For, we are not only assured of such spiritual resistance, but we are also assured of our security in the Christian walk: that "neither death nor life, nor angels nor rulers, nor things present nor things to come, nor powers, nor height nor depth, nor anything else in all creation, will be able to separate us from the love of God in Christ Jesus our Lord" (Rom 8:38–39). This is not a self-contradictory portrait. Rather, readers are to understand that our security in Christ is simply not as automatic as one might assume. We are not mere pawns playing in God's cosmic chess match against Satan. We are active participants who freely call on the name of the Lord (or not). As beings who must resist enemy combatants, one side has yet to win and the other has yet to yield. However, at the same time, we are assured of victory through our Lord Jesus Christ (1 Cor 15:57) but only if we continue to abide in him.

Curiously, the term "spiritual warfare" is not found as is in Scripture. Instead, it is more of a convenient theological nomenclature that is meant to describe what the Bible has to say about adversarial forces operating against God and his creation. It is a military allegory for the manner in which the Christian is in a struggle with an Other. This Other is not some mere obstacle or bump in the road, it is, rather, a vicious, malevolent, oppressive, and deadly set of personal forces that are actively seeking our demise. These are agents acting in tandem with one another and with and through earthly forces toward the same anti-Christian endgame: the dissolution and disintegration of the church. Our only consolation is that these beings, as spiritual agents, have natural and divine limitations that prevent them from any wholesale genocide. And, most importantly, they are not nearly as powerful as God.

That such conflict is "warfare" signals to us that the conflict is a significant, existential, and an ongoing threat to our Christian walk at the hands of opposing forces and powers. That such conflict is "spiritual" is a way to call out the supreme source of that Christian oppression, namely, that it is found in an aggregate of intelligent beings that are not resident members of the physical universe. Like God and his angels, their residence is otherworldly. And yet they are not far from us. We have come to know them as Satan and his demonic cohorts. I offer the following, then, as a working definition of spiritual warfare in going forward:

> *An unrelenting intercommunal conflict (for some reason or other[4]) between two or more rival populations including, among others, human beings and having been inaugurated by members of an otherworldly population.*

The "populations" involved will be spelled out in detail over the course of part I. But to be brief, they involve the communities of God and his good angels, the devil and his evil cohorts (i.e., these "members of an otherworldly population"), and neutral human beings in their various societal constructs (whether agencies, governments, churches, or whatever). It is a struggle because the warring communities are pursuing mutually exclusive destinies. It is "unrelenting" because the struggle has endured throughout all of human history and will continue until the return of our Lord (although one can win battle after battle and continue to be a conqueror). And it is "intercommunal" because it involves interactions between communities belonging, respectively, to the physical world (i.e., human beings) and to those "in the heavenly places" (Eph 6:12).

While this does not capture the entirety of all that is involved in spiritual warfare, it avoids any of the entrapments of any particular model of spiritual warfare on offer. For, as we shall see, some deny the existence of certain communities altogether (i.e., demons) while others just misunderstand the manner of combat to be waged. Nevertheless, the core of what spiritual warfare involves concerns the various struggles Christians, both individually and communally, find themselves in while living lives in obedient devotion to Christ. By being a Christian, one is forsaking any ultimate allegiance to anything other than Christ—including oneself! And such allegiance will be in perpetual tension with other forces vying for that dedication.

Let us now consider how this book will serve to meticulously fill out what spiritual warfare is and is not and what we as Christians need to do to be adequately equipped to endure such conflict.

---

4. There are a variety of reasons why such conflict might ensue. I do not want to presume up front what the conflict entails or why for they vary from circumstance to circumstance. Instead, I mean to zero in specifically on *that* such conflict occurs and with whom.

HOW TO USE THIS BOOK

It is my hope and prayer that this book is accessible to all levels of readership. In other words, I hope that for those unfamiliar with theological and/or philosophical depth will nevertheless benefit from this distilled but rigorous journey into thinking about spiritual warfare. At the same time, I am confident there is enough substance and rigor for even the most seasoned theologian or philosopher. Whether pastor, priest, parishioner, professor, or pedestrian, one will be able to navigate and appreciate and benefit from the material contained herein. And, finally, this book is not only a theoretical work that is *about* concepts and notions of spiritual warfare, but it is a practical work that implements some life applications of what I will argue is at the heart of spiritual warfare. That is, believers will not be left to wonder how to implement the teachings about spiritual warfare on their own. I will offer up some helpful and realistic suggestions and things both ordinary and mature folks can do to combat on the authority of Christ those spiritual forces in high (or is it low?) places.

As such, this book is divided into four parts. Part I talks about the communities of those involved in spiritual warfare: God, the angels, Satan, the demons, the world, and the flesh. Each chapter therein is devoted to a brief but substantive discussion about what these beings are and what we are entitled to know about them as they relate to the larger notion of spiritual warfare. Part II serves as an everyman's commentary on a substantial cross section of biblical passages where spiritual warfare metaphors are used. This is to give readers the fundamentals of what Scripture means when it talks about spiritual "armor" and "weapons" without being influenced by what contemporary authors mean by them. (If nothing else, it serves as a great curriculum for weekly Bible studies.) Part III is mostly about models of spiritual warfare that are dubious or downright false. It begins my argument for what spiritual warfare is against the backdrop of what it is not. And the section culminates in a defense of what spiritual warfare looks like when we take everything we know (including the deliverances of philosophical reflection) into consideration. Part IV consists of chapters on practical advice, including how to live an ethical and intellectually maturing life and what that means. It discusses how anyone can become equipped to be knowledgeable about Scripture and how one can defend the faith and why that's important for Christian living.

This book is essentially building a case for how to think about spiritual warfare reasonably and responsibly even though it will no doubt be an imperfect book on the subject. The stakes are high, for not only are few Christians able to successfully navigate through the conflict due to rampant misinformation, but our very spiritual well-being will be upended and the kingdom of God will stall with us if we do not reverse course and consider what a reasonable and responsible model of spiritual warfare ought to be. I am fully aware of my limitations in that I do not, for example, share in all of the same experiences had by my brothers and sisters residing elsewhere in the world. This is a big world with radically different cultures and perspectives. However, I believe it is an important contribution to a serious conversation few of us are having, namely, a reasonable and unassuming way to navigate through the extreme views of spiritual warfare. These extremities were once famously and eloquently posed by C. S. Lewis nearly six decades ago and bear repeating here:

> There are two equal and opposite errors into which our race can fall about the devils. One is to disbelieve in their existence. The other is to believe, and to feel an excessive and unhealthy interest in them. They themselves are equally pleased with both errors and hail a materialist or a magician with the same delight.[5]

Indeed, no Christian wants to be either overly skeptical or overly fantastical about the world of Satan and his cohorts. However, though cited with much enthusiasm by a number of authors on spiritual warfare, just about everyone thinks they have found the middle ground. Since most of them often pose models that are extravagant and even magical, we must look at where such models have gone wrong and, in their stead, argue for one that suitably fits something closer to what Lewis was hinting at. And the skeptic is also not off the hook. Our current age is filled with too much skepticism about God, angels, demons, and the supernatural worldview of Scripture. But denying that these things exist or relegating them to mere metaphors, allegories, and symbols is to commit the same kind of error as those who champion the more exotic models: falsehood. If the arguments are successful enough, then, despite the cloudiness and misdirection of other well-intentioned Christian authors, we may finally be able to uncover what it means to truly follow in the Conqueror's tread.

It is my hope that in the following pages there are useful discussions about the notion of spiritual warfare that are not only faithful to Scripture but provide clarity and thoughtfulness and end up being beneficial to every reader who desires victory in Christ. While I do not believe that this book is the last word on the subject, nor do I intend it to be, I hope it stimulates further thinking and offers some very useful, practical tips on how to grow in your walk with the Lord Jesus in equipping you to stand your ground against the enemy.

---

5. Lewis, *Screwtape Letters*, ix.

2

A Prolegomenous Defense of Spiritual Warfare as Conflict

HISTORICALLY SPEAKING, PUSHBACK OVER whether spiritual warfare involves personal conflict with supernatural beings is nothing new. But that pushback was generally given by Enlightenment theologians who otherwise dismissed the existence of supernatural beings like angels and demons. However, a less anti-realist criticism has arisen as of late. In their recent work, *Demons and Spirits in Biblical Theology: Reading the Biblical Text in Its Cultural and Literary Context*, John H. Walton and J. Harvey Walton object to the idea that there is an active spiritual conflict between celestial beings and human beings (what they identify as "conflict theology"). And their position is explicitly not motivated by a disbelief in the existence of celestial beings. For them, Satan and his demons *do* exist but are not *adversarial* beings that oppose human beings and/or God. Instead, they are seen as mere agents of chaos and ruination in much the same way that some dangerous and predatory animals are for humans.[1] While there is much to be said by way of criticism,[2] I want to focus here a bit on their objections to spiritual warfare as "conflict theology."

---

1. Walton and Walton, *Demons and Spirits*, 298–99.
2. There is, to be fair, much to be said by way of appraisal too, for they have some excellent things to say about certain Old Testament passages. For example, they have a lot of good insights in their treatments of Deut 32, Job 1–2, Ps 82, and Dan 10. They also serve as a decent counterbalance to the amount of metaphysical stock Michael S. Heiser puts into the mythologies of the wider ancient Near East.

Their first objection is preliminary and aimed primarily at philosophers who use Christian demonology to harmonize the reality of evil and suffering in a world sovereignly created and governed by an all-good, all-powerful God (such harmonization is sometimes called a "theodicy"). There is something philosophically attractive about blaming Satan for the ills of society and for the rampant destructive forces of nature that often lead to harm and premature death in both human and animal alike. If God exists, one can attribute all the evil and harmful aspects of reality to an anti-God—a śāṭān. If good comes your way, it is easily attributable to an all-good God. But if disease or disaster come your way, better to attribute them to Satan rather than to a God who only wants the best for his creatures—or so the story goes. Since human beings have adversity and struggle, it follows that Satan has some amount of influence and power over us. The Waltons complain (and rightly so) that while this approach might offer an answer to the problem of natural evil, it entails a version of Christianity that is "little more than a nominally theistic derivative of secular humanism."[3] Their complaint is rooted in a concern that God's goodness is defined by how well it accords with "human happiness and the value of self-will" as often celebrated by secularists.[4] So, when conflict theologians offer proof texts for spiritual warfare, they allegedly assume this dubious "secularist" notion of God's goodness and ignore the scriptural text-in-context.

I find this to be a rather poor objection for two reasons. First, no advocate of any serious theodicy (that is, any defense of God's justice in the face of existing evils) defines God's goodness as *that which promotes human happiness* and evil as *that which detracts from human happiness*.[5] Evil of any sort has always been understood as a *privation of the good* or *that which is contrary to what God intends*.[6] That there is an occasional intersection between what God intends and the promotion of human happiness is merely incidental.[7] That is, the fact that sometimes doing the right thing *can*—on occasion—lead to some kind of personal reward is not to say that this is how God intends to respond to human virtue in the here and now. John Hick,

---

3. Walton and Walton, *Demons and Spirits*, 279.
4. Walton and Walton, *Demons and Spirits*, 279.
5. I am aware that some authors on the topic of spiritual warfare often do suppose that human happiness in the present life is somehow implied by or consequential to God's goodness (e.g., Schnarr, *Art of Spiritual Warfare*). However, these are not recognized philosophers of religion or theologians writing on theodicy.
6. E.g., Augustine, *Enchiridion*, XXIV.
7. In point of fact, there are many things that are considered "naturally evil" that have no bearing on human happiness at all, such as tornadoes that might ravage unpopulated deserts or dying stars collapsing lightyears from earth.

following the second-century theologian Irenaeus, makes it very clear that "God's purpose was not to construct a paradise whose inhabitants would experience a maximum of pleasure and a minimum of pain."[8] Instead, it is a place where spiritual and moral maturity ensue. And the only way that can happen is if there is a certain amount of evil or adversity that is permitted to obtain. In short, evil is something to be expected within a properly Christian paradigm. Second, the Waltons assume that such supporters of spiritual warfare do so because human free will is so important in "conflict theology" that it needs to be preserved at all costs. The Waltons think that "conflict theologians" are rather Nietzschean, so to speak, in that these theologians allegedly assume that "the free exercise of self-will constitutes the highest good."[9] But this is a serious misunderstanding of theodicies based on free will. The value of free will isn't because it's the highest good; it's because it is considered a necessary condition for *even being a person*. A human being with no free will is no more a person than is a zombie or an animal operating out of instinct.[10] Even if someone's reading of Scripture is solely *motivated* by a Nietzschean need to elevate the significance of free will, it still says nothing about the truth or falsity of the claims made about spiritual warfare that "conflict theologians" might make. It is both a straw man and a red herring.

Moreover, the Waltons ignore the fact that self-proclaimed Protestant Reformers and/or theological Calvinists (i.e., theological determinists) have usually insisted that no creature is free in the relevant, *libertarian* sense. That is, such theologians deny that human beings even have the kind of freedom that allows them to, apart from any constraints, act or refrain from acting. So, *they* would not be motivated to resolve any tension between one's (libertarian) free will and the presence of natural evil since those following the traditions of the Reformation have no problem whatsoever rooting (natural) evil in the actions of God. However, these Reformers are avid supporters of such conflict theology. Spiritual warfare must therefore be assessed on the merits (or demerits) of the arguments or proof texts themselves, not on what may allegedly motivate those arguments or proof texts. So much for the Waltons' argument as it is based on a faulty understanding of God's goodness and the import of human freedom.

The Waltons raise a second argument against the conflict understanding of spiritual warfare. Their argument is loosely based on Augustine's

---

8. Hick, *Philosophy of Religion*, 45–46.

9. Walton and Walton, *Demons and Spirits*, 278.

10. The bald mention of "free will" here need not be understood as *libertarian* free will. One can be open to what kind of free will human beings have while acknowledging that only human beings (in the wider animal kingdom) have it.

reasons for why God himself is not evil, that is, since "there is too much order and too much *function* to account for, that could not be explained if God were evil."[11] The Waltons cite one of the fathers of the church, John Chrysostom, as one who uses this insight to show that demons could not have the kind of power over people and environment that gives rise to "conflict theology":

> This observation of cosmic order is actually one of the strongest arguments *against* conflict theology, as expressed by John Chrysostom[12]: "If God had entrusted the whole of this world to [demons'] authority, they would have confused and disturbed everything. . . . And I would ask this of those who say [that the world is under the authority of demons], what kind of disorder they behold in the present, that they set down all our affairs to the arrangement of demons?"[13]

The Waltons then characterize Chrysostom's argument as implying that "if demons are what conflict theology claims them to be, and have the power that conflict theology requires them to have, the world should be in a much greater state of disorder than it is."

There are two problems here, the first of which involves their use of Chrysostom. When read in context, Chrysostom is not saying what the Waltons attribute to him *at all*. What Chrysostom is pushing back against is the pervasive belief at the time that every evil that happens, including mischief and harassments from demons, does so apart from the governing providence of God. That is, that the evils that happen do so without God having any mitigating control over them. In the run-up to the passage of Chrysostom that the Waltons quote, Chrysostom prefaces his remarks by exemplifying in the life of Job how "a Demon arranges matters when God allows him to use his own power" and that, from this, one can witness the savagery of demons.[14] And before discussing Job, Chrysostom cites the Gerasene demoniac story where the swine are cast over a cliff by demons. He uses this case as an example of how God permits such catastrophes so that others may "learn their wickedness."[15] So, this leads to some important context: When Chrysostom asks what it is one observes that leads them to think that the world's affairs are left "to the arrangement of demons," he means a state of affairs *where God is not in charge*. He is *not* saying, arguing, or

11. Walton and Walton, *Demons and Spirits*, 280.
12. From T. Brandram's translation of *De Diabolo Tentatore* in Chrysostom, "Demons."
13. Walton and Walton, *Demons and Spirits*, 280.
14. Chrysostom, "Demons," 184.
15. Chrysostom, "Demons," 183.

implying that demons do not in fact disturb human affairs at all. He is arguing more modestly against those who "dare to say that Demons administer our affairs"—that is, that demons substantially and providentially control our fate.[16] So, not only is the argument nonexistent in Chrysostom, but he seems to make clear, contrary to the Waltons, that demonic harassments can, do, and have taken place in a world under God's providence.

Nevertheless, there is a substantive problem with the Waltons' argument regardless of whether it belongs to the historical Chrysostom or not. That is, the conclusion that there can be no cosmic conflict does not follow from there being "too much order" and "too much function" in the universe. The argument may do well to establish that *God* is not evil, but it is unclear how it establishes that there is no kind of evil that gives rise to conflict. Consider any "good" country where some form of terrorism is present (particularly those countries whose governments are not aligned with such terrorists in any way). The fact that there are pockets of terror that occasionally erupt does not entail or imply that such an initially designed country will observably be in utter disarray or that its nation will somehow be under the dominion of those terrorists. The presence of (occasional) terrorist acts along with pervasive terrorist and anti-government propaganda is not itself a predictor of the loss of any nationwide order or function. To say otherwise is terribly naïve. Moreover, the presence of "too much" order and function in the universe, regardless of whatever excesses "too much" might refer to, is not incompatible with there being a subdued though very active counterforce of deception and chaos moving against swaths of innocent people. A well-organized and highly refined society that is designed to be so can still suffer from aggressive influences operating from within. And certainly nobody thinks that spiritual warfare is anything quite as disruptive as, say, a nuclear holocaust. So, order and proper function can persevere despite eruptions of conflict; and this means that the presence of conflict is no indicator of the absence of order and proper function.

I have another objection to the Waltons' argument from there being "too much order" and "too much function." It seems to assume that the kind of demonic activity in mind in spiritual warfare is such that *nature itself* would be observably ravaged so as to appear disorderly and dysfunctional

---

16. In the introduction by W. R. W. Stephens to Chrysostom's homily, Stephens explains what it is Chrysostom is pushing back against: "In an age of great depravity there seem to have been many who tried to excuse the weak resistance which they made to evil, both in themselves, and in others, by maintaining that the world was abandoned to the dominion of devils, or to the irresistible course of fate" (Chrysostom, "Demons," 177). Again, Chrysostom's point wasn't to deny any kind of spiritual warfare, but to deny that the world had been abandoned by God to the uncontrolled powers of darkness.

(or, less than "too much order" and "too much function"). But why think that? It may be that spiritual warfare has nothing to do with nature or anything physical directly. It might, rather, have to do solely with *nonphysical* things involving the psychological, moral, and intellectual. Perhaps the kind of conflict that spiritual warfare involves is purely cognitive, having only to do with temptations, promptings, falsehoods, deceptions, and the like inflicted on victims. And, as I have argued at length in my own works,[17] I do not think Satan and his demons even *have* this kind of access to nature by which to adversely affect it. The Waltons would have to show, if there is to be any expectation about a diminished order or function in the universe, that spiritual warfare is *not* this.[18] On both counts, then, the assumption that "conflict theology" implies that there would be less order and function than what we have does not follow.

Having dispensed with the Waltons' objections, there is no reason to think that spiritual warfare does not involve some kind of cosmic conflict as minimally defined in the previous chapter (i.e., as an unrelenting intercommunal conflict between two or more rival populations including, among others, human beings and having been inaugurated by members of an otherworldly population). However, there are some positive indications we can point to up front that suggest that spiritual warfare indeed involves some measure of conflict.

First, as we will see later in Part II, there are warfare metaphors that *prima facie* involve interpersonal conflict. These metaphors are likewise used in defining what spiritual warfare is. For example, certain parcels of armor like the shield, helmet, and breastplate (which minimally reflect the notion of *defense*) are famously attributed to the ideal Christian that stands against spiritual foes in the face of adversity (Eph 6:11–17; 1 Thess 5:8). And there is no question that Ephesians 6 in particular is about such spiritual warfare, for verse 12 says that armor-clad Christians surely "wrestle . . . against the spiritual forces of evil in the heavenly places."

Second, the explicit equating of the Christian walk with "war" and "warfare" is offered in 2 Corinthians 10:3–4. Therein the apostle Paul writes that "though we walk in the flesh, we are not waging war according to the

---

17. E.g., Guthrie, *Gods of This World*, 202–19.

18. The Waltons offer a third objection based on the notion that (some) sufferings and evils have no explanation if they are not attributed to the works of demons (pp. 280–83). For according to this model, God generally wants human beings to be happy. That some are not is seen in some cases as evidential support for some kind of anti-God, demonic activity. But this is not an objection *to spiritual warfare*; it is an objection to *a heterodox interpretation* of spiritual warfare—one not held by the majority within Christian history. As such, I'm all too happy to accept the Waltons' criticisms of the tenets of Word-Faith theology and such.

flesh. For the weapons of our warfare are not of the flesh but have divine power to destroy strongholds." It is hard to *not* see this as conflict—a conflict with fortified "strongholds" no less. And it is worth noting that Paul here is speaking about such warfare *in the present tense*. For, it is in the context of us currently "walk[ing] in the flesh." As such, we presently wield "the weapons of our warfare." Verse 5 goes on to define such weaponry as us "destroy[ing] arguments and every lofty opinion raised against the knowledge of God, and tak[ing] every thought captive to obey Christ." But only *personal enemies* can assail with arguments and opinions. And it is personal enemies who erect strongholds to protect their cause.

Third, the famous apocalypse of the New Testament, the book of Revelation, likewise symbolizes a current and/or an eventual conflict that (some of) the saints will be involved in. Revelation 11:7 speaks of "two witnesses" that will be in direct conflict with "the beast." Now, without taking a position about who these "witnesses" are and what "the beast" represents, at a minimum it envisages a conflict between representatives of God and representatives of Satan (for "the beast" is said to be animated by Satan himself in Rev 13:2; cf. 12:9). Revelation 11:7 speaks of the "two witnesses" and says that "when they have finished their testimony, the beast that rises from the bottomless pit will make war on them and conquer them and kill them" (cf. 13:7). While this manner of conflict—indeed, *war*—is depicted as being quite literal (i.e., at the hands of human beings), it is an indirect assault at the hands of Satan himself. Since the foes of God will fail to convert Christians to the pagan religion of the oppressing "beast" (13:11–18; 15:2), its only recourse will be to exterminate those who refuse. It is a spiritual warfare that spills over and sometimes becomes a rather physical and often bloody warfare.

Therefore, not even a demonic realist such as the Waltons can successfully object to the notion that spiritual warfare seems to involve conflict. But as to what it involves and what it doesn't, and what it looks like in the lives of Christians, this all has yet to be discussed at length. We will begin our exploration of these pressing issues in the upcoming pages beginning with Part I. In Part I, then, I will offer a thorough discussion about the supernatural combatants involved. We will see more clearly who these enemies of conflict are along with some comforting insight about the contrasting identity of God and his angels who collectively help us to endure.

PART I

The Theater of War

The enemy roars
And attempts to destroy me,
His plans newly laid
Are awaiting each day.
A pilgrim, a stranger,
I face His revilings,
Rejoice in the furnace
And shout on my way.

—"The Conqueror's Tread" by Florence Potter (1902)

3

The Enemy Triumvirate

THE RECENT SURGE OF superhero movies reminds us of the common attitude that an enemy is bound to be an equal but opposing force to the hero or the innocent. Superman has his Lex Luthor. The Avengers have their Thanos. And God has his Satan. However, construing Christian theology along the lines of a comic book hero-villain story is bound to mislead us on many levels. For example, ancient Zoroastrians and Manicheans believed that God had an equal though evil counterpart and thus they were correspondingly potent forces pitted against each other. This is to say that they were pretty much equally matched, though God always had the upper hand in the end (phew!). Though most do not confess it openly, Satan is sometimes viewed as a genuine threat to God's power and sovereignty. This is, after all, what it means to be "superstitious"[1] and why many people take ritualistic precautions to ensure their health and well-being in the chance that our enemies might overwhelm God's protections. But we will soon see that this is an incorrect portrait.

This chapter and the one that follows are designed to correctly profile the primary opposing spiritual forces of spiritual warfare in operation. The current chapter shall specifically focus on who the enemy is (we shall treat the identity of God and his good angels in later chapters). What we will find is that a proper understanding of the enemy amounts to something more than a singular villain in the drama of human experience. That is, there isn't

---

1. Plutarch once defined superstition as an irrational fear of "sour and vindictive" demons (Plutarch, "Of Superstition," 169).

just a singular counterforce to righteousness that is on the move. There are others. But, unlike the Zoroastrians and Manicheans, we will not encounter a multifaceted enemy that can overwhelm God or manage victory over him.

Now, most Christians are already somewhat familiar with the figure of Satan, the putative archenemy of God. In fact, other than God, Satan is the most familiar character in Scripture despite the fact that many other figures, like the prophet Isaiah, are mentioned more times than him. And yet it is a testament to the impact that Satan has in the universe. The very concept of spiritual warfare itself entails that there is an enemy combatant—someone with whom one is in a state of warfare. People typically do not engage in warfare with nonliving things or events even though we often treat such things with a warfare attitude: "I was *fighting* with my printer all day"; "Cheryl was *bombarded* with questions"; "The Children's Hunger Alliance works at the *front lines* of the *war* on poverty," and so forth. But this is clearly to consider the opposition, whatever it might be, as a mere obstacle and not as a combatant proper. Such combat language is intended only to highlight how experientially significant and challenging the difficulties can be.

Scripture instead portrays the source of our struggles in spiritual warfare in personal terms. The reader is not left to wonder whether the opposition to one's spiritual well-being is an inanimate object or some impersonal event. For rarely is there a biblical denunciation of a mere abstract circumstance instead of a person as if something called "bad fortune" or "comeuppance" randomly clashes against aspiring followers of God. That which opposes God is far more personal and nefarious than some abstract "furniture" that populates the universe. More accurately, the New Testament speaks of a spiritual adversary with whom human beings must contend. And any obstacles that come into our pathways are often intelligently, even if malevolently, designed. Being so, they are not beyond the control or power of God.

But, as we may already suspect, it is rather evident in Scripture that Satan is not the only explicit figure of opposition. In fact, the Old Testament has little to say about this Satan figure specifically (though implications of his presence in hindsight are perhaps discernible). While passages here and there draw a focus to Satan (or "the *śāṭān*" as the case may be), the spiritual assaults against God's people are often very physical and are carried out by opposing nations and people seeking domination and conquest. For example, the New Testament is notorious for its depiction of Rome as not only an oppressor, but a "beast" seeking both the political as well as religious submission of its enemies. And if attempts at forcing its citizens to submit to the Roman Empire failed, it would result in their torment and destruction. If the book of Revelation indeed indicates something of the future, then Christians have not seen the last of such an oppressive "beast" regime. Even now a number of Christians in various parts of the world are enduring unspeakable suffering at the hands of regional autocrats, militants, and terrorists. Scripture often generalizes this "beastly" opposition to God's children as "the world" (e.g., Jas 4:4; 2 Pet 2:20; 1 John 3:13; 4:5). It is an unidentifiable aggregate not only of those outside of the fellowship of God but of those who are in direct opposition to it. Their goal, like that of ancient Rome and Babylon, is to either command Christians' obedience to its ungodly mores or to remove them altogether by any (violent) means necessary.

Lest we think Satan and the world that he governs encapsulate the entirety of the enemies of God and his creation, one more is mentioned by name—and his name is "the flesh" (e.g., Rom 8:3–13; 1 Pet 2:11). The New Testament reveals that the Christian is locked in a different struggle from that of a personal enemy; he is locked in a struggle with himself. More specifically, he is locked in a struggle with one of his *natures*. This enemy actually lives much closer than the others, for it dwells in our very person. The flesh is not quite the tangible integument system that holds us and our insides together; rather this flesh is a *side* of us—an alluring and captivating side of us. It is the locus of the temptations and shortcomings that befall everyone and have been enfleshed in us since conception. But, unlike Satan and the world, this assailant does not have a distinct consciousness. It is not the indwelling of a demon who steers us down the wrong paths of life for its own pleasure. The flesh is an impersonal force or instinct that beckons our indulgence irrespective of the contrary wishes of others and even of ourselves. It commands us but says nothing. It moves us but has no hands. It drowns out the voice of conscience but doesn't make a sound. And it cannot be destroyed lest we destroy ourselves. Its tokens are undoubtedly familiar to us: lust, pride, covetousness, hatred, envy, etc. These tools wielded by the flesh are relentless and indiscriminate.

We now get the impression that the enemy is not merely a singular villain ensconced somewhere in or beyond the cosmos, but an aggregate of enemies cavorting together in precipitating the downfall of those bearing the image of God. This is not too far from the truth, as far as Scripture is concerned, but it is not quite the complete portrait. Instead of a convergence of "like-minded" villains coming together for a single purpose (like a council or a board), all of these things opposing the Godly are extensions of the initial enemy himself, i.e., Satan. This is to say that Scripture portrays Satan as the mastermind behind rogue regimes and oppressive societies and as a stoker of fleshly desires. It is an unholy trinity of malevolence reaching across dual realities. That Satan directs oppressive regimes and societies is possibly, though questionably,[2] attested in Daniel 10:13, 20 (for something demonic—or perhaps even Satan himself—is the prince "of Persia" and "of Greece"). But it is most assuredly attested in Revelation 2:12–13, where Satan is said to have his "throne" in Pergamum—imagery that connotes authority and rulership. That Satan directs and/or affects the inhabitants of the world is evident in Luke 22:3–4 as well as 2 Corinthians 4:4.[3] In fact, Satan's union with the world is rather intimate as one who "is in the world" (1 John 4:4) and is considered the "prince of the power of the air" (Eph 2:2). Satan's use of the flesh (i.e., his exploitation of it) is implied by Mark 1:13 (cf. Matthew 4:1; Luke 4:2); Matthew 6:13 ("the evil one," *ponērou*); and 1 Corinthians 7:5. It is no surprise, then, that there are scriptural references to all three as if integrated into a unitary, tripartite enemy (emphases mine):

> And you were dead in the trespasses and sins in which you once walked, following the course of *this world*, following *the prince of the power of the air*, the spirit that is now at work in the sons of disobedience—among whom we all once lived in the passions of *our flesh*, carrying out the desires of the body and the mind, and were by nature children of wrath, like the rest of mankind. (Eph 2:1–3)

> I write to you, fathers, because you know him who is from the beginning. I write to you, young men, because you are strong, and the word of God abides in you, and you have overcome *the evil one*. Do not love *the world* or the things in the world. If anyone loves the world, the love of the Father is not in him. For all that is in the world—*the desires of the flesh* and the desires of the eyes and pride of life—is not from the Father but is *from the world*. (1 John 2:14–16)

This tripartite alliance makes, then, for a perfect storm of trouble in the life of the believer. And yet, if Satan were out of the picture, one expects that the auxiliary forces under his initial influence would not cease their destructive efforts. It would be a sort of satanic inertia where initial temptations and corruptions of our minds continue to be entertained by struggling believers even long after Satan has gone AWOL. But we are not empowered enough to test that hypothesis (though a day may come when we will![4]).

---

2. E.g., Walton and Walton, *Demons and Spirits*, 186–97.

3. Some push back on the idea that 2 Cor 4:4 has *anything* to do with Satan. For they see the "god of this world" mentioned there to be a reference *to God*. For my response, see Guthrie, *Gods of This World*, 36–37.

4. Cf. Rev 20:1–3.

Now, this inevitably raises a question about whether or not the world and possessors of the flesh are culpable for their sinister actions. If Satan is indeed the mastermind and director of the other two components of the enemy triumvirate, then he must be the sufficient cause of what they do. And if Satan is the sufficient cause of what they do, then neither the world nor the possessors of the flesh are acting freely. And if they are not acting freely, then they are not culpable for their actions. Accordingly, as expressed by critic Don Cupitt, "[e]xplanations of moral phenomena which have recourse to the Devil or devils must be repudiated because they are a device for shuffling off responsibility." Miguel De la Torre and Albert Hernández complain that to say of any behavior, whether of the world or of the possessor of the flesh, "the devil made me do it" is demonstrably problematic, for it implies that

> Nazi concentration guards can torture all week long and still attend worship services on Sunday mornings. Politicians can lead armies to war under false pretenses without addressing the tens of thousands, if not hundreds of thousands, who are killed or maimed because, after all, our intentions were pure–it was the enemy who was really evil.[5]

Such concerns can be addressed in either of two ways. First, the defender of such a triumvirate network can embrace a *compatibilist* notion of freedom and responsibility. This is to say that even though human beings can be construed as regime leaders or individuals with fleshly natures and that they are also determined by Satan to engage in moral wickedness/sin, nevertheless they remain free insofar as they are agents who act out of their own desires and for reasons in service to those desires. That is, one's freedom is *compatible* with one's being determined to do this or that. For compatibilists, the fact that an agent is determined by his or her circumstances and nature is not to say that they are not responsible for what they do. However, such a move, despite having able defenders,[6] is bound to be an unacceptable resolution for many to the problem at hand since acting freely and being determined seem *incompatible* with each other. But for those willing to embrace it, even in the name of "mystery," it quickly resolves the tension between Satan's agency and human free agency. Incompatibilists, such as I, will not prefer this approach. But a great many self-identified Augustinian Calvinists no doubt will.

---

5. De la Torre and Hernández, *Quest for the Historical Satan*, 198.

6. E.g., Narveson, "Compatibilism Defended"; Helm, "Human Beings"; Bignon, *Excusing Sinners and Blaming God*.

A second solution is nevertheless available. It is easy to deny the premise that suggests that Satan's influence on human agents is in fact deterministic. Scripture, for one, treats Satan's influence on human beings along the lines of *suggestions* or *promptings* (John 8:38, 44; Acts 5:3–4; 1 Cor 10:13; 1 Pet 5:8–9; Jas 1:14–15; 4:7) and not as deterministic, constraining causes of human behavior. As the eighteenth-century devotional work *The (New) Whole Duty of Man* makes clear, blaming the devil for being the sufficient cause of wickedness or temptation "is an error arising from a very false notion of the devil's power of tempting men; it being nothing more, but like that of wicked men tempting one another."[7] The enemy triumvirate, then, is more of a network of collaboration or collusion in that human beings freely act on the basis of a convergence of satanic influence and the circumstances and predisposing natures of those acting. I imagine it wouldn't take much for Satan to convince anyone to sin or to inspire political regimes to oppose God's people. And it seems that this can be done without violating a notion that sees human freedom as being incompatible with a satanic determinism.

Accordingly, Satan is poised as the ultimate agent behind the spiritual assaults against the believer through his exploitations of the predispositions of the world and the flesh. It is imperative, then, that we, in concert with Paul's cautioning, not be "outwitted by Satan [by being] ignorant of his designs" (2 Cor 2:11). In the chapters to follow, we shall explore in more detail who these enemies are, beginning with the primal adversary, Satan. We shall take great care to facilitate a proper understanding that is faithful to both Scripture and sound reasoning. Our objective will be to systematize what it means to refer to God's threefold enemy. Following those analyses, we will look to the heroes of the drama.

---

7. Allestree, *New Whole Duty of Man*, 326–27.

4

The Satan

THE FAMILIAR DESIGNATION "SATAN" is based on the transliterated Hebrew word śāṭān, which means "adversary" or "accuser." It is a term designating a function much like it does in a court case (where an "adversary" is one who functionally opposes the other side). Despite this, "Satan" *can* be used as a proper name. But, then again, just about *any* descriptive Hebrew word could be used as a name.[1] The point is, "Satan" is not necessarily something that would appear on Satan's birth certificate, so to speak. As such, the term (whether capitalized or not) can be used to refer to any personal agent—whether human, angel, or otherwise.[2] We have only a handful of passages in the Bible that utilize some form of śāṭān, which could refer to the (temporary) function of a good angelic being or to the more familiar villain of tradition. First Chronicles 21:1 ("Then Satan stood up against Israel and moved David to number Israel"), for example, gives us no information

---

1. For example, "Abraham" is deliberately given to Abram because it means "father of a multitude of nations" (Gen 17:5); "Michael," which means "who is like God" is the name of the archangel probably because he is "one of the chief princes" tasked with presiding over Israel (Dan 10:13)—a role generally reserved for God himself (Deut 32:8–9). Such also obtains in the Greek, for Simon is given the name "Peter" because he metaphorically becomes "the rock" (Matt 16:18) and Saul becomes "Paul," which, ultimately from the Latin, means "small" or "little" (Acts 13:9)—a possible reference to his self-effacing perception among his peers (1 Cor 15:8; 2 Cor 10:1, 10).

2. The same goes for *diabolos* in the Septuagint (the ancient Greek translation of the Old Testament), which takes on the meaning of "slanderer." None of these terms are what philosophers (e.g., Saul Kripke) call a "rigid designator"—that is, a term that essentially picks out the same being even if the world were arranged differently.

about the identity of this personal adversary. Given its parallel account in 2 Samuel 24:1, it makes identifying the one who "numbers Israel" less likely to be the more familiar Satan of a later Judeo-Christian demonology:

> Now again the anger of the LORD burned against Israel, and it [or *he*] incited David against them to say, "Go, number Israel and Judah."

Given what little is said here, it is plausible that the *śāṭān* of 1 Chronicles 21 just is an agent of God.

In Job 1–2, these chapters use the noun along with the definite article in describing the adversary (*haśśāṭān*, or "the satan"). Given the context of Job, the presence of the *śāṭān* before God, the manner in which the *śāṭān* interacts as a courtroom accuser, and the fact that he is "among" the angels (1:6; 2:1) might suggest that the *śāṭān* is merely one of the fellow angels carrying out a more functional role (something like a court-appointed attorney).[3] There is no definitive indication that the *śāṭān* is himself the notorious archenemy of God or the chief of demons. However, it seems evident that *haśśāṭān* is no mere mortal. He is, after all, among the heavenly angels (viz., the "sons of God"). That he is one of them is only a possibility, for there is nothing about *haśśāṭān* being "among them" that entails his sharing their identity. That God appears to be *surprised* at Satan's presence from among the angels ("The LORD said to Satan, 'From where have you come?'") suggests that he is likely *not* merely one of them.[4] If it should turn out that Satan is some kind of deviant supernatural being (a *former* angel perhaps), then Job's account accords well with this idea. But given that Job itself is a part of the Wisdom literature, we're not supposed to take Job as giving us unadulterated history either. It reads more like a hypothetical scenario for the purpose of challenging a longstanding principle (i.e., that prosperity always results from righteousness and suffering from sin and rebellion).

We turn to another Old Testament passage that might indicate that the *śāṭān* is the supernatural villain of lore, namely Zechariah 3:1–2:

> Then he showed me Joshua the high priest standing before the angel of the LORD, and Satan standing at his right hand to accuse him. And the LORD said to Satan, "The LORD rebuke you, O Satan! The LORD who has chosen Jerusalem rebuke you! Is not this a brand plucked from the fire?"[5]

---

3. Num 22:22 designates the "angel of the LORD" as *śāṭān*, which might further suggest that *śāṭān* was more of a role than a proper name.

4. Walton and Walton, *Demons and Spirits*, 217.

5. If the *śāṭān* were merely role-playing as an accuser, it could be doubted that he would have been scathingly rebuked in the way described, but no definite conclusions

While it remains possible that an angel is playing the śāṭān here, the strong rebuke finds a New Testament connection. Jude tells us about a dialog between Michael the archangel and Satan—a dispute, rather, over the body of Moses. Michael responds to Satan, "The Lord rebuke you!" (Jude 9). This rebuke echoes the reprimand of Zechariah 3 and may imply that the original "Satan" of Zechariah 3 is indeed the same Satan as understood in a more developed way in the New Testament. However, it is also possible only the *language* is recalled while being applied differently in Jude.

A REBEL FROM HEAVEN?

But do not Isaiah 14:12–19 and Ezekiel 28:13–16 describe in intimate detail through their pronouncements the rebellion of Satan in heaven? This is a tricky question because while Christians have asserted this since Origen proposed it, the passages once again are not that clear. Moreover, the imagery found in these passages closely echoes certain rebellion elements of what are called "combat myths" found in Canaanite and Babylonian predecessors.[6] These pronouncements are considered to be a part of the genre of prophecy and what is called "oracular poetry," which, in the Old Testament at least, uses symbolic cosmic language so that readers can feel the gravity of God's intent without intending to literally describe actual events.[7] For this reason, we must be careful about such symbolism when used in Scripture as the same goes for the so-called messianic passages of the Old Testament regarding Jesus. While the original messianic passages are not necessarily forthcoming about a divine messiah or even a singular person, they tend to be taken that way by some Rabbinic Jews, some in the New Testament, and by the later church.

Below I cite the relevant Isaiah and Ezekiel passages in their entirety with the *caveat* that we cannot draw any hard conclusions about them given their immediate context as taunts being explicitly directed at the leaders of oppressive regimes at the time. First, let us look to Isaiah 14:12–19, which reads in full:

---

can be drawn. As Marvin Tate notes: "Nevertheless, the usage of the verb is not sufficient to establish that 'the śāṭān' in Zech. 3:2 is the Devil, or even a devil figure, with implacable opposition to the will of God" (Tate, "Satan in the Old Testament," 464). Whatever one mines from the passages, by the time Judaism matured in the second century BC, śāṭān eventually took on the attribute of being a personal appellation.

6. Forsyth, *Old Enemy*, 134–42.
7. Walton and Walton, *Demons and Spirits*, 220.

> How you are fallen from heaven, O Day Star [or Lucifer], son of Dawn! How you are cut down to the ground, you who laid the nations low! You said in your heart, "I will ascend to heaven; above the stars of God I will set my throne on high; I will sit on the mount of assembly in the far reaches of the north; I will ascend above the heights of the clouds; I will make myself like the Most High." But you are brought down to Sheol, to the far reaches of the pit. Those who see you will stare at you and ponder over you: "Is this the man who made the earth tremble, who shook kingdoms, who made the world like a desert and overthrew its cities, who did not let his prisoners go home?" All the kings of the nations lie in glory, each in his own tomb; but you are cast out, away from your grave, like a loathed branch, clothed with the slain, those pierced by the sword, who go down to the stones of the pit, like a dead body trampled underfoot.

One of the preceding verses, verse 4, makes it clear that this is a proclamation against the "king of Babylon." Since Satan is not a king of any earthly nation, much less of Babylon, it is hard to see this as a connection to him. It is also questionable that Satan's original sin would have been something so presumptuous as the expectation that he could exceed God's glory.[8]

On the other hand, this could be a cryptic or *indirect* reference to Satan since it refers to this being having fallen from heaven—a familiar portrayal of Satan's origin. However, the king's "fall" ("you are brought down") is not a *consequence* of his hubris but a reality check on his subsequent humiliation before the Lord despite his pretentious boasts.[9] That is, God is reinforcing the king's inferiority in the face of his self-exaltation. We in the contemporary world are so deeply entrenched in a tradition that identifies Satan with "Lucifer" that we sometimes ignore what the passage is really saying. Anyway, as it turns out, to suppose that "Lucifer" is the person's name here is as mistaken as supposing that every mention of "god" in the Bible is always in reference to Yahweh (e.g., Exod 7:1). The word translated "Lucifer" (*hêlêl*) just means "day star" and should not necessarily be seen as a proper name much less an exclusive reference to a fallen angel or cosmic rebel. If I refer to a corrupt child as a "holy terror," I'm not identifying the child by name. I would just be colorfully describing the child's perceived characteristics. Moreover, the loftiness of this "son of Dawn" who strives to "ascend" over God and his heaven is not an unusual description of human beings when

---

8. I say "exceed God's glory" because, contrary to tradition, the passage does not imply that the king sought to *replace* God. His desire to "make myself like the Most High" is not an indication of usurpation.

9. Walton and Walton, *Demons and Spirits*, 218.

one considers that many corrupt kings and magistrates have often deified themselves as they lie drunk in their own power (cf. Ezek 28:6–10).

Second, similar considerations apply to Ezekiel 28:13–16, which reads as follows:

> You were in Eden, the garden of God; every precious stone was your covering, sardius, topaz, and diamond, beryl, onyx, and jasper, sapphire, emerald, and carbuncle; and crafted in gold were your settings and your engravings. On the day that you were created they were prepared. You were an anointed guardian cherub. I placed you; you were on the holy mountain of God; in the midst of the stones of fire you walked. You were blameless in your ways from the day you were created, till unrighteousness was found in you. In the abundance of your trade you were filled with violence in your midst, and you sinned; so I cast you as a profane thing from the mountain of God, and I destroyed you, O guardian cherub, from the midst of the stones of fire.

At face value, it is indeed difficult to see references to the recipient of this taunt as one who was "in Eden" and is a "guardian cherub" as referring to anyone but Satan. Satan, after all, was likely the one in the garden of Eden who tempted Eve into disobedience—right? Assuming that to be the case, the description of Eden and such appears to not be about geography as much as it is about imagery. Consider that here "in Eden," which is itself traditionally held to be in Iraq, there is also "the holy mountain of God." But the "holy mountain" is not in Iraq; it is in Israel (Ezek 20:40). The presence of precious jewels and "stones of fire" signals that this is about imagery and not about topography. In fact, the expulsion of Satan is thought to be an expulsion *from heaven* and not from any earthly province ("I cast you as a profane thing from the mountain of God"). Add to this the explicit identity of the one being taunted as "the ruler of Tyre" (v. 2) and, like Isaiah 14, we have diminished reasons to think this is a reference to Satan much less to an expulsion of a wider heavenly entourage.

There is some caution to exercise in the other direction, however. We should not be so shortsighted as to think that such taunts, though directed at earthly leaders, may not be indirect references to Satan. It may be that the rulers of Babylon and Tyre are earthly parallels to or typological representatives of Satan, which is why the authors employ the heavenly language of "Eden" and "holy mountain" and such. Perhaps these leaders' rebellious attitudes mirror those of the original rebel. This is certainly a possibility. But, aside from speculation, it surely puts the cart before the horse. For one must already have good reason to think that Satan was indeed a former angel whose ambitious loftiness to be greater than God led to his demise. If Satan was a good angel—the highest ranking one at that—it is a wonder that he would have been so obtuse as to think he could overthrow the God of the universe.[10] Pride is one thing, but Isaiah 14 gives us the indication that the "king" sought utter dominion and "shook kingdoms" that, on Scripture's timetable, did not yet exist anyway.

This is all we need say here about Isaiah 14 and Ezekiel 28. While these passages may allude to Satan and his origins directly or indirectly, we cannot take these as proof texts for the existence of the traditional Satan. We must look elsewhere for firmer conclusions to draw. One such consideration is to think about how *else* such a being might have arisen. Satan is obviously the *de facto* villain in the New Testament. Since only God is the creator of everything that is, then Satan's existence is the direct result of God's intention. This leaves us with whether God creates moral wickedness directly or whether Satan might have been something benign in his original state. The former option seems unconscionable, not to mention unscriptural (Jas 1:13).[11] And if we are left with the option that Satan must have been a morally innocent creature in the beginning, that he might have been one of the good angels looks plausible. What else would a morally innocent, nonhuman, purely spiritual being who is not Yahweh be anyway? It is initially plausible at least that he be one of the (former) good angels in God's company.

Some have attempted to find scriptural validation of this probability by appealing to Jesus' comments that he saw "Satan fall like lightning from heaven" (Luke 10:18) and the Revelator's comments that Satan, who had a "place in heaven," nevertheless ended up being "thrown down to the earth" (Rev 12:7–9). But Jesus, in the case of Luke, is not referring to any historical instance of Satan's fall but observing the cosmic significance of Satan's *present* defeat in the wake of the demons being subject to the seventy-two followers of Jesus (Luke 10:17). And Revelation 12 concerns, not a pre-Adamic fall of Satan and his minions, but a conquest that took place at the time of Jesus's crucifixion and/or some future conflict bearing some significance in the defeat of Satan.

Perhaps there was a wider angelic fall. This may provide the missing puzzle piece for where to place Satan's origins. Second Peter 2:4 reports that

---

10. Schleiermacher, *Christian Faith*, 161; Bamberger, *Fallen Angels*, 203.

11. One might point out that God indeed does "create evil" (ASV) as reported in Isa 45:7. But the "evil" in mind there is not moral wickedness; instead, as some translations clarify, it has to do with "calamity" (ESV) and disaster. These are morally neutral acts even if they are unpleasant. Death by execution, for example, is a "calamity" upon the body, but considered by many to be a morally permissible, if not morally obligatory, response by the state if the accused is a murderer.

"God did not spare angels when they sinned, but cast them into hell . . ." Jude 6 (being in part based on 2 Peter 2) reports that "the angels . . . did not stay within their own position of authority, but left their proper dwelling." That these angels abandoned their "position of authority" indicates strongly an angelic apostasy. The Greek word *archēn*, which is variously translated "position of authority" (ESV), "domain" (NASB), "limits" (NLT), and "principality" (ASV), connotes here a transgression from one's original situation or placement. Indeed, they willingly "left" their "proper dwelling" (*oikētērion*), which further supports this. The curious consequence that is threatened as a result of this apostasy is described variously as "hell" and "chains." But these descriptions likely serve a purpose other than to connote the eschatological lake of fire as mentioned in Revelation 19–20. "Hell" and "chains" probably refer to some kind of intermediate punitive restriction that had been imposed on them by God (similar to Satan's being "bound" in Revelation 20:2–3).[12] Peter's choice language ("cast into hell/Tartarus" in 2 Peter 2:4) makes it look like an exile of sorts. This gives the impression that these formerly good angels were exiled and forever "chained" due to their wickedness (or "darkness") "until the judgment of the great day." It parallels the punitive exile of humanity from the garden of Eden (Gen 3:23–24) as a consequence that will not be reversed until the consummation at the second coming of our Lord (Rev 20:1–2). Unlike human beings, however, these apostatizing angels will never return (Matt 25:41; Heb 2:16). That there was an angelic fall is thus a plausible understanding of Jude and 2 Peter.

By way of summary, it is likely that some angels freely fell from heaven ("their proper dwelling") for having sinned. If Satan is not a being distinct from the angelic race, then his own fall is likely implied by this report of what appears to be a rebellion followed by an expulsion.[13]

MISCELLANEOUS TITLES

Elsewhere in Scripture, Satan is known by other designations. These designations further define his adversarial nature in particular ways that reveal just *how* he is adversarial. For example, he is (likely) the serpent of Genesis 3.[14]

---

12. Being "in chains" is elsewhere used metaphorically in this way, e.g., Job 36:8 and 38:31.

13. There is an additional passage that is often brought up in defense of an angelic fall, namely Gen 6:1–4. Since a discussion of this passage would take us far afield, I shall address this passage later in a more applicable context. In terms of its would-be contribution here, if it should turn out that Gen 6 indeed teaches an angelic fall, we simply would have further support of a conclusion already derived in this section.

14. I defend this identification at length in *Gods of This World*, 33–36.

The point of the designation is to highlight his "craftiness" and superiority over other created things (see Gen 3:1). He is thus depicted as "tempter" in Matthew 4:3 and 1 Thessalonians 3:5. He is also "Beelzebul" (Matt 10:25; 12:24, 27; Mark 3:22; Luke 11:15, 18–19), which was a way (coined by the Pharisees?) to identify the real power behind the Canaanite god-hero Baal. After all, demons were considered by Second Temple Jews to be the animating powers behind the "idols" of nations in opposition to Israel (cf. Ps 96:5, LXX).

Satan is called "the evil one" (Matt 13:19, 38; John 17:15; Eph 6:16; 2 Thess 3:3; 1 John 2:13–14; 3:12; 5:18), which is, I would expect, for obvious reasons—not the least of which is because he "prowls around like a roaring lion, seeking someone to devour" (1 Pet 5:8). He is also known regally as a "prince" (Matt 9:34; 12:24; Mark 3:22; Luke 11:15; Eph 2:2) of this world and of "the air" (possibly referring to this realm which sits "below" heaven, so to speak). He is also more generically called the "ruler of this world" (John 12:31; 14:30; 16:11). It is not surprising, then, to find the apostle Paul theologizing him to be something even grander—the "god of this world" (2 Cor 4:4). From these designators, we can see that this adversary—this *enemy*—is destructive of the things of God. That God now resides in his people through Christ and not in temples (Acts 17:24) makes us more vulnerable, as if exposed to a predator. These epithets for his authority and power underscore the fact that his capabilities exceed those of ordinary persons and are nothing to be trifled over. The enemy retains enough influence to make life a living hell. As such, this raises the important follow-up questions we now need to answer: What kind of thing is Satan and what can he do?

THE NATURE OF SATAN

Satan is not the originator or creator of any fundamental essence or fixed reality. That would be the sole prerogative of the being who is God. And evil is not the sort of thing that is fundamental to God's nature, perhaps for obvious reasons. But, just to press the point, if evil were in some sense a part of God's nature, it would be a fundamental value since God is the ultimate ground of everything that is, including moral values. And if it is a fundamental value, then to align oneself with it would be a moral *good*, for God is the standard and metric of what is good (with evil being something that also resides in his nature). For this reason, evil would not be evil in the sense that it is a deviation, privation, or a transgression from that which is good. Evil would be a part of that ultimate ground of goodness. This is not only not how we intuit evil, but it is also incoherent.

Equally problematic is that our moral duties are rooted either in the commands issued by God (i.e., a divine command theory of ethics) or in the moral law God hardwires into nature (i.e., a natural law theory of ethics) since, in either framework, moral duties originate in the divine nature. This would mean that all of God's commands and the instances of natural law, where evil is commanded or imbued by God, must accord with evil. But this can't be. For evil consists of anti-values (or vices) that are incompatible with and contradictory to God's other values. An eternal essence cannot consist of both Justice and Injustice. *That's impossible!* And if we emend this to say that, instead, God's essence consists of Injustice and not-Justice, then we should never be able to regard instances of injustice as evil. Such acts of injustice would, by virtue of proceeding from the divine nature, be construed as acts of goodness. But we clearly do not regard unambiguous acts of injustice to be in any sense good but, rather, evil. It is for these reasons that evil is posterior to and a deviation from that which is good. And that goodness is grounded in God. So, God cannot be the direct cause or originator of moral evil. If that is true, then some other agent is the direct cause or originator of moral evil.

Now, perhaps this agent of evil, being free at least in some point of his life, was not always evil. He too might have been good once upon an eternity only to give rise to evil at some later time (this follows from the first observation, namely, that God cannot be the direct cause or originator of evil). But in order for such a being to be capable of transitioning from being good to being evil, he would have to have a certain distance, so to speak, from God's nature. Such a being could not be a *part* of God's nature, like the individual persons of the Trinity are, on pain of contradiction. But, as I have already argued, if that being were eternal and yet evil, it would not be the sole, fundamental reality. There would have to be something that sets the standard for what it means for deviant acts to be evil. It follows that a being that is evil must be a being separate from God.

Would that evil agent be eternal? We could posit that he was "eternally generated" so that he is both eternal as well as one that owes his existence to God. But we have no reason to suppose that such a being is eternal unless it is necessary to affirm this in order to explain some other feature of God's universe. And I can't imagine what such a reason would be. Would it be a personal being? If we say that the eternal-person-who-isn't-God is more like an abstract object or a Platonic Form—something that is impersonal but immaterial and eternal—then not only would it not be a person, it would not have any causal powers (for abstract objects and Platonic Forms, if they exist, are not persons and have no causal powers). Nor could it have transitioned from good to evil since abstracta and Forms are *fixed* essences. They're not people that can change their minds and follow other trajectories. It follows that any being of evil that exists and isn't God is contingent—something created even if eternally generated. Although, I have to say, for reasons of special revelation and on the assumption that he is an angel (see below), I think such an agent of evil would not be eternal (Ps 148:2, 5; cf. Jude 6).

This aligns well with the traditional Judeo-Christian outlook: that Satan is the primary agent of evil who, at some point in the past, was a morally innocent being who later fell from that state of moral innocence. So, what kind of being is Satan if not a part of God? Here, we must punt to what Scripture has to say. If we do not know when Satan was created (when the universe was or before), then we cannot determine whether Satan might be a material being or not. According to Scripture, Satan and his minions are variously identified as "evil spirits" (*pneumatōn ponērōn*; e.g., Luke 7:21; 8:2; Acts 19:12–13; cf. Judg 9:23).[15] And given that "angels" are the wider celestial company preceding humankind, it is simpler to think that Satan would have been part of that aggregate and not some third category of being. Recently, there has been much ado about whether there is a "divine council" of gods that are beings hierarchically above the angels but still something less than Yahweh. While I am not personally convinced that the biblical authors literally, rather than typologically or for reasons related to genre, adopted ancient Near Eastern myths about overlords and divine councils,[16] nothing theological hangs on this. Let's just consider any and all celestial beings that aren't God to be "angels" in order to advance the conversation.

Not surprisingly, the good angels are also described as "spirits" (*pneumata*; Heb 1:14). Accordingly, there is a certain metaphysical understanding that surfaces, for Jesus himself indicates that "a spirit does not have flesh and bones" (Luke 24:39). Spirits are therefore fleshless and boneless things. Moreover, God is also "a spirit" (John 4:24) who, as a consequence of being a spirit, is utterly intangible (John 1:18; 1 Tim 1:17). And it is simpler to take "spirit" uniformly—that is, that it is the same kind of thing across the board whomever it applies to, unless there are any reasons to think otherwise. Finally, Scripture reports that the good angels must undergo a special manifestation in order to be seen and interacted with by physical beings (e.g., Gen 19:1–3; Num 22:31; 2 Kgs 6:15–17; Judg 13:2–21; Heb 13:2). This fact punctuates the previous observation, namely, that they are not naturally material or even corporeal. Thus, it is reasonable to conclude that a biblical "spirit" refers to a *thoroughly* or *purely* immaterial being and

---

15. For more on "evil spirits" and its implications, see Guthrie, *Gods of This World*, 170–74.

16. So, Walton and Walton, *Demons and Spirits*, esp. 36, 177–211.

not to something that is physical or even polymorphous (composed of both physical as well as nonphysical properties). These facts together indicate strongly that the spiritual nature of Satan is, along with his cohorts, purely immaterial.[17]

The Knowledge of Satan

The knowledge that Satan has is, like humans and animals, probably something that accumulates over time. For this is the lot of finite beings (something that Satan likely is). This is to say that probably Satan did not begin from a point of infinite or maximal knowledge since he likely has not been around for all eternity. On this basis, it is more likely he would have progressed from a state of no or limited knowledge. For the only way a being can have maximal knowledge is for it to have had that knowledge from eternity since, as I will argue, finite beings probably cannot achieve a maximum quantity of knowledge no matter how much time lapses. To see this, consider first that knowledge is knowledge *of* something, namely propositions. Propositions are statements of content that are susceptible to being either true or false. Now, consider some high value representing the increasing, total quantity of propositions one comes to know throughout his past-finite life as he endures into the unending future. Let's call it F_n where F_n is the running total of all distinct facts that a finite being can know (F_1, F_2, F_3, . . .). At any given moment in the future, this being's F_n will be the product of every distinct F that he comes to know (e.g., that today is Labor Day in the United States). Since the perpetual future is always becoming and new facts are always obtaining, there will be no last F that can be known, for an additional day or moment will always succeed the current one. And the only way history can be in a finished state is for it to have obtained all at once. This evidences the fact that one cannot obtain maximal knowledge one fact at a time. So, for a temporal being like Satan is likely to be, it is not a possible achievement for such a finite being who endures into the unfinished future to become all-knowing one fact at a time. This means that there are only two ways someone can otherwise be all-knowing: either one is eternal and endures timelessly, thus having all knowledge necessarily and in a single vision, *or* one is imparted the knowledge of all future propositions in a single vision as given by God (from whatever starting point one

---

17. For an extensive defense of the pure immateriality of Satan and his demons, refer to my book *Gods of This World*. Also see my doctoral dissertation, "A New Metaphysics for Christian Demonology," which focuses narrowly on the subject of the metaphysics of demons.

arbitrarily picks). The first option is already ruled out on the assumption that Satan is not a timeless, eternal being.

Perhaps the second option is available. Perhaps Satan has come about his all-knowingness all at once by God. Though it is likely true that Satan began to exist a finite time ago, he could have been created with the totality of knowledge imparted to him. It is here that we must defer to our scriptural knowledge on the matter. Unfortunately, there is no *clear* indication of Satan's knowledge having limitations, but some implications can be teased out. First of all, in Matthew 24:36 (paralleled in Mark 13:32), Jesus reports about "that day and hour" in which he will return. Regarding when that day comes, he insists that it is something "no one knows, not even the angels of heaven, nor the Son, but the Father only." If "angels of heaven" is a sweeping designator that includes the fallen angels, then Satan does not know at least one thing about the future, namely, when Christ will return. And that suffices to say that Satan is not all-knowing.[18] Second, if he *were* all-knowing, it is difficult to think that Satan would have carried out his scheme with Judas at his first coming (Luke 22:3; John 13:27) had he known what Jesus's endgame was in the drama of salvation—unless one were to assume that Satan will have achieved exactly what he wanted despite ending in defeat, but that seems like an unlikely possibility. It is simpler to suppose that Satan is not all-knowing than that he intends his own defeat. Third, if Satan was indeed one of the good angels, then if the angels, including Michael, have limited knowledge, we should expect the same of Satan. And this much is also established by Matthew 24:36 (discussed above). It is a fact that may also be underscored in 1 Peter 1. Therein Peter writes about how the Old Testament prophets preached about the coming of the grace of the gospel (1 Pet 1:10–11), something those prophets didn't know at first when these things should obtain. It is this very grace and its fulfillment, says Peter, that is among the "things into which angels long to look" (v. 12). This eager desire or longing implies an ignorance on the part of the lookers (the angels), else it remains a mystery as to why anyone should desire looking into something they already know fully. And finally, that the underling demons in general are demonstrably ignorant of certain things (Matt 8:29 [Mark 5:7; Luke 8:28], Acts 19:15) may also lend itself to underscoring the ignorance of Satan, especially if he is one of them (cf. Matt 9:34; 12:24).[19]

---

18. I am assuming that the concept of "all-knowing" is something that includes all future-tense propositions. Open theists, like Gregory Boyd, deny that God definitively knows propositions about the future.

19. God asks of Satan in Job 2:3 whether he has "considered my servant Job . . . ?," which could imply the ignorance of Satan. But it is unclear just how much this is a transcript of the conversation. It could be an imagined conversation projected onto the lips of

Philosophically, there is another way to establish (or underscore) the limited knowledge of Satan—one that does not depend on assuming his finitude or having acquired it in a single vision. This alternative way depends on Satan's having transitioned from being good to being evil. Consider that no one performs an action unless they think that it is at least good (or neutral) in some way, either for oneself or for someone else. Even criminals and abusers who perform wicked acts do so because they believe such acts to be good (or neutral) in some sense at least for the offenders (or for others, like Robin Hood did). Supposing that Satan did have infinite or maximal knowledge, he would know the truth value of every moral fact as long as moral facts are propositions that are true or false. This is to say that he would know that it is true that "abuse is wrong" and that it is false that "being selfish/prideful is good." He wouldn't *believe* that the action that would precipitate his fall would be a good thing, since he would know already that it is false that it is a good thing. In order for him to have fallen from grace, as it were, he would have had to have been mistaken about what he believed about what the good was in that moment. But, on the assumption of his omniscience, he knows every moral fact without fail and, so, would not have believed wrongly about what he thought was good (for him) at the time. He would, instead, have believed his action to have been wrong and would have refrained from doing it. So, if he were all-knowing, then he would not have transitioned from good to evil. But he did. Therefore, he must not be all-knowing.

Thus, in virtue of Satan's finite origin and the scriptural implications of Satan not having all knowledge, we have good reasons to think Satan is less than omniscient. Also, given his transitioning from good to evil, Satan's knowledge is one that must be limited. But, to query further, to what extent is Satan's knowledge limited? Granting that Satan is not *all*-knowing, it does not follow that he is ignorant of *any* future propositions. According to Revelation 12, he seems to know one thing about the future. In that chapter, there is a "loud voice from heaven" (v. 10) that reports that the devil "knows that his time is short" (v. 12). So reported, there is indeed something in particular Satan foreknows. However, this could simply be, as the church has historically insisted, a matter of gifted insight. One can know that their

God and Satan at the discretion of Job's author. Or, the question itself could be seen as a rhetorical question with no epistemic significance implied (cf. Gen 4:6, 9–10). Perhaps we could appeal to the famous warning issued by Peter that "Your adversary the devil prowls around like a roaring lion, seeking someone to devour" (1 Pet 5:8). While one reading of "seeking" (where the Greek term implies "investigating" or "searching") seems to give the impression that Satan does not *now* know who it is he can "devour," it is possible to read "seeking" in the sense of "seeking out" or "striving for," as is the case in Matt 12:46, which then does not lend itself to any such ignorance on the part of the seeker.

time is short for reasons other than intrinsic foreknowledge. But if Satan does not have all knowledge, including all knowledge of the future, then it is simpler to say that Satan has no knowledge whatsoever in the first moment of his existence excluding, perhaps, self-knowledge. Like fellow finite intelligences, Satan begins with a blank slate and must come to know things only through those means at his disposal.[20]

In conclusion, we can offer a pretty reasonable case that Satan has limited knowledge and is not therefore all-knowing. But it is no mystery that he is crafty and quite knowledgeable in his own right. But to what extent Satan is not all-knowing is not clearly understood, though we can reasonably guess that Satan comes to know what he knows in much the same way we do—through incidental contact with others and his awareness of the realms in which he finds himself.

The Powers of Satan

Much of what Satan can do appears to be in part rather well known in Christian circles. Satan, as his Hebrew "name" indicates, is a being who opposes the will of God, including matters of truth, sound doctrine, and virtue. By extension, he opposes believers for he is "the accuser of our brothers" (Rev 12:10). The instruments of such opposition appear to include temptation, deception, and the propagation of false and heretical teachings. Jesus's words about the average thief's trinity of opposition nicely sums up what Satan's itinerary likely involves, namely, "to steal and kill and destroy" (John 10:10). Peter considers the devil's adversarial nature (he uses *ho antidikos*, which means "the adversary") to be such that he "prowls around like a roaring lion, seeking someone to devour" (1 Pet 5:8). The metaphor of a predator is appropriate in that Satan's actions are naturally destructive to those plagued already by various weaknesses as he seeks to satisfy his own hunger for human failure.

As an adversarial force, Satan's primary weapons of influence consist of moral deterioration and religious apostasy. Accordingly, he traffics in temptation to sin as well as the inculcation of false doctrines and moral compromises in widening the rift between human and God. We might say that these are satanic actions brought about through *cognitive* powers aimed at unsuspecting targets. This is to say that Satan's mode of influence is not physical or by any kind of supernatural acts of wizardry, but rather through intellectual or mind-to-mind influence. As a helpful visual, think of this as

---

20. For some discussion about whether Satan can know our inner thoughts—that is, whether he can read our minds—see appendix B.

a form of *telepathy*. Satan, like his demons, is able to communicate directly with us (viz., our spirits). And this makes sense given that Satan is an immaterial spirit himself. The one who adheres to a materialist account will have a much harder hill to climb in explaining the interaction, but at the very least she should see such cognitive interaction as an instance of mind-to-mind communicability—whatever that might look like to her.

Not many contemporaries dispute whether Satan can do anything *physical*, for we easily imagine that Satan, allegedly equipped with extraordinary power, can manipulate matter at his discretion (as long as it is permitted by God). Christians throughout much of history have taken it for granted that Satan can perform miraculous feats for his own purposes—counterfeit miracles, as it were.[21] From enacting apparitions to causing earthquakes, Christians have surmised that Satan and his minions can directly interact with our physical universe apart from any human proxies. While this is certainly possible, I am inclined to think that this is not among the diabolical powers in Satan's arsenal. My reasons for this are fourfold:

1. That immaterial things can causally act on material things is initially improbable.
2. The good angels, from whom the demons derive, lack such an ability.
3. There are no unambiguous passages in Scripture where Satan performs such miracles.
4. The prospect of a creative power to generate diseases and perform miracles inappropriately attributes divine powers to demons.

The strength of the improbability mentioned in (1) is based on the intuition that purely spiritual things cannot directly interact with physical things. Just in terms of distinct physical objects, the less dense an object is, the less likely it is to interact with any solid physical object. Steam, for example, cannot for the most part (perhaps under no circumstances) move rocks, whereas water and ice can under the right circumstances. Once *all* physical elements are removed, even if there is a phantom that remains, there is nothing left to produce any kinetic energy. Spirits are immaterial things and, so, are not naturally equipped to move upon physical objects.

Regarding (2), Scripture suggests that angels likely derive their ability to interact with the natural world, in one way or another, from God—that

---

21. A number of Christians associate Paul's mentioning of "false signs and wonders" (2 Thess 2:9) as a reference to these kinds of powers Satan allegedly perform. Against this, however, is that "signs and wonders" does not always mean miracles. The fact that they are "false" (*pseudous*; from this word we derive "pseudo-" in English) strongly indicates that they are not actual manipulations of nature and its forces.

God is the one who makes them visible (Num 22:31; 2 Kgs 6:17) and directly empowers their activity (Rev 7:2) when the occasions require. I will expand on this in chapter 8, but suffice it to say here that if the good angels indeed lean on God for their activity in this world, this leaves little chance that Satan and his demons can otherwise do so without any such divine intervention. Of course, we do not expect that God would specially empower someone like *Satan and his demons* as they seek to carry out moral wickedness on this earth. This would make God an accomplice to evil—a surely unconscionable alternative to denying that God assists his enemies.

Space does not permit a full defense of (3), but the few passages that possibly suggest that Satan has the ability to interact with the physical universe actually do not do so. To give one example, Job is reported to have been afflicted by Satan with skin lesions (Job 2:7). This suggests that Satan can indeed act on human skin. However, apart from whether the book of Job is giving us a straightforward historical description or not, it is not clear just what condition Job suffered. If he suffered from hives, then such a condition can readily be brought about by stress. And this could be accomplished strictly by Satan cognitively influencing Job—someone who was in the process of *losing everything*. What could be more stressful than that? There are other passages that may be accommodated in similar ways, such as the case of a woman "bent over" for eighteen years (Luke 13:11), whose condition could have been *willed* by an evil spirit influencing her to a life of improper posture; and the men who were made deaf and mute (Matt 9:32–33; 12:22) might have something to do with a *conversion disorder*—something that has no known physical cause. What remains are vague passages about satanic power and authority and passages where Satan either possesses someone, tempts someone, or influences someone to falsehood. And these need not be construed as physics-based activities.

And (4) seems to me obviously true. If Satan can indeed perform miraculous feats comparable to those of God's prophets and even Jesus himself, it is a wonder how divine miracles would prove anything. For example, if most of the nature miracles can be copied, then no nature miracle vouches for the divine origin or sanction of anything. One must look to something else to do the work of divine accreditation. But that completely disregards the purpose of miracles! In Scripture, that is the very reason why they obtain at all (see John 3:2; 10:25, 37–38; Acts 2:22; 2 Cor 12:12; Heb 2:4). Moreover, if Satan can indeed cause things like physical manifestations—where the manifesting spirit takes on a hominid body endowed with organs and such—then Satan would have the ability to create something like a human being. I cannot help but think that this encroaches upon the divine prerogative of God as the sole creator of any and every organism. Surely this conflicts with King David's declaration: "There is none like you among the gods, O Lord, *nor are there any works like yours*" (Ps 86:8; emphasis added). If Satan can create human bodies, his works would indeed be like the Lord's.[22]

Consequently, I am convinced that when all four of these reasons are considered *together*, it mitigates against the idea that Satan would have any such matter-interacting powers sufficient to produce miracles and such. We must consider any alleged satanic miracle to be nothing more than spiritual deception and chicanery. Thus, Satan's powers must be relegated to the cognitive and do not enable him to directly[23] impact the physical.

CONCLUSION

We have seen that Satan is a personal, spiritual being who is probably a fallen angel along with his compatriots the demons. He opposes God and, by extension, his creation. He can tempt us into moral failure and manipulate us into falsehood. It seems clear that Satan is the primary enemy of all that is holy and does what he can to ensure that God's righteousness continues to be tarnished by and ultimately dies with the human race. Though he is a force to be reckoned with, his power does not approximate God's—not even a little bit! For his powers are limited to cognitive interactions and nothing more. This much we can know with a high degree of probability. And, as the saying goes, better the devil you know than the devil you don't. We will now move on to say something about "the world" as the second part of the enemy triumvirate.

---

22. An expanded and more detailed defense of these four points can be found in my *Gods of This World*, 202ff.

23. I say "directly" here to allow for the fact that Satan could indeed cause things in the physical world *through* his interactions with human minds. In the aforementioned case of Job, Satan can cause skin lesions on him by inducing mental stress in Job. The condition would thus be purely psychosomatic, a phenomenon perfectly consistent with some form of stress-induced urticaria (see Kimyai-Asadi and Usman, "Role of Psychological Stress in Skin Disease").

5

The World

SATAN IS NOT THE only personal actor in the theater of war. The universe is obviously populated by, among other things, human beings. Collectively, human beings are often referred to as "the world" in the New Testament. Despite the misleading impression of its Greek word, *kosmos*, not all references to "the world" pertain to the planet itself or the universe at large. Take, for example, the most iconic passage—John 3:16. Therein we are told that "God so loved the world . . ." despite the fact that, according to a passage earlier in John's Gospel, "the world did not know him" (1:10). Though I imagine God loved, and still loves, the *planet*, these words are unmistakably referencing the human population. Other passages beyond the Gospels confirm that "the world" is a regular designation for a wider humanity. And this aggregate at least shares a solidarity in mutually opposing God's will (Acts 17:31; 19:27; Rom 3:6, 19; 4:13; 1 Cor 1:21; 4:9; 6:2; 11:31; 2 Cor 5:19; Gal 6:14; Heb 11:7, 38; Jas 4:4; 2 Pet 2:5; 1 John 2:2; 3:1; 4:5c, 14; Rev 3:10; 12:9).

This is significant insofar as one must understand that "the world" is neither impersonal nor unitary. And, despite its solidarity, it is not always comprised of complete like-mindedness. For sometimes "the world" refers to yet-to-be-believers (John 6:33) while in other contexts it refers to never-to-become-believers (1 Cor 11:32). Furthermore, there is no question that "the world," when used negatively, encapsulates a set of human adversaries distinct from the devil. Jesus's words in John 15:18–19 illustrate this perfectly:

> If the world hates you, know that it has hated me before it hated you. If you were of the world, the world would love you as its

own; but because you are not of the world, but I chose you out of the world, therefore the world hates you.

Despite such a bleak promise, Jesus goes on to show the solidarity we will have with the Holy Spirit and our God and how that translates into victory for the believer (John 16). But the point here is that the world—that is, the world that *hates*—is systematically in opposition to Christ and his disciples. In fact, outright hatred and not mere opposition are Jesus's choice words. The image cast by Jesus here is one of deliverance and conjures up images like that of the rescue of Noah's family from the flood (Gen 6–8) and the rescue of Lot's family from Sodom and Gomorrah (Gen 19). Appropriately, Walter Wink has considered this use of "the world" as "the Domination System."[1] He does so because the world is comprised of organized groups of fallen human beings that belong to this or that institution and seek to force others to conform to its nefarious mission and values. And these institutions are willing to eradicate any who would stand in their way. The ultimate outcome, whether it be carried out through conversion or annihilation, is *domination*. "The world" thus represents the establishment and is something that wields both political influence and military brute force in its desire to dominate. Consequently, it is a zero-sum game.

The apostle Paul also talks about how the world and the believer are of two different "spirits." Paul writes that "we have received not the spirit of the world, but the Spirit who is from God, that we might understand the things freely given us by God" (1 Cor 2:12). The comparison of the Holy Spirit to the "spirit of the world" is meant to be a play on words. The "spirit of the world" is not a personal being as is the Third Person of the Trinity. Rather, the world brings its own countenance, and it is in stark contrast to God. It entails having a tendency and an orientation—a penchant, really. Our disposition to sin is why we like being admired by the world and seek its accolades (cf. Matt 6:16). We are, by default, card-carrying members of its community. In turn, the world will come to recognize this shift in one's orientation away from "the spirit of the world" and toward Christ and will cease its reciprocated love and replace it with unmitigated hatred (John 15:19).

Even though followers of Jesus are encouraged and supported by the Spirit, this is not sufficient to stave off the temptations of some to compromise. To the compromisers within the church, James has these biting words: "You adulterous people! Do you not know that friendship with the world is enmity with God? Therefore whoever wishes to be a friend of the world makes himself an enemy of God" (Jas 4:4). It is explicitly stated here that

---

1. Wink, *Engaging the Powers*, 13–104.

the world is indeed at enmity with God, for each person who befriends the world is considered "adulterous" and is oneself "an enemy of God."

Thus the world, so understood, hates the things of God and stands in enmity with him. But the world is not something above and beyond the aggregate of human beings any more than a "stamp collection" is anything above and beyond the totality of one's collected stamps. This is important for, as Scripture indicates, being at enmity with God as a member of the world is a remediable condition. One can freely exit this camp and become an adopted child of God (John 1:12).

Though properly distinguished from other forces like Satan, the world does not act *independently* of other forces. Indeed, the First Epistle of John points out that "the whole world lies in the power of the evil one" (1 John 5:19). This gives the justified impression that the world may not be all bad after all but, rather, is a victim. For it is being influenced and exploited by Satan. If Satan is indeed the serpent of the garden of Eden and the *haśśāṭān* from among the "sons of God" in Job, then his power over the world is evident *even on God's own soil*. That Satan is the "ruler of this world" (John 12:31) and "the god of this world" (2 Cor 4:4) reflects his ascendancy and influence he has over the world. It appears that the world has been subjugated by Satan, but this does not mean that its inhabitants cannot be rescued.

Jesus's prayer to the Father regarding his disciples, then, is very apropos: "I do not ask that you take them out of the world, but that you keep them from the evil one" (John 17:15). The world is not an intrinsic evil force; it is a malleable aggregate of people who just happen to be under the blinding influence and jurisdiction of Satan. That Jesus does not desire to take us out of the world just yet finds a certain amount of tension with Paul's later statement that the light can have no fellowship with the darkness (2 Cor 6:14). But the tension is relieved once we accept that one can be *in* the world and not *of* it (John 15:19; 17:16). As it turns out, all the world is a stage—a stage comprised of human beings that are susceptible to external forces vying for control and dominion. But since Satan had become our *de facto* ruler and god, every human being is thus born into his adversarial kingdom—a kingdom in opposition to the kingdom of God. Since all of us are predisposed to sin and inevitably commit it, we are thoroughly separated from God and under the influence "of [our] father the devil" (John 8:44). Satan is thus the world's default patriarch whether we like it or not. And because God has a presence in everyone's lives, we are all inwardly groaning for release from Satan's black-hearted family.

We have to be careful, though. When we become Christians, our exodus from the kingdom of Satan and into the kingdom of God does not guarantee our fidelity to God. For, just as *haśśāṭān* had come from among God's heavenly hosts to unleash harm on righteous Job, there is no province or "safe zone" in which we can be sheltered from his assaults. As Jesus tells us, the kingdom of God is among us (Luke 17:21) and we are not, for as long as we live, physically removed from the world—the same world that is under the ongoing influence of Satan. We become unwelcome aliens residing in a foreign land.

Therefore, a systematized expression of "the world" based on what has been said up to now can be expressed as follows: the world is a malleable aggregate of human beings that are, by default, under the general control and influence of Satan. Though one can defect from this unintended allegiance to the devil, this does not remove the external influence the world can have upon the individual. And once one's allegiance and orientation change to the things of God, one becomes nothing more than an alien hostile occupying enemy territory. To wit, one has not *left* a relationship with Satan and the world; one has merely *altered* it. The Christian has shed her old uniform and has donned the distinctive colors of the Enemy—the Enemy in the Lewisian sense in that, from the point of view from the kingdom of Satan, God is the adversary. The follower of Jesus has become a light on the hill that cannot be hidden (Matt 5:14). To the open-minded, it is a beacon. To the stubborn and resistant, it is an illuminated target. It marks, not the end of any spiritual warfare, but the beginning of it.

6

The Flesh

LIKE "THE WORLD," THE designation of "the flesh" takes on a number of meanings depending on how it is employed in Scripture. On the one hand, it is a literal referent—referring to the integumentary system enshrouding each person and animal (e.g., Gen 2:21, 23–24; Exod 12:8; Lev 4:11; Isa 22:13; Ezek 39:17; Luke 24:39; John 1:14; Acts 2:31; Eph 5:29; 6:12; Phil 1:24; 3:2; 1 Tim 3:16; I Pet 3:18; 1 John 4:2; Rev 17:16; 19:18, 21). By extension, it's often used as a Semitic reference and metonym for "living being" (e.g., Gen 6:12–19; Deut 5:26; Ps 56:4; Isa 40:5; 66:23; Jer 12:12; Matt 16:17; Luke 3:6; John 17:2; Acts 2:17). On the other hand, it has a figurative connotation. In particular, "the flesh" sometimes refers to the pull of our sinful desires that are hard-wired, as it were, by virtue of belonging to the race of *Homo sapiens* (e.g., John 8:15; Rom 7:15, 18; 8:3–13; 1 Cor 3:3; 2 Cor 1:17; 10:2–4; Gal 4:29; 5:17, 19; Col 2:23; 1 Pet 2:11; 1 Pet 2:18; 1 John 2:16; Jude 23). It connotes the side of human nature associated with passions and desires.

While many Greek philosophers consider the literal interpretation to be on point, being enfleshed is not itself a sinful thing. The surest evidence of this is the fact that God intentionally and willingly created a physical universe, the concluding result of which is unequivocally deemed "good" (Gen 1:31). Second, God deliberately became incarnated as a human being in the person of Jesus of Nazareth and, yet, remained sinless (2 Cor 5:21; Heb 4:15). Third, the eschatological promise of a physical, bodily resurrection for all believers (Rom 8:11; 1 Cor 15:52; 1 Thess 4:15–17; Rev 20:4–6) shows that a permanent physical state is indeed a (supremely) good thing. So, "the flesh" is not to be understood along these lines. It must be something else.

It is evident that "the flesh," being cast in Scripture as an occasional enemy to our spirituality, is intended in the figurative sense. So used, it refers to a repository of sinful desires within the self that physically impels the self's will toward actions that are morally wrong. In that sense it is possibly but not necessarily a force of spiritual opposition. The flesh is not an autonomous being as if it had a will of its own and some measure of volition; however, it surely opposes the properly ordered spiritual will. Let us consider a helpful illustration used by Plato's mentor, Socrates, in book 9 of Plato's *Republic*. Socrates asks his dialogue partner to peel back the veil, so to speak, about what goes on in each human being. Within each person is a shepherd that represents the seat of consciousness and self-will. But there are animals, including a lion, present that the shepherd (who is a rational intellect) domesticates. These animals (and specifically the lion) represent the various passions of the flesh. If these animals should be inordinately overfed, they begin to increase in strength and eventually overpower and threaten the host intellect (the shepherd). But if they are tamed and fed modestly, they can be used in proper service to the host. Thus, says Socrates, the passions ought to be subservient to the rational side of each person, not the other way around.

When one gives in to a passion, she is feeding and growing that passion. In turn, the passion becomes a bit more of a potent force, making it increasingly difficult to resist. If an external mind, like a demon, could incite one to give in to this or that passion, then the rational self grows weaker. Such a diminution of the rational self becomes a recipe for ongoing sin by one's becoming a slave to those growing passions. And ongoing sin, in turn, is a recipe for rupturing one's relationship with God. Ironically, the flesh has become an enemy because *we*, having been created for fellowship with God and proper community with others, have instead allowed it to become so. We literally become our own worst enemy.

As it turns out, the various lexical uses of "the flesh" are not utterly unrelated to each other after all as though its literal connotation were something entirely different from its more figurative use. A number of the sinful desires we have are indeed rooted in the physical body. And beings in this world are naturally enfleshed creatures. The point here is that though having sinful desires rooted in the flesh is a sufficient condition for being a physical person, being a physical person is not a sufficient condition for having sinful desires.[1] Our physical bodies simply have a series of desires $D_1, D_2, \ldots D_n$

---

1. I would add that neither is it a *necessary* condition, for if Satan, an immaterial

that can be activated or sustained by oneself or be exploited by any invading or parasitic spiritual (=cognitive) influence. Think of mental images or thoughts. When a thought is recalled, it is merely the self's bringing up of an idea or image that already preexists in one's conscious or subconscious mind. But thoughts can also be recalled via the prompting by a friend, relative, lover, or enemy. Desires are no different in this respect. While one can certainly have and entertain desires on her own, they can also be prompted by an external mind. Desires, then, can be pawns utilized by demonic forces that seek to assail the Christian. As noted, the flesh is not an independent enemy and has no will of its own; rather, it lingers as a force of temptation that we ourselves can succumb to if we willfully dwell on or actively seek it, or if something outside of us coaxes us to do so. As such, *being tempted* is not the sin. It is the willful, even if temporary, surrender to the temptation in the bringing about of a moral (and/or theological) transgression that is a sin.

Some of these desires that can be used for ill include sexual desire, the desire for wealth, the desire for power, the desire for fame and importance, and even the desire to be spiritual. Now, these desires are not inherently wrong to have. Certainly the last one isn't. When they arise, we do nothing wrong. However, when we take over the desire and actively sustain it (or do nothing to curtail it), and perhaps yearn for unscrupulous ways to satisfy it, then we transgress God's moral rectitude.[2] If we are able to channel our desires within the boundaries of God's moral framework, then we do nothing wrong. For example, sexual desire in and of itself is not immoral. In fact, it is a fringe benefit to the procreative process. But if one focuses that sexual desire in a way that transgresses God's moral system, say by turning it into lust or by acting on the desire with another outside a marital context, then one has lost that bout with the flesh. That person has done something wrong amidst the pleasant feelings of satisfying the appetite. The subsequent euphoria that is now part of one's first-hand knowledge of what acting on desires leads to makes any subsequent resistance to the initial desire all the more difficult. We venture from the "what if?" into the "so that." And the "so that" is not a hypothetical conjecture, but a pleasant and vivid memory. Pity the person who knows what it is like to abuse drugs and wants to abstain more than the one who wants to abstain and has not (yet) touched a mind-altering substance.

---

being, did indeed fall from grace, then there are sins one can commit apart from a physical constitution. Also, though animals certainly have desires rooted in their flesh, these are not sins; for sins can only be committed by someone with the relevant autonomy and volitional will.

2. I discuss later how Christians can discern for themselves the moral difference between a proper sexual desire and an improper one (=lust) on pages 242–244.

Therefore, the flesh is part of the human being's furniture. It is an aggregate of desires rooted in human physiology. To have physical desires is obviously not a bad thing. But such desires, if not made subservient to oneself and tamed, become a force for sin. And that force can by exploited by either Satan or the world in meaning to do us harm.

THE THREEFOLD ENEMY

This concludes our exploration about who the enemy is. On the one hand, the enemy is threefold—comprising of Satan, the world, and the flesh. Satan, God's and our spiritual adversary, seeks the ruination of the Christian and all that is holy. The world is chaffed by righteousness and holiness, thus seeking to silence us by deconversion, suppression, or execution. The flesh seeks nothing of its own accord, for it is not a person but an aspect of a person. And yet it opposes our spirituality and our desire for fellowship with God and righteous living. But since neither the world nor the flesh are intrinsically adversarial or immoral things, they are used by us and other persons, as well as the devil himself and his minions, to snuff out the light of Christ within us.

It is important for Christians to know what we are up against. But since Satan is the only force that is wholly independent of us and has no longer any neutral aspect to himself, then even if we can master our flesh and successfully evade the ire of the world, Satan can step in and still use those things against us despite our best efforts. And the more successful we are, the more we invite Satan's retaliation. It is in this sense that our spiritual war against the threefold enemy reduces to being ultimately "against the rulers, against the authorities, against the cosmic powers over this present darkness, against the spiritual forces of evil in the heavenly places" (Eph 6:12). We are in a no-win situation except, thankfully, that we are not engaging the battle alone. God involves himself in the combat and pleads with us to conform to his instructions that will best empower us to stave off the assaults of the triumvirate enemy.

Since God is the key to our spiritual rescue, he is the enemy of our enemy. As such, we would do well to cover an analysis as to who God is. Knowing God, after all, is the primary aim of the Christian walk. It is the basis on which victory is to be had in spiritual warfare. To this we now turn as we advance toward learning what it means to build up our countermeasures.

7

The Enemy of My Enemy: God

"The enemy of my enemy is my friend," so goes the nineteenth-century quote. It is a more recent iteration of an Indian proverb that dates back to the fourth century BC. It happens to describe our present subject appropriately in two ways. First, in recognizing that Satan, the world, and the flesh oppose not only God but each of us, "the enemy of my enemy" implies that God indeed returns the conflict. Second, the saying implies such a God is my friend. Scripture certainly indicates that those who actively side with God are properly his friend (John 15:14–15; Jas 2:23). Conversely, anyone who is a friend of, say, the world is himself made an enemy of God (Jas 4:4).

In this chapter, we shall consider the nature and powers of God—the one who is the ultimate enemy of my (our) enemy. This is considerably important to do in cashing out a full understanding of the nature of spiritual warfare, for it involves, among other things, the status of combatants on both sides. A failure to understand the nature, powers, and liabilities of the combatants will yield a failure to map out a successful pathway to victory or even what that should mean. Moreover, that God, as we shall reveal, is the ultimate being should bring us considerable comfort, for God cannot be overwhelmed and himself conquered. It will also help us better appreciate the strengths and weaknesses of models of spiritual warfare currently on offer. Having already addressed the nature of the threefold enemy that opposes God, then, we now turn to the concept of God itself.

THE NATURE OF GOD

Any project that proceeds to address the nature of God is bound to be working under some obvious epistemic restrictions. For example, one cannot transcend the physical universe in order to have sensory access to God via the conventional five senses. And God, as traditionally conceived, is not the kind of thing that could be accessed this way even if we could. Thus, we have a severe *scientific* limitation, namely, that we cannot empirically detect God as he is and where he is (if indeed it makes sense for him to be any*where* at all). Despite being a logical limitation, it would be a mistake to suppose that this in any way makes knowledge of God an impossible or elusive thing. After all, one does not have empirical access to moral values, semantic truths, or even causal powers. And yet, few discount the reality of morality, truth, and causality.

Now, I'm not saying God is anything like an abstract value or a semantic property. What I am saying is framed purely in the negative, namely, that one cannot discount God's reality simply because God is inaccessible via a certain truth-detecting methodology. This is true about other matters as well. For example, one cannot determine whether Caesar crossed the Rubicon in 43 BC with a microscope or a voltmeter. One cannot determine the atomic weight of helium with the shovels and brushes of archaeology and paleontology. To speak more broadly, one cannot utilize the deliverances of one kind of science to settle issues pertaining to other kinds of science or other avenues to knowledge. While the Pythagorean theorem is quite useful in determining the length of the hypotenuse of a right triangle when its other sides are known, it cannot tell you whether the triangle in question *actually exists* or *what it tastes like* (assuming these things could be true of triangles).

Assessing the nature of God must derive, then, not from science but from the deliverances of theology and philosophy. Both disciplines are appropriate in facilitating our knowledge of who and what God is and what he is capable of. In this section, we shall discuss the nature of God by summarizing the findings delivered up by the tools of Scripture and reason. We shall also, along the way, consider a couple of sticky questions that have additional bearing on the nature of God.

God Is Immaterial

Genesis 1:1 clearly implies that God is something other than the universe he has created: "In the beginning, God created the heavens and the earth."

In the absence of a more technical word like "universe," the ancient phrase "the heavens and the earth" was their way of connoting the entirety of physical creation. Elsewhere Solomon asks, "But will God indeed dwell on the earth?" His answer immediately follows: "Behold, heaven and the highest heaven cannot contain you; how much less this house that I have built" (1 Kgs 8:27). In the New Testament, a Samaritan woman queries Jesus about which province true worshipers of God are to worship him (Samaria vs. Jerusalem). Jesus's response is the following:

> Woman, believe me, the hour is coming when neither on this mountain nor in Jerusalem will you worship the Father. You worship what you do not know; we worship what we know, for salvation is from the Jews. But the hour is coming, and is now here, when the true worshipers will worship the Father in spirit and truth, for the Father is seeking such people to worship him. God is spirit, and those who worship him must worship in spirit and truth. (John 4:21–24)

This passage reveals two relevant things. First, God's true worshipers will worship him "in spirit" and not from a mountain in Samaria or in Jerusalem. This indicates that God is not *in this or that region* as much as he is *in truth*. Unlike the figure of Zeus in ancient Greece or El in Canaanite lore, God does not reside on any particular mountain. And no religiously significant location is sufficient to make one in more worshipful proximity to God. Instead, it is one's *orientation* that gives one an audience with God, namely, being "in spirit and in truth."

That a "spirit" in the ancient world sometimes connoted a kind of incorporeal, ethereal substance serves as the backdrop for why God would not necessarily be confined to a particular spatial region. This is not to say that his being a spirit is *ipso facto* an indication that God is outside of space and, so, cannot be in any location.[1] Rather, God's being a spirit is a guarantee that God cannot be *limited* to this or that location. The conventional wisdom was that spirits could arise anywhere or in any place. That having been said, the implication of John 4 and other passages of Scripture is that God is devoid of *any* of the physical attributes normally attributed to human beings. For God is "not man . . . nor a son of man" (Num 23:19), unlike *Homo sapiens*. God is "through all and in all" (Eph 4:6), unlike limited and localized physical objects. God is "immortal" and "invisible" (1 Tim 1:17; cf. Col 1:15), unlike any human being. God is "in heaven" (Matt 6:9; Col 4:1), unlike anything physical. God is "from everlasting" (Ps 90:2) and the creator of everything outside of himself (Col 1:16), unlike any physical and

---

1. E.g., Thomas, "Spatial Location of God."

(some) nonphysical objects (which also happen to be temporal and among the things created). The ongoing language of Scripture is quite indicative of his transcendence and utter otherness. The convergence of all of the biblical data makes it difficult to think that God would himself be anything physical or even *quasi*-physical (like a phantasm or a ghost). The simplest assessment, barring any reason to think otherwise, is to conclude that God is thoroughly immaterial.

God Is All-Knowing

Scripture has no systematic or meticulously spelled-out doctrine of God's knowledge, but it certainly offers up plenty of passages that indicate that there are no limits to that knowledge. God knows everything from the private "secrets of the heart" (Ps 44:21; cf. Acts 15:8) to the expansive extent of our universe (Ps 113:5–6). His knowledge is detailed and meticulous and without fail (Matt 10:29–30). Even the imagery used of God ("eyes") conveys his universal and penetrative knowledge of every single person (Prov 5:21; 15:3; Heb 4:13; Rev 5:6; 19:12). By virtue of God being the universal creator and sustainer of all that there is (Col 1:16–17), it is implied that he would have knowledge of everything. The most reasonable conclusion is that God is *all*-knowing rather than merely *immensely* knowledgeable. For if God has a boundary to what he knows, this would cry out for an explanation (Why would he only know, say, 95.7 percent of all knowable things and not everything?). But infinite or maximal knowledge would not need an explanation, particularly for a fundamental reality whose existence is (metaphysically) necessary. This is especially true since God would not conversely lack any knowledge (i.e., that God would have 0 percent of all knowledge because he would at least be self-aware).

God Is All-Loving and All-Good

If there is an attribute of God's that needs no introduction, so to speak, it is the love of God. Scripture is replete with references to God's love. And, yes, that includes the Old Testament as well as the New (Deut 7:8; 2 Chr 2:11; Ps 146:8; Prov 3:12; Isa 48:14; John 16:27; 1 Cor 8:3; Heb 12:6; 1 John 4:7). The love God has is not exactly like a filial love or the love of a best friend. It most certainly is nothing like the love of food or a romantic love. If God loved us like one loves food, then he would not preserve us but, rather, consume us. If he loved us romantically, then he would desire us sexually. This would be a confusion of the kinds of love one can have. Similarly, our love for God should also not confuse other forms of love. For example, if we loved God like we do our children, then we should attempt to educate, feed, and nurture God. The love of God is as clearly a different form of love, as brotherly love is clearly a different form of love from the love of ice cream. It involves God's treating of those who bear his image with an esteemed adoration and mutuality, and as beings with intrinsic meaning and value.

The supreme love God has seems to be entailed by the kind of nature that he has. God obviously has desired to create a universe populated by embodied beings capable of moral reasoning and responsibility. A God that did not love would likely not have created such a reality. And that God has in fact created *persons* (beings having volitional consciousness and autonomy), rather than only creating animals or inanimate objects, suggests that God has created such beings to have liberty. These are also necessary in order to make any reciprocating love a reality. The way the universe is populated does not seem like a probable arrangement for a God that is not loving.[2] But if God is loving, it is simpler to think that God, as the ultimate ground of being, is not only loving but infinitely and maximally loving. To be anything short of *all*-loving would complicate God's nature and would require further explanation in much the same way limiting God's knowledge would.

As for God's *goodness*, more specifically his being all-good, this follows from at least two considerations. First, if God is in fact the greatest conceivable being, as Anselm had proffered during the Middle Ages, then such a being must be morally perfect. For if God were anything less than morally perfect, this would entail an imperfection. Accordingly, God would not be God. The other superlative attributes provide additional warrant for thinking that God's being the greatest conceivable being is not only a possibility (leading to his necessity?) but a pretty good bet. Second, that God is a person, and so free, and his being all-knowing, and so omniscient, also lend themselves to his moral perfection. For if God freely chooses his actions, then, like human beings, he does so because he believes he is accomplishing some good or some neutral act either for himself or for another. If God is omniscient, then God knows every moral fact (that "murder is wrong" is true and "it is okay to torture babies for fun" is false, etc.). It

---

2. Even if one takes into account the evils that obtain in this world, the fact that something like human beings exist the way that they do bearing such liberties along with the capacity for acts of compassion and virtue and the ability to enjoy certain pleasures are indicative of some measure of love on the part of our Creator. For evil to be a mitigating problem one must suppose those evils to have no place in the advancement of God's love in his universe. But it is beyond our cognitive capacities to assess whether any evils that obtain do not serve to maximize that love throughout all time and into eternity. As such, it is possible to be maximally loving and, yet, permissive of various evils to take place.

would reasonably follow that God, knowing all moral facts and believing that he always does what is either good or neutral, will only do that which is good or neutral. We could add a third reason for God's all-goodness, which ranks as the most obvious for the vast majority of Christians, namely, that Scripture endorses it: e.g., Num 23:19; Ps 19:7; Matt 5:48; Mark 10:18 (Luke 18:19); 2 Pet 3:14; 1 John 3:5; Heb 7:28; Rev 4:8.

Therefore, God is not only loving and good but he is *all*-loving and *all*-good, which is to say that he is omnibenevolent as well as morally perfect. This is in stark contrast to Satan, who approaches humanity as a predator and destroyer.[3] It also contrasts with the world, which only loves those who are aligned with it. The flesh itself, on the other hand, is not a moral agent and so neither goodness nor badness are properties of it. It is strictly a natural reality that just is.

God Is All-Powerful

Here we're talking about the capabilities or "powers" of God. Now, it is nearly impossible to think that the Scriptures support any level of divine power other than that God is all-powerful. For the Bible speaks of him as being the "Most High" (e.g., Gen 14:19–20; Ps 83:18; Acts 7:48), indeed even "the Almighty" (e.g., Gen 17:1; Ruth 1:20–21; Job 27:10–13; 2 Cor 6:18). That God is the sole creator of the universe (Isa 44:24) reveals that God's power is quite superlative. And since it is simpler to consider God's power to be without arbitrary limitations (i.e., maximal), then God is indeed all-powerful, which is to say that he is *omnipotent*. This is to be expected particularly if God's other attributes are equally maximal.

However, despite such straightforwardness, there are generally two opposing concerns associated with a proper understanding of God's omnipotence. First, there is the concern that God might be able to do the logically impossible; that is, that God can bring about logical contradictions like a square circle or a married bachelor. René Descartes once surmised that it is possible to imagine that 2 plus 3 might not equal 5 and that we are only deluded to think so by a secretly manipulative and sinister God.[4] The force of our assurance of mathematical "truths," Descartes suggested, possibly lies not in the "proper" arithmetic itself but in God's diabolical deception in us

---

3. It would be wrong to conclude, for any reason, that Satan is *maximally* evil or the paradigm of moral imperfection. All that is implied by one's having an evil nature is that one acts deliberately in more sinister ways than in benevolent ways (however that may be cashed out). Satan's being evil does not entail his being a *summum malum*.

4. Descartes, *Meditation* I.

every time we add 2 and 3. Thus, the instantiations of contradictions may merely be an *epistemic* problem and not a metaphysical one. That is, that the problem allegedly lies in our inability to *imagine* what the right answer is and not in the *reality* of mathematics itself (where something is the case but we, due to our cognitive limitations, can't conceive of it). From this, it is argued, it follows that God can indeed do the impossible. But if God can do the impossible, then he can bring it about that he exists and does not exist at the same time (or could end his own existence despite being eternal). The problem with this *universal possibilism* is that such "things" are not things at all; they are just semantically incoherent claims that are linking together otherwise meaningful ones when used in isolation. Consider barking and the property of being a non-barker. Taken independently, these are meaningful properties. But you could combine them and write out the statement: "the barking non-barker." This is no longer describing something that really exists despite our inability to conceive it. It is a self-negating statement that describes *nothing at all*. Any entity that might exist can always be described appropriately in terms that do not self-contradict. That God cannot perform contradictions would not be a limitation, for there is no *thing* that God cannot do. Rather, anything that can be done in accord with his other attributes (e.g., his being all-loving), God can do. Thus, theologians have typically stipulated God's omnipotence in terms of God's being able to do what is logically possible for a God to do. And if God is indeed the ultimate ground of being, and so of logic itself, then any violation of the laws of logic would amount to a violation of God's own nature. Since this is an impossibility that would amount to assailing his own nature, it follows that God cannot do the impossible, for God cannot oppose God.

The second concern is that God's being omnipotent may be an empty truism. This is to say that if we adopt the stipulation that God is omnipotent if and only if God can do anything that is logically possible for that being to do, then no matter what God is he would be omnipotent. To see the potential problem here, consider Alvin Plantinga's thought experiment where God is a being that cannot do anything but scratch its own ear.[5] As it turns out, this being is doing everything it is possible for an ear-scratching-only being to do. Therefore, such a being would also be considered omnipotent for it is in accord with the definition of omnipotence, that it can do anything that is logically possible for that being to do. It seems to me, though, that this is not a strong concern. For an ear-scratching-only being has limitations not already evident in a being who would be in God's position (that

---

5. See Plantinga, *God and Other Minds*, 170; see also Wierenga, *Nature of God*, 28–29.

out of all the possibilities that lie ahead for God in the beginning, some of them, including the world we have, might not have been brought about or brought about differently). Moreover, though it is true that this being cannot itself do anything other than scratch itself, its being an ear-scratching-only being to begin with is inexplicable and by itself explains nothing else. It has built-in limitations not implied by being an ultimate being. Whereas God's "limitations" (like being unable to kill himself or to sin) would not be inexplicable but sensibly bound up in what it means to be the ultimate and necessary cause/ground of everything else. This is to say that one cannot swap out God with another being in God's position who does not bear the same essential but delimited "limitations."

Thus, it is wrong to include the impossible among God's powers and it is questionable, if not also wrong, to render omnipotence as something that could apply to anything with limitations under an arbitrary set of circumstances. Nevertheless, as we shall see, Scripture certainly gives the clearest indication of God's abilities far surpassing those of an ear-scratching-only being.

In Scripture, God's powers are delineated in three ways. First, God *permits* certain things to obtain. This is to say that God does not directly and intentionally act in the bringing about of certain actions (such as the rebellion of Satan or Judas's betrayal of Jesus), and yet if he did not permit them, then they would not have obtained. In this sense, God controls the events in the most passive and hands-off way. Second, God brings about certain things *through mediation*. This is to say that God acts through some person or event or set of events and/or persons in order to ultimately bring about something (such as God's using ancient Israel to drive out the Canaanites). In this sense, God intentionally and actively moves person x toward the production of y and does not bring about y apart from having moved on x to do so. Third, there are things that God does *directly and without mediation*. These acts involve things like miracles. For example, when God heals someone directly and such does not obtain (and perhaps could not obtain) by any other way, then it is a miracle. Whether we are speaking of healings or resurrections, such powers exhibited by God do not depend on mediation.[6]

---

6. We must recognize that sometimes healings take place only when the afflicted undergo some ritual on their part (John 9:6–7; Jas 5:14–15). But this is not the same thing as God acting through some normal medium that could otherwise bring about a healing without God's direct intervention. For example, in John 9:6–7 Jesus restores a blind man by applying mud to his eyes. Mud is not itself a healer of blindness and, so, there is no expectation that such a healing might have obtained apart from God's intervention. Rather, the application of mud probably reflected a different purpose in the healing episode.

This third notion is the most significant in appreciating God's overwhelming opposition to any other celestial being, specifically the demons.

This third notion might lead us to say that *any* direct cause on God's part that exceeds the productive powers of nature is always a miracle. This would entail that anything God does directly and without mediation would be a miracle, including the creation of angels or the sending of fire down on Sodom and Gomorrah. In one sense, these things are indeed miracles as we might casually use the term. But Scripture indicates that a miracle also serves as a "sign" or a testament to the credential of or by God (e.g., John 9:16; 10:25). And this credentialing aspect of "sign" is not necessarily present in things like the destruction of cities (at least not a "sign" in the same way; cf. Jude 7). We might prefer to regard those acts instead as something more broad like "special acts of creation." However, it is evident that miracles, so understood, are exclusively performed by God when not only does God perform special acts of creation but when those acts serve to accredit some person or doctrine in the eyes of onlookers. As Nicodemus himself acknowledged to Jesus, "Rabbi, we know that you are a teacher come from God, for *no one can do these signs that you do unless God is with him*" (John 3:2; emphasis added). They are visible demonstrations of God's power for authenticating some doctrinal or prophetic notion or person.

As can be seen in view of the last chapter, Satan does not even approximate these attributes. This means that in terms of pitting the abilities of God and his enemy against each other the situation proves to be quite unmatched. If Satan cannot so much as manipulate matter, much less perform a special act of creation, then Satan is completely and thoroughly impotent with regard to the physical world. Even if Satan could manipulate matter, he could not create worlds or call fire down from heaven. There can be no concern or threat to God's providence and sovereignty at the hands of his archvillain. Satan's relative potency is no obvious match for God's omnipotence. But we should not be so myopic to conclude that Satan can wreak no significant havoc or that God can have no morally sufficient reasons for permitting him to do so. Nevertheless, we can appreciate the boundaries, or in the case of God the lack thereof, in the mutually opposing celestial forces that populate the theater of spiritual warfare. Indeed, Satan does not have such comparable power for his limitations are many and could have been otherwise. This should be a great comfort to the followers of God and a great terror to those that viciously oppose him.

THE SUPREMACY OF GOD OVER SATAN

The attributes of God testify to the superiority of such a being over any would-be rivals. When we consider the threefold enemy of the previous chapter (Satan, the world, and the flesh), it is apparent that none hold a candle to the power, majesty, and glory of God. God's attributes are superlative and maximal such that we can, with Moses, confidently declare that "there is no one like the LORD our God" (Exod 8:10). God is personal, eternal, ever-present, all-knowing, all-loving, and all-powerful. God is not just the ultimate version of what these things represent; he is the metric and gold standard by which all others are measured.

But God's superiority does not guarantee a spiritual life free of conflict. In fact, we are promised nothing of the sort. And when it comes to Satan himself, we are accosted by him and his demons' destructive ways. Though the superiority of God does not guarantee immediate relief, we can rest assured that nothing happens apart from his sovereign control. For whatever obtains does so for reasons that may or may not be disclosed to us, but always for reasons consonant with the divine will. Since God is all-loving, he does not permit the destructive powers of the enemy out of some sadistic desire to see us tormented. Our confidence and destiny are in God's hands because something *good* is ultimately being preserved (Rom 8:28). Moreover, God does not wage war separately from us. He has not created a bordered heaven on earth, so to speak, that he places us in in order to protect us from all harm. Instead, we are participants, willing or not, that must strive to withstand the assaults of the enemy in whatever form it takes.

We will endure much, but in the end the threefold enemy will not endure at all. That is God's promise. This should be both a comfort to us as well as a call to be responsible in how we both understand spiritual warfare and how we practice it. And our victory, if we endure to the end, is assured for "the victory belongs to the LORD" (Prov 21:31).

8

Angels: The Good, the Bad, and the Fallen

THERE ARE NOT JUST multiple forces on the dark side of the fence. On God's side, there is also a race of beings called "angels." Like the demons under Satan's command, God has created and enlisted an aggregate of beings he uses in the climate of spiritual warfare. Though human beings can and often do flout their responsibilities to God, the angels do not fail to actualize them at God's behest. However, as we have suggested already with respect to Satan, there must have been a rebellion that led to the exile of some of these angels. This might be expected if angels had been given a certain amount of freedom (volition) and responsibility and were not placed in any ultimate beatitude. That is, angels were probably not put into a position relative to God where God's presence would have prevented them from any rebellious decision-making. Conditions might have been quite analogous to that of Adam and Eve, who, despite being created in a morally innocent state, nevertheless succumbed to temptation. If Satan was in fact the impetus for this rebellion and the angels' subsequent exile (Jude 6), then angelic beings populate both sides of heaven—those under God's direction and those under Satan's.

In this chapter, we shall explore the angelic component to the chain of command in the hegemonies of God and Satan. Since angels—both good and fallen—are often mentioned in some key warfare passages in Scripture, we shall seek to uncover what their role is and how we should think about them. Like the forces of God, Satan, the world, and the flesh, the subject of angels is equally riddled with mystery in the grander drama. That mystery has, unfortunately, given way to rampant and often uncritical speculation about the nature and powers of good and evil angels alike.

In this chapter, we shall explore what angels are and what they can do with a view toward clearing up some misconceptions relevant to spiritual warfare. Since this book's focus is limited to spiritual warfare, we shall only consider a systematization of their role insofar as it relates to the subject. This will therefore not be a complete analysis of Christian angelology or demonology.

THE GOOD: THE ANGELS OF GOD

One of the peculiarities of Scripture is the existence of a race of beings identified as "angels"—peculiar because it is curious why God would need or want a race of beings with which to mediate his will on earth. But it is certainly not inconceivable (after all, God uses the church to mediate his will to the unevangelized). Popular perceptions of angels tend to revolve around angels as supernatural beings in service to human comfort, rescue, and, in a word, happiness. They are seen by many as agents of the universe that occasionally intercede for our benefit. They make themselves available to gentle souls who call upon them, or permit them their work, in righting some wrong or in saving us from certain doom. Some have even claimed to have photographed these emissaries of hope. As for their appearance, they are often depicted as winged creatures that are mostly female, though around Valentine's Day the ancient Homeric imagery of the cherub takes over: chubby babies with disproportionate wings donning bows with arrows and seeking out unsuspecting lovesick mortals as they work to promote the most cosmic matchmaking system ever. And some think that upon our deaths, those of us who were beloved on earth become postmortem angelic protectors of those we have left behind. Sounds nice, doesn't it?

But this is almost entirely wrong, at least as far as Scripture goes. Angels do not have material properties. Instead, they are explicitly identified as "spirits" across the board (Heb 1:14). And we know that "a spirit does not have flesh and bones" (Luke 24:39). Accordingly, they lack physical properties like "wings" or "chubby faces." This is also perhaps why they do not partake in romantic relationships (Matt 22:30; Mark 12:25), for if they lack anything physical then they are sexless. Though they are described as having wings in Scripture (Exod 37:9; Ezek 1:4–25; 10:5–22; Rev 4:8), the ascriptions are merely representative of their ability to oversee and protect and/or their ability to attend to a situation swiftly (Ps 18:10), which are all in line with their ministry to human beings.[1] They are to be unequivocally distinguished from the human race (1 Cor 4:9; 1 Pet 1:12) as beings that likely preceded us (Gen 1:26a; 3:24). That people and not angels go on to the resurrection at the end of the ages further establishes their distinction from us. For God, "it is not angels that he helps, but he helps the offspring of Abraham" (Heb 2:16). So, they cannot be the products of human death as they are distinctly different kinds of beings. And, no, heaven isn't calling for another angel when a loved one passes on (which would amount to an afterlife of *burden* rather than of *rest*!).

As far as Scripture is concerned, only two good angels are mentioned by name: Michael and Gabriel. Michael (Hebrew: *mîkā'êl*; "one like God") is considered one of the highest-ranking angels (the "archangel"; 1 Thess 4:16; cf. Dan 10:13, 21 and 12:1) and is the only one reported to confront Satan directly (Jude 9; Rev 12:7–9). Gabriel (Hebrew: *gabrî'êl*; "man of God") pops up now and then throughout Scripture (Dan 8:16; 9:21; Luke 1:19, 26) but he, unlike Michael, is not given any such special status or rank. To what extent being an archangel or "prince" or whatever is meant to be an official rank or just a way to denote a special level of importance is not made clear. Equally unclear is whether being a cherub(im) (Gen 3:24; 2 Sam 22:11; Ezek 9:3; 10) or a seraph(im) (Isa 6:2, 6) is supposed to be an indication of *function* or of *species* (or both?). But even if we were told which, it may not be enough to tell us just what that means in relation to other angels.

Aside from these specifics, we should back up and take a more systematic look at the nature, knowledge, and powers of angels as far as we can reasonably discern. Let us turn to these matters now.

The Nature of Angels

An "angel" (Greek: *aggelos*; Latin: *angelus*; Hebrew: *mal'āk*) in Scripture is itself a reference to a *function* of someone or other and not so much to a *being*. It literally means "messenger." And that doesn't involve any speculation about the nature of who is delivering that message. The term is quite often used in reference to a kind of being that is somewhere between the divine and the mundane. This is implied by the New Testament in reference to Jesus's incarnation, which made him for "a little while lower than the

---

1. Other things in Scripture, including God and even the wind, are said to have wings and they are clearly meant as metaphors (e.g., Ps 63:7; 91:4; 104:3; 139:9; Jer 48:40; Mal 4:2). The wing motif is captured well in Jesus's lament in Matt 23:37: "O Jerusalem, Jerusalem, the city that kills the prophets and stones those who are sent to it! How often would I have gathered your children together as a hen gathers her brood under her wings, and you were not willing!"

angels" (Heb 2:7, 9; cf. Ps 8:5) only to end up to be elevated above them (Heb 1:4). They, like any other creature, are also "subjected" to God (1 Pet 3:22) and were at some point created by him (Ps 148:2, 5). They are appropriately *intermediary* beings in terms of both their nature (they are spirits but not God; they are finite but not human; they are higher than human beings but lower than God) as well as their office (they obey God and render services to him and on his behalf to others).

The ancient Greeks believed that something like the angels (they preferred the term *daimon*, from which the English derives the word "demon") could be good or bad. They believed that angels could be people—a "golden race of human beings"[2]—or maybe not even persons at all. For the *daimon* might just be something abstract like fortune, luck, or fate. The Persians and Babylonians had a more developed sense of these beings that approximates more the Judeo-Christian doctrines of angelology and demonology. In fact, that proximity has led some since Celsus in the second century to suppose that Jews and Christians just plagiarized their views. But early thinkers like Origen (AD 184–253)[3] thought that perhaps it was the Persians and the Greeks who borrowed from Jews and Christians in filling out their (later) views of angels and demons. Neil Forsyth thinks this is a "complicated" one to answer but that Origen is at least "partially right."[4] And it is clear that, as far as Mithraism is concerned, there was certainly some copying of Christian doctrines prompted by the desire to curry favor with those who would otherwise not respond well to pagan myths. That angels (*daimones*) were often depicted as fickle beings with natures fusing a heavenly (=spiritual) substance together with an earthy (=material) one further suggests a discord between a developed Judeo-Christian angelology and other ancient views of the *daimon*.

The concept of angels in the canonical works of the Old and New Testaments reveals two things. First, the biblical writers did not just copy straight from their ancient neighbors despite some interesting similarities. No self-respecting Jew or Christian would have blindly intimated the teachings of a pagan in order to solidify their distinction from the world. Second, the differences are too significant to ignore. For the ancient Greeks thought of "demons" (=angels) as good or bad and that they might be mysterious impersonal forces of good fortune. But nothing about this notion parallels what we have in either Jewish or Christian angelology. Moreover, the Greeks considered such intermediary, hybrid beings to exist so that God's

2. Hesiod, *Works and Days*, II.121–39; Ferguson, *Demonology*, 40.
3. Origen, *Against Celsus*, VI.42.
4. Forsyth, *Old Enemy*, 88.

commerce with human beings would even be *possible*. In Judaism as with Christianity, this is not a problem. God directly interacts with whomever he pleases (e.g., Exod 33:11). Moreover, the angels of the Greeks are also necessary in order to bring communications back to the gods. Again, this is neither Jewish nor Christian. That God uses angels is no different than his using prophets, apostles, teachers, etc. in the dissemination of the gospel to the people. It is an option and one that he delights in exercising.

As for *how many* angels there are, Scripture seems to be unclear about any specific amount. One could probably set a numeric range from however many nations there were in Genesis 10 (Deut 32:8[5]) to an undisclosed "multitude" (Luke 2:13; Rev 19:1), which is potentially so large as to be innumerable (cf. Rev 7:9). So, there are a lot, and that's all we can say about that.

The Knowledge of Angels

Like the number of angels, it is equally unclear how much knowledge angels have precisely. For surely their knowledge exceeds that of the average human being (e.g., 2 Sam 14:20). And from the mere fact that angels do not die off, and on the presumption that angels can continue to learn, one imagines that they can certainly amass far more knowledge than the oldest human being to ever live. On the other hand, they naturally lack physical bodies with which to have access to any empirical knowledge vis-à-vis the five senses. But lacking a body is not pertinent to having other forms of knowledge. It just means that their knowledge, at least for those who have not had the privilege of embodiment, must primarily be propositional and unmediated.

It is unmediated for the simple reason that they lack any constituent parts—organs and limbs and such. When human beings gather, say, visual information, it must proceed through the mechanism of the eye and optic nerve in tandem with the operations of the physical brain. Angels, as immaterial beings, would lack vision in this sense. As Thomas Aquinas writes, "[a]ngels do not have bodies naturally united to them . . . Hence, only

---

5. The passage reads: "When the Most High gave to the nations their inheritance, when he divided mankind, he fixed the borders of the peoples according to the number of the sons of God." If one accepts the notion that the "sons of God" here are angels, then there appears to be a numerical correspondence between the list of then-existing seventy nations in Gen 10 with the number of angels. It is inconclusive, however, whether the "sons of God" are angels here (cf. Deut 14:1). For more on Deut 32:8, see appendix C, "On Territorial Spirits."

intellect and will of the powers of the soul can belong to them."[6] Accordingly, they would likewise lack the ability to hear, taste, smell, and touch. But this does not mean that they would not have some undisclosed means of receiving, say, imagery (such as human beings do when we dream, where there is visual imagery when there is no corresponding visual input to the eye at that moment). As such, there is no reason why an unembodied mind cannot still receive informational input through other means.

As for their having propositional knowledge, this is easily conceivable. One can know, for example, that 45+193=238 or that triangles are three-sided figures wholly apart from any physical constitution. Aquinas seems to think that God gives such knowledge to angels directly and by virtue of their ontological proximity to God.[7] But, as Aquinas also recognizes, they can draw inferences.[8] Or it is possible for one to derive knowledge from the communicative interactions of others. Since angels can communicate with God and fellow angels, and vice versa, they can acquire such propositional content without having to behold objects in the world numbering 45 and 193 or having to see objects shaped in a triangular fashion. And once an angel receives some basic propositional content (like axioms, laws, quantities, facts about shapes, etc.), he could further infer additional propositions. For example, if an angel knows that a right triangle is 90 degrees, then he could envision putting two of them together back to back and having an isosceles triangle. This would be new knowledge that could be arrived at without any additional external input.

Can angels know the future? Not in the same way that God does. If they can know the future, it would not be relevantly different than how human beings can gather enough insight to draw inferences about what is to come. For example, to borrow an example from Aquinas, an angel can know that the sun will rise tomorrow, not because he timelessly knows the future, but because he is already familiar with causes and can predict what would obtain, all things being equal.[9] It would be as one predicting the weather or as one predicting a stock market crash. Since angels are finite, contingent beings, they are not omniscient. And if they are not omniscient, we should not expect them to know the future with laser precision or to know the sum total of all that can be known (cf. 1 Pet 1:12).

---

6. Aquinas, *Summa Theologiae*, I.54:5.
7. Aquinas, *Summa Theologiae*, I.56:2–3; I.57:1.
8. Aquinas, *Summa Theologiae*, I.57:3.
9. Cf. Aquinas, *Summa Theologiae*, I.57:3.

The Powers of Angels

Angels serve a variety of functions. They are sometimes employed to guard the people of God both literally (Gen 48:15-16; Num 22:22-35; Exod 23:20) and figuratively (Ps 91:11). And there is little doubt that they actively involve themselves in human affairs in general (e.g., Gen 19; Exod 33:2; Acts 12; Heb 13:2). Regardless of why God chooses to operate through angelic beings instead of directly, it is evident that this is a common mode of his acting. We should probably expect nothing different when it comes to spiritual warfare, especially if God's angels are portrayed as agents who take on spiritual adversaries directly (perhaps Dan 10:13, 20-21; Jude 9; Rev 12:7-9). However, these portrayals are not forthright descriptions about what takes place between angels and demons. They're often cast in symbolic terms and are literarily designed to narrate something else with angels being used as images with which to convey it.

In assessing the powers of angels, we have already gathered from our discussion about Satan and his powers that angels likely cannot interact with the physical universe unaided. That is to say that unless God operates on their behalf and empowers or materializes them as the occasion demands, they do not otherwise have the independent power to do anything particularly extraordinary. This might be the case so as to easily credit God for any supernatural goings-on that sometimes occur, in (at least) biblical history. Since they are spiritual beings, it is not difficult to accept that they can naturally communicate with fellow spirits (Jude 9) as well as embodied ones like human beings (e.g., Dan 10:5f.)—even if only through visionary or auditory contact.

Given their finite existence and their dependence on God, their abilities are nowhere close to being able to rival those of God. Perhaps this is additional reason why we should not be quick to think of Satan's departure as the product of a power grab instead of as a moral failing and a falling way.

THE BAD AND THE FALLEN: THE DEMONS OF SATAN

The Greek New Testament term for "demon" is *daimon(ion)*. The term itself antedates its usage in the New Testament and is used twice in the Greek translation of the Old Testament, the Septuagint, to refer to idols (Deut 32:17 and Ps 106:37). The Greek here replaces the Hebrew term *shed* ("devils"). But in terms of these demons or "devils" spoken of in the plural, no clear demonology is ever spelled out. We're vaguely aware of the Satan of

Job (which is Wisdom literature and not pure history) and in a couple of bits of other Old Testament books. But in no case is there any insinuation that Satan himself is the chief of demons who runs his own cosmic military unit, so to speak. The reason for this may not be difficult to imagine. Consider that in the New Testament, God is revealed to be Trinitarian for the first time; and even then it's only implicit. But this Trinitarian understanding helps us to meld the figures of the Old Testament into a composite portrait of God. For example, it is perplexing that in the opening verses of Genesis God creates the heavens and the earth (v. 1) only to have "the Spirit of God . . . hovering over the face of the waters" (v. 2). This might have been glossed over by ancient rabbis as simply an expression of God's extended presence, but the New Testament's biographical comments about the Holy Spirit reveal that this is indeed a person separate from the Father but one that is united with him in the one deity (e.g., John 16:7, 13; cf. Acts 5:3–4 [1 Cor 8:6]; 2 Cor 3:17). Indeed, it is often that the New Testament makes more explicit some of the cryptic sayings and teachings of the Old Testament. So, we should not be surprised by the lack of detail pertaining to God's enemies, particularly if we are lacking a similar trend in reference to someone as important as God himself.

The King James Version of the Old Testament employs other terms to refer to superhuman beings that are neither God, angel, nor human and these are "familiar spirits" (e.g., Lev 19:31; 20:6; 2 Kgs 23:24; Isa 8:19). However, this designation is only a particular way of referring to someone's *practice*. That is to say, these passages refer to *people* who are those said to have or to consult with so-called familiar spirits. Whether there *are* familiar spirits is simply left out of account. Other translations will have something like "medium" rather than the full "one who has/consults with familiar spirits." It is like "necromancer," which could also be rendered as "one who consults the dead." To refer only to "the dead" when "necromancer" is intended would be misleading. "Familiar spirits" likely derives from the fact that mediums claim to make contact with postmortem family members, friends, and sometimes sworn enemies (hence they are *familiar*).

There are possibly other designations of demons found in the Old Testament: "satyr" (*sa'iyr*) and "evil spirit" (*rā'āh rūaḥ*). Though "evil spirit" is mentioned once (Judg 9:23), it happens to harbor an unclear connotation as to whether it is a "spirit that causes disaster" (which could be God himself or an angel) or a spirit that is itself evil (though it is unclear if it is in the moral sense; more on this in a moment). On this, the New Testament is less obscure, for it mentions evil spirits in a few places (e.g., Matt 12:45; Luke 7:21; 8:2; 11:26; 19:12–13; Acts 19:11–19). And it is evidently clearer that these are in reference to demons. As for the Old Testament use of "satyr"

(Isa 13:21 and 34:14), it is more obscure for nothing more is clarified about it except that the Septuagint does replace *sa'iyr* with *daimonian*. However, it may only be a reflection of rabbinic beliefs at the time and not so much a divinely ordained clarification of the Isaiah passages.

Despite being called "evil" spirits, are they *morally* evil or just *naturally* evil? John H. Walton and J. Harvey Walton see demons as mere creatures of chaos, preferring to see "evil," whenever it describes demons, in the non-moral sense of being a natural evil like a tornado, a disease, or suffering. They explicitly write that "demons are *not evil* . . . [but] they are extremely dangerous and can be extremely inimical to healthy human life" and equate them to "such things as *wild animals* or *viruses*."[10] While I agree that demons are often depicted as agents of ruin and uncleanness (the majority of passages on demons would seem to suggest this), this is not excluded by their also being adversarial and morally evil if in fact Scripture designates them as such. After all, the devil himself is clearly referred to as an adversary in 1 Peter 5:8 ("Your *adversary* the devil . . ."), but he is immediately described in predatory-animal terms as one who "prowls around like a roaring lion, seeking someone to devour." So, we ought to focus on what Scripture says.

The controversial identification of Satan as a demon aside, I think there are some indications that demons are implied to be more than just naturally destructive. First, Revelation 16:13–15 depicts demons as bellwethers assembling "the kings of the whole world" for a cosmic battle with God at Armageddon ("they are demonic spirits, performing signs, who go abroad to the kings of the whole world, to assemble them for battle on the great day of God the Almighty"). Inciting and moving people to oppose God is what Satan is described as doing and yet such adversarial opposition is attributed to "demonic spirits." Undoubtedly this portrays them as something a bit more hostile and wicked than a predatory animal or a disease. Second, Paul warns Timothy in 1 Timothy 4:1 about "deceitful spirits and teachings of demons." While "deceitful spirits" could just be an idiom for describing heretics, the "teachings of demons" (*didaskaliais daimoniōn*) suggests something else. Whatever we make of "of demons," it must mean one of two things: either it is a reference to the teachings being advocated by the demons themselves (="demons' teachings") or, more likely, it is a way to characterize the teachings that are in stark contrast to God's (="demonic teachings"). In the former sense, their adversarial nature would be obvious. Nevertheless, as understood in the latter sense, it is difficult to see how the teachings "of demons" is not also to be construed in an adversarial sense. For, as Paul continues, these teachings are about local heresies. What makes

---

10. Walton and Walton, *Demons and Spirits*, 298.

the teachings demonic here is that they are *false* (vv. 2–3) as well as profane (vv. 4–5). If demons are merely analogous to wild animals and are mere agents of chaos and nothing more, then Paul's description of these heresies as "teachings of demons" seems out of place. Finally, and most obviously, if demons just are fallen angels, and fallen angels are clearly described as adversarial and morally opposed to God (2 Pet 2:4; Jude 6; Rev 12:7–9), then demons are adversarial and morally opposed to God. (I will argue in a moment that demons are in fact the fallen angels.)

Now, the Waltons' observation that demons tend to behave like wild animals is interesting but does not support their thesis that they are merely like wild animals even if one dismisses the counterexamples I offered above. In fact, I cede that demons, when mentioned as "demons" or as "evil spirits," do *overall* tend to be portrayed as agents of natural evil, chaos, ruination, and ritual uncleanness—something distinct from being moral opponents or adversaries. But the Waltons' conclusion doesn't follow from this concession. Even supposing that they're right, couldn't we say that the New Testament authors might have selectively used "demon" and "evil spirit" when specifically intending to cast them as agents of natural evil? Who's to say? This would be especially reasonable if, as the Waltons further suppose, the biblical writers were employing elements of mythography for narrative effect. Of course, we have to remember that their hypothesis nevertheless assumes that demons are not the fallen angels, which I think is a crucial assumption here (a point we will consider in a moment). And it is presumptuous because we already know that biblical authors do this in other contexts. They may use "the devil" instead of "Satan" (1 Pet 5:8) or "heavenly host" instead of "angels" (Luke 2:13). But this is no standalone indication that there are two different kinds of beings in either case. Likewise, we would need an argument to justifiably conclude that demons are something distinct from fallen angels.

So, *are* demons fallen angels or do they only *derive* from the fallen angels? This controversy depends on a number of factors surrounding what we are to make of the "sons of God" in Genesis 6:1–4.[11] As such, before Genesis 6 can be used in support of a particular understanding of demonology, it will have to surmount approximately three prohibitive firewalls. The first firewall, which is perhaps the most obvious, has to do with *interpretation*. That is, it must be more probable than not that the referent "sons of God" has to do with fallen angels and not something else. The fact of the matter is that there other interpretations that make this passage too controversial

11. This is most recently found in Payne, *Satan Exposed*, 63ff.; and it is most ably defended by Michael S. Heiser in his *The Unseen Realm*, 103ff. and his *Demons*, ch. 5. I push back against this view in my *Gods of This World*, 227–33.

to use as hard data. Perhaps the "sons of God" refers to deviant kings and magistrates who fancied themselves as demigods and exploited women in attempting to foster tyrannical dynasties of their own (cf. Gen 4:18–24).[12] If this is at all a live option, then we should be hesitant to adopt anearth-shattering doctrine on the basis of so controversial a passage as Genesis 6.

The second firewall is one that is predicated on *style*—that even if the "sons of God" are to be understood as angels, we are still far from an origin story for demons. One would have to surmount the old problem of the genre of this part of Genesis. An advocate of the fallen angels view must insist that this account *intends* to convey unadulterated history apart from the use of any literary strategy (i.e., poetry, apocalypse, etc.). Since the first eleven chapters of Genesis are normally considered a separate genre from the rest of the book (of the patriarchs), these first eleven chapters—the "primeval history"—are considered at least in part to incorporate the literary device of myth. That is, Genesis 6:1–4 is no more about what *really* happened than Psalm 89:10's poetic assertion that God actually "crushed" a sea monster named "Rahab" is. Myths are sometimes used to support a wider narrative, even if the narrative has a historical core. Why not think that, in order to punctuate to the reader how awful antediluvian human beings were behaving, the author chose to use the imagery of myth to show that their sins were so bad it's *as if* semidivine beings were behind it all?

The third firewall to be surmounted involves the *metaphysics* entailed by the angelic interpretation. To suggest or imply that these beings are finite immaterial spiritual beings makes it metaphysically impossible to square with a number of implications: (i) that good angels without bodies can nevertheless feel lust, (ii) that as finite beings they can create a new kind of living person (their hybrid offspring) with human women,[13] (iii) and that they impart to their hybrid offspring/creation the peculiar condition of having their spirits wander the planet upon death rather than pass on into an afterlife. While an adherent may be willing to affirm a series of mysteries here, such implications give critics every reason to doubt the fallen angels view of Genesis 6 altogether. Aware of this metaphysical awkwardness, theologians William F. Cook III and Chuck Lawless have suggested that maybe the immaterial angels here possessed human beings on earth by which they

---

12. See Kaiser et al., *Hard Sayings*, 106–8.

13. Heiser makes space for supposing that the "sons of God" may not have engaged *sexually* with the daughters of men but, rather, "fathered" their offspring in the same sense that God "fathered" the nation of Israel through Abraham and Sarah (*Unseen Realm*, 188; however, Heiser seems to neglect this alternative understanding in his *Demons*). Nevertheless, that God, whose prerogative it is, can create at will is hardly a good reason to think that any finite immaterial being like an angel can do the same.

carried out their sexual shenanigans.[14] This certainly would accommodate the angelic view of the text and how they could nevertheless engage sexually with the "daughters of men." But if this is how it went down, then any offspring produced would not have had any genetic material distinct from the physical parents. It trivializes the interpretation into a view that does no work to explain how embodied demons are supposed to arise from such sexual unions. Accordingly, Genesis 6 does nothing to account for the origin of demons. Therefore, what all three of these firewalls prevent is any good reason to think that demons are something distinct from fallen angels.

Aside from the (bad) negative case in Genesis, there are positive reasons to think that the fallen angels and demons are not distinct creatures. First, it is the simplest hypothesis. Supposing that demons and fallen angels are completely different beings means that there are two kinds of villains in the universe. One kind of villain is challenging enough to explain (i.e., how could evil come about in God's heavenly realms?). Without any positive reason to think the two are separate, we should prefer a much leaner metaphysic here. Add to this the fact that fallen angels and demons share a number of striking attributes: both are spiritual beings (Eph 6:12), both are "evil" (Luke 8:2; 2 Pet 2:4–9), both can be exiled (Mark 6:13; 2 Pet 2:4), both are headed up by Satan (Mark 3:22–26; Rev 12:7–9), both retaliate (Luke 11:24–26; Rev 12:7), and both are appointed unto judgment (Matt 8:29; Jude 6). That fallen angels and demons share these characteristics and that fallen angels are *never* distinguished from the demons either explicitly or implicitly makes seeing them as the same set of villains the simpler view. And if we're not permitted to reason this way, then on what basis would there be to identify, say, "unclean spirits" with demons? Why think these two sets of villains are the same except through a similar inference strategy? How we answer this is likewise how we answer the original question about fallen angels and demons.

Second, aside from the simplicity of the hypothesis, there is a significant absence of "demons" being mentioned in Jesus's statement that the unrepentant will depart to "the eternal fire prepared for the devil and his angels" (Matt 25:41). But in Matthew 8 it is the *demons* that seem to fear this eschatological fate long before Jesus ever consigns anyone to it (i.e., Matt 25:41–46 and possibly Luke 16:19–31). When Jesus confronts two men who are demon possessed in Matthew 8, the demons respond: "What have you to do with us, O Son of God? Have you come here to *torment us before the time*?" (v. 29). Assuming that the "torment" here is the torment of hell (cf. Rev 20:10), then the lack of mentioning demons in Matthew 25 might

---

14. For a recent example, see Cook and Lawless, *Spiritual Warfare*, 16.

likely be due to the fact that the demons *just are* the angels for whom hell is prepared. This is something we would expect if this is the case. There is a third point, though not unrelated to the second, that bears mentioning. We have a reverse situation in which it is the demons that are mentioned but not the fallen angels. In 1 Corinthians 10:20, the apostle Paul says "that what pagans sacrifice they offer to demons and not to God. I do not want you to be participants with demons." Notice that "demons" and not "fallen angels" are the contraries here. If we include the fact that hell "was prepared for the devil and his *angels*," pitting demons and not the devil's angels against God is even more baffling if the two are not referring to the same entities.

Are these knock-down arguments? Of course not. But the arguments given here, especially when taken together, constitute a powerful inductive case for identifying demons with the fallen angels. If the two are indeed distinct villains in the cosmic scene, there must be some positive evidence for that. Until that is accomplished and the prohibitive reasons surmounted, we should presume them the selfsame villains.

Let us now ask: Where do the demons reside? Are they located in the air or underground? Popular lore, influenced largely by Renaissance literature and art, would have them living in hell. But hell is a judgment that has yet to obtain (Rev 20:10); it is even less clear that hell is a place where beings endure, for it may refer to a punishment of destruction or annihilation. But never mind that. As for their current abode, Paul speaks of them residing "in the heavenly places" (Eph 6:12). This is apparently the same realm—or perhaps just the same *kind* of realm—wherein God himself dwells (1:20).[15] However, as Walter Wink has suggested, "the heavenly places" might refer not to some outer location, but to a power that has "suprahuman quality" and is something "bigger than life."[16] Wink's argument for this is predicated on what is meant by the various powers said to reside "in the heavenly places." By combing other New Testament passages, it is apparent that at least *some* references are to earthly regimes and governments (e.g., Titus 3:1). But this neglects the significance of context, particularly when it comes to Ephesians 6. Therein, Paul has not only invoked the well-understood figure of Satan (v. 11), but he seems to be arguing for precisely the *opposite* point, namely, that true Christian opposition is *not* against "flesh and blood." Paul is intentionally pointing to "the man behind the curtain," who is not some physical inhabitant, ruler or otherwise, of this world. He has already made it clear that Satan is a "spirit that is now at work in the sons of disobedience"

---

15. One need not think that God and Satan (along with his cohorts) therefore all reside in the selfsame community or kingdom of God, as it were, for Satan and his apostate angels have been exiled from their original position (Rev 12:7–10).

16. Wink, *Naming the Powers*, 86; cf. Wink, *Engaging the Powers*, 164.

(2:2). Chapter 6 would seem to be a careful reminder of this fact that such spirits truly do animate our earthly enemies and are the *real* enemies indeed. That this is also where Christ dwells and from where blessings derive (1:3; 2:6), the "heavenly places" is likely a generic reference to what we would vaguely call the supernatural realm.[17]

Much of what we know about the nature and powers of Satan and those of angels will naturally carry over into a discussion about demons. Since Satan is understood to be the chief of all evil spirits, one expects that anyone under his charge can do no more than he. In virtue of sharing the same kind of nature, the demons, like their angelic counterparts, are also capable of communicating with fellow spirits, whether embodied or not. This is perhaps most dramatically illustrated in what are called "demon possessions" or "demonizations" found in the New Testament (e.g., Matt 8:28; Mark 3:22; 5:15; Luke 8:36; John 13:27; Acts 19:12). It is less dramatically illustrated in the context of Satan's ability to tempt us (Matt 4:3; 1 Thess 3:5) and to incite people to act in certain ways (1 Chron 21:1; Acts 5:3). It is less obvious that demons can directly interact with physical creation without acting *through* the souls of rational beings.

This demonology has profound implications for our understanding of spiritual warfare. For one, spiritual warfare should likely not be seen as a physical form of combat. Demons have no hands or limbs with which to assault their victims since they lack physicality. They're also not likely responsible for things like poltergeist activity and some forms of alleged hauntings as these would require demonic beings (which are supposed to be immaterial) to interact with physical objects and/or human sense receptors. If ghosts (or whatever) are postulated to be moving objects around the house, this too would involve the incredible notion that the immaterial can directly affect the material.[18] We must imagine the primary terrain of spiritual warfare to be, well, spiritual.

CONCLUSION

We have seen that there are underling beings God has created in service to him and his purposes in creation. These beings—angels—were initially created good. Some of them are bad and we refer to them as "fallen angels" or "demons." Their existence is likely due to their having (freely) fallen from

---

17. Also see Hoehner, *Ephesians*, 169; Fowl, *Ephesians*, 35–39 and 203–5.

18. For more on demons and the paranormal, refer to appendix D, "Paranormal Activity and the Occult." And for more on what purely immaterial beings can and cannot do, refer to our discussion on the powers of Satan in chapter 4.

an initial state of grace. As rebellious and evil spirits that can cognitively or spiritually interact with us, they are genuine threats to our physical and spiritual well-being. However, God ensures that, on occasion, he (perhaps through his angels) does in fact guard us from these evil spirits. But we should not imagine such skirmishes to be physical or something like hand-to-hand combat. This gives us a clue that whatever spiritual warfare is about, it does not involve any physical or literal combative prowess on our part.

To round out our understanding of what Scripture has to say about spiritual warfare, we will transition from discussions about the participants of warfare to a survey of scriptural references to spiritual warfare apart from any preconceived ideas or model of spiritual warfare that might otherwise skew our appreciation for what the Bible has to say on its own.

PART II

Warfare Language in the Bible

But the greatest thing by far is to have a command of metaphor. This alone cannot be imparted by another; it is the mark of genius, for to make good metaphors implies an eye for resemblances.

—Aristotle, Poetics 1459a.4

9

Biblical Metaphors for Spiritual Warfare

THIS NEXT PART WILL continue to prepare us for what spiritual warfare is by turning our focus away from the combatants involved and turning to the content of what Scripture has to say about those combatants as well as how Scripture variously describes warfare activities. This brings us to the biblical vocabulary of warfare itself. This will give us a picture about what warfare is and how it is conducted by those involved. However, I want to emphasize up front that Scripture—specifically the New Testament—does not give us a systematic theology about spiritual conflict but, rather, incorporates a previously established belief that such conflict occurs (one that is largely derived from the Qumran community).[1] The biblical authors seem to take it as given that their audiences already know that there is a kind of cosmic conflict involving, among others, human beings. But the chosen way this is communicated in the teaching passages is through *metaphor*. So, let us consider what this means for the present discussion.

We already know that things like swords, shields, arrows, and breastplates—the usual features of warfare imagery—are used in both the Old and New Testaments. Battles are waged, kingdoms fall, and leaders conquer their foes. But not all warfare language is used literally in Scripture. Specifically,

---

1. E.g., Eph 6:12's "For we do not wrestle against flesh and blood . . ." = "*Because* [*hoti*] we do not wrestle against flesh and blood . . ."). The "because" implies that the reason (the powers that lie behind the curtain, so to speak) was known and acknowledged already by the audience. See Arnold, *Power and Magic*.

when talking about spiritual matters, the device of metaphor is used, and for good reason: real military warfare was a common and familiar fact of life. Nations constantly warred against nations and everyone had to eventually make use of the sword. And since such warfare was often a battle for control and sovereignty between people groups or kingdoms, it is an apt frame of reference for what is going on in the life of the Christian since spiritual warfare is as significant as, if not more so than, the ordinary human experience of national domination. So, by using warfare imagery, the biblical authors could paint a vivid, memorable, and familiar picture about how participants relate to each other in the grand cosmic battle over our souls.

Now, the ancient world was no stranger to the use of metaphor. Plato, to give a nonbiblical example, used "light" as a metaphor to represent truth and illumination.[2] New Testament readers will recognize a similar usage of the metaphor (e.g., Matt 5:14–16; Eph 5:8; I John 1:5–7; 2:8–10). In fact, from agriculture to sports, the Bible does not shy away from using a broad range of metaphor types. And why not? Metaphors enhance our understanding so that we can wrap our minds around the meaning and significance of what is being communicated—even vividly. Warfare metaphors were no exception when used in the ancient world. And neither are they relegated to the ancient world. We in the twenty-first century are quite familiar with this kind of talk. For examples: we talk about how certain individuals and institutions in this world may "declare war" on us, but we might take care to "pick our battles"; we may "zero in" on a certain "target," but occasionally we may have to fend off "friendly fire"; we may aspire to "divide and conquer" others, but pity us if they are "locked and loaded" and respond with a "take-no-prisoners" approach.

Scripture uses the metaphors of warfare and battle quite frequently. To appreciate better the Christian's own involvement in what is to be emphasized as *spiritual* warfare, we must take care to recognize that this is not something the Christian literally does when she is said to engage in such warfare; that is, the Christian does not wield an actual shield and sword in taking down her enemies and oppressors. Scripture uses warfare imagery as a way to describe the spiritual conflict that is evident all around us as well as that which is not so evident but all around us nonetheless.

---

2. Plato, *Republic*, VII.

WARFARE METAPHORS AND APOCALYPTIC LANGUAGE

While Scripture uses the metaphor of warfare with which to depict the struggles of the Christian walk, warfare metaphors are sometimes merged with an apocalyptic style of writing (or genre) with which to convey the significance of those struggles. That is, while the Bible uses symbols like "the shield of faith," "the breastplate of righteousness," and "the sword of the Spirit" as metaphors for certain Christian virtues and practices, sometimes the Christian struggle is depicted by the imagery of combating angels, roiling sea monsters, flying dragons, coiling serpents, and devouring lions. Neil Forsyth associates such things with the ancient "combat myth" as employed by various ancient civilizations such as Babylon, Canaan, and Greece.[3] Forsyth's hypothesis is that the biblical writers consciously incorporated the combat myth to portray the kingdom of demons as a rebellious, roguish empire hell-bent on defeating their overlords. Since the earliest iterations of Satan in the Old Testament tend to lack those elements often present in combat myths, it is possible that the biblical writers later availed themselves of them in filling out a larger doctrine of demonology at some point after the Jewish exile. This is *not* to say that the biblical writers *copied* those myths thereby *inventing* a doctrine of demonology, only that such myths were familiar, convenient, and useful ways to understand spiritual warfare.[4]

There are other examples of the benign uses of myths-as-frameworks in understanding real events. For example, John calls Jesus the *logos* of God (John 1:1, 14), which is likely a deliberate reference to the Greek myth of the *Logos* of the demiurge. Jesus is cast as a unique principle or expression—the Word—of God through the *Logos* myths of Philo and Heraclitus. While Jesus isn't *that Logos*, the comparison helps us appreciate the uniqueness of Christ's identity in the Father and as proceeding from the Father as the selfsame God. The authors of Genesis, Job, the Psalms, and Isaiah also seem to avail themselves of various creation myths in establishing or arguing for the superiority and uniqueness of Yahweh as the sole and supreme creator of the universe. And the early ante-Nicene fathers used Platonism in general

---

3. Forsyth, *Old Enemy*.

4. Why would a biblical author use a pagan combat myth in order to describe some reality? We can only speculate, but it may be because, given that there was no real straightforward scientific way of describing significant otherworldly events, it was familiar enough to make the point—and to make it forcefully as well as memorably. Take, for example, how scientists talk about the origin of the universe. They speak of it in mythological terms such as its being a "creation event" having been inaugurated at "the big bang." Neither of these are necessarily scientifically precise descriptions but they do provide memorable and appropriate ways of looking at what they are meant to refer to.

as a familiar framework through which to understand the natures of God and creation and the supremacy and transcendence of heavenly things over earthly things.

Never is the incorporation of demonology-plus-combat-mythology more evident than in the last book of the Bible: Revelation. In Revelation, the penultimate conflict of powers is construed in both spiritual and cosmic terms. It features metaphors and personifications of cosmic and beastly beings, which are used to punctuate the significance and seriousness of what is and/or is about to happen. Images of flying locusts with human heads and scorpion tails (Rev 9:3–9) and those of warring dragons (12:7–9) convey to the reader that there is a serious and calculated demonic threat to Christian livelihood. Our consolation is that such demons are no match for God, whose ability to defeat them is so assured that it is Michael, the archangel, and not God himself, who defeats Satan. This might also be the case in Daniel's vision of the archangel battling the "prince of (the kingdom of) Persia" and, subsequently, the "prince of Greece" (Dan 10:13, 20).

Far too often the apocalyptic elements of Daniel (and, of course, those of Revelation) are construed by many in the modern West as straightforward, literal descriptions of warring territorial spirits.[5] Daniel's vision is often taken this way as if the vision was a peering into the spiritual realm in order to see what was *really* going on. I grant that this may be a possible understanding. However, it is not the most natural one given the literary context (a "vision" no less). Accordingly, I am hesitant to take an apocalyptic passage like Daniel 10 as a straightforward description of unfiltered reality. That is, Daniel's vision does not intend to convey raw, unfiltered images of what is transpiring.

Wait! Is this to say that angels and demons are not real beings? Not at all. The invoking of spiritual agencies, especially in apocalyptically charged contexts, is not to affirm that such beings are indeed present and doing the things ascribed to them. Figures like Isaiah and Solomon, for example, use the presence of certain animals in their narratives to make a point. Isaiah refers to various predatory animals that will make their way to Babylon and Edom when they are decimated by God (Isa 34). Included are hawks, owls, ravens, hyenas, goats, and other "wild animals" (vv. 11–15). The point isn't that these animals indeed will gather in the ruins of Israel's enemies, but that the invoking of such animals is merely to conjure up the right kind of familiar imagery that connotes destruction, desolation, and slaughter. Likewise, Solomon in Proverbs speaks about those who spurn their parents and says that they "will be picked out by the ravens of the valley and eaten

---

5. See appendix C, "On Territorial Spirits."

by the vultures" (30:17). Again, readers would not expect parental disobedience to literally invoke predatory animals from the sky. Nevertheless, the animals mentioned really do exist. Perhaps similar imagery is being used in the case of Daniel 10. That is, by invoking divine beings, the author(s) is not interested in saying what is really out there, but, rather, the invoking of such beings is a way for the author(s) to punctuate the spiritual significance of national conflict.

Furthermore, I consider the imagery of dueling angels to be a framework through which to understand the significance of what is happening. Angels are immaterial beings; they cannot engage in hand-to-hand combat with anyone without being made corporeal. So, it is not the case that Michael is *physically*, even if literally, intervening on behalf of Daniel; rather, the imagery of Michael's intervention signifies that the God who has since abandoned Israel for her transgressions (Ezek 10; 11:1–13) has not forgotten the faithful. It is not even clear if the princes of Persia and Greece are even *demons* as we often suppose.[6] For they may just be other angelic beings merely representing the cosmic interests of contrary empires. Regardless, the point is that apocalyptic language often involves the merging of the combat myth with spiritual warfare—not to describe what supernatural combatants are really doing, but to reveal the spiritual significance of international conflicts with Israel.

GOING FORWARD

Even though Scripture uses disparate modes of symbolism, nevertheless, spiritual warfare focuses on actual combatants, real spiritual weapons, existing citizens, and a genuine arena wherein the drama plays out. There really are demons vying for either control over or the destruction of God's creation. There really are angels under God's command that are dispatched in service to human beings. There really are opposing forces: God and Satan. And there really is a heaven of reward and a hell of judgment. The war is real. It's just not real in the sense of being physical and (in most cases) straightforwardly defined. So, how are we to understand what spiritual warfare is amidst the noise of disagreement by those writing on the issue today? Well, it begins with a sensible and unbiased approach to how the Bible uses the language of warfare in telling the story of Christian conflict.

In the chapters to follow, we will explore a vast array of relevant passages from both the Old and New Testaments that utilize such warfare imagery. We will not look to *every* instance of a warfare metaphor and so this

---

6. Keener and Walton, *NIV Cultural Backgrounds Study Bible*, 1445.

will not be an exhaustive study. But enough passages will be mined so as to give us some indications about what is going on in the theater of war. Accordingly, we will look at a healthy cross section of warfare language in the Bible and allow the Bible to speak on its own terms on each occasion where such warfare language is implemented. Let this serve as a sort of everyman's commentary—a forthright and uncomplicated discussion about how this or that instrument of war is being used metaphorically and what it means in its original context. This being the intent here, we will not yet proceed to a full systematized theory of spiritual warfare. That can only be accomplished after we have explored where the Bible speaks on this issue and to what these metaphors apply.

Consider what follows in the next few chapters to be the last part of our fact-gathering mission wherein we are looking for the most relevant and significant passages specifically utilizing the language of spiritual warfare. Since the notion of spiritual warfare is only specifically taught through the use of such metaphors, we can only discern what is being said by becoming familiar with how those metaphors are normally used. This study, then, is not intended to be full presentations of the teachings inherent in each of these passages, for such teachings are often treated in more detail and depth in a variety of ways all throughout Scripture. In what follows, we will limit our discussion to focus on warfare language, and we will do so topically. That is, we will look at those metaphors *categorically*: those that pertain strictly to attack, to defense, to retreat, to victory, and those that do not quite fit under any of these. And there will be a discussion of the key passages that make up those categories. As such, this part of the book functions as both a repository of data on spiritual warfare and as an opinion-free Bible study on the relevant passages.

10

Metaphors for Attack

ONE OF THE MOST common categories of metaphor in spiritual warfare is, of course, the attack metaphor. This is understandable given that the Christian life is one that ought not to be idle. Rather, she must assert herself for the sake of the gospel of Christ in advancing the kingdom of God both locally and globally. When the Christian begins to advance, opposition and resistance become inevitable. This means that the Christian is one who must ready herself to take on those that would stand in her way no matter the cost. Let us take a look at those metaphors that ultimately are made to convey this message.

ARROWS

The Psalms utilize the metaphor of arrows in a number of places (e.g., Ps 7:13; 45:5; 64:7; 127:4) and it occasionally occurs outside of the Psalms (Job 6:4; Ezek 5:16; Hab 3:9, 11, 14; Eph 6:16). As we are aware, arrows are projectiles or missile weapons found most prominently in premodern warfare. They are, of course, also used in the context of contemporary archery and sport hunting. That they are often used *at a distance* is apt to imply that there is some degree of separation between two (or more) opposing parties. Sometimes the arrows are described in terms of their cut or in how they are felt, such as their being described as "sharp" (as in Ps 45:5). Indeed, to be opposed to the one with the arrow is to invite a piercing reality! Sometimes God is said to be poised to reign down upon the unrighteous a judgmental strike of flinging arrows from above. In some cases, to underscore a high level of fury, these metaphorical arrows are described as "fiery shafts" (Ps 7:13). Such imagery accentuates the presence of judgment. Indeed, God will harshly judge the unrepentant such that their nefarious plans may even result in their own self-destruction (v. 16).

The direct and penetrative aspects of arrows are common themes in the use of the metaphor. Psalm 64:6 tells us that "the inward mind and heart of a man are deep." Nevertheless, God's "arrow" (v. 7) successfully and painfully penetrates his enemies. For them, it is quite the reality check in how fast this arrow is deployed! For "they are wounded suddenly" and without delay. On the other hand, not all of God's arrows proceed directly from him. Couched in simile, the "arrows" of God in Psalm 27:4 are *personal*; that is, they represent the children of the godly. The meaning here is that one's having children is a testament to one's honor given that it is God who ultimately makes such a child-rearing reality possible. Having descendants, and so a multiplication of oneself, increases the number of warriors that can engage conflict. So, God indirectly deploys his arrows through one's lineage.

But God is not the only one armed with arrows. Sometimes it is the opponents of God who wield them. The psalmist in Psalm 64:3 uses arrows among other metaphors to refer to the sting of an enemy's verbal assault. That these attacks are launched "secretly" (v. 5) conveys the notion that sometimes verbal vitriol often seems to come out of nowhere. Verse 6 makes it evident that this vitriol is slander in the ongoing attempts to tarnish the righteous. Such slander is sometimes, thanks to God, a pitiful irony: it becomes the ultimate downfall of the slanderer (v. 8). Indeed, the arrows of the enemy can be turned inward. Habakkuk 3:14 also reveals a bit of irony in that God is able to pierce the enemy "with his own arrows," signaling that the enemy's reign of terror will be their own undoing. And this will be the case even when the situation seems utterly hopeless (v. 17).

There are other examples of the verbal assaults of enemies being described as arrows. Jeremiah 9:8, for instance, notes that the enemy's "tongue is a deadly arrow; it speaks deceitfully." The same goes for Isaiah 42:9. These missile weapons are not projectiles that cause physical or spiritual harm; they are *words* that, in their own right, cause other kinds of unruly harm to others and to oneself. It ought to remind us of what James tells us in the New Testament, noting that he chooses a different metaphor—fire:

> the tongue is a small member, yet it boasts of great things. How great a forest is set ablaze by such a small fire! And the tongue is a fire, a world of unrighteousness. The tongue is set among our members, staining the whole body, setting on fire the entire

course of life, and set on fire by hell. For every kind of beast and bird, of reptile and sea creature, can be tamed and has been tamed by mankind, but no human being can tame the tongue. It is a restless evil, full of deadly poison. (Jas 3:5–8)

The mutual point is that the tongue is potentially incredibly destructive, though James notes an irony, namely, that the same tongue that scorches is the one that superintends.

CONTEND

In Jude 3, readers are implored to "contend for the faith." Now, this *could* be more of a sports metaphor than a warfare one (boxers, for example, are also called "contenders"). But contending in the military sense is more likely given that the faith is under siege by "certain people [who] have crept in unnoticed" (v. 4). The scene is adversarial and not merely competitive. They are "ungodly people, who pervert the grace of our God into sensuality and deny our only Master and Lord, Jesus Christ." Heresy was rampant in the first century and it was no game. It was war, indeed. It still is. And it is incumbent upon the readers of Jude to defend the faith of the saints against those who reduce God's grace to a *dis*grace. While Marlon Brando *could* have been a contender, Christians are called to be nothing less!

DISARM

There is a verse in Paul's letter to the Colossians that sounds a bit like it could have been a plotline for HBO's *Game of Thrones*. This passage, Colossians 2:15, reads as follows: "[God] disarmed the rulers and authorities and put them to open shame, by triumphing over them in him." Twice in chapter 2 Paul makes mention of "elemental spirits of the world" (vv. 8, 20), which are, alongside "human tradition," cast as that which underscores worldly opposition to Christ and his wisdom. Understanding what the "spirits" are might expand our understanding of who these "rulers and authorities" of verse 15 are (they might be the "rulers" and "authorities" of Ephesians 6:12 or they might just be human institutional powers[1]). But, in the absence of a clear indicator, the understanding of 2:15 can proceed from either viewpoint.

---

1. For the latter interpretation, see Wink, *Naming the Powers*, 77–82. I am somewhat sympathetic to Wink's specific understanding of the passage here. But it is not at the exclusion of evil spirits being behind these who teach such false philosophical notions which seems to be suggested by a related passage, 1 Tim 4:1–5.

We can note that 2:15 also uses other warfare metaphors, including "triumphed" and "put . . . to open shame," although these are not exclusively warfare metaphors. But let us zero in on the "disarmed" one for now. *How* this disarming was done is explained in the previous verses, namely, that believers have been "filled in [Christ], who is the head of all rule and authority" and that we were also spiritually circumcised, buried with him in baptism, and made alive through our deliverance from our trespasses (vv. 10–14). It is the "philosophy and empty deceit" of the world (v. 8) that assaults us. This makes spiritual warfare here a matter of recognizing the lordship of Christ over "rulers and authorities" so that "no one may delude you with plausible arguments" (v. 4). Some of this worldly philosophy and deceit apparently involved "asceticism" and "the worship of angels" and were being promulgated by those (falsely?) testifying to visionary experiences (v. 18) and denying the one from whom all the elements of life derive (v. 19). Given the believer's superior position over such deceivers, no one need accept their regulations (20). It is the ascetic's philosophy that has been used as a weapon but has been blunted by Christ, thereby rendering those who wield it disarmed. And it is blunted because it advocates for a pathway to holiness that will not work (v. 23) and otherwise ignores the one who has power and authority over such "elemental spirits." So, it is evident that the disarming of the "rulers and authorities" obtains through the accreditation of Christ and our relation to him. The result is that such rulers have been shamed through the demonstration of Christ's own authority and supremacy—the one who has such authority by fiat as the one who created everything "visible and invisible," including any and all "rulers or authorities" (1:16).

FIGHT

As with "contend" in Jude 3, Scripture also uses "fight," which doubles as a warfare metaphor if we let it. First Timothy 6:11–12 and 2 Timothy 4:7 are good instances of this. The emphasis in either case is one's call to endure and persevere through opposition. This endurance involves the grounding of oneself in, among other things, an optimally moral lifestyle—a lifestyle that must radiate from mere confession to action, for it was declared publicly. And both passages have in mind that such a fight is something to be endured to the end (cf. Matt 10:22; 24:13; Mark 13:13).

When we get to Revelation, the fight language used is unambiguously one of warfare. In 13:4, an unnamed "beast" is said to be empowered by its patron, Satan (v. 2: "to [the beast] the dragon gave his power and his throne and great authority"). It is likely to be identified as the Roman Empire and/

or something like it (see vv. 11–18; ch. 17; cf. Daniel 7). Those that "worshiped the beast" ask the question, "Who is like the beast, and who can fight against it?" Undoubtedly, this comes across as a rhetorical question but is meant to be a parody of the kinds of things rhetorically asked of God (e.g., Exod 15:11; Jer 49:19). In response, Revelation seems to declare that Christ is both willing and able (19:11). As king of a glorious anti-Rome (or anti-whatever), Christ empowers his church (19:13–14) and his angels (12:7; 20:1–2) to become victorious over their draconian oppressors. Though Rome touts its deified status, as have many other regimes in the ancient world, the true God will soon bring her and those like her to ruins. Indeed, even the *last* battle belongs to the Lord (cf. 1 Sam 17:47)!

SPEAR

Habakkuk 3:11 describes how, metaphorically of course, the "sun and moon stood still in their place at the light of [God's] arrows as they sped, at the flash of [God's] glittering spear." Not only do we have the familiar arrows (see "Arrows" above), but we have the use of a melee weapon this time—the spear. The show-stopping spectacle of God's "glittering spear" is a testament to his unparalleled ability not only to conquer victoriously but also immediately. And even then, the spear had only been brandished but not yet used. It was only because of that spear and the accompanying arrows that the "sun and moon stood still" (cosmic rhetoric indicating just how show-stopping God's actions were). Sometimes the threat of force is just as good as using it; and when it's God's, it's understandable that that would be enough!

SWORD

The sword is one of the most familiar attack weapons in Scripture. In Deuteronomy 33:29, the author speaks metaphorically of the "sword of [Israel's] triumph," which results in their enemies "fawning to you, and you shall tread upon their backs." God is himself said to be that sword. He is a sword in the sense in which he conquers and "treads" on Israel's enemies. Such a demonstration of Israel's imperviousness is why her enemies will then end up "fawning" after God. Elsewhere God is also said to ready a sword of his own (Ps 7:12). But in Deuteronomy 33:29 God *is* the sword wielded by his people, which connects well with the later New Testament, wherein the sword represents the very words of God. When we get to Isaiah 49:2, the passage presents the image of Isaiah himself as a conqueror who has been ordained to be so ever since conception (v. 1). That Isaiah's "mouth" is "like a sharp sword" makes it evident that the conqueror is also an aggressor for righteousness and salvation. The metaphor of having a sword in his mouth there refers to his calling to be a proclaimer and declarer of God. It's sharp because it is an unmistakable contrast to the compromising messages of the unrighteous.

Of course, such weapons can also be used in the wrong hands. Like the arrow, the metaphorical sword is reported to be wielded not only, so to speak, by God and his people but by evildoers. For example, Psalm 64:3 speaks of evildoers who "whet their tongues like swords." It is a picture of the harmful words they may hurl at the righteous (recall the discussion about the tongue in the section on "Arrows" above). While we may have the word of God, we must be wary of the contrary words of the enemy!

As we turn to the New Testament, we have Jesus in Matthew 10:34 mentioning a sword. But this sword represents something negative ("I have not come to bring peace, but a sword"). It is a sword *of division*. It is going to be inadvertently wielded by the followers of Christ as clarified by Jesus's words in the next verse: "For I have come to set a man against his father, and a daughter against her mother, and a daughter-in-law against her mother-in-law." This is not to say that Christ is sanctioning enmity within the household as if he were, say, anti-family, rather it is that by being followers of Christ one is, in effect, going to be strongly (violently?) opposed by their loved ones (as Jesus himself had experienced[2]). This sword is in fact a sword of impending division, though I am sure Jesus wished it would not be.

In the later New Testament, we have a return to its positive use. It is vividly depicted in Ephesians 6:17 as the "sword of the Spirit." This sword is unrelated to the one of division just mentioned in Matthew. Here, Paul tells the Ephesians that they must wield this sword, which appears to be associated with the authoritative teachings of God, particularly as they relate to the core gospel message ("the word of God"; cf. Acts 13:5, 7, 46; Rom 9:6; 2 Cor 2:17; 1 Thess 2:15; 1 John 2:5). However, the "word of God" of these other passages is translated from *logon tou Theou*. By contrast, in Ephesians 6:17 we have a different Greek referent: *rhēma Theou*. Some think that the *rhēma* of God refers to a special piece of revelation that is tailored specifically for the individual (one usually given for the benefit of the receiver). However, this is inconsistent with the fact that the armor of God is a *collective* endeavor—that it is in reference to the church body as a whole and not merely to individuals. Whatever this *rhēma* is, it must also apply on a corporate level. Still, others insist that the *rhēma* of God is the witness of the Holy Spirit (since it is called the "sword *of the Spirit*" [*machairan tou pneumatos*] and not the "sword *of God*"). This may be on the right track, but it does not

---

2. Mark 3:21, 31–32.

yet clarify how one uses it to combat the opposing powers. It turns out that there might not be a relevant difference insofar as the terms *rhēma* and *logos* often appear to be used interchangeably: both refer to "saying" (cf. Luke 2:50 and Rom 13:9), both refer to "fact" or "matter" (cf. Luke 1:4 and 2 Cor 13:1), both refer to "speech" (1 Cor 10:10), and both even refer to the very proclamation of the gospel (cf. 1 Cor 15:2 and 1 Pet 1:25). While there is perhaps a nuanced difference, context seems to be more important as to the meaning of "word" regardless of which Greek term is employed.[3] That it is the word *of God* being depicted as the sword *of the Spirit* may be to emphasize that the word is under divine inspiration (whether it be, broadly speaking, referring to "[a]ll Scripture is breathed out by God [*theopneustos*]" [2 Tim 3:16a] or to a delimited confession of one's identity in Christ as we find in Rom 10:8–9). That Paul, just a chapter earlier in Ephesians, declares that Christ cleanses the church "by the washing of water with the word [*rhēmati*]" (5:26) suggests that it is that which brings about the church's holiness. Whether it be the gospel message, all of Scripture, or a confession of one's identity in Christ, it is the vehicle through which the church stands apart from the jurisdiction of opposing (demonic) powers.[4] It is what Christ has taught and represents that is to be wielded as an offensive weapon.

Though it is the only explicit attack metaphor used here, it may not be the only means of attack discussed in Ephesians 6 (see comments on Eph 6:11–17 on pages 92–95). Prayer and supplication, though not represented by metaphors, are also mentioned in the same chapter (v. 18). Nevertheless, it is elsewhere evident that one combats sinister spiritual forces by means of *sound doctrine* (1 Tim 4:1–7; 2 Tim 2:15) and *righteous proclamation* (Rev 1:16). That Paul couples the word of God with prayer also in 1 Timothy 4:5 as a composite recipe for "good" and "trained" (v. 6) should incline us to see that such spiritual attack weapons are designed for doctrinal fidelity, a sturdy witness, and ethical holiness. It is a sword packed with a great deal of moral and intellectual punch.

In Hebrews 4:12, the "word of God" is not only instructive but divisive as punctuated by the invoking of the image of a *"two-edged* sword." This double-edged weapon represents just how deep sound doctrine can cut. For it not only wards off falsehood and impiety enacted by others, but it judges the self and reveals our own inner wickedness. This divisiveness

---

3. It is very much like how there are two words for "death" with no relevant dissimilarities—*thanatos* (e.g., Rom 8:38) and *nekros* (e.g., Jas 2:17).

4. The "sword" may also share some commonality with the "sword" as used in Hebrews (4:12) as well as in Revelation (2:12, 16; 19:21). In Hebrews, it seems to take on the connotation of "Scripture," whereas in Revelation it takes on the connotation of proclamation—specifically of one's witness of Christ.

is not intended to be *destructive* but *healthful*. The penetrative ("piercing") aspect of the word in Hebrews is such that it can compel the hard-hearted to turn in repentance to God and that it can further repel any potential disobedience. Its duality implies obedience and holiness on the one hand while warding off temptation and disobedience on the other.

Revelation repeats these motifs throughout its pages (1:16; 2:12, 16; 19:15, 21). We have in these various passages a "sharp" and often "two-edged" sword that proceeds from the "mouth" of Christ. Each of these descriptors is significant. The sword itself represents, not surprisingly, the words of God, but not so much in the doctrinal sense. It is more or less being used in the prophetic sense of proclaiming divine judgment (cf. Isa 49:2). The adjectival "sharp" peppers this imagery, emphasizing the harshness and precision of that proclamation and how much it will not be well received by some.

Speaking of a sword being "two-edged," this is often overlooked in Christian circles. We fancy ourselves wielding the "sword of the Spirit" that "divides joint and marrow" but neglect that such a sword cuts in two opposing directions. That is, the sword judges not only the unfaithful but also the faithful. The unfaithful are judged for obvious reasons: they are in (violent) opposition to God. The faithful are judged because of their doctrinal and moral failures (cf. Rev 2:12–16). Its proceeding from the "mouth" of God or his surrogates means that such judgment is being proclaimed with divine authority. Thus, one is being condemned either for belonging to Satan and his on-earth opposition against the saints or for compromising the faith and the virtues of Christian living.[5] Everyone, and not just unbelievers, is put on notice.

WEAPON(S)

In 2 Corinthians 10:4, Paul makes mention of the "weapons of our warfare" (on "warfare," see "War(fare)" in chapter 14). And just four chapters earlier, Paul makes mention of "the weapons *of righteousness*" (6:7), which, unfortunately, are not clearly disclosed. That they are "for the right hand and for the left" likely indicates that "weapons" refers to the *total* armament at one's disposal. One imagines something like a shield in one hand and a sword or lance in the other. This is apropos to the context since Paul is referring both to faithful "endurance" (v. 4; the "shield") as well as "truthful speech" (v. 7a; the "sword").

---

5. See Blount, *Revelation*, 45.

11

Metaphors for Defense

THERE ARE NOT JUST metaphors for attack but also for defense. This is important to emphasize mostly because spiritual warfare is not an engagement we participate in apart from the provisions of God. Rather, God *is* the provision in the sundry ways he both empowers and delivers the faithful. Hence, we find some passages that focus on and celebrate God as our bulwark against opposing forces of darkness.

ARMOR

In Luke 11:21–22, we have an early reference in the New Testament, by Jesus no less, to the armor metaphor. On the heels of Jesus's Beelzebul controversy (where he is defending his use of exorcisms against the absurd charge by the Pharisees that he has enlisted the powers of darkness in bringing about those exorcisms), he presents the illustration of a "strong man." This strong man is an armed soldier of sorts who stands guard of his home and possessions. When he is overtaken by someone else even stronger, he is defeated and then pillaged for spoils—even the very armor on his back. What Jesus is expressing here is that Satan is in fact the strong man standing guard over the world ("his own palace"). It is Jesus, with his power of exorcism, who overcomes Satan and takes ownership over what now belongs to him. This is one of the few warfare passages that does not quite involve the saints as much as it is Jesus himself acting alone. Jesus is unilaterally overcoming the evil one and rendering him vulnerable to ultimate conquest. Indeed, "[t]he reason the Son of God appeared was to destroy the works of the devil" (1 John 3:8c). It should be noted that the work of exorcism is not only at the hands of Jesus. For followers (Mark 6:13) and even uncommitted imitators of Jesus (Matt 7:22) are somehow being used to expel demonic forces.

Exorcism serves the same purpose as Jesus's healing ministry. It publicly demonstrates his power and authority over the heavens and earth. For Jesus does not heal and exorcise *in the name of the Father*, but he does so on his own accord and with his own authority. But those Jesus has enlisted to expel demons do not have that kind of authority in themselves. They must do so in his name if they are to do it at all.[1]

The metaphorical use of armor also pops up in the later New Testament's most iconic passage on spiritual warfare: Ephesians 6:13–17. Undoubtedly, this is the most extensive expression of what constitutes the "full armor" (*panoplian*) according to the apostle Paul; however, it is not the only place where he mentions it (e.g., 1 Thess 5:8; cf. 2 Cor 6:7). In the most celebrated passage of Ephesians, we have a list of metaphorical armor to be donned by the Christian that enables one to "stand" against "the rulers, against the authorities, against the cosmic powers over this present darkness, against the spiritual forces of evil in the heavenly places" (v. 12). The context is surely one that sees our Christian conflict to be against railing demonic forces from a reality distinct from but in a remotely governing connection to the physical one (cf. 1:20); indeed, the demonic realm is not shut off from the physical realm (3:10). Rightly so, Ephesians 6 has been the centerpiece for many a sermon pertaining to the struggles and conflicts Christians tend to have with forces beyond their control. But such a conflict is not without an immediate context as it pertains to the city of Ephesus. As Clinton Arnold explains, there was a concern among the Ephesians that the pervasive pagan belief in and practice of the magical arts might actually fail to stave off the assaulting powers of magicians and demons.[2] Christians likely considered Ephesus's patron deity Artemis (cf. Acts 19:24–27) to be among the demons seeking its (Christian) citizens harm.[3] A typical citizen would thus be worried that gods or demons or incantations or curses (or whatever) might overwhelm any countervailing magic one might wield, thus bringing ruination

---

1. I shall have more to say about the relationship between exorcism and spiritual warfare in chapter 16.

2. Arnold, *Power and Magic*, 14–20. Arnold offers insightful background here: "Ephesus had a reputation for a prolificity of magical practices ... Magic was primarily concerned with the acquisition of supernatural powers and the manipulation of the spirit world in the interest of the magician ... [And] Hellenistic magic ... was widely practiced in the area to which the epistle was written and it was chiefly concerned with 'power' and supernatural 'powers'" (20).

3. Arnold, *Power and Magic*, 20–37.

to oneself. Since the Christian Ephesians would not have the pagan resources of magic and curses to rely on in their quest for self-preservation, nor the protective powers of Artemis,[4] they would have Christ himself, who is far superior to any defensive magic or divine power a pagan might utilize.[5]

It is the *manner of warfare*, then, that this armament is meant to represent that has invited quite a bit of disagreement and confusion for those of us in the twenty-first century. John H. Walton and J. Harvey Walton believe that one is "misguided" if he or she assumes that "the message of Ephesians is fundamentally an instruction to believers (for all time) about how they should deal with manifestations of power."[6] Instead, they find that the passage has more to do with how the Christian culture better confronts its fears than the wider pagan culture, particularly given that the Ephesian culture is replete with claims to destructive magic and spiritual beings in high places. For the Christian in particular, Paul's emphasis on appreciating the supremacy of Christ ought to assuage any fears we may have that spiritual beings might assault us and be victorious. The emphasis of Ephesians 6 here is to say that when *Christians* as opposed to *non-Christians* (i.e., superstitious pagans) are confronted with spiritual forces, it is the Christian who has nothing to worry about. Ephesians 6 is not about how to engage such powers as much as it is about being reassured of victory in a sovereign Christ. And so, the "warfare image should not be interpreted to be affirming a literal combat with literal enemies," which otherwise would *reverse* the intent of the passage, namely, to alleviate and not intensify any fears over destructive magic or nefarious spirits.[7] Regardless, it is at least possible to accept the Waltons' commentary here while still believing that, beyond the Ephesian-pagan context, one continues to stand against spiritual forces by donning the armor (to be addressed in a moment). In fact, if demons exist and are indeed the powers at work in opposing the Ephesian Christians, it is difficult not to see this as at least *some* form of conflict, even if only indirect (insofar as the Waltons are right, it has nothing to do with some kind of *direct* conflict with evil forces). So, let us now turn to focus on just what that metaphorical armor might represent.

In today's day and age, many have become accustomed to seeing the passage as, contrary to the Waltons, an instruction manual on how to combat literal, spiritual enemies through certain spiritual practices (like prayer). And it begins with beyond-context speculations about the armor metaphors

---

4. "The devotees of Artemis feared the demonic realm, or the spirits of nature, and considered their goddess more powerful than these forces and thereby called upon her as their protector and deliverer" (Arnold, *Power and Magic*, 27).

5. Arnold, *Power and Magic*, 56.

6. Walton and Walton, *Demons and Spirits*, 254.

7. Walton and Walton, *Demons and Spirits*, 257.

themselves. A number of Christian pastors and teachers like to say that the warfare metaphors employed in Ephesians 6 are a reflection of Roman gear—gear that only operates defensively, save the sword. This might be true (more on this in a moment). But the armor described here was also present in pre-Roman militaries, not the least of which are noted quite specifically in the Old Testament long before the founding of Pompeii. For example, 1 Samuel 18:4 mentions a soldier's "belt," 1 Kings 22:34 a soldier-king's "breastplate," Psalm 60:8 (cf. 108:9) a "shoe," 1 Chronicles 5:18 a "shield," 1 Samuel 20:20 "arrows," and 1 Samuel 17:5 a "helmet." We also have mention of a sword but, as tradition would have it, this was the exception to the other defensive military accessories. Thus, all of Paul's listed armor is, so we have heard, intended for defense while the "sword of the Spirit" functions as the primary weapon of attack (for more on the sword, see "Sword" in the previous chapter).

Most readers have lost the significance of Paul's descriptions here by overlooking the prepositions "of truth," "of righteousness," and "of faith." These are often treated as distinctively Pauline, as if Paul were metaphorizing the soldier's gear out of the blue and for the first time. But the careful reader of Ephesians will recall that these themes have been discussed earlier in the correspondence. Moreover, these metaphors that represent them were already present in the Old Testament, including Isaiah 11:5 and 59:17. This hardware in the Old Testament represents the role of Yahweh and his Messiah and what will be accomplished through them. And what they will accomplish is far from a passive endurance of stresses imposed from without. Rather, God actively combats opposing forces in bringing about salvation and maintaining righteousness. This has led some commentators to consider that what Paul is really asking the Ephesian Christians to do is to don *Christ himself*[8]—the one who is in himself the revelation of Yahweh and the anticipated Messiah of Jewish antiquity. For as Paul says elsewhere, we must "put on the Lord Jesus Christ" (Rom 13:14). Only then will we become "more than conquerors," for it is only accomplished unequivocally "through him who loved us" (8:38). The better part of Ephesians is about the equipping of the Gentile saints to be well anchored in Christ as Paul himself has been (ch. 1–3) and to actively build up the extended body of Christ through sound doctrine and moral virtue (ch. 4–5). Most curiously, 4:20–24 connects some of the familiar elements of the armor—i.e., "righteousness," "holiness," and truth (from "put away falsehood" in v. 23)—when he tells the Ephesians "to put off the old self . . . and put on the new self." Full immersion in Christ, both individually and collectively, seems to be in Paul's mind

---

8. E.g., Powlison, "Classical Model," 92–98.

and that it is the *kind* of life lived in Christ that characterizes one who truly foregoes their pagan ignorance and their desires borne out of deception.[9]

Ephesians 6, then, serves to summarize these components in the choice metaphors of warfare spoken of elsewhere in Ephesians and beyond. For some commentators,[10] such an engagement is *not* a passive situation where the Christian is expected to hunker down and wait out the enemy's assaults. Even if the armor is seemingly defensive, Roman battalions would stand in the sense of wearing down their enemies before ultimately striking back.[11] It was a tactic used as an offensive strategy. Moreover, the imagery might mean that the Christian is to actively engage her surrounding culture by being and doing what Christ himself was and did—something not obviously (only) characterized as a defensive posture. For example, the righteousness of Christ was an aggression against the religious establishment of Jewish legalism, his truth was an active force of freedom (John 8:32), and his salvation was a threat to Roman imperialism. Perhaps Paul is not calling the saints to weather a storm; he is, rather, calling on them to *make* one! But it must also be noted that other able commentators see the armor as mostly defensive—that it is a call to intercultural (i.e., Jew and Greek) unity in the face of opposition.[12]

Perhaps much gets lost in Paul's call for us to stand since he might not be suggesting by this that Christians are to merely *endure* or take it on the chin, as it were. Rather, he might be suggesting that we stand *up* as opposed to remaining *sitting down* (cf. Acts 14:10). If the armor is offensive, and we either directly or indirectly engage enemy spiritual forces, it might be a call to arms in our being at the forefront of moral and theological revolution. If primarily defensive, then it might be a call to stand firm on our witness and to guard it against demonic assaults. Either way, the armor amplifies a communal life of truth, righteousness, peace, readiness, and faith without the church ever silencing her bold proclamation of her witness to Christ. And one thing is for sure: the supremacy of Christ ought to be of great comfort to us amidst the conflict.

---

9. For a more detailed explication of the armor, see the subsection "An Integrative Approach: The Armor of God" in chapter 18.

10. E.g., Powlison, "Classical Model," 92–98; Arnold, *Exegetical Commentary*, 451ff.; Neufeld, *Armour of God*, 109–31.

11. Morris, "Ephesians 6:10–17."

12. E.g., Fowl, *Ephesians*, 203; Keener, *IVP Bible Background Commentary*, 553f.

BREASTPLATE, HELMET, AND GARMENTS

Isaiah 59:17 reads: "He put on righteousness as a breastplate, and a helmet of salvation on his head; he put on garments of vengeance for clothing, and wrapped himself in zeal as a cloak." It is increasingly evident that Isaiah's conqueror dons the same armor and clothing that Paul will likewise describe in Ephesians 6 (see above). And, like Ephesians, the armor represents a spiritual war—a spiritual war centered on the Messiah. But it is Isaiah who first explicates the "breastplate" as righteousness and the "helmet" as salvation. It is noteworthy that Isaiah here describes the armor as "garments *of vengeance*," which *may* indicate that the familiar spiritual armor might not merely be defensive after all.

FORTRESS

A very common warfare metaphor in the Old Testament is that of a fortress (e.g., 2 Sam 22:2; Ps 18:2; 31:2–3). This is decisively warfare language as a fortress is a fortified military stronghold that wards off invading and attacking armies. Such is a fortress mostly because it is intended to be impenetrable. The image, when it is used of God, is meant to capture the fact that God actively fights on our behalf, and he does so without there being a concern that he would be overwhelmed or defeated by an enemy. That God is all-powerful is a property of God firmly embedded in the fortress motif. And the fruits of his being a fortress are all the same: deliverance and salvation. It is no wonder that the fortress figures in many hymns and worship songs celebrating such salvific and protective care.

GUARD

Paul says that God is our "guard" and that he guards us "against the evil one" (2 Thess 3:3). Paul implies to yet another provincial city that there are assaults by a supernatural *someone* who is not of this world. And only God is the successful protector—a protector who will not ever fail to protect us provided we do not fail in our obedience (v. 4) lest we become vulnerable.

The guard motif continues in the letters to Timothy (1 Tim 6:20; 2 Tim 1:12–14). In these passages, it is not so much that God is doing the guarding—though he does as we see in 2 Timothy 1:12—as much as it is that Timothy himself is commanded to do the guarding (1 Tim 6:20). This reveals that the one being guarded is a cooperative reality, one involving God on the one hand and the saint on the other. God is both able and willing to guard us from "false 'knowledge,'" but it is something from which we must ourselves also guard against. It is our turning to God in Christ that allows us to maintain our fidelity to virtue and doctrinal truth. We guard ourselves by turning to God and he, in turn, does not fail to *finally* guard us.

HEDGE (BOUNDARY)

We may often hear some in contemporary prayer groups pray for a "hedge of protection." It is a phrase found in Job 1:10. No, this is not an allusion to the spiritual effectiveness of landscaped bushes; it is an extension of the shield metaphor found prominently in the Psalms. For it reveals that God not only protects but also sets boundaries. In fact, according to the Job passage, this hedge protects not only Job's person but also his wider livelihood. Now, we are all aware of what happens to poor Job in the ensuing chapters, but this only illustrates that God's protection is not always a protection of isolation from harm but a kind of protection that empowers one to endure it. This is the heart of Job as a commentary on the human suffering that will befall even the righteous, "[f]or God speaks in one way, and in two, though man does not perceive it" (33:14). Indeed, human suffering is one of the languages of God and so we ought not to expect to always or even usually be protected from it (cf. 1 Pet 2:20; 3:17; 5:9; Rev 2:10). Nevertheless, it is the prerogative of God to lift the hedge as he sees fit even if it inevitably results in injury of both person and property. *God permits some evils for reasons we may or may not ever discern this side of the grave.*

SHIELD

One metaphor that is found prominently in the Old Testament is God's being our shield (e.g., Gen 15:1; Deut 33:29; 2 Sam 22:3, 31, 36; Ps 3:3; 5:12; 7:10; 18:2; etc.; Prov 2:7; 30:5). To Christians, it is a familiar one as it is one of Paul's iconic metaphors for faith in Ephesians 6 (see above). What each of these passages indicates is that those positioned in an appropriate way according to God's ways are under divine protection. This protection means different things for different circumstances. Sometimes such protection is literal and physical, as in God's protection of one from earthly enemies in battle (2 Sam 22:3; Ps 3:3). At other times it is God's protection from vice and moral infidelity (Prov 2:7). And this protection is not just of individuals but of the corporate elect of God (Deut 33:29) as evidenced by Israel's perpetuity. However, we ought not to confuse perpetuity with effortlessness or lack of failures along the way, for Israel's endurance involved difficult exiles and a frequent straying from God when temptation arose.

12

Metaphors for Retreat

Though Scripture promises that the faithful will eventually be victorious through the empowerment and presence of Christ in us, this is also accomplished in part by not engaging in either direct or indirect conflict that would be foolhardy. Sometimes one must avoid the conflict altogether. You might say that there is the occasional call for the saints to go marching *out* and not always *in*. For victory is not always brought about by overwhelming the opposition but sometimes by fleeing the assaults altogether and allowing God to work in other ways and for different reasons.

It is worthy of noting that Scripture sometimes says that it is the enemy who does the fleeing—perhaps as an indication that some Christian posturing is a lost cause even for the devil and his angels. So, both affirmations about the need for the Christian to sometimes back down and the fact that the enemy sometimes flees reveal that spiritual warfare gets a bit more nuanced than the usual fighting and deflecting. Let us take a look at those metaphors reflecting the various instances of retreat.

FLEE

We do not often think of fleeing as a feature of wartime, but it is often appropriate to do if the risk is too high. In the case of 1 Corinthians 6:18, this flight metaphor is attached to the Corinthian Christian, who is encouraged to "flee" from "youthful passions." While it would be incorrect to think that Paul is advocating an asceticism (which would run aground with his comments aimed at married couples in the following chapter), he is referring to the lure of the flesh, which is felt most strongly in one's youth. That one flees this and turns instead to "pursue righteousness" indicates that this is an intentional pursuit one must purpose for themselves. In short, the admonition is for us to focus not on the deliverances of the flesh but on self- and other-building "fruits of the Spirit" (cf. Gal 5:17–25).

Four chapters later, in 1 Corinthians 10:13–14, we have Paul's famous declaration that "No temptation has overtaken you that is not common to man" and that "God is faithful, and he will not let you be tempted beyond your ability, but with the temptation he will also provide the way of escape, that you may be able to endure it." Now, it is no secret that one of the literal tactics of Satan is that of temptation. Temptation is no metaphor. And yet this passage indicates that there is always a road to victory over that temptation. Of equal importance is that that road to victory is not one any Christian carves out on her own. It is "the way of escape" that is provided for us by God himself. And this will require that we "endure" the assaults of temptation as they arise. But the end of verse 14 offers a curious command. Paul says to "flee from idolatry." Here, one's fleeing sounds like a scenario where one is surrounded by the enemy and/or behind enemy lines. One is thus being encouraged to *not* take on her enemy in this circumstance, as it were. Instead, your best bet is a quick exit.

While we're on the subject of temptation, the "temptation" of verses 13 and 14 pertains specifically to a temptation to *idolatry*. Like adultery, casual flirtation with pagan deities will endanger the spiritual welfare of the Christian. And this can occur even if one has fully participated in the sacraments of Christ. For even the ancient Hebrews did this in the wilderness (vv. 1–4) and a lot of good it did them![1] So, the call to "flee" (*pheugete*) from such idolatry is appropriate. It is a willful and proactive abandonment of anything that might lead to a compromise where the Christian may find herself simultaneously "drink[ing] the cup of the Lord and the cup of demons" (v. 21). And one must flee just as one should if in the presence of untimely sexual temptations that prompt fornication and immorality (6:18). It is a removal of self from the circumstances altogether in order to preserve one's fidelity to God and his holiness. In short, it is a battle one should not engage. And she may reliably look to God to find her escape route.

In 2 Timothy 2:22, Paul tells us that sexual immorality is unique in that it is the only sin that depends on one's being embodied. Beings like angels would not be intrinsically capable of things like sexual immorality—a considerable strike against the fallen angels view of Genesis 6:1–4, incidentally.

---

1. So, Proctor, *First and Second Corinthians*, 80.

As advice for the young Timothy, Paul tells him to flee from sexual immorality for it is rooted in the body, which is the influential abode of the flesh. And the flesh is the instrument of the world (1 John 2:16). To entertain the flesh is to thereby sin against one's own body. And it is that body that is intended to be one's permanent abode in God's everlasting paradise (Rom 8:11; 1 Cor 15:51–54; 1 John 3:2). Sin caused our separation from God, but it is our reunification with God that now prompts us to separate from sin.

Fleeing is not only a normative response for Christians, but it is also a response that the enemy, the devil, sometimes entertains himself. It is a flight prompted by the Christian's submission to God as we read in James 4:7 ("Submit yourselves therefore to God. Resist the devil, and he will flee from you"). Such fleeing obtains as a result of one opposing pride and humbling oneself (vv. 6, 10), come what may. And pride, which is a form of idolatry, is elsewhere said to be something that will lead the believer to fall under the "condemnation of the devil" (1 Tim 3:6). In the face of pride, *we* should flee; but in the face of humility, *Satan* will flee.

FLIGHT

The concept of taking flight is not too dissimilar to fleeing in the sense of a forfeiture or retreat. In the Psalms, we have situations where, amidst the use of other spiritual warfare metaphors, the enemies of God are said to "take flight" (Ps 21:12; 48:5). Such a flight tends to obtain at the prospect of God's demonstrative power over his enemies. In Psalm 48:5, it appears to be merely at the sight of what God has done for Mount Zion that motivates the flight. Like "flee," "flight" connotes the enemy's futility of a situation before God and prompts the combatant(s) to tuck tail and run. This is no doubt meant to convey both the ease and surety that God will be victorious in any would-be conflict. However, we would be wise to appreciate that such victory is not always immediate and literal, though sometimes it is (Josh 23:10). Sometimes God is with us and yet leads us or accompanies us into failure (Judg 1:19)! But we can be assured that God will *finally* be victorious and put all enemies to flight, for this is a truth that is promised in the apocalyptic portions of Scripture.

TURN AWAY

Proverbs 29:8 says that "[s]coffers set a city aflame, but the wise turn away wrath." This simple but profound saying reflects a truth about *tactics*, namely, that the practice of wisdom involves diffusing a conversation before it gets out of hand—violent, even! In an age of social media, where passions run high, it is almost impossible to say something that will "turn away wrath." However, the truly wise can manage the kind of response that will keep the peace as well as convey the truth. Of course, we must recognize that no matter how conciliatory you are, sometimes your attempting to quell the hotheads in a dialogue is bound to fail. But at this point the scoffers in your situation are not violently motivated *by you* but by *your cause for Christ*. And when there is personal persecution over such a cause, all you can do is "[r]ejoice and be glad, for your reward is great in heaven" (Matt 5:12).

13

Metaphors for Victory

LIKE ANY GOOD STORY, the cosmic story of spiritual warfare is one that ends happily. God and his "soldiers" will ultimately overcome their enemy triumvirate despite having been bloodied up along the way. And the way Scripture captures such victory is no less in military terms. Thus, we shall include the metaphorical vocabulary of how the war will end, which is no less significant than the vocabulary of the battles themselves, for it offers us a significant light at the end of the tunnel.

COMMAND AND MEET

Paul assures the Thessalonians in his correspondence with them (1 Thess 4) that even though some Christians have already died, it is the resurrection of Christ that assures us of their future. In fact, we will be with them on that glorious day when Christ returns. The inevitability of Christ's return is a great comfort to us and so we need not "grieve as others do who have no hope" (v. 3).

It is the language of the second coming that is being bathed in a bit of warfare language. For when Christ returns, he will "descend from heaven with a cry of command, with the voice of an archangel, and with the sound of the trumpet of God" (v. 16). After that, those of us who have not yet died "will be caught up together with them in the clouds to meet the Lord in the air, and so we will always be with the Lord" (v. 17). The promise is one of union with God as well as *re*union with our loved ones. It is a message of hope. And the assuring language surrounding it reveals Jesus's credentials. The "cry of command" emphasizes the sovereignty of Christ. And the "trumpet sound" punctuates the fact that this hope is a fulfillment of God's salvific promise, not to mention that it decisively identifies Christ as the apocalyptic "son of man" of Daniel 7:13. (We'll defer talking about the trumpet metaphor until the next section.) But there is something to be said about the fact that we will "meet" Christ "in the air." It may not sound like warfare language, but there is actually something very political about what these words mean.

This passage about an aerial meeting has invited quite a bit of eschatological speculation. In fact, it is the bedrock proof text for a number of Christians today who anticipate that God will rapture his church out of the clutches of an impending seven-year period of tribulation. The doctrine of the rapture construes Paul's message here as being about the saints, who will literally ascend into the sky and be ushered into heaven. And then there are those who demur. Regardless of what one makes of this atmospheric ingathering (I myself am not convinced that this as indicative of such a rapture[1]), the language intends to reflect how dignitaries and nobles are greeted and then escorted (cf. Matt 25:1). As a dignitary is greeted at the border by an entourage, so are we, as Christ's entourage, said to escort Jesus back to this world (cf. 1 Thess 3:13). In this case, it is "the air" where the reunion occurs. This is significant, not because it is conveying an anti-gravity ascension into the sky (just like it doesn't in John 12:32 when Jesus says, regarding his ascension, "I, when I am lifted up from the earth, will draw all people to myself"), but because "the air" means something else. It is a this-worldly province currently under the tyrannical jurisdiction of Satan (Eph 2:2). Put simply, it is the atmosphere of the devil's rule and, yet, it is the territory where we will reunite. This telegraphs to the Thessalonians that Satan's power and rule will be no more, for we will all be gloriously resurrected and thus no longer susceptible to the power of death (cf. Heb 2:14). It is quite easy to see why this gives the Thessalonians ample reason to "encourage one another with these words" (v. 18).

The takeaway message here is hope, and so Paul is choosing his words carefully. This is so because elsewhere (2 Thess 1:6–8; Rev 20:7–10) it is clear that such a hope is really one that comes *after* an interim battle. Such hope, then, is the fruit of Christ's victory, for it is a hope that comes

---

1. The doctrine of the rapture seems to have things completely backwards here. For the passage, as well as every other "coming" text, is about Christ coming unto his people, not the people coming unto Christ! And we shouldn't read too much into "caught up" (*harpazō*) since, as a passive verb, it is expressing only that such an ingathering is due to the unilateral providence and power of Christ to resurrect (cf. John 6:44; 11:25).

TRUMPET

Isaiah 27:13 promises that there will come a "day a great trumpet will be blown" heralding the salvation of Israel. Israel, being no stranger to exile as they were driven into the desert by the Egyptians centuries earlier, is in another state of exile in Assyria. And the promise to the Israelites is that they will return from being scattered back to "the holy mountain of Jerusalem." As such, the imagery here is eschatological (which is to say that it looks forward to the victory of God at the end of human history). The curious expressions "in that day," "the holy mountain," and "a great trumpet" along with the chapter's finality of God's vengeance are all telltale signs that this is in view. Indeed, God will vindicate his people after they have endured a period of exile. In ancient battles, the blast of the trumpet would, among other things, mark the end of the conflict (cf. 2 Sam 2:28; 18:16).[2] It was also used to herald the king (2 Sam 15:10; 1 Kgs 1:34; 2 Kgs 9:13). Outside of battle, it was to inaugurate the spiritual salvation of God, for on the ritual Day of Atonement the trumpet was to be sounded (cf. Lev 25:9). The metaphor of the trumpet came to represent the supreme vindication, kingship, and salvation of God.

When we get to the New Testament, a similar theme is echoed in Jesus's Olivet Discourse as found in Matthew 24:31 ("And he will send out his angels with a loud trumpet call, and they will gather his elect from the four winds, from one end of heaven to the other"). As Jesus narrates, the scene of his return ultimately concludes with him returning to this world to "gather his elect." Paul may have had a similar understanding of the event when he wrote 1 Thessalonians 4:16 (see previous section). The similarities with Matthew 24 should not be missed: both speak of the Lord's descent (among the "clouds"), an angelic accompaniment, a trumpet call, and an ingathering of God's people. However, I shall resist interpreting this as the *same* event in order to move on to focus on the more pressing trumpet imagery.

Both Jesus and Paul use the metaphor of a trumpet to drive home the understanding that with Christ comes ultimate victory. He is not just another announced victor; he is the apocalyptic "son of man" of Daniel, who

---

2. Or, as the case may be, it would also be used to mark the *inauguration* of something terrible, such as war (e.g., Exod 19:16; Jer 6:1; Ezek 33:3–5; Joel 2:1).

will finally judge the wicked and reward the righteous. It also likely connects to the seventh trumpet of Revelation 10:7 and 11:15. The trumpet on the Day of the Lord is always blasted by the archangel, which gives it further apocalyptic significance, for Michael the archangel was thought by many to be Israel's national guardian angel. Moreover, it is undoubtedly a final fulfillment of Isaiah 27:13.

The significance for spiritual warfare is that such a trumpet marks the *end* of the spiritual conflict. And it is only ended by God himself. To the ears of the righteous, it is the sound of everlasting rest and comfort. To the ears of the wicked, it is the sound of ultimate loss.[3] *We* do not bring about final victory; rather, only God in Christ finishes the lifelong struggle by destroying the seemingly undestroyable: Satan, the power of death, and those who have relied on such powers in afflicting the saints. And praise be to God that the trumpet will one day be blown!

---

3. Rev 8:7—9:14 ("The . . . angel blew his trumpet . . .") uses the "trumpet" in a way that does not involve the announcing of the arrival of a king or of ushering in salvation. Instead, these only signify the occurrences of divine judgments. The presence of angels as those meting out judgment might be meant to punctuate the notion that all such judgment is brought about *indirectly* (possibly because the outcome to these forms of judgment do not bestow final judgment). God seems to only dish out human judgment on earth by proxy in Revelation. Only those awaiting the second death earn the privilege of God's direct judgment (Rev 19:20). And this judgment has only one terrible outcome for the wicked.

14

Miscellaneous Metaphors

AND THEN THERE ARE those metaphors that have no specific category in which to place them. Some metaphors are about certain accessories utilized in battle. Others are mere accompaniments during or at the inauguration of a war. And then there is general talk of war and peace, which are themselves neither weapons, armor, nor accessories of any sort but are about the presence or absence of conflict altogether. In this chapter, we shall end our exploration of warfare metaphors by addressing these miscellaneous terms, which are no less important in filling out an ultimate study on spiritual warfare.

BELT

Isaiah 11:5 makes a reference to a special future Davidic king whose "[r]ighteousness shall be the belt of his waist, and faithfulness the belt of his loins." He will come with the "Spirit of the LORD" (v. 2). Messianic expectations in the Old Testament certainly give the impression that this figure will be a conqueror who will vindicate the elect of God and will settle his theocracy once and for all. This conqueror comes with the "belt of his waist" and the "belt of his loins" signifying righteousness and faithfulness. This imagery is famously invoked by Paul in the New Testament in Ephesians 6:14.

BUGLE

While Paul in 1 Corinthians 14:8 does not directly speak of a bugle as an element in spiritual warfare *per se*, he is offering a battle analogy. It is the bugle that, if sounded inappropriately, "gives an indistinct sound," thereby confusing soldiers as to whether it is a call to arms. Paul wants to show the importance of not promoting confusion in the exercise of certain spiritual gifts (e.g., the gift of tongues) in an improper way. But this analogy has wider application, even in warfare. For anything that we do to combat darkness must not be ambiguous or vague. We should purpose to be very clear about how to combat things like heresy and moral vice. This is especially true if we are leading others to be victorious. If we muddy the waters with obscure tactics and undue compromises, we would in effect be playing to the battalion cacophonies instead of a more distinctive and appropriate song like "Reveille."

CAPTIVES

Most of us are aware that Jesus has come to "set the captives free." This bumper sticker expression likely derives from Luke 4:18 and is, indeed, a true statement. Let us look at what Jesus himself says in full in Luke 4:18:

> The Spirit of the Lord is upon me, because he has anointed me to proclaim good news to the poor. He has sent me to proclaim liberty to the captives and recovering of sight to the blind, to set at liberty those who are oppressed.

The words themselves derive from Isaiah 61:1 and were uttered to comfort those who were marginalized. It is evident from his citation that Jesus himself also sees the oppressed as prisoners of war. In light of the fact that the church is to continue its endeavor of world evangelism, it is incited to, among other things, right the wrongs perpetuated by acts of social injustice and the like. But there is also a spiritual dimension here that we can appreciate.[1] That is, each person is held captive by the enemy triumvirate: the world (Col 2:8; 1 John 5:19), the flesh (Rom 7:3, 6; Gal 3:23), and the devil himself (Rev 2:10[2]). The present reality is dually under the province of

---

1. It is not uncommon for passages that apply to the literally oppressed and marginalized to double as statements directed to those that are *spiritually* oppressed and marginalized—that is, to those who have been taken in by the world, the flesh, and the devil himself. Compare, for example, the literal poor of Luke 6:20 with the "poor in spirit" of Matt 5:3.

2. However, one's "captivity" appears to be, in the wake of Jesus's victory, a matter of

a wicked "prince" (political tyranny) and "god" (religious tyranny), for Satan seeks to control both our national and spiritual allegiances. We can glean this from Jesus's own temptation in the wilderness, where Satan actively seeks Jesus's political (Matt 4:8–9) as well as spiritual (v. 9) devotion.[3] If we rebuff the devil's attempted ascendancy over us, then his final recourse is to destroy and even kill those who refuse his lordship (Heb 2:14).

It is unclear whether Paul intends a similar connotation for "captive" in his letter to the Ephesians. Therein, Paul modifies a Septuagint reading of Psalm 68:18: "Therefore [the Psalm] says, 'When he ascended on high he led a host of captives, and he gave gifts to men'" (Eph 4:8). These "captives" could be living and/or deceased saints—including believers who were once oppressed but are now in God's presence.[4] Or they could be Satan and his cohorts. In other words, maybe Paul is saying that Jesus didn't lead a "host of captives" *out* of captivity but *into* captivity (for the passage says nothing either way). Regardless, Luke 4:18 is evidence enough that we, as heirs to salvation, are captives who are set free.

But being captive isn't something only applied to our condition under the enemy triumvirate. The term is also applied to the Christian as a way to *remedy* her captivity. Paul says in 2 Corinthians 10:5 that, along with "destroy[ing] arguments and every lofty opinion raised against the knowledge of God," we are to "take every thought captive to obey Christ." In context, it seems to refer to a pressing need to take control of the conversation in some way (for more on this passage, see "War(fare)" below). That captivity connotes a sense of

---

choice. Cf. Luke 11:21–22.

3. It seems to me that Satan is not seeking anyone's devotion because he has a thirst for power and self-worship; rather, it is probably because in so doing, each person who capitulates ultimately separates herself from God and subsequently leads others to do the same.

4. Some see 1 Pet 3:18:19–21 as a similar reference, where it is alleged that upon Jesus's death, he descended into the abode of the deceased (i.e., those who died under the Old Covenant) and announced their promised salvation. This interpretation seems unlikely to me. Most importantly, those who receive the proclamation are only those "in the days of Noah, while the ark was being prepared" (v. 20). Moreover, the grammar of v. 19 is ambiguous, for it could be either that Jesus *indirectly* "proclaimed to the spirits in prison" through the spirit or that it was "the spirit" himself who did so. That the ark of Noah's flood "corresponds" (v. 21) to how baptism saves our "appeal to God for a good conscience" (v. 21) shows that God doesn't abandon those who endure evil but eventually saves them. Peter might only be meaning in verse 19 that God delivers no less than Jesus through his suffering and death and that this is something even the disobedient during Noah's day were witnesses to. That is, that the same "spirit" who made Jesus alive again is perhaps the one who had proclaimed, through the flood event, that God delivers those who suffer for the sake of righteousness. I find this explains well the preceding verse (1 Pet 3:17): "For it is better to suffer for doing good, if that should be God's will, than for doing evil." Why? Because, as evidenced by Jesus and Noah and his family, God will inevitably deliver his people.

overcoming and conquering is clear enough (cf. Rev 2:7, 11, 17, 26; 3:5, 12, 21; 21:7; see "Conquer(or)" below). Though our victory is in Christ, we should not lose sight of the fact that it entails effort on our part too—effort in the face of adversity and active resistance by malevolent and destructive forces.

CONQUER(OR)

Paul famously tells the Roman Christians that "we are more than conquerors through him who loved us" (Rom 8:37). To conquer means to overcome by some measure of force. It clearly has military overtones as we often speak of famous historical events like the conquest of Alexander the Great or the conquest of Sargon of Akkad. Quite often the military concept is metaphorized—even romanticized—as when we might say that Don Juan DeMarco "conquered" many women during his exploits. Clearly enough, the term denotes one's ability to finally overcome something or someone, usually but not necessarily against their will. In context of the Pauline usage (Rom 8:31–36), he is talking about the Roman Christians conquering any kind of force that seeks to "separate us from the love of Christ" (v. 35). This includes any opposing *immaterial* force too (vv. 38–39). The imperviousness of Christ's love for us is obvious from the fact that God, in advance and with perfect insight, sovereignly elects those "called according to his purpose" (v. 28) and that these will, accordingly, be "justified" (v. 30). Nothing can get in the way of that except, possibly, one's willing departure from faith (4:16).[5]

Indeed, we know that Christ conquers and that, through him, we are made to conquer. This much is implied by Luke 10:19–20. But what does it look like for believers themselves to conquer in a way that properly distinguishes between the intrinsic, sovereign majesty of Christ and the lowly sinner saved by his grace? The book of Revelation uses this metaphor quite a bit to help us cash this out. In God's letters to the seven churches of Asia Minor, the notion of conquering occurs quite frequently. Here is a list of references in Revelation depicting the nature of the one who conquers:

1. The one who conquers is the one who does not abandon one's love of Christ and doing good works (2:5–7).

---

5. I am not interested here in disputing about whether salvation is something that can be foregone or not. The present wording surely accords more closely with those holding to an Arminian-Wesleyan notion of conditional security. But to those holding to an Augustinian-Calvinist notion of eternal security, we might just say that *nothing at all*, including lack of faith, can separate one from the salvific love of Christ. Our present discussion does not hinge on any doctrine of the perseverance of the saints.

2. The one who conquers is the one who is willing to die for Christ (2:9–11).
3. The one who conquers is the one who resists immorality and false doctrine (2:14, 17, 20, 24–26).
4. The one who conquers is the one who is alert to avoid infidelity (3:2–5).
5. The one who conquers is the one who is authentic (and not a liar) before God (3:8–9, 12).
6. The one who conquers is the one who does not blur the distinction between virtue and vice (3:15–16, 21).

Each of the churches are declared to be guilty of something, which often involves their compromising the faith in some way. Accordingly, they are issued these edicts to check their attitudes, predispositions, carnal desires, and ignorance before God. For one's inheritance of the kingdom of God is on the line. Consequently, "[t]he one who conquers will have this heritage, and I will be his God and he will be my son" (21:7). However, "as for the cowardly, the faithless, the detestable, as for murderers, the sexually immoral, sorcerers, idolaters, and all liars, their portion will be in the lake that burns with fire and sulfur, which is the second death" (v. 8; cf. Rom 6:23). With the added contrasting vices, it is made even clearer what it means to conquer in the name of Christ and how significant it is that we do so.

So, while God is in supreme control as to ensure that none of his chosen will fall from grace, the means of his doing so are captured in the last book of the Bible. It is the convergence of God's sovereignty with human responsibility. Regardless of how this tension may be philosophically resolved, one thing is for sure: in order for Christians to be conquerors, we must be faithful unto the Lord, cling to his virtues, and rebuff vice and doctrinal falsehoods.

HORSES AND CHARIOTS

In yet another apocalyptic context, we have some mixed imagery in Revelation 9:7–9. The passage reads in full:

> In appearance the locusts were like horses prepared for battle: on their heads were what looked like crowns of gold; their faces were like human faces, their hair like women's hair, and their teeth like lions' teeth; they had breastplates like breastplates of iron, and the noise of their wings was like the noise of many chariots with horses rushing into battle.

Despite being heavy on warfare imagery, it features unlikely enemies not often associated with war: "locusts" that arise out of a "bottomless pit" (vv. 2–3). That God unlocks this pit with a "key" is a familiar image of authority that reflects the prerogative of God to do the unlocking (cf. Isa 22:22; Matt 16:19; Rev 1:18; 3:7; 20:1). Along with cosmic disturbances (again, these are just images), these locusts dish out a measure of harm (viz., retributive justice) against those who do not belong to God, for these are in violent opposition to him (Rev 9:4). It is evident that the use of "locusts" here is meant to be connected to the locusts of the Egyptian plagues that ravished Egypt during the days of the Hebrews' captivity (Exod 10:3–19; Ps 105:34–35). The fact that they appear as "horses prepared for battle" invokes Jeremiah 51:27 and Job 39:19–20. However, the most obvious connection Revelation 9's horse-like locusts have is with Joel 2:1–4:

> Blow a trumpet in Zion; sound an alarm on my holy mountain! Let all the inhabitants of the land tremble, for the day of the LORD is coming; it is near, a day of darkness and gloom, a day of clouds and thick darkness! Like blackness there is spread upon the mountains a great and powerful people; their like has never been before, nor will be again after them through the years of all generations. Fire devours before them, and behind them a flame burns. The land is like the garden of Eden before them, but behind them a desolate wilderness, and nothing escapes them. *Their appearance is like the appearance of horses, and like war horses they run.* (emphasis added)

The imagery not only has locusts appearing as horses, but it even mentions a darkness that we seem to have in Revelation 9:2. The connection here is unmistakable, for it truly is a judgment that heralds "the day of the LORD."

Revelation 9:7–9 goes on to describe these "locusts" in military terms. This is not surprising given that in Joel 2 these "locusts" are foot soldiers. So, John the Revelator says that they are donned with "breastplates like breastplates of iron." No doubt this is meant to underscore the fact that they are impervious and invulnerable, probably because God is providentially permitting the unleashing of this hoard for his own purposes. Despite not taking these locusts literally, they do signal to the reader that such judgment by proxy is selective, temporary, and unstoppable. The locusts originate from "the bottomless pit" and have a "king over them the angel of the bottomless pit" whose "name in Hebrew is Abaddon, and in Greek he is called Apollyon" (v. 11). Given that this is not merely *an* angel but *the* angel, we are prompted to make the connection with verse 1: the "star fallen from heaven to earth." And it is in Luke 10:18 where we are told that Jesus saw Satan fall like lightning from heaven thereby possibly clinching the identity of the sinister angel in question. Therefore, Revelation 9 indicates that these horse-like locusts are probably demons or demon-controlled (Parthian?) soldiers. But they operate under the control of God, who permits them their havoc for the sake of God's meting out retributive justice.[6]

In this context, we learn that demons indeed play a role in assaulting others. How this might be carried out is not quite clear in Revelation 9. But the interesting human targets of these demons are not believers but unbelievers (v. 4)! Indeed, demons are apparently against *any* kind of person—believer or not. This is probably because even those without "the seal of God on their foreheads" still have a chance at repentance (cf. 6:10–11), and what demon wouldn't want to stop that?

KINGDOM

Jesus often framed his own messianic reality in Levitical terms: that Jesus is the King of kings among us. It was in Jesus's own modeled prayer that we, as emulators of him, pray: "Your kingdom come, your will be done, on earth as it is in heaven" (Matt 6:10). The Gospels are filled with references by Jesus of the "kingdom of God," the "kingdom of heaven," and the "gospel of the kingdom." It was this kingdom preaching that fueled the accusations against him as one who would unseat the Roman emperor. And this culminated in the ultimate mockery hurled against him as "the King of the Jews" (e.g., Mark 15:18, 26). Kingdom language is about as warfare oriented as you can get, for it establishes one's national and, in this case, spiritual allegiances in opposition to others.

Luke 11:18 reveals a counter-kingdom to the one heralded by Christ. In this controversy over Beelzebul, Jesus is responding to the accusation that his kingdom power derives from Satan. By way of response, Jesus points out the obvious: kingdoms pitted against themselves would be self-defeating; therefore, Jesus's power does not derive from Satan. Jesus's remarks also reveal another truth: that the power of Christ is greater than that of Satan. For Jesus is acknowledged to "cast out demons." The charge of being in cahoots with Satan is evidence that Jesus's power was not in question. They only

---

6. In 1 Cor 5, readers can see that God uses Satan to judge an unnamed adulterer. In meting out this kind of judgment, the Corinthians are implored to "deliver this man to Satan for the destruction of the flesh, so that his spirit may be saved in the day of the Lord" (v. 5). In this case, the judgment is likely one of correction. For it seems that the "flesh" that is to be "destroyed" here is a reference to out-of-control sexual passions in need of quashing. The "flesh" here is not the physical life of the person but part of the tripartite enemy we introduced in chapter 6.

sought an alternative, nefarious interpretation in order to deny that Jesus, the one opposing the chief priests, was indeed the promised Messiah.

PEACE

Warfare language includes not only metaphors of battle and conflict but also metaphors of what is often called *jus post bellum* ("justice after war"). This is to say that there remain obligations even when we are in between conflicts and not actively engaged in combat at the moment. When one operates under God's provision and direction, and focuses on "whatever is true, whatever is honorable, whatever is just, whatever is pure, whatever is lovely, whatever is commendable, if there is any excellence, if there is anything worthy of praise" (Phil 4:8), the result is "peace" (Phil 4:7–9). It is a peace that "surpasses all understanding" and continues its abiding influence. This is not to say that *God* surpasses all understanding but that it is his *peace* that does. This peace is the harmonious contentment we experience when we bathe ourselves in virtue and truth. And it is not something that is instilled unilaterally by God. It is an active way of human living on our part that insulates us from the spiritually negative consequences of entertaining vice. That it is *we* who are to "think about these things" in bringing about what is honorable, just, etc. evidences the fact that our virtue is one that must be maintained and not passively taken for granted; for our very being can still be upset by the enemy triumvirate that seeks to destroy that peace in God.

WAR(FARE)

We would be remiss not to make mention of an obvious term, "war" or "warfare," which is often used to describe some kind of spiritual, aggressive tension. We find most uses of "war" or "warfare" as they are used in the spiritual sense to be found in the New Testament, beginning with Romans 7:22–23. In this war passage, the context pertains to a sort of conflict between two "laws"—that of God in the inner person ("the law of my mind") and that of the flesh (viz., "the law of sin that dwells in my members"). As the apostle Paul suggests here, he is made a sort of prisoner of war ("making me captive") by such passions. The notion of such "laws" coming into conflict no doubt represents the unimpeachable reality of both God's spirituality and the flesh's carnality. Each of us struggles and is bound to struggle with this tension and therefore it is as a law. But God is just as resilient, so we can, like a law, count on him.

In the much-celebrated passage of 2 Corinthians 10:3–6, the Corinthian Christians are being upheld to an ideal standard in that our "war" against the assaults of the flesh is a different kind of assault from that of the flesh:

> For though we walk in the flesh, we are not waging war according to the flesh. For the weapons of our warfare are not of the flesh but have divine power to destroy strongholds. We destroy arguments and every lofty opinion raised against the knowledge of God, and take every thought captive to obey Christ, being ready to punish every disobedience, when your obedience is complete.

The Corinthian (i.e., Christian) response to adversity is to be a calculated one—one effective enough to "destroy strongholds." These "weapons of our warfare" involve the destruction, not of our assailants, but of "arguments" (*logismous*) and anything detracting from knowledge of God. That Paul then implores the Corinthians to "take every thought captive to obey Christ" is a signal for them to control the conversation. The "thought" (*noēma*) here is likely referring to a scheme or design plan since this is how Paul uses the term earlier in 2:11 when Paul warns of the devil's "schemes" (*noēmata*).[7] The chapter itself begins by warning of "the flesh" (vv. 1–2) and anticipates "someone [who] comes and proclaims another Jesus than the one we proclaimed" (11:4). Thus, as Clinton Arnold summarizes, "the critical thrust of [10:3–6] is directed against Christological heresy."[8] It is clearly a doctrinal and ultimately a moral combat narrative, for the saints utilize such "weapons" in order "to obey Christ"; and they are poised to "punish every disobedience" in the process.

As we venture outside of the Pauline corpus, passions once again take center stage. In this case, we have a war metaphor used in James 4:11 and 1 Peter 2:11. That our flesh, viz., passions, "are at war" within us and that they "wage war against your soul" are clear indications that our spiritual lives are supremely threatened by our passions. James even indicates that such passions are what drive all intramural quarreling amongst fellow Christians (this should not be confused with the edifying need for moral reprimand and doctrinal correction). We quarrel when we lack the discipline of honest and reflective disagreement leading to some kind of unifying compromise if not a full-blown solution (a unifying solution such as we find in Acts 6:1–7).

According to the last book of the Bible, specifically in Revelation 2:16, war is not always between Christians and the enemy triumvirate. Sometimes it is God himself who acts directly, and on our behalf, in response to

---

7. This contrasts with a less careful reading by those who take "thought" to be something more generic like a mental image as in one's having a "thought life" (e.g., Moore, *Praying God's Word*, 7–8; Meyer, *Battlefield of the Mind*, 3–4).

8. Arnold, *3 Crucial Questions*, 54.

wrongdoing. That such war in Revelation is carried out by "the sword of [Christ's] mouth" is a common indication that this is an ideological (theological) correction—that the gospel is the remedy to heresy. And that makes sense given verse 15's commentary that the readers here are followers of the (undisclosed) doctrines of "the Nicolaitans."

In Revelation 12:7–9, there is a "war" that "arose in heaven" between Michael the archangel and Satan. Despite Revelation being a book that includes talk about the victory of God at the end of human history, much of it regards (in part) the contemporary scene of Christians living under oppressive Roman rule. It may be that the war "in heaven" is not a reference to a distant exile of Satan and his hoard; rather it may be a more recent reference to the conquest by Jesus on the cross given that verse 5 seems to refer clearly to Jesus ("a male child, one who is to rule all the nations with a rod of iron, [and] caught up to God and to his throne"). This cosmic battle scene reveals the significance Jesus's crucifixion has in the human struggle against the forces of darkness (cf. v. 10: "Now the salvation and the power and the kingdom of our God and the authority of his Christ have come . . ."). Again, the war that "arose in heaven" is being inaugurated by God himself through Christ in what is undoubtedly a war with clear victory at its end. Praise be to God!

As a continuation of the events of verses 7–9, the war of the dragon transitions from being directed at Christ to being directed at the "offspring" (v. 17). These are the saints of God. Revelation 13:7 later has the "beast . . . of the sea" (13:1; cf. 11:7) not only at war with the saints but as something that is permitted to "conquer" them. (The beast is either Emperor Nero of Rome and/or a Roman antitype yet to emerge.) Accordingly, the saints are, once again, brought directly into a war precipitated by one that roots itself in Satan (13:4).[9]

So, the empire strikes back. In Revelation 17:13–14, followers of the beast return that war to the Lamb (Christ). However, Christ in turn will end up conquering them as the final chapter of the struggle. And that victorious conquest will be shared by the saints who are aligned with Christ. Victory indeed belongs to the Lord. And this victory is couched in unmistakable Old Testament terminology that is generally reserved for conveying unmatched supremacy (e.g., Deut 10:17; Ezra 7:12; Ezek 26:7; Dan 2:47).

CONCLUSION

One of the takeaways here is that warfare language is not exclusive to only one type of genre. It is a device that transcends its genre. The use of the

9. Indeed, the relevance of Eph 6:12's depiction of "spiritual forces of evil" as that which drives the rulers and powers of this world gets dramatically realized here in Revelation.

metaphors involved span the apocalyptic and poetic as well as the historical and biographical books of the Bible. There is no literary limit to the occasion of wanting to use such metaphors in addressing the various struggles and conflicts the believer has in relation to the threefold enemy. But we must not lose sight of the fact that the goal of such warfare is not only to enrich the self but to advance the kingdom of God. The weight of the latter is surely heavier than the weight of the former. This means that sacrifices will be made, often to our dismay.

As it turns out, God will unify two pathways: the path to growing the kingdom of God will ultimately meet the pathway to the enrichment of ourselves. God will not fail to bring abundant life to those who put God's kingdom before their own. For he promises a resurrection for the saints and a restitution of a universe for us to inhabit. The conflict that is assured for the believer brings equal and corresponding assurance that God will bring about everlasting peace and life to those enlisted in his army.

But, what do all of these metaphors amount to? While we may appreciate what each passage means when it speaks of "sword" or "shield," it is not always clear how these things are to be implemented in the lives of Christians—especially today! We may agree that the sword of God is Scripture, but it is unclear how we are to wield this particular weapon so described. Does it mean that we are simply to *chant* various scriptural passages amidst a spiritual crisis or does it mean that we are to be scripturally *savvy*—knowing what its teachings are when confronted with scheming lies? These are crucial questions that lie at the heart of systematizing what spiritual warfare is and will be the focus of the next few chapters.

We shall begin by exploring how some models of spiritual warfare neglect not only the core teachings of Scripture but also a philosophy of demonology that allows us to make sense of such teachings. In so doing, we shall consider models of spiritual warfare that tend to fit into, if I may borrow from Aristotle, the mutually opposing errors of *deficiency* and *excess*. A model that sees Satan as a fictional or symbolic figure strikes the average Christian as being a deficient description, for it eliminates Satan as a reality. A model that sees the general practice of spiritual warfare to be tantamount to magic and superstition is bound to be one of excess. Therefore, we shall consider what spiritual warfare is *not* before proceeding to consider what spiritual warfare *is*. And we shall do this with the accompaniment of both Scripture and philosophical reflection. Only then can we have a fully informed and reasonable understanding about the metaphysics and methodologies that underlie the theater of the Christian's spiritual war.

PART III

Spiritual Warfare

[W]e would be foolish in our journey as Jesus' disciples if we failed to avail ourselves of spiritual warfare principles and acknowledge the presence of demonization when circumstances warrant it.

—J. P. MORELAND, THE GOD QUESTION, 209

15

Spiritual Warfare Is Not Mythology

THE WORD "MYTHOLOGY" is an ugly word even to those who would unwittingly advocate for what it applies to. This is so because the word has come to mean something like "made up" or "fiction." And while this might accurately describe the heart of what most of its supporters are saying, "mythology" means more than or something distinct from out-and-out fabrication. Talk of spiritual "mythology," then, might mislead the reader to think that this model of spiritual warfare entails that Satan and demons do not exist—period. But the mythologist's position is more nuanced than that. It is more accurate to say that this is an attempt to *reassign the meanings* of terms like "Satan" and "demons" to refer to something other than literal superhuman, malevolent spirits as previously defined. Advocates will insist that given our increasing scientific understanding of the world along with our desire to preserve the integrity of Scripture, such terms must be repurposed to preserve intellectual integrity. It is a salvage operation that seeks to maintain the language of demonology while updating its meaning. As such, it really is a form of *concordism* in that there is a concerted effort to define "Satan," "devils," "evil spirits," "demons," and other such monikers in accordance with what would be scientifically acceptable by today's standards. If a boy is said to have "a spirit that makes him mute" (Mark 9:17), then this "spirit" must be a prescientific way of alluding to the unknown condition itself and not to some spiritual agent that might instead be responsible for the condition. Jesus' subsequent rebuking of the "spirit," then, is probably him using a certain amount of theater as a way to publicly demonstrate himself as the healer of the boy's otherwise natural condition.

This "spirit" is not really a personage; it is a condition being expressed as a personage because prescientific people did not understand the nature of diseases and genetics. It's possible the boy's muteness was due to myasthenia gravis or cerebral palsy, they might say. But since ancient peoples were unaware of neurological disorders, they merely adopted a vocabulary that served as a placeholder for something that was not familiar to them. And thanks to our enlightened understanding two thousand years later, we can better define what a "demon" truly is. Since this subcategory of the mythological model of spiritual warfare involves changing (updating?) word meanings, let us refer to it as *the semantic model* (though there are differing views about how demonological language ought to semantically represent aspects of reality). This is a pretty straightforward way that some mythologists attempt to retain their intellectual integrity while denying the existence of real demons.

But not all mythologists are satisfied with this kind of biblical interpretation. Indeed, other mythologists feel like it does a disservice to the purpose of using such language. They do not redefine the words "Satan" or "demon" to accommodate the contemporary science of the time. Instead, they believe that the biblical authors and actors really do mean to refer to such beings but for nonliteral reasons. That is, the biblical authors and actors intentionally used a familiar mythology (=Second Temple demonology) in order to make a larger narrative point that does not mean to endorse the existence of things like devils, demons, and fallen angels. Let us consider an example of this procedure being done in another context. When certain prophecies are foretelling the desolation of a city, they sometimes speak of various animals coming in and making their home there in the wake of its destruction. Isaiah 34:4–17, in proclaiming the future destruction of Edom, mentions how birds such as hawks, owls, and ravens along with land animals such as hyenas and goats will be gathered together in her ruins as a "resting place." Though things like ravens and goats just happen to exist, this isn't the point of invoking animal migrations into Edom. The point is to punctuate the utter permanence and completeness of Edom's destruction. There is no genuine expectation that these particular animals will actually converge on Edom's ruins. And the messaging would still work even if these animals didn't really exist but were only believed to exist or were a part of some entrenched cultural lore.[1] As with Isaiah's animals, so it is with the invoking of demons.

1. Here is a modern example to help illustrate the point further. Suppose a pastor declares from the pulpit: "God created the Big Bang singularity that gave rise to our physically expanding universe. If he can do that, then he can certainly restore the earth in the

This approach provides these particular mythologists wiggle room among conservative Christians to see "Satan" and "demons" as indeed referring to otherworldly beings but without committing them to the view that the biblical author himself means to affirm their real existence. The mythology is merely being invoked to, like Isaiah's animals, make a different point not related to the reality of such beings. Accordingly, these mythologists are content to be agnostic about the existence of such beings. Let us refer to this subcategory of mythology as *the accommodation model*.[2] This is to say that this view sees the biblical writers and actors accommodating audiences with their cultural mythologies at the time, not as a means of affirming the existence of mythological beings, but as a way to make a larger theological point.

Those who side with the semantic model consider talk of demons to be fluid. What they say and what is written about these events are open to interpretation and speculation. Consequently, the authors and actors themselves were probably just using the language of demonology as a placeholder for this ignorance. Those siding with the accommodation model believe that talk of demons is not fluid but in reference to what any Jew at the time would have understood. Instead, they prefer to say that the biblical authors and actors intentionally invoked such beings so understood, not to say that they're real, but as a literary device in making a point in their narrative.

The mythological model is, for most, motivated by a desire to preserve Scripture at the hands of higher criticism. Science, we are told, has unquestionably shown us that there are no such things as demons as the traditional church has defined them. And maintaining biblical integrity *and* scientific credulity require a new interpretive strategy when it comes to demonology. After all, the Bible has a lot of nice things to say to just throw it all away because of a superstition or two. What better way is there, then, to save face in the presence of both the theologian and the scientist then by demythologizing the diabolical for modern audiences? To see what's wrong with this approach to spiritual warfare, we will need to turn to a separate analysis of the semantic model and the accommodation model.

---

future!" If scientists should conclude tomorrow that there really is no singularity and that the universe is not really expanding, this would not impugn what the pastor has said. Why? Because the pastor did not say what he said in order to *teach* that there was a big bang singularity and that we're in an expanding universe; rather, he was only referring to the "mythos" of what scientists have told us in order to make the point that restoring the earth would not be hard for a God who created the entire universe (regardless of whether what the science currently says is descriptively right or not). So, along the same lines, a biblical figure can coopt references to supernatural demons while denying that they in fact exist.

2. I am following Merrill F. Unger, who calls this "the accommodation theory" in his *Biblical Demonology*, 91. Unger traces it back to the nineteenth-century Presbyterian pastor Archibald Alexander Hodge.

THE SEMANTIC MODEL

Recall that this view uses more contemporary explanations to define what a "demon" or "devil" is when used in Scripture. The German theologians Friedrich Schleiermacher and David Friedrich Strauss and the Swiss theologian Karl Barth were three of the key instigators of this kind of model.[3] For Schleiermacher and Strauss, the demonic was nothing supernatural. It was to be understood as an abstract evil that is merely being personified in the person of Satan and his demons. For Barth, he not only thought the demonic didn't exist as something distinct from the physical (something in line with his predecessors), but he also insisted that it is not something that is reducible to it. Instead, talk of Satan and his demons is meant to represent "nothingness." And such "nothingness" refers only to a privation of the good—that is, that demons are a reality that can be experienced but only insofar as they reflect an *absence* of something good. In physics, coldness is the absence of heat; black is the absence of light. And, yet, coldness and blackness are no less real than heat and light. But neither do they have any positive ontological status in creation—i.e., they're not substances or "things." Thus, demons are real but only insofar as they represent a lack of good in some person, event, or action.

Some contemporary mythologists try not to follow Schleiermacher and Strauss, especially when it comes to spiritual warfare. However, there are those that do continue to follow Barth's tradition.[4] Still, there are those that are more sensitive to church tradition but are less impressed with the kind of Enlightenment materialism implied by Schleiermacher and Strauss. Instead, they seek to adopt an understanding that is less materialistic when it comes to the semantics of demonology and satanology. This is the approach taken by a more recent and highly influential scholar of spiritual warfare, Walter Wink.[5] Like his predecessors, he explicitly distinguishes

---

3. See Schleiermacher, *Christian Faith*, II.1 (esp. 161–70); Strauss, *Life of Jesus*, §55 and 56 (267–73); Barth, *Church Dogmatics*, §51:3 (477–531).

4. Amos Yong, for example, thinks that the good angels are in fact spiritual beings. However, he sees angels as emergent realities that do not exist apart from "interpersonal, social, and cosmic relations" in the physical world (*Spirit of Creation*, 217). And when it comes to demons, he follows Barth in that "they lack their own being or onticity" altogether and are, instead, "privative" of any good (219–20).

5. See especially the second installment of Walter Wink's famous "Powers" series, *Unmasking the Powers*. The first installment, *Naming the Powers*, is of equal importance; the third is apropos to how on such a model one actually engages spiritual warfare and is appropriately entitled *Engaging the Powers*. *Engaging* is the largest of the trilogy and is his crowning achievement. According to his preface, it is the final result of "almost three decades of my life" (xiii).

between how we today talk about adversarial demonic powers and how the biblical writers about talk about them when he writes: "We use the same words but project them into a wholly different world of meanings. What they meant by power and what we mean are incommensurate."[6] And it has not been good, Wink laments, that the principalities and powers mentioned in Ephesians 6:12 "have long since been identified as an order of angelic beings in heaven, or as demons flapping about in the sky."[7]

But he is no materialist. For even though he says that we should never "capitulate to the past and its superstitions," nevertheless we must "bring all the gifts our race has acquired along the way as aids in recovering the lost language of our souls."[8] This cryptic "lost language of our souls" is his way of agreeing to oppose materialism and anti-supernaturalism but without the same kind of demonic realism proffered by traditional orthodoxy.

For Wink, demonology is not a binary theology where we only have materialism on the one hand and "demons flapping about in the sky" on the other. Wink instead wants to salvage the vocabulary of demonology that does not pay homage to such trenchant materialism. So, he suggests that a "demon" is something that emerges from the physical. It is, among other things, "a will to power exerted against the created order" that arises in and out of individuals as well as those of societal organizations.[9] It is not the emanation of a phantasm or a literal spiritual reality, but an evil presence (something like a "mob spirit") that is found in like-minded individuals and groups. And, contrary to materialism, it is not something to be identified with or reducible to anything physical. Consider the massive political protest that took place on January 6 of 2021 in Washington, DC. Eventually, some of the protesters started rioting and stormed the Capitol building with the intention of causing damage and disarray. Wink might have interpreted this through his demonology as a case where a "spirit of insurrection" emerged from the crowd. It subsequently animated some in the crowd to engage in egregious and violent behavior. He would say that this "spirit" was present and real but was not literally a standalone personal being. Contrary to his materialist predecessors, Wink's approach allows for one to believe that demons exist, not as something that is scientific or a part of nature, but as something irreducible to nature. But, in solidarity with his predecessors, it also means that one does not have to construe demons as literal discarnate, evil spirits.

6. Wink, *Naming the Powers*, 4.
7. Wink, *Engaging the Powers*, 3.
8. Wink, *Unmasking the Powers*, 2.
9. Wink, *Unmasking the Powers*, 59.

Wink is right to lament that materialism is indeed the fashionable thing to hold on to today for those opposing classic demonology. And he is equally right to push back on that approach. I applaud him for that. But, ironically, it is difficult not to think of his own view as just another unwitting iteration of materialism. For the demonic (or angelic) spirit to be found in individuals and collectives is not to inch any closer to the discarnate beings of traditional Christianity. His good and bad angels *just aren't* discarnate spirits of any sort! To refer to them under the new vocabulary no more realizes the demon than does, say, the theist who wants to preserve talk of God but only uses "God" as a mere symbol for a supreme inner force for good (all the while denying that there is an unembodied transcendent creator and sustainer of the universe). We must consider his endeavor to avert materialism and preserve spirituality nothing more than a failed attempt to have his devil's food cake and eat it too.

But a project like Wink's is understandable when we come to see that the classic models of spiritual warfare have been tainted with the overlay of fringe traditions, popular lore, fanciful storytelling, and outright fiction. We have neglected the original teachings of the Old and New Testaments. Enter the contemporary ensemble of "the Devil's biographers."[10] These "biographers" claim that the story of Satan and his cohorts has evolved. Accordingly, they declare that the traditional portrait of Satan and his demons has evolved into something that is all wrong. The later biblical and postbiblical concepts of such beings that emerged is, so they say, nothing but a set of stolen viewpoints that have been taken from other religious cultures of the time and repackaged for Judeo-Christian consumption. Indeed, these "biographers" agree that the concept of Satan seems to have evolved drastically from the original portrayals in the Old Testament to the later church traditions.[11] This is supposedly an indication of deliberate doctrinal adjustment with every subsequent generation of biblical authors. Satanology is a theology, they argue, that has been heavily influenced by various external religious and cultural systems. These "biographers" find the waters of Satanology so muddied that they either suspend judgment about Satan as a real figure of history or actively dismiss his existence altogether.[12] However, they

---

10. This was a phrase coined by Samuel Taylor Coleridge in describing John Milton and others writing biography-style works about the devil (Coleridge, *Poetical and Dramatic Works*, 137).

11. E.g., For example, Kelly understands the original Satan to be an "obnoxious functionary of the Divine Government" (*Satan*, 2)—a mere instrument of God. He is not an exiled angel who subsequently presides over his own kingdom of demons in autonomous opposition to God and humanity.

12. Forsyth (*Old Enemy*), Niebuhr (*Nature and Destiny of Man*), Bamberger (*Fallen*

all acknowledge the practical advantages of using Satan imagery since evil is often too perverse to be seen as just another form of vicious human activity. Their unanimous insistence is that anyone wishing to preserve the integrity of Scripture or to take it in earnest can and should take Satan seriously without taking him literally. And this paves the way for Wink and friends to do just that in cashing out what they think spiritual warfare is about.

Wink's approach stands apart from what you would expect a traditional antirealist model to do, mostly because he *does* want to offer up a physically transcendent model of spiritual warfare as taught in Scripture. Unlike the biting critics outside of Christianity, Wink holds a profound respect for the Bible as a professing Christian himself. For him, we cannot ignore talk of Satan and his demons any more than we can ignore talk of God, miracles, and resurrections. The terms are there. The challenge is how one is to appreciate (or appropriate?) Satan imagery vis-à-vis spiritual warfare if such beings do not actually exist the way Christians typically have understood them.

Wink's view truly is idiosyncratic. For he thinks the demonic represents the inner aspect of an individual, a people, an organization, or a government when those institutions or individuals threaten our Christian (ethical) values. A government that would force its citizens, say, to oppress a minority would consist of two aspects: an outer aspect, which is the governmental forces and infrastructures themselves (i.e., the physical), and an inner aspect, the demonic "spirits" that "emerge." Demons are real only in the sense that vice, hatred, and any anti-Christian antipathy are imposed on others by a person or regime. It comes across as a sort of pantheism where demons are not anything distinct from those in power. But it is not an atheism where such things are declared not to really exist. These are real

---

Angels), Pagels (*Origin of Satan*), Almond (*Devil*), and Wray and Mobley (*Birth of Satan*) appear to suspend judgment about whether there even is a real Satan—choosing to remain agnostic on the question of Satan's literal existence. De la Torre and Hernández are more aggressive in their conclusion and overtly deny the existence of a literal Satan (*Quest for the Historical Satan*, esp. 179). Where all of these "devil's biographers" seem to be on the same page is that the vocabulary of demonology, if it is to be employed at all, must be accommodating to those who do not believe in actual discarnate malevolent spirits but also want to accept the teachings of Holy Writ.

As a side note, none of these scholars ever outright argue *against* the literal existence of Satan (although Bamberger comes close). Instead, they presume his nonexistence for a number of familiar reasons (e.g., "It's superstitious nonsense!" or "It exonerates the real villains!" or something along these lines). This is understandable. For if our sole or primary reason for being demonic realists to begin with is due to the New Testament's presumably reliable depiction of Satan and his demons, then everything hinges on a proper theological understanding of what the relevant terms mean (e.g., "Satan," "god of this world," "demons," "fallen angels," "evil spirits," etc.).

things and are potentially malleable. As such, our work is cut out for us. For, unlike the traditional demon, Wink's demons can ultimately be changed and rehabilitated—preferably through nonviolent resistance, of course.[13] By transforming evil regimes and institutions, one effectively "exorcises" the malevolent forces that animate them. This, Wink assures us, is a biblically faithful spiritual warfare. And it avoids the fanciful talk of "demons flapping about in the sky."

Now, mythologists along the harder lines of Wink et al. do nothing to attempt to convince their readers that demonic beings do not exist (again, because Wink denies that this is in fact what he is doing). They, like many demonic anti-realists, are content just to *assert* or *imply* their nonexistence on the basis perhaps of what others have "responsibly" concluded and that any affirmation of their existence is nothing short of superstition and backward thinking.

Wink's own dismissal of the diabolical is based on his uncritical appeal to Enlightenment thinkers. For example, he quotes Morton Kelsey writing about how there is "no rational place" for the devil and so "the devil was as good as dead."[14] Wink then proceeds to do what other anti-realist theologians tend to do: he asserts that whether one believes in Satan or not is neither the right question to ask nor one "of any real urgency."[15] The better focus is, instead, about what Satan is *really* like. For, he believes, one must oppose popular Christianity's misguided notion of Satan as a "two-dimensional bogeyman."[16] How convenient! Now he doesn't have to offer *any* reasons to deny Satan's literal existence. He can just mention how a small aggregate of the intelligentsia dismiss demonic realism, direct us away from chasing up such questions, caricature the opponent's viewpoint as superstitious, and declare victory for his favorite model that has no positive evidence to commend it.

But Wink's "argument," if we even want to call it that, is too permissive since it is unclear why one cannot do this with *every* tenet of Scripture. In fact, these same Enlightenment thinkers (including Schleiermacher and Strauss) have also treated the resurrected Christ and God himself in similar fashion. They reasoned that these things cannot be real and that, for the sake of scriptural integrity and the Christian community, we must consider the next best (liberal) interpretation—even if it is contrived out of whole cloth. But given good reasons to think otherwise, the allure of a theological

---

13. Wink, *Engaging the Powers*.
14. Wink, *Unmasking the Powers*, 9.
15. Wink, *Unmasking the Powers*, 10.
16. Wink, *Unmasking the Powers*, 9.

liberalism loses both its force and its interpretive luster. Consider, contrary to fact, that Santa Claus is a real bearded fellow living at the North Pole with elves and eight tiny reindeer. It seems that we would have to abandon in good conscience any further attempts at mythologizing Santa as "the spirit of giving" as the right response to inquisitive children concerned about how one man can accomplish a global distribution of gifts in less than twenty-four hours. Parents would no longer have to salvage the Santa legend in the face of such "truth." Well, what's true of counterfactual Santa would be true of factual Satan. If there were good reasons to think such beings really existed, all this redefining-the-terms business would be moot.

A RESPONSE TO THE SEMANTIC MODEL

A believer in demons will just assert that because the Bible talks about and refers to demons therefore demons exist. That seems straightforward enough. However, as we already have seen, the fact that Scripture brings them up is not enough because we have seen that alternative interpretations of the diabolical are available. And if they are available, then the mere scriptural mention of "demons" or "Satan" is not enough to settle the question. After all, as also noted, Scripture speaks of monsters and beasts that often defy anything we might find in the animal kingdom (e.g., Ps 104:26; Isa 27:1; Dan 7; Rev 9; 13:1–3). The fact of the matter is, we're not supposed to take these descriptions literally. So, why should we not likewise take what Scripture says about Satan and his demons in a nonliteral way? Below are five reasons, based mostly on the exorcism stories of the Gospels, why the demonic realm is something we are not supposed to sweep under the rug of mythology.

The most important factor in support of taking descriptions about demons literally is how they are described in various so-called possession cases. These demonic possessors are not just violent aggressors; they are personalities that are concerned only for themselves and not those of existing governmental powers. In the episode of the Gerasene demoniac (Mark 5:1–20; Matt 8:28–34; Luke 8:26–39), when Jesus confronts the "legion" of demons, they seek their own asylum in a neighboring herd of pigs. No such asylum is asked for by the demoniacs they inhabit. This is an odd request if the demonic *just is* an expression or symbol of sinister human forces within the possessed. Furthermore, it makes no sense that there should be an exorcism of the human oppressors they inhabit followed by a relocation of the demons into nearby animals. If demons are not subsisting things independent of the human persons and institutions they inhabit, to speak of expelling a demon into an animal makes about as much sense as expelling, say, one's "moral compass" and relocating it into your pet cat. Transmigration is not a feature of abstract things. But such an expulsion and relocation make perfect sense if the inhabitants are personal and discarnate by nature.

Second, in at least two cases, there is a demonic presence *in the very house of God*. In the story of the Capernaum demoniac (Mark 1:21–28; Luke 4:31–37), there is a demon-possessed person amidst an active and sacred synagogue. Despite the demoniac submitting to Jesus' teachings, the demon's identity is not revealed until Jesus confronts him (that is, the "unclean spirit" goes unnoticed in the gathering until Jesus singles him out). This isn't representative of some intra-Jewish schism because it is a single man involved. Nor does it represent Capernaum in general for the same reason. And there is no evidence that the group here was in any way a divided clan; on the contrary, we have every reason to think that the congregants were open to what Jesus had to say (cf. Mark 1:27–28). What in the world could this isolated demon possibly symbolize? Or, *pace* Wink, what regime or abstract form of social injustice does this "demon" represent or supervene on?

There happens to be nonpossession instances we have in the Old Testament, particularly in the case of the book of Job. In Job 1, Satan arises and does so not from some outside world system or some villainous faction of Jews, but from the inner court of God's presence (1:6). Satan found himself among the angels of God after having surveilled the world. It's not clear how such mythology can plausibly play out in this scenario other than to dismiss the passage as something else entirely (i.e., that Job is a complete fable or mere poetry because it is Wisdom literature). But this harsh conclusion is unlikely given that Job himself is treated as a historical person (Ezek 14:14, 20). Nevertheless, it's true that the book of Job is likely not a transcript of the celestial goings-on. But why think that nothing about its depictions is even approximately true? That any cosmic scene would have been invented by an Israelite itself supposes that *this is the kind of thing that was believed to have occurred*. When Jesus invokes a parable, for example, the kinds of dialogue he invents reflect how people really are. Take the parable of the rich man and Lazarus in Luke 16. If Jesus is depicting a reversal of fortune between the two, then that is the kind of thing that happens, whether the details about burning fire and large chasms are true or not, between God-followers and God-haters. That Satan is depicted as coming from among the "sons of God" in Job is because the author(s) considered that kind of thing could occur. Moreover, we could further question why the later burgeoning Christian community would have refrained from deleting these things from their Scriptures for fear of giving readers the impression that these sinister aspects obtain in the highest levels of God's presence.

Third, in addition to the noted Gerasene and Capernaum demoniacs, all of the demon possession cases read as straightforward accounts. They do not have literary signs of being parables, mini-apocalypses, or mythologies.[17] (I am not suggesting that none of the accounts are free of embellishment, however, which is in fact a different question.) When one reads about a "beast" in Daniel or Revelation, the writing is always clearly one of apocalyptic symbolism. But the Gospels are not of this genre and neither are the specific exorcism accounts. So, the grounds for appealing to symbology in explaining the ongoing plight against the demonic is literarily out of place.

Fourth, and most perplexing, is that the possessions of demons do not always fit Wink's associating the demonic with social injustices. For example, we have the account of the Syrophoenician woman's daughter (Mark 7:24–30; Matt 15:21–28). In the story, it is the daughter of a socially marginalized woman that is possessed. The woman herself is not. This is odd because the possession is supposed to be in some sense symbolic or a psychical expression of the tyranny of a corporate system. Why would the woman, the one who governs her household, be free of this and not her child, who is otherwise under the guidance and guardianship of her mother? Well, I suppose we could regard the daughter's condition to be physical, say a bout with epilepsy or some such ailment. Either way, it is merely the mother's *interpretation* that her daughter is possessed. But then the remedy is curious. It is the woman's somewhat irreverent response to Jesus that facilitates the daughter's deliverance. The daughter is then delivered *from a distance* as the result of this conversation that she was not even around to hear! If Jesus was delivering her despite the woman's incorrect diagnosis, one must imagine Jesus supporting what can only be construed as a false premise. And Jesus never accommodates himself to the lies of a pagan.[18]

Fifth, and perhaps the most troubling for the semantic-mythological view, is the uniqueness of Jesus's approach to exorcism. If Jesus and his "biographers" are interested in employing myth as a way to represent disease and corrupt institutions alike, one would imagine that in order for the narrative to make sense, he would have simply borrowed from Jewish or pagan sources. But, in the cases of Jesus's exorcisms, these are too distinct from any would-be pagan or even Jewish counterparts. For example, unlike other exorcists, Jesus does not use any special incantation or formula in order to drive out demons. Nor does he invoke the authority of another sage or mystic as the rabbis did but he chooses instead to act on his own authority. Nor

---

17. Blomberg, *Historical Reliability*, 3ff.

18. In fact, quite the opposite is true. Jesus never seems to miss an opportunity to correct the bad theology of his critics (Matt 5:21ff.; 23:2–36) as well as those of his friends (Mark 10:17–18; John 9:2–3; 20:24–29).

does he utilize charms like amulets and talismans as Apollonius of Tyana and the other mystics did. Attempts to dismiss the stories of exorcism as adopted myth fail to take into account the substantial differences between the Gospel portraits and those of pagan and Jewish sources.

Now, not all mythological models of spiritual warfare attempt to redefine the semantics of demonology. There are models that think the biblical authors and actors in fact used such demonological terminology to intentionally refer to discarnate, supernatural beings as a form of accommodation to the historical audience. However, we're not supposed to think that the authors and actors were in fact endorsing such things by invoking such myths. Let us now take a closer look at this accommodation model followed by a response to it.

THE ACCOMMODATION MODEL

In their recent book entitled *Demons and Spirits in Biblical Studies*, John H. Walton and his coauthor, J. Harvey Walton, propose this second kind of mythological model. While the Waltons themselves do not consider their views as mythology *per se*—for they seem to affirm the existence of demons explicitly[19]—their own take is to say that the biblical authors themselves purposely *incorporate* the mythologies of the "cognitive environment" in which they wrote as an instrumental means of underscoring certain points unrelated to real demons that they wished to make in their particular narratives.[20] This is to say that while demons may or may not be spiritual realities, their existence and nature are neither being *affirmed* nor *endorsed* (nor *denied* for that matter) when Scripture brings them up, even if such mentions fall on the lips of Jesus himself. Instead, they are being invoked as literary devices by the authors and actors because their audiences would have been familiar with the images employed. They would have already believed in them. The Waltons want Christians to understand that the "Bible's information content should . . . not be seen as a list of various facts but rather as a *message* that its author intends to *communicate*."[21] Because it's a message and never anything like a reportage of "various facts," the authors and actors of Scripture can incorporate known mythologies in service to that message.

It is important to clarify that the Waltons' view is not one that sees the Gospels or the Epistles as using "Satan" or "demons" or "evil spirits" as symbols or abstractions. Neither do they see the New Testament as inventing

19. Walton and Walton, *Demons and Spirits*, 298–99.
20. Walton and Walton, *Demons and Spirits*, 55ff.
21. Walton and Walton, *Demons and Spirits*, 14.

mythologies or naïvely adopting them approvingly from other cultures. Instead, they propose, the use of such mythologies is deliberate *from a literary standpoint*. That is, the biblical authors and actors incorporate these (false?) tenets of pagan religions when they happen to serve, say, the gospel message (e.g., Acts 17:28–29). The Waltons insist that it is a way an ancient writer or speaker would have written or spoken to an ancient audience where that audience would not have considered the writer or speaker to be supporting or embracing such mythology. Since the biblical writers are not just reporters of facts (if they are reporters of facts at all), they have an interest in deliberately crafting literary works that accommodate the superstitions of their audiences. Because their audiences already believed in such superstitions, an author or actor could use the familiar mythologies to add significance to their thoughts and actions.

To illustrate, consider how the Old Testament invokes certain well-known mythological beings such as chaos monsters. In the Old Testament, we have such monsters as Leviathan, Behemoth, and Rahab (Job 3:8; 40:15; 41:1; Ps 74:14; 89:9–10; 104:26; Isa 27:1; 51:9). These creatures had been well-understood by the neighboring cultures of the ancient Near East. Though such creatures are brought up in Scripture, they are not being affirmed to exist. Rather, they are brought up because the audience would have understood the references in the context of their literary narratives and it would have driven home the larger points being made about, say, God's sovereignty over even the most chaotic elements of nature. Casting such chaos in the familiar lingo of Mesopotamia would help drive home the understanding that God is greater than any would-be villainous monster.

Such incorporation of cultural myths in a nonliteral way is not unique to the ancient world. In today's "cognitive environment," we still sometimes do the same thing. For example, we may wish to elicit someone's opinions about heaven or what it takes to deserve it. To do so, we might inaugurate such a conversation by asking, "So, when you die and show up at the pearly gates and St. Peter asks you why he should let you in, what are you going to say?" The question seemingly has Catholic overtones, but it is not intended to *endorse* a Catholic notion of heaven (which really isn't a Catholic notion) or any other Western pop cultural variant for that matter. Rather, the point is to quickly orient the listener to a conversation about salvation. It is obvious by the question that one wants to know what the other thinks is the standard by which one can merit eternal life. In no way is the questioner affirming literal "pearly gates" or a cosmic concierge desk headed up by the apostle Peter. In this sense, the question's theological elements clearly mentioned in the New Testament ("pearly gates"[22] and "St. Peter"[23]) merely function as *screens* or *filters* that determine who deserves to pass through into eternal life and who does not.

The Waltons insist that when mythological images, including images of demons, are being literarily employed, it is because they "convey function, not phenomena."[24] Instead, "they are tools used to tell the story. The text talks about demons, but only as a means to an end to talk about something else."[25] This, in their opinion, is true even of the Gospel accounts that are purported to be literary works along the lines of Greco-Roman biographies. For those who think that the Gospels are straightforward reportages of eyewitnesses, the Waltons demur and make it clear that they think that "the Gospel narratives are not *history* as we commonly understand the term."[26] If all they meant was that the Gospels are not like modern-day documentaries in how they, for example, always maintain a chronological order, take care not to leave out any details, etc., then that would be trivially true. Ancient works didn't always follow chronology and sometimes left out details. But the Waltons mean *much* more than that—something far more controversial: "The Gospels are not reminiscences wherein authors gush about incredible things they saw Jesus do using all of the details they can remember; they are finely *crafted* works of literature and everything they include is intended to help convey its chosen message."[27]

With this kind of alleged emphasis by biblical authors on style and message over facts, including the Gospels, it is a wonder how anyone should find *any* historical value to what the Gospels or Scripture in general convey *about anything whatsoever*. As long as a Gospel author's "chosen message" is anything but the conveying of facts, there are no limits to what one could deny. But if there are limits to seeing the Gospels as not including and endorsing any facts whatsoever, why draw the line at talk of demons? That is, why is talk of demons just the useful incorporation of mythographic imagery but talk of God or the Son of God are not? Just where do the Waltons draw the line between history and a literary *façon de parler*?

---

22. Rev 21:21.
23. Matt 16:18.
24. Walton and Walton, *Demons and Spirits*, 36.
25. Walton and Walton, *Demons and Spirits*, 51.
26. Walton and Walton, *Demons and Spirits*, 230.
27. Walton and Walton, *Demons and Spirits*, 238.

A RESPONSE TO THE ACCOMMODATION MODEL

The problem with an accommodation model such as that proposed by the Waltons is that while most New Testament scholars and commentators prefer to attribute at least some core factuality to a Gospel, given that the genre is thought to in some sense approximate Greco-Roman biographies,[28] the Waltons offer no line of demarcation as to what is historical or not within the Gospels themselves. They simply declare without argument that the Gospels are artistic literary works and "not reminiscences wherein authors gush" about what Jesus said and did, only to cherry-pick which messages in the Gospels are historical and which are not—declaring (again without argument) that any reference to exorcism, Satan, or demons is merely the literary or rhetorical accommodation of what was believed within the wider "cognitive environment." *We're supposed to just take their word for it.* But since they think Jesus is a true historical figure who died and rose again for the salvation of humankind, they offer no way to demarcate when the Gospels are reporting history and when they are intimating ahistorical images for the (literary?) sake of their readership. The Waltons owe it to their readers to defend what makes these seemingly straightforward exorcism stories, especially those that have no antecedents within their "cognitive environment," ahistorical, even if within the narratives no one is interested in outright saying, "Oh! By the way, demons *do* exist." Is it really necessary for an author to have to say this in order to see the exorcism stories as being historically descriptive?

---

28. E.g., Keener, *Christobiography*; Blomberg, *Historical Reliability*; Carson and Moo, *Introduction to the New Testament*. The way many (not all) New Testament scholars understand the Gospels as Greco-Roman biographies perhaps goes too far. For some think that the Gospels are intentionally using an ancient literary style of writing such that the Gospel authors can assume a creative license in knowingly passing things off as history when, in fact, they know they're not reporting history. See Licona, *Why Are There Differences in the Gospels?* and Burridge, *What Are the Gospels?*. A blistering criticism of this approach has been recently offered by Lydia McGrew in her two books *The Mirror or the Mask* and *The Eye of the Beholder*. The overall point here isn't to establish precisely how one is to take the Gospels, but to note that one ought to *at least* take them as historical. Any dehistoricizing of any particular subject within the Gospels would have to be supported by argument. One cannot, as the Waltons seem to, merely *say* that the Gospels are "crafted" literary works in order to conclude without any specific support or argument (knowing that the Gospels at least *contain* straightforward history) that talk of demons is one of those areas where the authors felt free to incorporate a known mythological falsehood in order to tell a different story. Just because a modern-day movie, for example, may tout itself as merely being "based on true events," where poetic license leaves the writers the creative freedom to invent dialog and fabricate events, one cannot use this fact alone to say that any given event cast in the film is therefore not true. One would need other reasons—reasons that perhaps rely on eyewitness testimony or other nonfictional sources of relevant history—in making that case.

But someone might protest, "Is there not clearly any unhistorical material in the Gospels?" Of course! But we have in those instances some kind of implicit or explicit in-text tagging (i.e., clues that signal to the reader that there is a shift from taking what is said literally to something else[29]) about how to receive the content. When Jesus proceeds to speak *parabolically* or begins to speak *apocalyptically*, these involve clear indications of hypotheticals, folk stories, or typological symbolism. So, overall, we have genre and specific tagging that tip us off about when to set aside our notions of wooden literality with very few exceptions.[30] But when Jesus is speaking about Satan and demons or the Gospel writers are writing about Jesus's dealings with demons, such communications are not couched in parable, apocalypse, poetry, or any recognizable ahistorical tagging. They obtain in the same straightforward, historical reportages as do his confrontations with the scribes and Pharisees. (And yet, the Waltons do not see fit to think that references to "scribes" and "Pharisees" might merely be the literary products of a wider "cognitive environment.")

Moreover, when the Old Testament authors or characters are discussing Satan, there is no "cognitive environment" in which to understand him. One might be tempted to find Satan parallels in the ancient Mesopotamian world, but any closer inspection of such stories quickly reveals an absence of such parallels. If one grants that "Satan" and "the Satan," wherever the

---

29. Consider, for clarity's sake, a modern-day example. Amidst what might be a rather straightforward historical report, an author may seek to clarify what he is writing about by interrupting his reporting with a story preceded by "Once upon a time . . ." Moderns would know that this would be a familiar tag informing the reader that what follows is not necessarily to be taken as historical fact. Perhaps the author means to cite a fairy tale or an old fable, both of which are fictions, in his quest to clarify his attitude about the event on which he is reporting.

30. There are a couple of candidates that could be exceptions to this. One is perhaps Jesus's referring to Peter as "Satan": "But [Jesus] turned and said to Peter, 'Get behind me, Satan! You are a hindrance to me. For you are not setting your mind on the things of God, but on the things of man'" (Matt 16:23; paralleled in Mark 8:33). Clearly Jesus is not intending to identify the chief of demons with Peter. But it seems to me that this is *precisely* how readers/listeners know the claim to be nonfactual in its not being a literal identity claim. While it could be a mere metaphor, it may actually be a way of signaling to Peter that he is under the influence of a literal Satan perhaps in much the same way Judas was (cf. Luke 22:3; John 13:2). Another passage *might* be Luke 10:18, where Jesus says, "I saw Satan fall like lightning from heaven." One might imagine that Jesus is not actually referring to a literal Satan as much as he is making the point that *adversity itself* is retreating in the presence of Christ's kingdom power. But, why think that? Any would-be "literary device" being used here need not be "Satan" as much as it might (more likely) be in Satan's "fall[ing] like lightning." That is, a literal Satan, and so his hold over humanity, is being rapidly diminished at the sudden inbreaking of the kingdom of Christ through his disciples.

character(s) appears in the Old Testament, is anything like the Judeo-Christian conception outlined in chapter 4, then such a figure is very much *unlike* what we find in the mythologies of early Mesopotamia.³¹ Only in later, Second-Temple Jewish thinking did a consistent "cognitive environment" about Satan arise. Supposing that "Satan" would have been singularly understood by an Old Testament audience vis-à-vis the ancient Near East is terribly anachronistic.

For these reasons, the intimation of myth, however it's being done, does not play well as a viable interpretation of Jesus's exorcisms and teachings. It makes no sense for a biographer or a writer of an apologetic memoire to suddenly use the genre of myth in order to describe *to Second-Temple Jews* something *they* believed to be literal while offering no didactic correction to their theology or not carefully couching such imagery in a more clearly identifiable nonhistorical context. The accounts of Jesus's exorcisms come across as straightforward, ancient, and original, and are always seamlessly a part of the flow of a larger historical set of occurrences. By contrast, the instances of Jesus intimating things that are not necessarily true are always tagged somehow to be so.³² In fact, these accounts are so straightforward

---

31. Space does not permit a detailed defense here, but something needs to be said by way of support. Indeed, the diabologies of the ancient Near East (ANE), such as those of Sumer, Babylon, and Canaan, are spectacularly dissimilar to that of Judeo-Christian diabologies. The first dissimilarity of note is that while ANE combat myths have rebellion narratives, we do not have any kind of rebellion myth in either the Old or New Testaments (though we do have passing mention of a rebellion in 2 Pet 2:4 and Jude 6). Even so, no consistent reason is ever given for the various rebellions in ANE myths. These facts have led some, like Kelly (*Satan* and "Reviewed Work"), to suppose that Satan is not a rebel at all but merely an opposing officiate of God's heavenly court. Second, unlike Judeo-Christian diabologies, the rebels of the ANE are typically spatio-physical beings—often linked with a natural phenomenon like trees, oceans, and rivers. Satan is not. Third, it is not clear in the ANE rebellion myths, particularly among generational-gods myths, *who the real rebel is* since the good guy is defined tautologically as whoever ends up being the one who is victorious in battle (!). Fourthly, the high god in ANE myths (if he is not in the process of seeking that high status) never deals directly, if at all, with his adversary. But the Second Person of the Trinity of God (=Jesus) does. Fifthly, the ANE rebels are sometimes divinely appointed to their position if not directly endorsed by the overlords. We find an example of this in Gilgamesh's conquest of Humbaba (or Huwawa), who is appointed by the high god Enlil to oversee the cedar forest (*Epic of Gilgamesh*, tablets II, IV, and V). The hero, Gilgamesh, is later reprimanded for his assault on Humbaba because Enlil himself put him there (tablet VII). The God of Scripture, by obvious contrast, did not deliberately set Satan up to oversee "the air" (Eph 2:2) or "this world" (2 Cor 4:4).

32. E.g., Jesus gives an object lesson about how even the littlest amount of faith can yield significantly positive consequences. He mentions the "mustard seed" which, he says, "is the smallest of all seeds on earth" (Mark 4:31). The mustard seed is actually not the smallest seed. But never mind. We know we are not to take Jesus here to be teaching

that there are even somewhat embarrassing details in some of these stories not redacted out of such accounts (e.g., such as Jesus being upbraided by the Syrophoenecian woman and, in the Gerasene demoniac story, the destruction of a community's livestock that incites the residents to chase Jesus out of town). There is also at least one undesigned coincidence in two of these demoniac stories in particular that would also support the exorcism narratives as eyewitness reports and not as accommodating literary narratives.[33] In fact, there are undesigned coincidences all over the Gospels that would further reveal that they are not fanciful works of literature but more straightforward accounts of the goings-on in the life of Jesus altogether.[34] If these exorcist accounts are indeed eyewitness accounts and are straightforward presentations of actual expulsions of real demons, then the mythologist's

---

about botany; rather, he is appealing to what was perhaps believed by locals even if falsely. How do we know this? Because of the clear in-text tagging in the previous verse (30): "and [Jesus] said, 'With what can we compare the kingdom of God, or what parable shall we use for it?'"

33. An "undesigned coincidence," a term used by William Paley in the eighteenth century, refers to how a certain inexplicable awkwardness or an unexplained fact gets inadvertently explained by an independent witness or source. For example, suppose police were interviewing people who claim to be eyewitnesses to a violent attack where a homeowner was hit in the head by another with a frying pan in his living room. Suppose someone who claims to be an eyewitness reports that the attack was spontaneous and that the assailant immediately picked up the frying pan off the floor and struck the victim. This raises a question about the awkwardness of the description: why would there be a frying pan *on the living room floor*? Suppose further that another who claims to be an eyewitness says that he only saw the two people in the room fighting but didn't see much. And the reason he didn't see much, he says, is because he was behind a plastic tarp in the kitchen, where he was busy helping to renovate it. *That explains why there would be a frying pan on the living room floor, for any cookware would surely have been relocated out of the kitchen and into a nearby room.* If an eyewitness were *inventing* his story, he most likely would have taken care not to include any awkward facts without, at least, explaining away any awkwardness. The presence of such an undesigned coincidence serves as evidence that what is being reported is not invented and is not being concocted with other *faux* eyewitnesses. I find that the Gerasene demoniac account is just such a case. In the episode, the demons are expelled from the men and sent into a nearby herd of pigs. The awkward question that comes up here is why there would be an aggregate of *ritually unclean* animals in a knowingly Jewish region near the Sea of Galilee. It turns out, thanks to the Jewish historian Josephus (*Antiquities*, XVII.11:4), that Caesar annexed various cities, including the region where the expulsion took place. After such annexation, the community would have become increasingly secularized and would have had relaxed standards over their livestock. And a Gospel author would not have anticipated that Josephus would have added that little detail in order to salvage the odd presence of pigs in a seemingly Jewish community. In my book, I also suggest another possible undesigned coincidence that pertains to the Beelzebul controversy. See Guthrie, *Gods of This World*, 143 for that discussion.

34. See McGrew, *Hidden in Plain View*.

interpretation is not only misplaced, but it is a defiance of the true work of Christ when it comes to his particular ministry of exorcism.

Whatever the specific mythological model one considers, almost all these mythologists harbor a foregone conclusion: Satan and his demons either do not really exist or cannot be known to exist. As such, mythological models of demonology are only belief worthy if and only if such beings do not exist in the way proffered in this book. I would hazard to say that even Wink and the Waltons would agree that such models turn on whether we have good reasons to think that Satan and his demons do exist so understood. I think the scriptural testimony establishes this. But, in what follows below, let us consider some additional, nonscriptural reasons to think that they literally do exist—reasons that intersect with the historical case based on Jesus's exorcisms.

CONTEMPORARY EXPERIENCES OF THE DEMONIC MIGHT SUGGEST A LITERAL DEMONIC REALM

The contemporary experience of the demonic, if good, would perhaps suggest that what happened in Jesus's day continues to be happening today. And if these are not myths today, then neither were they then. For, how odd would that be for there to be confirmation of demons today only to deny that they were around when Jesus was? Thus, if what follows gives us plausible grounds for thinking that demons do exist (today), then we have confirmation of the existence of demons outside of Scripture. In turn, this evidence would indeed bolster the historical case defended from Scripture above.

Now, having a religious experience is often seen as a very private thing. That is, onlookers cannot benefit from whatever closeness or feelings you acquire from your relationship to God. But that you have those vivid experiences at all should not be dismissed simply because they are private. Think of the general experience of pleasure. If someone experiences a pleasure not shared by others submitting to the exact same conditions, that is no reason to dismiss *your* experience. The fact that many testify to feelings of cosmic unity or feelings of being in God's presence or feelings of forgiveness and favor give many a foundation for believing in the reality of God without turning to sophisticated philosophical or scientific arguments.

As it turns out, many also testify to having *diabolical* experiences. What are "diabolical experiences"? Like religious experiences, they are experiences that seem to be imposed on one from a source other than oneself. But *un*like religious experiences, diabolical ones are not feelings of love, unity, and the lot. Instead, they often involve feelings of fear, threat, and malice. These too might derive from an external source for those experiences. In both kinds of private experiences, some experiences might come in the form of a *voice* that seemingly derives from an alien source.[35]

It is difficult to determine from an outsider's perspective and to everyone's satisfaction whether any kind of supernatural experience is legitimate just as it's nearly impossible to determine from an outsider's perspective and to everyone's satisfaction whether someone's feeling of not being alone is grounds for believing that one is in fact not alone. Unless we're talking about miracles, there is one feature that certain internal experiences of the diabolical have that religious experiences do not: the ability to be experienced by outsiders in ways that authenticate the person's inner experience. What I am talking about here is demon possession. If someone is genuinely demon possessed, whatever that may look like, it is expected that there will be outward signs that would reveal the presence of an invading demon. Demon possessions are rarely regarded as occurrences that cannot be detected by outside observers.

And while it is difficult to say what conditions are necessary for diagnosing someone with possession, there may be some sufficient conditions that reveal a possession case. According to the recent testimony of psychiatrist and professor at New York Medical College Richard Gallagher, some signs of demon possession involve the various victims's ability to "[speak] various foreign languages previously unknown to them," their ability to "exhibit enormous strength," and their "'hidden knowledge' of all sorts of things—like how a stranger's loved ones died, what secret sins she has committed, even where people are at a given moment."[36] Philosopher Phillip H. Wiebe suggests that an exorcism may confirm *in hindsight* that the possession case was indeed a demon possession: "finding that people regain their sight or hearing or mental wholeness after an exorcism in which evil spirits are commanded to leave a person, as though those spirits were causally

---

35. See Cook, *Hearing Voices*. Cook's work here is a brilliant and useful collection of historical and contemporary claims to hearing voices in alleged religious and diabolical encounters. Where I would disagree with Cook would be on his own attempted interpretation of those experiences (i.e., his "incarnational approach"). But readers can appreciate the fact that people from all walks of life—rich or poor, developed world or underdeveloped world, educated or uneducated, etc.—claim to have heard the voice of God, an angel, or a demon. This suggests that there is no natural predictor of voice hearing, which, in turn, suggests that voice hearing is not the sole product of, say, mental illness. This last point is emphasized quite well in the collaborative work of Cardeña, Lynn, and Krippner, *Varieties of Anomalous Experience*. Their contributors focus on a variety of "anomalous experiences" in general, however.

36. Gallagher, "As a Psychiatrist, I Diagnose Mental Illness."

responsible for producing the malady, adds credence to the claim that spirits might exist."[37]

As it turns out, many claimants throughout history report having had possession experiences that were multiply attested by the presence of cowitnesses. And many of the properties of what was witnessed involve at least some of the ones mentioned by Gallagher and Wiebe. Of course, one could just as easily dismiss these claimants as mad. But that is quite a sweeping dismissal in the face of eyewitnesses spanning different cultures and geographies, different economic backgrounds, and residing in different time periods throughout all human history. That there is little to gain and much to lose in publicly affirming such "superstitious nonsense" further suggests that the eyewitnesses at least *believe* that a demon possession has taken place.

And then we have the less invasive kinds of experiences reported by percipients. Take the recent case of Nikolas Cruz, the Parkland, Florida shooter who gunned down several former classmates and teachers at Stoneman Douglas High School. Many news outlets reported on an interrogation episode that was videoed and subsequently transcribed.[38] During the interrogation, Cruz not only acknowledged having heard "a voice in his head" but specifically acknowledged that it was a "demon." When the interrogating detective left the room, Cruz proceeded to chastise himself by saying things like "Kill me. Just [expletive] kill me."[39] He also said to the detective that he was instructed to "burn," "kill," and "destroy" anything. Cruz also confessed to using psychotropic drugs in previous attempts to drown out the voice. Now, this is not to validate what Cruz himself said, but it gives us a richer taxonomy about the kinds of diabolical experiences one can lay claim to. And such experiences cannot be disregarded on the question-begging basis of demonic anti-realism. Indeed, for someone unaware of being videoed, Cruz chastising "himself" seems most plausible if the voice seems to him to be alien and not his own.

But, you might be thinking, do not other experiences we deny as real also occur throughout human history? Take, for example, those that claim to experience alien conversations and alien abductions.[40] The primary reasons these alleged percipients believe their encounter to be, say, an alien abduction is likely because their experiences are often initially suggested by or are reinforced by therapists attempting to help the traumatized navigate

---

37. Wiebe, *God and Other Spirits*, 39.
38. E.g., Lynch, Toropin, and Gallagher, "Parkland School Shooter."
39. Lynch, Toropin, and Gallagher, "Parkland School Shooter."
40. For one high-profile example, consider one of Whitley Strieber's personal accounts as recollected in his novel, *Communion*.

their experience. Clinical psychologists, the primary people the experiencers confess these stories to, tend to not critique the legitimacy of the alleged victims' experiences in order to help manage their trauma.[41] Or the alleged victim actively and surgically seeks out someone in advance who is perceived to be sympathetic (i.e., confirmation bias). Aside from dubious uses of memory recall (e.g., hypnosis, guided imagery, meditation, free association, etc.),[42] the therapist may accommodate or even *facilitate* abduction language to describe the experience that will be construed by the victim as a ratification of their interpretation.[43] (As a result, one's extraordinary claims can pass into the night without any critical pushback.[44]) But nonvictim witnesses of something like a demon possession are under no such trauma. They may be rattled by the experience, but they are usually not *injured* by it. But when they share their stories with others, all they are bound to receive is pushback and marginalization. Their stories are seen as equally embarrassing as alien abductions and no one outside of a believing community will reinforce their experiences. And yet, these eyewitnesses fervently persist in their beliefs. Some, like Gallagher, may even convert from an agnosticism about demon possession to a full-throated endorsement of it!

At the same time, we must not be naïve about what these reports mean. We cannot simply say uncritically that we must therefore *believe* possession cases or of hearing demonic voices merely because we have such testimony and yet deny the use of multiple testimonies in validating claims to things like alien abductions. There have been enough people who have asserted that they have been abducted by UFOs to raise a few eyebrows. If we're going to accredit any supernatural experience because a few brave souls have recounted their trauma, then it appears we're going to have to accept a great many things that maybe shouldn't be accepted. However, there are some good reasons why things like alien abduction claims should not be on the same level as demon-possession and voice-hearing claims.

---

41. Jasun Horsley has recently scrutinized Strieber's various accounts and found them to be not only unreliable but often self-contradictory. See his *Prisoner of Infinity*.

42. In Strieber's case, his own (normal) memory recall is demonstrably unreliable. A number of times in *Communion*, he vividly recalls his having witnessed the 1966 shooting spree at the University of Austin, Texas only to denounce it on page 117: "For years I have told of being present at the University of Texas when Charles Whitman went on his shooting spree from the tower in 1966. But I wasn't there." Worse, he then reverses course a year later and proceeds to not only claim to be an eyewitness after all but then goes on to offer a detailed account of the event (*Transformation*, 88–90).

43. See Lynn and Kirsch, "Alleged Alien Abductions."

44. This is related to a point given by John Douglas in his eighteenth-century work *The Criterion*, 52 and 86ff.

For one, alien abduction stories do not have the cross-cultural thriving that demon-possession and voice-hearing cases have had. Possession cases and hearing voices obtain all over the world and have been claimed by human beings for at least three thousand years. That's a pedigree not yet enjoyed by alleged alien abductees. And, second, excluding the victims, possession eyewitnesses and voice-hearers are not being coddled for their experiences, unlike alleged alien abductees. The eyewitnesses to, specifically, possessions are unaffected by any direct would-be supernatural component. That is, none of the eyewitnesses outside of the immediate victim are themselves being invaded by alien spirits or having any comparable kind of experience. They are simply observing a certain kind of behavior *in someone else* that is best explained in their minds as a demonic possession. If we had any comparable scenarios in alien abduction stories where bystanders could observe a victim's abduction (whatever that might look like), then we might be having a different conversation. As it turns out, abduction experiences tend to be externally unwitnessed, private encounters experienced only by the victim who has been traumatized. And that makes demon-possession cases in particular far more interesting.

Moreover, the presence of any personal agendas should lessen our interest in alleged supernatural experiences. If an alleged percipient would gain something, say the validation of a preconceived belief, then this makes taking that alleged eyewitness at their word a bit suspicious.[45] Some eyewitnesses in possession cases lack any sort of agenda (as far as we know). Gallagher's role in one particular encounter he discusses is a case in point:

> I was inclined to skepticism. But my subject's behavior exceeded what I could explain with my training. She could tell some people their secret weaknesses, such as undue pride. She knew how individuals she'd never known had died, including my mother and her fatal case of ovarian cancer. Six people later vouched to me that, during her exorcisms, they heard her speaking multiple languages, including Latin, completely unfamiliar to her outside of her trances. This was not psychosis; it was what I can only describe as paranormal ability. I concluded that she was possessed.[46]

---

45. In *Communion* on pages 3, 30, and 49, Strieber claims to have been "indifferent to," ignorant of, and even skeptical of Ufology and ETIs in the lead-up to his alleged abduction encounter. But in a later book (*Breakthrough*) he contradicts that by acknowledging that in 1984 he had an interest in "a possible hidden government policy devoted to concealing evidence of extraterrestrials" (249) as well as his acknowledging a then-involvement with the Mars Anomalies Research Society Inc. (249–53). In an earlier short story he penned, simply entitled "Pain," he likewise contradicts his alleged disinterest in such things prior to his first encounter (see especially 283).

46. Gallagher, "As a Psychiatrist, I Diagnose Mental Illness."

Gallagher's conclusion is not a leap if what he reports is an accurate rendition of the events. Indeed, having such insightful knowledge and the ability to speak languages one hasn't learned before are not expected properties of someone dramatically exhibiting a mental disorder. And if one cares about his professional reputation and practice, transitioning from "skepticism" to belief is not necessarily something one would publicize, particularly if one is in a discipline like psychiatry, which is generally hostile to such ideas.

And then there is an *a priori* or principled objection offered by the Waltons to the evidential contribution of diabolical experiences. That is, that they think that nothing can ever be established on the basis of any empirical evidence if demons are indeed supernatural entities. They note that "[c]onflict theologians warrant their claim for the real existence of evil spirits by pointing to observable phenomena such as 'radical evil,' possession, and the results of 'spiritual warfare.'"[47] While they're right to criticize the lack of any calibration for what constitutes the presence of spiritual warfare or what precisely "radical evil" is,[48] they do pose the following dilemma for those that consider possession cases to be empirical evidence of demons:

> If a thing is "supernatural" it means that it cannot be known by the methods of science, period . . . If the scientific methods offered by conflict theologians to defend the existence of spirits are actually evidence of anything, it means that spirits are knowable by scientific methods and therefore are not "supernatural" after all.[49]

What is interesting is that this is not really an objection to the evidence nor an objection to the existence of evil spirits. Rather, they are arguing that the "conflict theologian" is not allowed to borrow from the deliverances of science in order to draw affirmative conclusions about the existence of demons. To do so would be to "scientize" demons. But this confuses the nature of precisely what is supposed to be scientific here. No one is suggesting that *demons themselves* are scientific entities or entities detectable by the instruments of science. That, of course, *would* entail that they are not

---

47. Walton and Walton, *Demons and Spirits*, 45.

48. I think their reasoning here is misguided too. Instead of seeing the "evidence" of "radical evil" and "spiritual warfare" as scientific or not, the more accurate problem with these evidential avenues is that there are equally probable counter-explanations if not better explanations than the ones conflict theologians offer. Horrific evils, if they can be consciously facilitated by rational, fallen angels, can be consciously facilitated by *any* rational, fallen being. And I have discussed the challenges of appealing to evidential claims of spiritual warfare elsewhere in chapter 16, so I refer the reader to that part of the book.

49. Walton and Walton, *Demons and Spirits*, 47.

ontologically supernatural. But that isn't what possession cases are doing. Instead, what *are* detectable are the behaviors and expressions and all the relevant circumstances of alleged victims of possession. Consider, for a parallel example, the deity of Christ. Certainly, Christ's being God is not itself scientifically verifiable (one cannot, say, extract some blood from Jesus and see that he has one hundred units of divinity). However, the occurrences of the miracles of Christ and his subsequent resurrection from the dead *are* scientific in that they are empirically verifiable. That is, someone wielding a video recorder could have captured the restoration of a man's withered hand, the raising of Jairus's daughter, and the postmortem Jesus himself exiting the tomb he was observably buried in. But the empirical nature of the eyewitness testimony is not to say that Christ's deity or miracles are themselves scientific in nature. For similar reasons, regarding the empirical evidence from diabolical experiences, the Waltons are confusing *the nature of the evidence itself* with the *nature of the explanation for that evidence*. So, this objection, which depends on a significant misstep about differentiating evidence from explanations, cannot even get off the ground.

For the reasons given, possession experiences, while not conclusive, should not be discounted for allegedly being on a par with alien abduction stories or for being inconsistent in attempting to empirically verify something supernatural. But, minimally, if the historical situation of Jesus's exorcisms are what they appear to be, namely, the genuine expulsion of evil discarnate spirits, then (some of) the ongoing reports of contemporary possessions deserve a hearing. No one is entitled to just lump the testimonies that do not fit one's naturalistic narrative into the same camp as the most dubious of experiences.

CONCLUSION

I pointed out that there are actually two species of the mythological model: the semantic model and the accommodation model. The semantic model implies or proceeds from the notion that demons as discarnate evil spirits do not exist. But if demons do exist, it is difficult to see what the purpose of crafting a mythological model would be. For the scriptural references to Satan and his demons would then just need to be taken at face value just as we would the real existence of a group referred to as "the Nicolaitans" (mentioned in Rev 2:6, 15). After all, we seem to have no support for their existence and who or what they are beyond their mere mention. And yet commentators do not take any liberties to mythologize them. I offered two main reasons to think that demons probably do exist where at least the historical (Scriptural) evidence seems to me to be the most compelling. Thus, the mythologist must address both reasons if their model is going to get off the ground. Otherwise, it is transparently a biblical salvage operation for the sake of saving face in the twenty-first century.

I then addressed the accommodation model, namely, that though Satan and his demons are mentioned in the New Testament—the Gospels in particular—they are not being affirmed to exist. Put another way, none of the New Testament authors or actors are endorsing the superstitions of the surrounding cognitive environment. They simply incorporate their mythologies for the purpose of colorfully supporting a different message they wish to convey. I primarily responded to this by pointing out that, unlike situations where that is going on in other contexts, we have genre and in-text tagging that indicate when we are not supposed to take what someone says and does literally. Since the exorcism stories in the Gospels seem straightforward and have all the markings of history reporting, there is no good reason to adopt the accommodation model. It just comes out of nowhere as a way to save face *and* appease conservative approaches to biblical inerrancy.

The ultimate conclusion I draw here, then, is that it is both unnecessary and unwarranted to posit a mythological model of any species. This means that the mythological model is likely false. And if the mythological model is likely false, we must turn to a better alternative if there is one, preferably a realist model. But *which one*? For not all realist models are the same. Some realist models of spiritual warfare involve quite extraordinary claims about what demons can do. In the upcoming two chapters, we shall explore the flip side of the mythological model: that spiritual warfare might involve exorcism and/or acts of wizardry that go beyond what one might expect of the demonic world. Therein I shall argue against such models in giving way to a more promising and sustainable model more consonant with Scripture and reasonable reflection.

16

Spiritual Warfare is not Exorcism

THANKS TO MODERN AUTHORS and filmmakers, we have all heard about the practice of exorcism apart from our reading of the Bible. It was William Peter Blatty's novel-turned-movie *The Exorcist* (1971, 1973) that thrusted exorcism into the limelight. No longer was the underground practice of exorcism a remote occurrence; it was now in full view of the general public. *The Exorcist* consequently paved the way for spiritual warfare to be construed by moderns as a form of supernatural expulsion. In the late 1980s, Christian storytellers followed suit. Among them was Frank Peretti, who penned his famous fictional novels, *This Present Darkness* (1986) and *Piercing the Darkness* (1988), which in part depict spiritual warfare along those lines. Spiritual warfare was starting to look like how the fictional Abraham Van Helsing was said to deal with vampires.

The remedy was and is equally dramatic: we must engage these hostile powers directly and expel them. It is war, after all. The decades following only managed to cement this idea more firmly in the minds of pop culture. Even today, the contemporary rise of viral videos on the internet and the prevalence of paranormal investigation "reality" shows are helping to publicly validate what is considered the best kind of physical evidence imaginable: demonic haunts caught on camera. That in today's climate many openly confess that they are witches (i.e., Wiccans) or that they are Satanists (i.e., members of the Church of Satan or the Temple of Set) suggests in the minds of many a demonic conspiracy of biblical proportions.

There is no question that our collective view of the world today is reenchanted. We now think more than we did half a century ago that the world is bewitched by spiritual forces that mingle with and even affect the physical universe. And contemporary missionaries are beginning to see how places like Africa and Indonesia are deeply entrenched in the belief of the inhabitation of spirits all around us. And these views are not just by those on the fringe. William Payne, in fact a missionary and theologian, has recently made this a big deal in his current book on spiritual warfare.[1] Indeed, our universe is seen as being haunted with unseen malevolent and domineering forces everywhere. There is no longer any question in the minds of many about this alleged reality.

So, what does all of this have to do with spiritual warfare? Unlike the anti-realist's mythological model critiqued in the last chapter, there are models of spiritual warfare that appear to take the matter more seriously. Such models are decisively realist. For most Christians, this is by no means surprising or controversial. After all, Christianity has always taught that such beings exist and can affect human affairs. However, we are not in agreement as to what extent Satan and his demons war with the saints or to what extent the saints can bite back. While Christians may agree overall with the cosmic infrastructure of spiritual warfare (i.e., that there are angels and demons, God and Satan), there is much disagreement about how spiritual warfare is to be conducted.

In complete opposition to what the hardline mythologists say, there is a warfare between human beings and literal spiritual villains. And this warfare involves, at least in part, *exorcising* these spiritual villains from people, objects, and even entire regions. The practice of exorcism is not a distinct discipline reserved for an elite few but is a pervasive practice available to the larger Christian population, for such warfare is affecting us all. C. Peter Wagner, a defender of exorcism as a feature of spiritual warfare, refers to this as "strategic-level spiritual warfare" (hereafter SLSW).[2] According to this notion, mature Christians are called to exorcise demons from objects and

---

1. Payne, *Satan Exposed*, esp. 14–23.

2. Wagner generically defines strategic-level spiritual warfare (SLSW) as a confrontation one may have with territorial spirits. His book (*Spiritual Warfare Strategy*) is designed to explain what this confrontation involves and why we ought to believe that it happens. SLSW is a broad category that is elsewhere called "power encounters." And this refers to any public demonstration of God's power over those of pagan deities and/or demons. One aspect of a power encounter is the expulsion of a demonic presence. For those specially called and prepared, they are to exorcise or "cast out" any regional or "territorial spirits" (demons occupying regions or people groups) in making way for repentance, discipleship, and sanctification. In a successful SLSW, one expels the demons and summons God.

regions in order to make way for societal repentance and godly revival. Such spirits that occupy regions are specifically identified as "territorial spirits." These territorial spirits are, according to Neil T. Anderson, "spirits [that] may take territorial rights and associate with certain geographical locations which have been used for satanic purposes."[3] While not all exorcisms have to do with territorial spirits, all territorial spirits are things to be exorcised if Godly spirituality is to prevail.

Some charismatics, but not all (e.g., the Assemblies of God), believe that exorcism is something that must be undergone in some Christians. For they believe that some Christians are in a demon-induced bondage to sin. These Christians are alleged to have fallen into a sinful enslavement that is being caused and sustained by an indwelling demon (one that is usually unbeknownst to the victim). The act of exorcising Christians of demon-induced bondage is known in most quarters as "deliverance." We thus have "deliverance ministry" for its emphasis on the ongoing mission of delivering fellow Christians from all kinds of demonic bondage brought about through possession and occupation. It is the exorcism of demons from fellow Christians. What distinguishes exorcistic models of spiritual warfare from other views, then, is that they involve exorcism as a major part of everyday spiritual warfare in the life of the believer and not just as an occasional remedy for an afflicted nonbeliever.

Below, I shall challenge the idea that exorcism is part of the spiritual warrior's combative repertoire. That is, I shall argue that exorcism is not really what spiritual warfare is about except that, when used to remedy nonbelievers who are afflicted, one could see it as an extension of the grander narrative that the kingdom of God has in fact subdued the kingdom of Satan. As such, exorcism is to be properly understood either as an extension of a healing ministry or of a ministry of miracles (or both). I will thus be arguing below that exorcism is not the right response to demonic forces directed against Christians as a means of opposing, standing against, or resisting those forces that threaten our spiritual well-being. As for other extraordinary features of contemporary views of spiritual warfare, I will have more to say in the chapter to follow this one.

TERRITORIAL EXORCISM AS SPIRITUAL WARFARE

It seems that if demonic beings are the source and cause of any spiritual tumult, particularly in a region or people group, it would not be unreasonable

---

3. Anderson, *Bondage Breaker*, 103.

to say that remedy comes in part by the demons' expulsion. Analogously, when we suffer from, say, a bacterial infection, it is true that we appropriately seek an antibiotic medication in order to rid our bodies of the offending microorganisms. This promotes the body's healthful restoration. The same goes for regional illnesses present in local epidemics, for we will quarantine the infected if need be. Why not think exorcism, then, to be an appropriate response to a spiritual assault—a quarantining, as it were—thus enabling the victims' spiritual renewal and openness to the gospel?

Exorcism (without qualification) is a practice that is relatively uncontroversial for most conservative Evangelicals and Catholics. However, there are some conservative Protestants who resist the notion that exorcism so understood is a viable practice for the church outside of the New Testament.[4] But the kind of exorcism is not quite what proponents of spiritual-warfare-as-exorcism mean (though it surely includes it). Rather, they are often extending the practice as a means of remedying *regional* (or corporate) possessions. When Wagner et al. speak of regional exorcism, they are referring to the exorcism of a territorial spirit. This is a part of what Wagner calls SLSW. Unlike the traditional purpose for exorcism, this one is more controversial for it is extending the object of exorcism to *locations* and/or *masses* of people. Let us refer to such exorcism for brevity's sake as "territorial exorcism." Now, some think, as already noted above, that SLSW also involves exorcism as a means of delivering *fellow Christian believers*—usually from habitual sins that seemingly cannot be overcome. Let us refer to this kind of exorcism as "deliverance exorcism." So, territorial exorcism has to do with the expulsion of demons from (occupied) provinces and deliverance exorcism has to do with the expulsion of demons from Christians.

The tools for such expulsions often involve a wide range of spiritual exercises. They involve individual prayer, corporate prayer, "binding," "speaking against," and so forth. By the territorial exorcist focusing not necessarily on an individual, but on a region of individuals, she can cast out the menacing spirit(s) from its/their stranglehold on a given people group (or any would-be people group that may be in the process of occupying that region). And the deliverance exorcist can extend the practice to that of demon-possessed Christians in the region or, to follow the parlance, "demonized" Christians (more on this terminology later).

One need not deny the notion of territorial spirits to object to territorial exorcism. Clinton Arnold, for example, holds to a modified notion of territorial spirits and yet denies that exorcism is the right response to

---

4. E.g., Powlison, *Power Encounters*, 91.

them.[5] So, while belief in territorial spirits may be a necessary condition for some acts of SLSW in our pre-evangelism, it is not a sufficient condition. As such, believing that there are territorial spirits of a sort is not enough to justify the practice of territorial exorcism. There must be an independent argument to justify it. For there are other conceivable ways to minimize demonic activity in regions and/or people groups that need not punt to an exorcistic approach. For example, it is possible that such territorial spirits lose their authority and power through the biblical and sanctifying maturation of those in the affected region. That is, it may be that if the people group were to seek God, pray, study the Scriptures, and practice Christian virtues, this would render the governing demonic powers useless. This alone might lead the demon to seek a different and less resistant populated region with which to start again. And yet, this approach would not involve exorcism.

There are essentially two independent arguments that have been offered up in support of the notion that spiritual warfare (in part) involves the expulsion of demons in ways that differ from the usual exorcisms found in the Gospels—the latter here being what Wagner refers to as "ground-level spiritual warfare."[6] These arguments can be parsed out as (i) the experiential argument and (ii) the scriptural argument.[7] Let us turn to these arguments now to see if the notion of territorial exorcism is supported.

The Experiential Argument for Territorial Exorcism

Most of the experiences reported tend to loosely follow the same kind of pattern:[8] one discovers that a people group claims to be under the control by a semidivine being (usually a patron deity). There are phenomena that appear to confirm alien spiritual rulership (rampant illnesses, pervasive sinfulness, feelings of dread/darkness, political upheaval, etc.). Some Christian missionaries and/or evangelists are then tapped to pray or speak against this semidivine being. The phenomena subside. The Christian missionaries then declare God's victory over the semidivine being and proceed to win over converts. All is now right in the region.

---

5. Arnold, *3 Crucial Questions*, 150–59.
6. Wagner, *Spiritual Warfare Strategy*, 22–23..
7. There is actually a third category—the argument from church tradition. But, as Wagner anticipates, Protestants will just wave away the import of church tradition. Others—typically cessationists—will dispute the reality of the accounts.
8. E.g., Payne, *Satan Exposed*, 71–86; Warner, "Dealing with Territorial Spirits."

Given the ubiquity of a doctrine of *animism*[9] throughout mostly non-Western cultures of the world, it is easy to see how incoming missionaries would find ample witnesses to a bare conception of territorial spirits (which is a concept closely related though not identical to animism[10]). Eyewitness testimony is, after all, why we believe central doctrines like Jesus's having been raised from the dead and other truths about him.[11] But, as Wagner suggests, the only reason why most Christians balk at the notion of such personal experience is because they have been conditioned (or poisoned) by the isolated anti-supernatural rationalism of the West.[12] Indeed they have. But pointing this out does not accredit just any claim to some supernatural occurrence. And yet Wagner claims, as do many others in the field, to have seen the effectiveness of praying against (i.e., expelling) territorial spirits. While not always successful, it has, they say, made a difference in their evangelism.

So strong is their confidence in personal experience that such experience may come pretty close to trumping Scripture itself. Religious studies professor Sean McCloud reports that "[p]hysical experience as proof is so crucial that some [SLSW] theologians suggest that biblical interpretation must be evaluated and judged through experience."[13] If this is true, it is alarming. And for Protestant theologians and missionaries to be thinking such things is quite bizarre if they are indeed consciously in line with the doctrine of *sola Scriptura* of the early Protestants. That is, that they ought to be elevating Scripture over any other would-be source of doctrinal authority.

Now, I don't dispute that experience is certainly a viable, if not one of the strongest, means of evidence gathering. But Wagner and friends fail to install any confidence in readers that they can distinguish between the actual evidence (or pure observation) and one's mediated interpretation of it.[14]

---

9. Animism is the view that there are otherworldly spirits that reside in any number of things that are not human (from trees to rocks). It may even be the entirety of the universe itself that is inhabited (i.e., *pantheism*).

10. The notion of territorial spirits, though somewhat related to animism, is not quite the same thing. For territorial spirits are *temporarily invading* spirits and not part of the permanent essences of the objects they inhabit. A human spirit constitutes both part of a human's essence and is a permanent fixture that is separable only by death. (I am, of course, merely assuming a particular anthropology here in that humans are alleged to be composites of body and spirit or soul. There is considerable debate about whether human beings have spirits so understood; I simply assert this anthropology in the interest of its being the majority position amongst Christians. It also happens to be my own view.)

11. Wagner, *Spiritual Warfare Strategy*, 43.//
12. Wagner, *Spiritual Warfare Strategy*, 47–48, 74–75.
13. McCloud, *American Possessions*, 8–9.
14. E.g., Löfstedt, "Establishing Authority," 12.

The problem this poses is easy enough to illustrate: Suppose there is a knock at the door. It could be a salesperson. It could be a parcel delivery service. It could be your neighbor. There are obviously a number of interpretations available here. Unfortunately, there is only one piece of evidence: the knock at the door. While such evidence effectively rules out some possibilities (it's not an elephant and it's not a tree), we have a long way to go to arrive at the right answer. We can add to the datum of hearing a knock the circumstances under which the knocking takes place. For example, suppose the knock occurs at one's house somewhere in the United States, and it is no place of any political significance. So, it's unlikely the Prime Minister of England. It's also not Halloween, so it's not likely going to be children seeking candy. I may have additional reason to believe that so-and-so was going to come over and visit me. This certainly increases the likelihood of this so-and-so being the mysterious knocker. But absent that kind of background information, there is a wide range of possibilities that one does not have to strain to accept. The problem becomes particularly acute when we don't hear the knock ourselves and are believing someone *else* who, being generally a questionable witness to such events, reports that there was a knock.

So, what entitles one to narrowly prefer one interpretation of some given experience over another, not to mention whether the experience obtained altogether? Well, sometimes the evidence is not enough to sufficiently whittle down the options. In the case of the mysterious knocker, we just do not know who it is until we gather more evidence. This could be accomplished by going to the door and looking through the peephole or by asking aloud for the person do disclose him-/herself. But the missionary experiences of the success of exorcism claimed by folks like William Payne, C. Peter Wagner, Derek Prince, Charles Kraft, John Wimber, and many others are not equivalent. In most cases, we cannot acquire more evidence like we can of the mysterious knocker. And if we can't do that, then we may never know if those reporting such events are even credible (and Wagner acknowledges the import of personal credibility as a major factor[15]). Thus, I think we need to set aside the credibility question for now. Credibility is not the end of the inquiry, anyway, but only the beginning. Nevertheless, there are other reasons such reports need not necessarily be taken as evidence willy-nilly for the use of territorial exorcism.

Generally speaking, the role that experience should play in the believability of an experiential claim is directly proportional to the evidential impact it affords. A "because I said so" approach will do little to move the needle of an outside skeptic though it will certainly make an impact

---

15. Wagner, *Spiritual Warfare Strategy*, 57.

on oneself (the one who experiences) if it's seemingly authentic. But even then, we can often misconstrue what our own experiences seem to be telling us. And only our missionary eyewitness can navigate that. While I would not presume to downplay or minimize any of the supernatural elements involved simply because they are supernatural, I do not think the vast majority of accounts are *interesting* enough to consider as confirmations of the utility of exorcism. And by "interesting" I mean something like "evidence conferring." In order to count as evidence, assuming no further investigation is possible or available, it must be the kind of experience that would be reasonably expected if territorial exorcisms are legitimate. If a different hypothesis explains what has happened with equal probability (or better), then what has happened is not evidence for territorial exorcism.

One way to make a claim interesting would be if there are not alternative explanations available that we do not have to strain to accept. To illustrate, suppose someone claims to have experienced a haunting in one's house as something caused by a deceased person because they hear odd sounds and doors slamming from time to time. If this is all one has to go on, it's easy to imagine the sounds being attributable to natural causes or, if you will, demonic activity (showing that this skepticism need not be motivated by an anti-supernatural bias). There is another factor that might prevent a claim from being interesting. If making the claim would be carnally self-serving, then it would be suspect. That is, if someone stands to personally gain in terms of, say, the advancement of one's career or in acquiring financial earnings, then the claim may be contrived for self-gain. Having such a dog in the fight will make us reasonably suspicious. A third factor for what counts as interesting would be if the event were witnessed by multiple people and such people could be (in theory) cross-examined. That should eliminate personal psychological factors that would otherwise taint the results. Fourth, it would make it interesting if something of significance resulted from the episode—something like the immediate toppling of a political regime or an immediate and unprecedented widespread conversion that took place in the region. If something like this obtained after a so-called territorial exorcism, with nothing else of significance concurring, then we might consider what happened to have some legitimacy for that exorcism—perhaps as something we could even predict and replicate elsewhere. And one final thought: it helps one's case when such claims are reported and/or documented in a timely fashion and not kept under wraps until a much later date. Stories deferred to later dates are more susceptible to embellishments and look increasingly suspicious.

Though this is not an exhaustive list of what might constitute evidence-conferring or "interesting" reports of territorial exorcisms based on experience, it does help prevent us from accepting just *any* extraordinary claim of personal experience as evidence. As such, it minimizes our need to chase down every single claim to territorial exorcism made. Otherwise, we should be busying ourselves not just with Christian claims to the extraordinary, but with non-Christian ones as well. So, only if there are any interesting claims out there so understood should we take them seriously. But it is apparent that most if not all of the claims offered fail to be unqualifiedly belief worthy. And yet, Wagner does not intend for people to necessarily take such experiences apart from the testimony of Scripture. He believes that Scripture is the final arbiter over such matters, thereby implying that the experiences are only as good as the scriptural evidence.[16] So much for the independence of experience!

We are inclined, then, to move on to explore what is allegedly the scriptural evidence for the practice of territorial exorcism as a constituent of spiritual warfare. This is the right arena for the advocate to make her case more convincingly.

The Scriptural Argument for Territorial Exorcism

Wagner asserts two things in his biblical defense. First, even if Scripture does not openly endorse territorial exorcism, nothing in Scripture prohibits it. And second, there are in fact instances in Scripture of such a practice. While he does not characterize his approach as one offering "proof," he does say that we "can find an abundance of biblical 'concepts' that will lead us to believe strategic-level spiritual warfare is valid."[17] (Recall that SLSW is the larger category of warfare-driven "power encounters" of which territorial exorcism is but a part.) As for the lack of prohibitions, the question is made irrelevant by the teachings to Christians on how to positively engage in spiritual warfare. If no instructions were given pertaining to the exorcism of anything like a territorial spirit, then one might (weakly) conclude that it is unnecessary to speak of the lack of prohibition. Since spiritual warfare centers around Satan as the ultimate source of conflict, it is reasonable to assume that exorcism ought to be a primary practice. But it is not so much as *mentioned* in the instructional portions regarding spiritual warfare. Bear in mind that Scripture also does not prohibit the use of garlic or the wearing of talismans as means to warding off demonic spirits. But we don't use such

---

16. This is why the Old Testament, for example, does not endorse focusing on the dazzling experiences of the supernatural rather than on the clearly established doctrines that make such experiences belief-worthy or not to begin with; e.g., Deut 13:1–3.

17. Wagner, *Spiritual Warfare Strategy*, 84.

things on grounds that such things are not already affirmed in Scripture. While merely not mentioning a potential tactic is not enough to discount it, one is not warranted in supposing it in the absence of any other positive reasons. It is therefore better for us inquire about these "biblical concepts" Wagner seems to affirmatively find in Scripture.

It turns out that none of his cited passages give us such indication that exorcism is used to expel demons from things or places. He cites Jesus's wilderness temptation as "the highest level of spiritual warfare ever recorded in history."[18] Though the temptation account does not involve a possession in the usual sense, it is nevertheless alleged to serve as a paradigm for this kind of practice—one that Jesus himself passed on to his disciples.[19] But, in what can only be a category mistake here, it is evident that the temptation narrative says nothing about an expulsion! The way in which Jesus handles Satan is not by "casting out" or "binding" him. Instead, Jesus rests on the strength of the Spirit of God (Matt 4:1) and on the promises of Scripture (v. 4). Satan sought to tempt Jesus into acquiring his messianic titles as prophet (v. 3), priest (v. 5), and king (v. 8) without having to endure subservience, suffering, and persecution. It is the religious equivalent of a get-rich-quick scheme. Jesus's response was to recall Scripture (the "sword of the Spirit") wherein it is implied that he stood against the schemes of the devil (cf. Eph 6:11) in ways that required him to have truth, righteousness, readiness, and faith—not to mention supplication in his fasting for forty days and nights. Unwittingly, the temptation narrative seems to validate the contrary idea that exorcism is *not* one of the tools of such engagement.

Wagner goes on to cite other alleged instances of territorial exorcism by Jesus, including Mark 4:39.[20] In this passage, Wagner says, we have mention of "the spirit who caused the storm on the Sea of Galilee."[21] I take it Wagner infers this from Jesus's rebuke of the wind and his speaking to the sea. But such an inference is beyond what we should think is going on here. The passage is merely using such terms to express his authoritative control over the elements. It is similar to Jesus's cursing of the fig tree (21:19), where we do not imagine that the fig tree was or has a demon.

---

18. Wagner, *Spiritual Warfare Strategy*, 119.

19. Wagner, *Spiritual Warfare Strategy*, 131.

20. Wagner mentions "Legion" in the episode of the Gerasene demoniac, but he just asserts that it might be a designation that represents "higher-level spirits" without supporting such a notion. More likely, "Legion" just represents a plurality that controls the demoniac—a collective, if you will—in much the same way a group of aggressors might describe themselves as an "army."

21. Wagner, *Spiritual Warfare Strategy*, 132.

Wagner then turns to the fact that Jesus equates himself to one who "binds the strong man" (Matt 12:29; Mark 3:27; Luke 11:21). He then suggests that the word "overcome" in Luke's account is interchangeable with Matthew's use of "bind."[22] That each believer is one who "overcomes" (1 John 5:4–5) licenses Wagner to equate it with "binding" (where "binding" is also directly ascribed to what disciples can do in Matthew 16:19 and 18:18). However, no one would ever make such a connection, or imply it, unless one were already fishing around in Scripture for any hints of direct demonic confrontations. It does not entitle one to conclude that all instances of overcoming are therefore instances of binding. And the mention of Matthew 16 and 18 is even more perplexing, for there the "binding" (i.e., constraining/forbidding) has nothing to do with exorcism (or any kind of demonic confrontation) at all![23] For there it is a *whatever* that can be bound, not a *whoever*. This is supported by the latter part of the promise ("whatever you loose on earth"), which should strike us as an awkward addition if understood as a territorial *summoning*. Indeed, it does not suggest that the Christian can *summon* or *sanction* a demonic presence. Therefore, to overcome does not mean to expel as if it were the contrary to summoning.

This brings us to the book of Acts. Wagner recalls the story of Simon Magus ("the magician") in Acts 8:9–25. Therein Simon sinfully requests to purchase the power of God from the apostles. Leaning heavily on the contribution of Susan R. Garrett, who is quoted saying that Simon is "endowed with the power of Satan" and "no mere con artist or cheap charlatan,"[24] Wagner pushes for a noticeably modest conclusion in that "this could easily be seen as strategic-level spiritual warfare."[25] If we set aside Garrett's dubious approach (which is to "reveal" that Acts is the embellished product of Luke's supernatural imagination), the grounds for associating Simon with being possessed vanish. Simon's sin was to demand that the apostles "[g]ive me this power also, so that anyone on whom I lay my hands may receive the Holy Spirit" (v. 19). This isn't the sort of thing Satan would ask for since the power he was seeking was *not* miracles (for he considered himself someone who could already do that; vv. 9–10) but *the receiving of the Holy Spirit* (vv. 17 and 20). Moreover, Simon was considered a believer (v. 13).[26] Instead,

---

22. Wagner, *Spiritual Warfare Strategy*, 147.
23. See Ice and Dean, *What the Bible Teaches*, 110–14.
24. Wagner, *Spiritual Warfare Strategy*, 171; cf. Garrett, *Demise of the Devil*, 75.
25. Wagner, *Spiritual Warfare Strategy*, 171.
26. There is space in Acts 8 to surmise that Simon may not have had the kind of belief that was salvific. This might be suggested by Peter's reprimand in verses 20–23, wherein Simon is denounced for his "wickedness," "gall of bitterness," and "bond of iniquity." One could argue that Simon only believed in the content of what was said (i.e.,

this must have been something Simon himself was honestly seeking but obviously for the wrong reasons. Secondly, Peter's response is that Simon's heart "is not right before God" (v. 21), which defies the normal insight an apostle would have in detecting the presence of demons, much less Satan himself. Peter would have openly identified and then cast out the afflicting Satan if Garrett were right about Simon. Thirdly, and most devastatingly, Garrett does not actually suggest in the cited passage that Satan was even present (as if to say that in Simon there was a territorial spirit as Wagner supposes[27]). Instead, as Garrett's quote indicates, Simon was simply endowed with the *power* of Satan, but this is not cashed out to be his *presence*. Even on its face, Wagner's push to have this "power encounter" involve the defeat of a territorial spirit falls flat. It is nothing more than the reprimand of a misguided believer.[28]

Acts 16:16–18 cannot be so dismissed. Wagner is right to address this as an explicit exorcism story.[29] But the issue is whether this is an instance of a territorial exorcism as defined above (or, in Wagner's vernacular, "binding . . . a spirit from the invisible world"[30]) rather than an instance of ground-level spiritual warfare (i.e., a conventional exorcism). Wagner is convinced it is the former because it "was an event that shook an entire city."[31] He has in mind the earthquake that released Paul and Silas from prison in verses 25–26. But the passage makes absolutely no connection between the

---

v. 14), not that he was necessarily a true Jesus-follower (cf. James 2:19). Nevertheless, it is difficult to think that Simon was not a real believer for four reasons: (i) he not only believed but was baptized (v. 13); (ii) he served alongside of Philip, who surely would have called him out if he were not a true brother in the Lord; (iii) what Simon is said to have believed was that which Philip preached, which included "the kingdom of God and the name of Jesus Christ," which seems to meet the threshold for what constitutes a saving faith (Rom 10:9–10); and (iv) the matter has a relevant parallel in Acts 19, where the Ephesians there are identified as "disciples" (v. 1), who likewise "believed" but nevertheless did not have the power of the Holy Spirit (v. 2). That Simon was reprimanded was an indictment, not on his salvation, but on his attempt to appropriate the power of the Spirit through purchase. Indeed, it looks like that it was an attempt by a misguided brother to buy the power of the Holy Spirit that was denounced by Peter.

27. "[I]t might have been nothing less than a territorial spirit Peter had encountered through Simon" (Wagner, *Spiritual Warfare Strategy*, 171).

28. Wagner goes on to address Acts 12 and 13 (*Spiritual Warfare Strategy*, 172–87), but, since these do not record any instances of exorcism, they are beyond the scope of our present analysis. One can maintain belief in the existence of territorial spirits without thinking that exorcism is the right response (indeed, Wagner himself suggests that the consistent responses in these two chapters is prayer and not exorcism, though it is possible he may be conflating the two).

29. Wagner, *Spiritual Warfare Strategy*, 188–90.

30. Wagner, *Spiritual Warfare Strategy*, 189.

31. Wagner, *Spiritual Warfare Strategy*, 190.

expulsion of the "spirit of divination" and Paul and Silas's prayer leading to their rescue. Wagner attempts to connect them by associating the spirit with regions (first Delphi and then Philippi). The reason is because the Greek designation for "spirit of divination" is more aptly translated "python spirit," which is a direct allusion to the Oracle of Delphi and the cult of Apollo. This much is true, but it adds no traction to the idea that the spirit is a territorial being since nothing in the text reveals that the spirit was possessing anything other than a particular person; and it was the particular person who was exorcised, not the region. The earthquake has no grammatical or conceptual link to this expulsion since their miraculous release follows their acts of prayer and worship, which occur much later at midnight (v. 25). It's just an independent miracle account.

The other passages Wagner brings up do not pertain to exorcism as such. Instead, he is bent on defending one's theological right to directly engage demonic spirits in order to subdue and resist them. Just in passing, I would say that one is not called to directly engage demonic spirits in the context of spiritual warfare. Appeals to Jesus's activities are actually evidence of the fact that any exorcism he did was of the traditional kind—the expulsion of nonregional demons from those afflicted by demonic possession. When there is such a possession case, the disciples are authorized to exorcise. But none of this informs what the discipline of spiritual warfare is all about when we arrive at the epistolic teaching material on the matter. Exorcism, like physical healing, is a remedy and a testament to nonbelievers that in Christ the kingdom of God has come. It is thereby not the means by which the Christian normally endures and combats the forces of darkness.

It would seem, then, that both the argument from experience as well as the argument from Scripture both fail to support the practice of territorial exorcism. That Scripture does not openly *forbid* much less endorse such a practice fails to appreciate the significance of the fact that the teaching material on spiritual warfare nowhere includes territorial exorcisms in the believer's repertoire. That truly none of the teaching passages about how to stand your ground include territorial exorcism is indeed striking, for we should expect at least a mention of it if it ought to be something of which the Christian should be cognizant.

THE PROBLEM OF "DEMON HUNTING"

The notion of territorial exorcism assumes that one can know that a demon is present. But in the absence of clear possession symptoms—that is, in the absence of obvious physical signs like violent convulsions, the speaking of foreign languages, the verbal confession of an invading presence, or whatever—there is no clear way to determine that an oppressive demon is present in some region or other. Consider a people group that might claim to be under the religious direction of some pagan deity. This would not be sufficient grounds for thinking that the indigenous people are *in fact* commercing with a supernatural being. We cannot be sure that the pagan people aren't just making it up or that they aren't merely thinking of their pagan icon as an objectification of their nationalistic principles like the bald eagle is for the United States of America. Even if American leaders and patrons worshiped the eagle, it would be no unambiguous indication that there is a malicious spirit present in the icon or its leaders. And even if its leaders *said* that they worship an unembodied evil spirit, it still would not follow that there is indeed a demon at the helm.

In fact, Ephesians 6:12 tells us nothing about the frequency of demons in the earthly powers that govern the nations. The significance of Paul's statement here is to explain that demons are *ultimately* responsible for the oppressive conditions they inflict on believers, but they are not *immediately* responsible for them or immanent in those situations. Demons need not be anything like puppeteers where they are always present as they move on their human agents to carry out their adversarial actions against the saints. Being blinded, for example, need not be something that is mystically sustained by a demonic presence. Spiritual blindness, like physical blindness, may just be a condition that was inaugurated at some time in the past and continues unabated to this day. Again, we have no way of knowing that a demon is actively present (that he is *here* in the *now*) when a human adversary is opposing us, even forcefully.

If we insist on exorcism as a means of ridding a nation, regime, object, or even a singular oppressor from the influences of the demonic vis-à-vis spiritual warfare, then we would be saddled with the uncomfortable task of what could only be called "demon hunting"![32] That is, we would have to be like the Ghostbusters in having to discern where demons are lurking so as to expel them. Sympathizers prefer, of course, a less stigmatizing nomenclature; they would prefer to identify their project of seek and destroy in more clinical terms—i.e., "spiritual mapping."[33] But, regardless of the nu-

---

32. Mary Garrison boldly embraces the designation in her *How to Conduct Spiritual Warfare*. One small start-up publishing company even dared to identify as Demon Hunter Publishing Company (see Meade, *Spiritual Warfare*). Kjell Sjöberg uses the metaphor when he says that some people "have been given a hunting instinct to track down the enemy's manipulations" (*Winning the Prayer War*, 60). Wagner cites this approvingly in his *Spiritual Warfare Strategy*, 31.

33. Otis, *Informed Intercession*; Holvast, *Spiritual Mapping*; Wagner, *Breaking*

ance, there is no surefire way to discern when, where, or if demons might be actively pulling the strings apart from the more manageable signs found in normal possession cases.

Well, one might push back and insist that there are some people groups who openly acknowledge that they are actively being occupied by a spiritual being. However, what's to prevent a demon from giving us only the *illusion* that there is a supernatural animating force behind this or that locale or regime? For a demon may very well influence a people group to lie or act like they are presently being inhabited by a spirit when they are not. Before there can be a call for expulsion, there must be unambiguous evidence of a demonic presence. Otherwise, what could end up merely being a diversionary tactic will have succeeded. Other than these notions imposing unrealistic and unlivable demands on laypersons, that Scripture gives us no such discernment criteria underscores the sentiment that exorcism just isn't the sort of practice we are supposed to employ when it comes to spiritual warfare. That conventional possession cases are even sometimes difficult to discern despite having some of the telltale signs is precisely why standard exorcisms themselves are rare.

DEMON POSSESSION INVOLVES NEITHER PLACES NOR OBJECTS

Speaking of the difficulty of discerning if and when demons are supposedly inhabiting regions, locales, or objects, it is questionable that this is even a (metaphysical) possibility. Now, it is obviously true that demons have been "cast out" of the afflicted in the Gospels and Acts. But the kind of expulsion that takes place is not a spatial one. Immaterial beings aren't located anywhere any more than God is. They are said to be "in" someone or other as a matter of speaking in much the same way the kingdom of God is said to be "within" (Luke 17:21, KJV) or "upon" (Matt 12:28; Luke 11:20) us. Thus, exorcism is not so much a form of *forced relocation* as much as it is *revoked* or *blocked jurisdiction*. To expel a demon is to cease its input into the victim's mind and body such that it is no longer "present." This comports well with the fact that when the "strong man" is "bound" by Jesus (Luke 11:21–22), he is not said to be deported or displaced.

Perhaps it is best to think of exorcism as analogous to locking out a specific computer from using a shared device like a wireless printer. Now, wireless printers allow multiple users to print documents without having to be in direct physical contact. But settings can be changed whereby current

---

Strongholds.

users can be forbidden from having any further access. Since demons are purely immaterial beings, this is a viable way to understand their access and control over a human being's mind and body without contradicting what it means to be purely immaterial. You can no more relocate a demon than you can the number 1. For numbers, if they exist concretely, also do not have location. In the same way that someone might be "separated" from God (a case in which spatiality does not play a literal role regarding an immaterial person), perhaps through exorcism one also gets (analogously) "separated" from their demonic oppressor(s). And, like God, it does not mean that they are outside of any contact. It just means that jurisdiction and/or cognitive influence has been minimized or eliminated altogether. Exorcism, then, likely just shuts off a certain level of influence a demon might have over a victim (kind of like shutting off one's ongoing access to a wireless printer). And describing such things in terms of geography is just a more familiar way of communicating it.[34]

However, I want to anticipate another objection here: if demons are not spatial beings and really do not get relocated, how does one explain Jesus's narrative about a certain demon, seemingly following an exorcism,[35] subsequently seeking rest in waterless *places* only to return with reinforcements to the victim from whom he was expelled (Matt 12:43–45; Luke 11:24–26)? This seems to have all the earmarks of demonic spatiality and interstate travel. Most New Testament commentators point out that during this time it was believed by many that demons often resided in desert or wilderness climates (cf. Luke 8:29).[36] This is supposed to serve as the backdrop to Jesus's statements here. If this is the right reading, then demons can indeed occupy places; and if places, then also provinces.

But can demons occupy places, even uninhabited ones, as the narrative implies to some? A couple of indications suggest not. First, it is clear that Jesus is using a series of housekeeping metaphors here. For he describes

---

34. This also seems to call into question the notion of territorial spirits. But such territorialism, if one so desires to maintain it, can be adjusted to accommodate the fact that demons cannot be located in space (see appendix C).

35. A number of readers see Jesus's introductory statement to the narrative in Matt 12:43 and Luke 11:24 ("When the unclean spirit has gone out of a person, . . .") as indicative of an exorcistic expulsion (e.g., Anderson, *Bondage Breaker*, 103). Given the proximate context of the Beelzebul controversy, which involves a dispute about Jesus's successful exorcisms, along with similar wording used in a more clearly exorcistic context (Luke 8:2), this is plausible. However, the term in question (*exelthē*, "has gone out") does not itself *require* one to read this as a forced exit (cf. Mark 1:35). For, presumably, demons can freely come and "go out" as God permits.

36. E.g., Fitzmyer, *Gospel According to Luke I–IX*, 514; Keener, *IVP Bible Background Commentary*, 81.

the place of the spirit's return as a "house" that is "empty, swept, and put in order" (Matt 12:44; cf. Luke 11:25).³⁷ As an illustration using obvious metaphors, the "places" of rest may also be read as representational if not also metaphorical (more on this in a moment). That a stressed-out individual living today might tell herself to "find your happy place" is not a clear indication that she is seeking a literal location for relief as much as she is seeking a state of tranquility. So, whatever we are to make of "places," it seems that all bets are off that this is to be taken without qualification given the presence of metaphors that fill out the narrative.

Second, these places are intentionally described as "waterless places" (*anydrōn topōn*; Matt 12:43; Luke 11:24). While this appropriates the Second-Temple Jewish notion of demons spatially residing in places like deserts or wildernesses (which is not an unreasonable conjecture apart from its context), this is bound to be misleading. Yes, deserts and/or wildernesses were the literal environments in which God's people were challenged and tempted (e.g., Ps 78:12–32; Jer 2:6; Josh 5:6). But it became a common theological motif for describing generally forsaken, depraved, and hostile environments and territories (e.g., Ps 74:14; 102:6; Isa 27:10; 21:1; Jer 2:6; Ezek 20:33–36; Hos 2:3; Joel 3:19).³⁸ As a motif, the "waterless places" to which the unclean spirit journeys is meant to capture those parts of the (populated) world where enmity and tribulation abound.³⁹ The unclean spirit's failure

---

37. It seems that "house" more likely refers to the wider environment in which the victim resides, namely, a wider people group—the entire populated world, perhaps. This is what it meant a few verses earlier in the context of the plundered "strong man" at the hands of Jesus (Matt 12:29; cf. Luke 11:17, 21). Indeed, it makes more sense of Jesus's expansive conclusion to the story in Matthew 12:45: "So also will it be with *this evil generation*" (emphasis added). That this is a warning about "this evil generation" makes the most sense in light of the "house" as a metaphor for a wider people group and not as a metaphor for the victim himself. The spirit's return with seven other cohorts to the restored "house" where the previously inhabited person resides perhaps indicates that retaliation will not only be from within, but from without—through the Jewish and Roman authorities increasingly hostile to Jesus and his disciples (i.e., the situation of "this evil generation").

38. E.g., Heiser, *Demons*, 198 n. 9.

39. Variants of *anydrōn* ("waterless [places]") are found in 2 Pet 2:17 ("waterless springs") and Jude 12 ("waterless clouds"). In both cases, "waterless" represents a *dysfunction*—a scarcity of water *where there should be*. Springs and clouds aren't the kinds of things that normally lack water. It parallels the use of "fruitless trees" as is also found in Jude 12. Jude is not meaning to invoke the image of, say, a literal fruitless tree like a pine tree. Rather, he is referring to a tree *that normally produces fruit*, such as a fig tree, *but fails to do so*. Likewise, judging by the passages in Peter and Jude, "waterless" signifies a similar absence (=a functional deficit) as it pertains to certain despots throughout history. Being linguistically and thematically similar, Peter's statement in 2 Peter seems to parallel Jesus's narrative quite strikingly: "For if, after [the delivered]

to find "rest" among the depraved is likely an indication that a demon's work is never done, even among his own. This is especially true if it mirrors the kind of "rest" God enjoys after the six days of creation, for his "rest" is not (merely) a cessation of work but is a state of post-work retrospection involving "enjoyment, approval, and delight" in what was accomplished.[40] This is a plausible reading. As such, there is no clear indication to think that Jesus is teaching that demons literally commute to spatial regions—deserts or otherwise—as if to escape to find relaxation from a tough day on the job unsuccessfully harassing urbanites. The imagery is there to convey the demon's inability to achieve his nefarious purposes.

Therefore, one need not, nor should, assume that the occurrences of possession and expulsion reveal any literal spatial ambulation on the part of demons. This sensible conclusion avoids the awkward notion that something immaterial can nevertheless have location. But if something immaterial cannot have location, then demons do not occupy locations—including physical objects. It is metaphysically more plausible that they can only occupy—in the sense of exercising ascendancy over—other minds. And if literal spatiality is not a feature of the demonic, then territorial exorcism so understood is wrongheaded.

DELIVERANCE EXORCISM AS SPIRITUAL WARFARE

One final discussion is worth having in this chapter and it pertains to whether deliverance exorcism is a proper mode of spiritual warfare. Since the notion necessarily depends on whether Christians can ever be possessed by demons, we will specifically focus on this matter. The reason why this issue matters is because there are Christians who seem to be either deeply entrenched in sins they cannot overcome or afflicted by certain psychological conditions that cannot be remedied. If we assume that any fleshly

---

have escaped the defilements of the world through the knowledge of our Lord and Savior Jesus Christ, they are again entangled in them and overcome, *the last state has become worse for them than the first*. For it would have been better for them never to have known the way of righteousness than after knowing it to turn back from the holy commandment delivered to them" (emphasis added to reflect Jesus's almost identically worded statement in Luke 11:26). That depraved communities are in mind makes this a reasonable reading of "waterless places" in Jesus's narrative of what appears to be a similar theme.

40. Collins, *Genesis 1–4*, 70–71. My thanks to Jonathan King for this insightful point in his forthcoming book, *Remythologizing Angels and Demons: Their Purpose in the Cosmic Kingdom of God* (Lexham).

or psychological force can normally be resisted when they obtain outside of a possession case (1 Cor 10:13), then the failure of one to overcome such forces might imply the presence of a nefarious demonic cause. Surely the overwhelming nature of what is tearing us down must be due to the direct actions of demonic beings seeking to hamper our Christian walk. It just makes sense! And it may even be a condition that afflicts *every* Christian.[41]

Like the alleged success of expelling territorial spirits, the success of, and so the truth of, deliverance exorcism seems to be defended largely on the basis of dubious personal experiences.[42] Such missionary experiences prompted Merrill F. Unger, the famous contemporary theologian specializing in Christian demonology, to move away from a skepticism about the possibility of Christian possession in favor of believing that it does occur.[43] This should not be taken to mean that experience is the *only* driving force for those opposed to the more traditional view. Rather, such experiences lead certain theologians to rethink their ivory tower approach to a subject that seems to be disconnected from the empirical approach of worldwide missions—particularly in underdeveloped countries.

However, much of what was said in the above section in this chapter on the contribution of personal experience vis-à-vis territorial exorcisms applies here too. The takeaway from that section is that just because a victim *feels* or *senses* the presence of a demonic offender, it makes it difficult if not impossible to frame it into a bias-free proposition. For one wonders if the victim just isn't confusing her interpretation of the occurrences with the nature of the occurrences themselves. We might feel plotted against or a part of some kind of local conspiracy when things go frustratingly wrong. That our printers malfunction just when we need them or that we seemingly encounter more obstacles on the road than usual when trying desperately to get to our destination might indicate for us that forces are colluding against us. And as for the more dramatic alleged demonic possessions of Christians at the hands of certain exhibitionist exorcists (think Bob Larson and Benny Hinn), there is little to commend the interpretation. These public encounters often lack the telltale properties that make the encounter a matter of evidential interest. For example, the Christian victim does not speak languages unknown to her. There is not any insightful knowledge given that the victim would not have known otherwise. And most Christian victims on display seem to be altogether healthy, physically stable, and in complete control of their bodily functions (other than a movie-style flailing of limbs

---

41. Hammond and Hammond, *Pigs in the Parlor*, 12.
42. E.g., MacNutt, *Deliverance from Evil Spirits*, ch. 3.
43. This led Unger to update his views in his book *What Demons Can Do to Saints*.

and such). It appears that we cannot discern between a possession case in these matters and someone merely acting the part or of someone who is suffering from an adverse psychological condition. Unless the experiences are met with the more interesting properties normally associated with the more indisputable possession cases, we are under no obligation to canonize the notion that demons can possess Christians on the basis of experience. Otherwise, why not embrace everything from alien abduction stories to astral projection?

On the one hand, it would seem that the traditional objection to the notion that Christians can be demon possessed is right: if one is possessed or owned by God, she cannot be simultaneously owned by someone else; therefore, a Christian, who is possessed (=owned) by God, cannot simultaneously be possessed by a demon. Accordingly, traditional theologians will distinguish between demonic *possessions* and demonic *oppressions*— oppressions being the most aggressive kind of demonic harassment that can befall Christians but not possession proper. But the nontraditionalist who affirms the possibility of Christian possession will point out that in a possession case one is in fact not being owned by the demon(s) at all. It is a misuse of the term. For the term *daimonizomai*, which is normally translated "demon-possessed," is actually to be translated "demonized." It does not denote ownership at all. This is significant because if all possession cases are actually *demonizations*, then it is not a question of ownership as much as it is a question of demonic ascendancy over the victim. Consequently, demonization implies that demonic influence can come in *gradations* with what we refer to as "possession" being the most tyrannical. This is to say that there are degrees or levels of demonization (from lesser forms of oppression to more debilitating ones). The more tyrannical ones require exorcism and the less oppressive ones probably just require the practice of the Christian virtues to ward off the oppression. Given the fluidity of the Greek here, there is space for thinking that Christians can still be demonized (=co-occupied by a demon) without being owned by the demon.[44]

Clinton Arnold, who pushes back against some of the radical thinking behind Peter Wagner's SLSW, nevertheless argues that, as a mere matter of co-occupancy, there is biblical precedent and support that such co-occupancy is possible given how the temples of God were sometimes co-occupied by pagan deities, such as what we find in 2 Kings 23.[45] Neil Anderson points to Jesus's brief discourse about the evil spirit who "has gone out of a person"

---

44. Unger, for example, says that a demon can enter into a person "as a squatter and not as an owner or a guest or as one who has a right there" (*What Demons Can Do to Saints*, 60).

45. Arnold, *3 Crucial Questions*, 82.

and then threatens to "return to my house from which I came" to "dwell there" with "seven other spirits more evil than itself" (Luke 11:24–26; Matt 12:43–45).[46] From this, Anderson reasons that "[d]emons can exist outside or inside humans." While I have already addressed this passage earlier,[47] it is understandable how one might take this to mean that demons can literally inhabit persons. For Arnold, they can reside in the periphery of the person while their core—the heart—may not be able to harbor such alien spirits. While an invader may be lurking in the bedroom or the bathroom, so to speak, he may not be permitted to have any occupancy in something as prominent as the living room.[48] Accordingly, says Arnold, "Christians can be profoundly influenced by evil spirits—even to the extent that it can be said that they are inhabited and controlled by demons."[49]

Before we address the merits of whether Christians can be demonized in the way Arnold imagines, I just want to say up front that we should resist the literalizing of the language of demonic inhabitation lest we end up formulating a doctrine about (evil) spirits solely by analogy to what ordinary physical beings can do. There are two reasons for why "inhabitation" language should be construed nonliterally: First, as was stressed a number of times already, immaterial beings do not have location (e.g., see 72–73 and 159–160). The prospect that they might be here or there in a molecular sense is a category mistake. Second, Scripture uses the language of inhabitation in referring to God, his Spirit, and his kingdom "dwelling" within us (Luke 17:21; John 14:10, 17; Rom 8:9, 11; 1 Cor 3:16) and/or within a "temple" (Matt 23:21); and yet, it is evident that we are not supposed to take such inhabitation literally (1 Kgs 8:27). Instead, "inhabitation" or "indwelling" likely serve as metaphors to describe how close or immanent someone's influence and control over us might be.[50]

But Arnold's apparent literalizing of "inhabited" does not dissolve his case altogether. For, apart from a literal inhabitation, a demon might still have some measure of power over Christians such that it would nevertheless qualify as a demonization proper. Arnold explains that, on his model, Christians may relinquish control when they choose to engage in overtly sinful and occultic activities. They would be giving the devil a foothold (Eph 4:27)—a way "into" the person, ripe for demonization. Arnold cites Acts

46. Anderson, *Bondage Breaker*, 103.
47. See 160–162.
48. Arnold, *3 Crucial Questions*, 87.
49. Arnold, *3 Crucial Questions*, 88.
50. Paul refers to how sin "dwells" in our hearts when he means to convey its power over us (Rom 7:14–23) and not that it is a bounded, material thing with coordinate location.

19 as a possible example of Christians being demonized.[51] He argues first that the "residents of Asia" were said to "hear the word of the Lord" for two years (v. 10) and "were now believers" (v. 18). During this time, "evil spirits came out of them" (v. 12), except for the failed exorcism of the seven sons of Sceva. If they were believers and, indeed, evil spirits subsequently left them, then surely this exemplifies that Christians can be demonized.

So, is Arnold's case for Christian demonization a strong one? Or are there better reasons to think that Christians cannot be demonized?

Arnold's appeal to Acts 19, at best, commits the fallacy of division. The fallacy of division is the wrongful inference that just because a group of people or things have a certain property (in this case, that they "believe"), it doesn't follow that every individual member of that group has the same property. A sports team may be good, but that doesn't mean that *every member* of the team is likewise good, for teams can succeed despite the shortcomings of a few. As a group ("Jews and Greeks"), the people group in Acts 19 may be Christianized (i.e., the Ephesians); however, that some within their ranks are demonized does not entitle us to conclude that those particular ones were likewise Christianized. Apart from this consideration, Arnold seems to have read too much into the account. For verse 18 only says that "many of those who were now believers [*polloi te tōn pepisteukotōn*] came, confessing and divulging their practices." The "of those" (*tōn*) refers to the wider community, which grammatically suggests that *some* from that community were believers, not that they *all* were (cf. 20:30). Moreover, that those in the province "heard the word of the Lord" hardly suffices to imply that they were full-on Christians (cf. Rom 2:13; Jas 1:22)—especially if they were dabbling in the magical arts (cf. Gal 5:20). And, finally, it is possible that they were once Christian believers but are no longer due to their lapses back into occultic heresy (cf. 2 Tim 1:15).

While it is true that *daimonizomai* does not denote ownership, it is not at all evident that demonization is anything that can befall Christians. In every instance where *daimonizomai* or one of its cognates is used, it always applies to nonbelievers. From the Gerasene demoniacs to the Syrophoenician woman's daughter, it is evident that these possession victims are outside of the fellowship. Consider the Capernaum demoniac who happens to be congregating at the local synagogue at the time; he is still an outsider (e.g., Mark 1:27; cf. Luke 10:15). Now, one might accuse me of an argument from silence in that just because the Bible doesn't mention that some of these demonized were believers, it does not follow that weren't. But the burden of proof here is to show whether any of these victims are in fact Christians

---

51. Arnold, *3 Crucial Questions*, 91–2.

because there is no *prima facie* expectation that this should happen. Scripture always treats demoniacs as *under the control* of their demonic assailants by means of (implied?) consent. But Christians would not knowingly consent to this unless they were not (any longer) Christians after all (more on this point in a moment).[52] It is at least initially implausible that Christians are the kinds of persons who are susceptible to demonization. We must look to arguments to overturn this predisposition.

In addition, there are problems with accepting Arnold's relaxed understanding of *daimonizomai* in its supposed applicability to Christians. For one, there is too much liberty being taken with the concept of being demonized. It is true that there appear to be analogous words in English suggesting that this could be a gradual thing. For example, we might speak of a country as becoming "secularized" or of a citizen who was becoming "radicalized" by terrorist propaganda. These things obtain gradually and to differing degrees. However, this is only true when participles like "secularized" and "radicalized" are preceded with a modifier like "becoming." When such a participle is being used to describe what something *is* or *has been made to be*, it implies that the notion has been fully realized. Thus, a "secularized nation" is one that is fully dominated by secularism. A "radicalized citizen" is one who is fully dominated by radicalism. Similarly, then, to speak of someone being "demonized" is to say that they are fully dominated by a demon. It is never being used in the durative sense in its various Synoptic usages as if it were in a state of becoming. It is not surprising, then, that the demonized are almost always seen as actually *having* or *being indwelt by* a demon.[53] So, while one's "being demonized" or "demonization" may be the better translation, it is no less a maximal condition—it refers to the complete takeover of and/or an inhabitation within the victim (whether explicitly consensual or not).

52. One might ask about children who are reported to be demonized. For example, recall the story of the convulsing boy in Mark 9:14–29, wherein the boy had been harassed "since childhood" (*ek paidiothen*). One might wonder how children, who are seen as innocent and perhaps even participants in God's salvation (Luke 18:16), could be made to succumb to such demonization. Here I say that to be outside of the fellowship would not entail that one is therefore an atheist, a Satanist, or some other form of anti-Christian. It just means one is in a state of nonbelief about such matters (think of Nicodemus in John 3:1–15, who was not necessarily opposed to the preaching of Jesus despite his current state of nonbelief). Underdeveloped children may be incapable of specifically gospel belief too. While a child would not be explicitly consenting to his/her demonization, such a child would perhaps not have the requisite belief (cf. Rom 10:9–10) that would insulate one from such an invasion. Therefore, that some children can be possessed is not a counterexample to the notion that being a Christian insulates one from demonization.

53. Gilhooly: "it is clear that the demonized are often inhabited by the demon" (*40 Questions*, 80).

At this point, the tension in Arnold's understanding reveals its weakness, thus forcing him to pull back a bit on how much ascendancy demons can have over Christians. While ordinary, nonbelieving demoniacs are obviously under the *complete* control of demonic beings, Arnold depicts demonized Christians as those who only "allow an evil force to have a controlling and dominating influence in his or her life" such that the demon can "reign" or "rule and dominate."[54] But rather than speak of the same kind of takeover that obtains in the undisputed demoniacs, he guards himself. He seems to be saying that Christian demonization is something just shy of a traditional case—that a demon's exertion is only an "extensive influence,"[55] a "decisive hold,"[56] a "near-total dominance,"[57] "operating powerfully,"[58] and to "a very high degree."[59] And yet, strangely, Arnold clearly identifies the demonization event as a maximal condition—something that *exceeds* even being "taken captive" or "devoured."[60] In fact, he writes, demonization is something specifically involving the "inviting [of] a demonic spirit to reside within him or her."[61] Surely he *wants* to distinguish demonized Christians from demonized nonbelievers. But, as he makes his case, it's evident that Christian "demonization" looks little like that of nonbelievers after all. Indeed, Arnold adds, most "of the ways that demons work against believers would not be described as symptoms of 'demonization' or inhabitation."[62] Might this be because, in the case of the still-Christian, it's *not* demonization?

Aside from concerns that he's artificially moving the goal posts here (and doing it very confusedly), there arises an important question regarding Arnold's model: What demarcates or distinguishes a demonized Christian from a demonized non-Christian? Why not straightforwardly think that such Christians have now apostatized and are no longer Christians, or that they never were Christians to begin with, thus availing themselves (still) to the demonization process? Scripture seems to be no less clear that those *ruled* and *dominated* by habitually and freely engaging in sinning are not in fact Christians (1 John 3:8–9; 5:18). Surely there is no soteriological

---

54. Arnold, *3 Crucial Questions*, 89–91.
55. Arnold, *3 Crucial Questions*, 93.
56. Arnold, *3 Crucial Questions*, 95.
57. Arnold, *3 Crucial Questions*, 95.
58. Arnold, *3 Crucial Questions*, 96.
59. Arnold, *3 Crucial Questions*, 97.
60. See the chart in Arnold, *3 Crucial Questions*, 101.
61. Arnold, *3 Crucial Questions*, 101.
62. Arnold, *3 Crucial Questions*, 101.

difference between a Christian who subverts her Christianity in service to the practice of evil and a nonbeliever who practices evil. It is a strange use of language to speak of a Christian who can be demonized in the same sense as a nonbeliever once the believer takes on the same properties of a nonbeliever without actually becoming a nonbeliever (!). It all looks rather forced here, for Arnold is facilitating a new kind of category that wreaks of self-contradiction: Christians who aren't (any longer) Christians but are still Christians at the same time. Paul seems to have no problem making the distinction, for, he says, there are Christians who "devot[e] themselves to deceitful spirits and teachings of demons" who are then unequivocally referred to as those who "depart from the faith" (1 Tim 4:1).

One final point is worth mentioning. As if the deliverance model was not problematic enough, it ends up being quite circular. On the one hand, one's enslavement to sin is alleged to be due to demonic invasion. This is the reason the Christian seeks a deliverance exorcism. *But*, it is demonic invasion that is alleged to be brought on as the *result* of the initial enslavement. That is, as one spirals deeper into sin and/or occultism, one opens the door to demonic inhabitation.[63] It appears that the demonic invasion is merely a consequence of the sin that has so ensnared the Christian. But it is the very thing that the deliverance exorcism is supposed to remedy. Perhaps what advocates mean to say is that once the demon invades, the victim is now locked in to his or her condition, making rehabilitation impossible without an exorcism. But whether the takeover is either explicitly or implicitly consensual, the behavior is still not something the "victim" *wants* to cease—otherwise it wouldn't be a consensual takeover! If the person has and continuously wills to escape her sinful practices, she is not consenting to the invasion. If the advocate insists that the invasion obtains *apart from* any consent, then the demonization process can fully obtain in *any* Christian believer *with or without* inviting such inhabitation, and that seems obviously wrong. Thus, if one is wrestling with finding victory over their sin, then they are not consenting. The demon inhabits regardless of their contractual attitude. If it is the sin itself that opens the door, then the root of the problem is not demonization at all but the sin that invites it. And if one freely gives (implied) consent to demonization, then he or she is not

---

63. Some may think of occultism as a special kind of straightforward doorway into the soul. Certainly, popular culture wants us to think that dabbling with dark magic is an attractor of demonic inhabitation. However, one needn't take this position (in fact, I do not; see appendix D). Rather, the minimal way one can see occultism as an attractor of demonic activity is to relegate it to a form of falling away from Christian virtues. Indeed, to dabble in any or all forms of witchcraft is to rebel against God and to reject his Word against such things (1 Sam 15:23).

being taken over, for the demon is only doing what the "victim" wants it to do, and that is inconsistent with one's being a Christian at all. Since the supposedly demonized Christian who seeks deliverance is not really consenting to the demonization, even if she is subconsciously (or tacitly) consenting by sinning, then the most reasonable remedy for the person is to deal with the sin itself since, in all scenarios, it ends up being the free act of sinning that drives the condition.

Therefore, both the silence of Scripture on any attributing of *daimonizomai* to Christians along with acknowledged symptomatic distinctions between apostatized Christians and demoniacs are probably significant. If to be Christianized is to be made fully dominated by Christ, it is difficult to see how one can be simultaneously demonized unless it is possible they have become *former* Christians (or were never Christians to begin with—something that would also include young children). This is at least as plausible as, if not more so than, the notion that Christians are not really inoculated from demonization. And I would not presume to have anyone's experience override what seems doctrinally and reasonably evident already unless someone's experience somehow is evidentially interesting enough to justify a reconsideration. But, then again, the experience of a demonized Christian may just be the demonization of one who is not (any longer) a Christian. For the natural reading of the demonization passages suggests nothing less than a complete takeover, something in tension with one's being a Christian in any meaningful sense. And since the term is only used of nonbelievers, and believers cannot in principle be taken over by any demonic presence just short of apostatizing, which is just to say that they aren't believers (anymore), then deliverance exorcism (the exorcism of Christians) is not a justified response. But even if we ignore that, the fact that one's sinning is the driving force for demonization or its sustainability in us is enough to focus on minimizing that sin, not expelling the demons that are allegedly influencing the victim. Christians who struggle with sin such that they have not relinquished complete control must seek remedy in other ways.

CONCLUSION

Mythological models are inadequate because they do not do justice to the metaphysics of Scripture, namely, that demons literally exist as nonhuman spirits. But exorcistic models are guilty of a different kind of error, namely, among other things, that they suppose that regions, objects, and Christian believers can be inhabited by demonic (territorial) spirits. Accordingly, they affirm that exorcism is the right response to those spirits as an extension of spiritual warfare. Not only do experience and the alleged biblical support not vindicate such a model, but, as I have argued, believing that an exorcistic response to a suspected territorial spiritual presence is appropriate requires certain beliefs that cannot be maintained under scrutiny.

This is not to say that exorcism of individuals is never an adequate response to a certain kind of demonic assault as long as it is of the traditional sort. This is to say that exorcism is appropriate when deployed as a form of healing from physical or psychological maladies reasonably deemed to be caused by the demonization process. We may even consider this to be an exceptional or irregular part of spiritual warfare proper,[64] though the teaching material in Scripture on spiritual warfare *never* suggests or implies that Christians are to identify if demons are present in a particular situation. Even so, possession cases are but rare exceptions. And it is certainly out of place when applied to Christians struggling with sin where the needed response is thought to be a deliverance exorcism. For there is no good reason to suppose that Christians can, even in principle, be (finally) demonized. Spiritual warfare must be about something else. Before we attempt to uncover what that is, there are other extraordinary components attached to realist models of spiritual warfare that must be addressed. This is the subject of the next chapter.

---

64. So, I am happy to agree with Gregory Boyd in considering healing exorcisms to be a part of a larger spiritual warfare framework (Boyd, "Response"). I would demur with him, however, over the *frequency* of such exorcisms—finding the coming of Christ's kingdom and the birth of the early church to be uniquely situated in a way where demonizations would have expectedly been more ubiquitous.

17

Spiritual Warfare Is Not Wizardry

THE FINAL DISPUTED MODEL we will consider is one that supposes spiritual warfare to be a set of mystical practices—practices that resemble but are nevertheless staunchly opposed to demonic sorcery. They include one's performance as a "prayer warrior," as one who decisively speaks aloud, as one who engages in "prayerwalking," and/or as one who enacts or negates supernatural curses. While the individual elements of the model seem to have nothing in common, they all tend to share the tendency toward incorporating familiar practices generally associated with magic and the "correct" ways in which to wield it; accordingly, I refer to this as the "wizardry model" of spiritual warfare.

In many ways, a wizardry model is the product of an outlook on spiritual warfare that parallels how characters see the force in the Star Wars franchise. There is a dark side (the Sith) pitted against an opposing light side (the Jedi), and this light side operates pretty much according to the same rules as the dark but with obviously different motives and intentions. The force—both good and bad—is a sort of magical undercurrent that permeates the universe. Both dark and light force powers can repel opponents, lift heavy objects, and provide secret knowledge. Differences abound too. While Star Wars traffics in science fiction and fantasy, it is not unlike how some popularizers portray spiritual warfare in the wizardry model.

According to such a model, the combat of spiritual warfare is perceived to be, like the Star Wars franchise, a sort of "light side" versus "dark side" where each side harnesses its own powers. The dark side of spiritual reality is often cast (either implicitly or explicitly) as being in possession of a set of magical practices that bring about ruination and death on God's people. Some of these practices involve the bestowal of supernatural curses on people or, through spellcasting and incantation, the summoning of the powers of darkness for the purpose of wreaking all manner of havoc in the lives of others. So understood, the contrastive acts of spiritual warfare by Christians are thought to be counterforces working for good—a literal tit for tat. Each demonic action is countered by a corresponding Christian action: Christians do not summon demons but, instead, God and his angels; Christians do not incant or cast spells, but they pray and recite the promises of Scripture aloud; Christians do not invoke curses on people, but they proclaim blessings and expel the agents of evil who cause such curses; Christians do not use crystal balls or a witch's brew in order to divine private facts about others, but they are given "revelation knowledge and the mind of God through His Holy Spirit" so one can "see as He sees."[1] This understanding really does envision spiritual warfare as a contest—almost a dualism, really—between the dark arts and the power of God. However, the "powers" of the blessed are perceived to be far more impressive than their accursed counterparts if wielded correctly.

Indeed, the model appears to be very Harry Potter-esque. And while I speak of "wizardry models" as such, it is not a nomenclature used by any of its proponents. In fact, often enough, many of its advocates think of their own approach to be something *unlike* magic, witchcraft, or incantation. It is ironic indeed. Nevertheless, the designation is my own, for the model involves the Christian seeking remedy by means of the intrinsically extraordinary (i.e., magical in its own right). Accordingly, this chapter is devoted to addressing some of these auxiliary practices that look to be nothing but Christianized versions of occultic and/or magical techniques often associated with the traditions of sorcery.

To their credit, wizardry models are certainly opposed to mythological models; and that is to be commended. For the Christian can and should be open to the supernatural. But wizardry models are not, however, opposed to exorcistic models. In fact, quite often proponents of wizardry models tend to adopt an exorcistic model as part of their more complete view of spiritual warfare. For, in their thinking, sometimes evil spirits need to be banished from a person, a province, or a physical object. However, not all holders of an exorcistic model are themselves advocates of spiritual warfare as wizardry. Nor does any exorcistic model entail it. I would hesitate, for example, to put Neil T. Anderson—an exorcistic model supporter—in the same camp

---

1. Alves, *Prayer Warrior*, 37.

as Derek Prince or Bob Larson. The latter two have been known to hold to a far more exotic, magical view of spiritual warfare; Anderson not so much. The point is, while the two models (exorcistic and wizardry) can cohabitate within one's worldview, one does not necessarily imply the other. Therefore, a critical evaluation of wizardry models is to be treated here distinctly from the exorcistic models. I will argue that such practices in this model are, like exorcistic models, more superstitious than shrewd. However, I do want to note that things like praying aloud and praying while walking are in and of themselves unproblematic practices. It is only the overlay of wizardry that makes them superstitious—that the practices themselves have been infused (by God?) with a power or the ability to release a secret power that can successfully ward off enemy combatants. Deep down they are doing things no different than a sorcerer operating within the confines of white magic.

So, in an attempt to avoid the errors of anti-supernaturalism, wizardry model advocates opt for an extreme form of supernaturalism. In fact, I find that their view really amounts to something more like super-*duper*-naturalism! As my assessments below will reveal, the Christian ought to abandon this super-duper-naturalism and ought to remain on the more moderate side of supernaturalism, all the while steering clear of anti-supernatural models like the mythological model. Let us, then, take a critical look at the various and mostly independent tenets of the wizardry model.

THE "PRAYER WARRIOR"

Let us begin by saying something about the "prayer warrior." Many suppose that the way Christians are to get things done is to go to the mattresses, as it were, and pray actively, verbally, and perpetually in bringing about victory over demonic foes. So far, this doesn't sound too problematic even for the most traditional among us. Elizabeth Alves imagines the prayer warrior as one who is "called to do spiritual warfare through prayer over Satan's strongholds until you win! . . . God is for you, and the battle is the Lord's."[2] Alves then equates the prayer warrior to the "watchman" of Isaiah 62:6–7, who must be vigilant in guarding the church—for hours if need be. Often, such prayers are designed to hold demonic afflicters at bay. In addition to warding off the wicked ones, she adds that prayers also have the power to stave off natural disasters. Still, nothing terribly controversial is proffered here.

It is certainly true that prayer is a crucial component of one's preparation in standing firm against those principalities and powers that war against us (Eph 6:12, 18). I also think the designation of "prayer warrior"

---

2. Alves, *Prayer Warrior*, 38–39.

itself, though not used explicitly in Scripture, is benign. However, the typical image of the prayer warrior seems to be influenced by notions more at home in exorcistic models of spiritual warfare. Just like in a typically envisioned exorcism, the expulsion process of the prayer warrior will often involve verbal commands to any invading spirits to depart and will be accompanied by ongoing recitations of prayers against darkness. It is here where things get a bit weird. For, one imagines the prayer warrior openly expressing commands to any nearby demonic oppressor to "leave" while "claiming" specific scriptural truths in the process.[3] If directed to a demonic invader, speaking verbally ensures that the invader hears the command loud and clear; and claiming certain outcomes or promises found in biblical passages is our way of realizing a usually positive truth for the situation at hand.

Prayer warriors, so understood, do not believe themselves to be merely stalwarts against demonic oppressors. They see themselves as active suppressors of grand events like natural disasters as they seek to mitigate their destructive impact (these are likewise considered by some to be events caused by demons).[4] Even the vernacular of the prayer warrior underscores the directedness of their involvement, for they often pray *against* this or that, as if the prayer itself were doing (meta-)physical work. In this sense, praying looks more like an incantation than it does a mere petition to God for an intervention. For the very nature of an incantation is that it is a kind of recitation of a magical formula that is used to thwart oppressive powers and natural evils, sometimes by calling on a certain patron deity.[5] Such a prayer warrior sees herself as one whose effectiveness of prayer is directly proportional to the forcefulness of her words. The harder, the longer, and the louder she prays, and the more she "claims" in the name of the Lord, the more she can affect real change in the world. This sort of incantational approach to being a prayer warrior seems to have more in common with witchcraft and sorcery than a biblical spiritual warfare.

While prayer certainly involves the calling on God for his intercession in the afflictions on people's lives, it should not involve the practices of "claiming" or incanting. Yes, the prayer warrior is ideally one who is faithful, persistent, and sincere. God honors that (e.g., Mark 9:29). But it

---

3. The notion of "claiming" is not always clear. For some, it seems to mean something like reassuring oneself of a truth in that it brings about or implements some promise or consequence tied to that truth. E.g., Moore, *Praying God's Word*, 136–39, 284–85. Others think of "claiming" to mean something more active like "facilitating" or "bringing about" (e.g., Prince, *Secrets*, 202). In either case, "claiming" seems to involve some level of implementation.

4. E.g., Omartian, *Prayer Warrior*, 18.

5. Del Olmo Lete, *Incantations*, 4–7.

is not a guarantee of an outcome any more than is the petition for healing or for a change of circumstances. This should be obvious given that no less a prayer warrior than the apostle Paul was unable to bring about remedy from whatever his "thorn in the flesh" was (2 Cor 12:7–9). While immediate results may not obtain, I do believe God adds counsel and further spiritual resources to the one who is prayerfully engaged in opposing evil—perhaps even more so if the one praying also fasts (Matt 4:2; 6:18; Luke 2:37; Acts 13:2–3; 14:23). God strengthens our resolve and gives us the grace to endure our circumstances, even if being delivered from them should be denied us. Prayer is indispensable for the one who engages in it since it helps fortify the believer in her posture against any forces moving against her. The prayer warrior ought to be, then, one who is successfully, consistently, and repetitively seeking God's protection, remedy, and deliverance come what may. She also seeks it on behalf of others, even aggressively so. But she is also aware that, while complete deliverance may not be immediate, or to the expected level, God will see to it via his Holy Spirit that we can endure to the end. It is this result that attends to all our other practices of spiritual warfare, for only by the power of God can we overcome. These characteristics are noble, but they are muddied by the sensationalists and the super-duper-naturalists, who have redefined the prayer warrior as if she were in the House of Gryffindor at Hogwarts.

As for the spiritual effectiveness of praying out loud, we'll consider this in the next section.

SPEAKING ALOUD

When exorcists are dealing with a possession case, they generally will speak aloud either to gain power over the invader or to issue a command of expulsion. Such out-loud declarations, though not prayers in themselves, are then thought to be more effective precisely because demons could not otherwise hear these commands and adjurations. This is then encouraged by well-intentioned teachers and pastors who desire that folks emulate the mode of the exorcist in their prayer lives in their plight to find general spiritual relief from "the spiritual forces of evil in the heavenly places" (Eph 6:12c). Beth Moore, for example, encourages readers to "[t]urn to several chapters and pray a number of Scriptures . . . out loud if possible."[6] But she prefaces that her approach is not a "name-it-and-claim-it philosophy,"[7] by which she means that one is not speaking aloud in order to bring about material goods

---

6. Moore, *Praying God's Word*, 12.
7. Moore, *Praying God's Word*, 9.

like riches and fame. Joyce Meyer likewise offers this recommendation: "I recommend that you not only purposely think right thoughts, but that you go the extra mile and speak them aloud as your confession."[8] As for reading Scripture, she says: "Read them, then read them over aloud, and use them as weapons against the devil who is attempting to build a stronghold in your mind."[9] Meyer makes it explicit that speaking aloud serves as part of one's "weapons against the devil," but we are not told how verbalizing mitigates this "stronghold."

But what about the idea that it seems reasonable that commands must be verbalized so that demons have something to obey? If a demon cannot hear what we say, how can it know it's being expelled? Neil T. Anderson defends this point:

> We are to defend ourselves against the evil one by speaking aloud God's truth. Why is it so important to speak God's Word in addition to believing it and thinking it? Because Satan is a created being, and he doesn't perfectly know what you're thinking.[10]

And again:

> As you go through these steps to freedom, remember that Satan will be defeated only if you confront him verbally. He is under no obligation to obey your thoughts. Only God has complete knowledge of your mind. As you take each step, it is important that you submit to God inwardly and then resist the devil verbally by reading aloud each prayer and statement (James 4:7).[11]

Satan can't read your mind, so you must speak aloud if your words are to be efficacious.[12] Moreover, it is bound up in what it means in James 4:7's call to "resist the devil." Charles Kraft likewise emphasizes and defends the importance of verbalizing our commands:

> When we assert authority over children or animals, we usually do it vocally. We command what we expect to happen. It is important that we realize, in dealing with spiritual authority, that the spirit world is always listening. So we can speak out what we expect to that listening world, and know we are heard. A useful way of asserting our authority is simply to say something like this: "I speak [protection, blessing, healing, etc.] in the name

---

8. Meyer, *Battlefield of the Mind*, 34.
9. Meyer, *Battlefield of the Mind*, 128.
10. Anderson, *Bondage Breaker*, 84.
11. Anderson, *Bondage Breaker*, 186.
12. For more on whether Satan can read our minds or not, see appendix B.

of Jesus Christ." Asserting our authority vocally is easiest with demons.... Any command we utter, therefore, that relates to the activity of enemy spirits will be heard loud and clear by them. And if our command is in accord with what God wants to do, it will be done.[13]

Unlike Anderson and Kraft, it is unclear whether Moore and Meyer agree that speaking aloud is that by which external changes are brought about or merely that by which there is a sort of change made *in us* (say, to psychologically embolden ourselves in the act). Although Meyer seems to advocate speaking aloud in facilitating a direct victory in spiritual warfare (in what *seems* like an exorcistic model), she later suggests that speaking Scripture aloud serves the purpose of helping oneself to internalize certain truths.[14] By contrast, Anderson is clearer about the expulsive nature of speaking aloud. For it is about Satan's "obey[ing] your thoughts" by vocalizing them, which implies that thoughts have the power to, upon speaking them, alter states of affairs. Aside from my having reservations about Satan not being able to hear our thoughts (see appendix B), Anderson thinks resisting the devil is to be in part accomplished through a vocal exercise. (Incidentally, James 4:7 does not indicate anything about vocalizing Scripture; it only reports that we must "resist the devil, and he will flee from you.") And Kraft implies that there is indeed a mystical power of speech ("asserting our authority"), not in the citing of Scripture, but in the form of vocalized commands aimed at demons themselves—the kinds perhaps uttered by exorcists.

Scripture affords no special power in the vocalization of Scripture, much less commands aimed at enemy spirits barring what goes on in an actual exorcism. And while it is plausible that a demoniac must hear the commands issued by an exorcist, it does not follow that this must be how *unembodied* demons can and will respond in nonpossession cases. It should be acknowledged, however, that verbalizing Scripture can help comfort and embolden the speaker and victim alike. Nevertheless, the idea that one must chant aloud this or that verse or command as a means of directly warding off an unembodied demonic assault (whatever that looks like in each situation) relegates spiritual warfare to something akin to Eastern mantra-speaking and occult-like incantational spellbinding. It sets up the demonic world as a world of magic and our response as one of fighting fire

---

13. Kraft, *I Give You Authority*, 52–53.

14. Meyer writes: "I learned Scriptures about the love of God, and I meditated on them and confessed them out of my mouth. I did this over and over for months, and all the time the revelation of His unconditional love for me was becoming more and more of a reality to me" (*Battlefield of the Mind*, 160).

with fire by countering its black magic with the white magic of God. This seems to relegate God's will and means to act to a law-like relation with a creature's relevant verbalizations. That is, if the creature can invoke the right words (say, by praying aloud Scripture x instead of Scripture y or z), then, like connecting a copper conductor to a power source, God's expulsive and protective powers can be (predictably) realized. But if vocalization is a necessary condition in bringing about relief, then in no case would silent prayers against the demonic work. And if that is true, then persons who are mute could never ward off their afflicters—an implication that seems counterintuitive if not outright absurd. Moreover, it is much simpler of an approach to see power rooted in the omnipotence of God and to not treat words or language as though they themselves release a certain amount of preestablished magical power through which spiritual fortification can be implemented. That smacks of pagan sorcery pure and simple.

That demons need to hear the commands remains problematic. It is assumed that demons, which are purely immaterial beings, have the ability to physically hear human vocalizations. But that seems wrong when one considers what it means to hear anything. Hearing is the ear and brain's translation of certain vibrations being caused by certain frequencies distributed through an atmosphere. Purely spiritual beings cannot be acted upon by physical perturbations in the atmosphere. Demons lack any medium through which they would hear anything. If we suppose that they supernaturally translate human audio signals, then we are supposing that demons have a power with which to directly interact with the physical, which now greatly complicates the matter. We would need an argument for this. If, on the other hand, spiritual warfare works differently than through one's vocalizing of Scripture for earless beings to hear (!), then that model would have fewer metaphysical commitments in its favor. As it turns out, Scripture only features verbalizations against demons in the strict context of possession cases.[15] And that is precisely the sort of thing one would expect if demons cannot by nature hear.

Perhaps advocates of speaking aloud could insist that it isn't the demons' hearing the vocalized Scripture that brings about relief at all; rather, it is because one vocalizes Scripture that prompts *God* to act and move so as

---

15. It is worthy of note that in the episode of the itinerant Jewish exorcists (the seven sons of Sceva) (Acts 19:11–20), the invading demon confesses ignorance about the one who attempts to exorcise him from a demoniac. This is so despite the probability that this is not the first time the exorcist spoke. If that is so, the demon's ignorance is perplexing, for he should have heard him in the past. Quite likely the reason for his ignorance is because the demon is encountering the exorcist for the first time by inhabiting someone who *can* hear.

to bring about relief. Since God is omnipotent, he could easily arrange it so that human vocalizations are immediately apprehended by him. God, then, responds by warding off demonic oppressors if and only if the Christian has spoken aloud. But if this is how speaking aloud serves us in doing spiritual warfare, then it makes audibility a necessary condition of God's hearing of our prayers and recitations. However, as everyone recognizes, God certainly hears the prayers and recitations of his people whether they be silent or not uttered at all (Ps 44:21; Matt 6:8)! Since that is true, then speaking aloud to fortify oneself in spiritual warfare is not necessary. And since demons cannot, *per* their nature, hear anything, speaking aloud is also not useful. Therefore, speaking aloud is likely not a component of spiritual warfare even if it affords a certain amount of psychological comfort to those who choose to do so; and that may be all the reason they need for that occasion. But let us not make it a biblical feature of spiritual warfare proper.

"PRAYERWALKING"

C. Peter Wagner defines "prayerwalking" as believers "gathering in small groups and walking the streets of their neighborhoods praying for God's blessing in every way on what they see or what God brings to mind as they move along."[16] John Dawson stipulates that individuals not in groups can do this as well.[17] Dan Crawford offers up a more artsy even if somewhat vague understanding of the practice: "*Prayer walking is intercession on location with information in cooperation against opposition for glorification.*"[18] I take it that this means that to be present in person on location makes one aware of adverse (spiritual and physical) conditions that rupture the relationship between community and God. One then can intercede on behalf of that community for remedy. Steve Hawthorne and Graham Kendrick consider it to be a form of "citywide intercession" and that prayerwalkers typically "belong to the places they pray for."[19] So far, this is neither controversial nor mystical.

However, Hawthorne and Kendrick continue:

> Many Christians feel besieged by evil. Rising crime and open hostility to Christ appear to be energized by stubborn spiritual evil. Prayerwalking provides a way to wage some of the

---

16. Wagner, *Spiritual Warfare Strategy*, 38.
17. Dawson, "Foreword," 7.
18. Crawford, "Unceasing Intercession," 4; emphasis original.
19. Hawthorne and Kendrick, *Prayer-Walking*, 12–13.

necessary spiritual war with your feet literally on the ground. It makes biblical sense to step out from a defensive, fortress mentality and come physically near to the people whom we know God longs to redeem.[20]

They give the impression that *increased proximity* translates into *increased effectiveness*. It's noteworthy that one need not be in a constant state of motion, as it were, as if there was some special power in ambulation.[21] That isn't what makes prayerwalking successful. Instead, the point is to become personally ensconced in one's city and neighborhood to better focus one's prayers on what's really going on in those environments. But, other than for informational purposes, proximity itself certainly seems to be key for the increased effectiveness of intercessory prayer. To explain why, Hawthorne and Kendrick continue:

> Walking embellishes spoken petitions with an undeniable body language that can be read in the heavenlies. The act of walking emboldens pray-ers to push through feelings of futility and intimidation. Entrenched evil can post spiritual "No Trespassing" signs which seem to enforce the misery of the status quo. Prayerwalkers gently defy such fraudulent claims of darkness over their community.[22]

But, they caution, prayerwalking can also invite a counterattack, for it "can magnify the hassles and hazards of everyday spiritual war"[23] if one is not adequately prepared to do it. Nevertheless, it is one of the aims of prayerwalkers "to expose, limit or displace the power of evil forces,"[24] thereby making it an overt act of spiritual warfare. And this is not just accomplished supernaturally but also quite practically, for "[p]rayerwalkers find themselves in a position to meet divine appointments, in which the timing of encounters or events points toward a direction for prayer."[25]

There is something to be said about how the practice of prayerwalking helps to focus the one praying so she can "push through feelings of futility and intimidation." This is a psychological truth about what such a posture does for the human psyche. I can see that it serves a similar purpose as fasting does for one's prayer life. It isn't the act itself (walking or starving)

20. Hawthorne and Kendrick, *Prayer-Walking*, 13.
21. Hawthorne and Kendrick, *Prayer-Walking*, 30.
22. Hawthorne and Kendrick, *Prayer-Walking*, 18 (cf. 24).
23. Hawthorne and Kendrick, *Prayer-Walking*, 27.
24. Hawthorne and Kendrick, *Prayer-Walking*, 40.
25. Hawthorne and Kendrick, *Prayer-Walking*, 20.

that mystically overwhelms the powers of darkness; it is the act that brings clarity, focus, and persistence in one's prayer life. When one is ably focused and persistent, the ones praying will not be like the ones who are waffling in their stance or the "double-minded" (Jas 1:6–8), who implicitly disbelieve in the kinds of changes that God can bring about. For this reason, prayerwalking can be a good exercise to help solidify and ground the ones praying. If it is presumed that the act of walking itself somehow contributes to an expulsive power over demons, then such a presumption is false. As for proximation automatically driving out demonic forces, this is highly doubtful given the ubiquity of demonic activity within the Christian church. We've been told already that even Christians can be oppressed and that there are others further insisting that we can be fully demonized! So, so much for proximity.

Aside from the fact that there are no positive reasons to think that ambulation or proximity have a kind of mystical contribution to spiritual warfare, we should be concerned when Hawthorne and Kendrick say things like "[w]alking embellishes spoken petitions with an undeniable body language that can be read in the heavenlies." This gives the impression that something of the power of God gets mystically amplified through physical activity. And yet not all advocates of prayerwalking think this to be the case. Still, others think that prayerwalking, in addition to the aforementioned, may also effectively expel demons from spatial regions. As for potential problems with this last point, recall our previous discussion in the last chapter about territorial spirits (i.e., "Demon Possession Involves neither Places nor Objects").

Nevertheless, defenses of the practice do exist. In chapters 4–6 of their book, Hawthorne and Kendrick defend prayerwalking with Scripture. They suppose that prayerwalking was something done by Abraham, Joshua, and even Jesus himself. From what I can tell, they are simply relaxing their notion of "prayerwalking" in order to find, at best, incidental connections with the practice as they've defined it. It turns out that substantial differences do abound, thus making such comparisons of no use. Take the specific calling of Abraham, for example, to envision the land to be occupied by the future nations under one's spiritual care. This hardly equates to the contemporary prayerwalker praying in a local neighborhood. They loosely associate events like "public worship" and Abraham's call to "walk the land" that God had promised him and his descendants (Gen 13:17) as a type of forerunner to Christian prayerwalking.[26] It is such a stretch that one could, on similar grounds, preach about something like "prayer*diving*" by pointing to Peter's faithful plunge into the Sea of Tiberias in order to draw closer to Jesus in John 21:7; or "prayer*mudding*" as a way to seek physical healing like the

---

26. Hawthorne and Kendrick, *Prayer-Walking*, 44–5.

blind man who had mud put in his eyes by Jesus before washing in the pool of Siloam in John 9:6–11! Clearly, these are not foreshadowing future day-to-day Christian practices. As prayerwalking supporter Crawford honestly and rightly concludes, prayerwalking "does not appear in the Bible, nor does any person actually practice prayer walking as we know it."[27] The special and unique circumstances of people who are told or who take it upon themselves to "walk" for one reason or another cannot themselves serve as templates for Christian prayer life. The instructions on prayer do not include any need to be on site or to ambulate. The individual reasons for the walks of prophets of old served specific purposes associated with the destiny of God's people not suited for the modern-day Christian (i.e., no Christian will be promised to be the father of all nations; no Christian will be promised to collapse the walls surrounding a city destined for the occupation of God's people, etc.).

There is a further worry other than an apparent wizardification of praying here. If the mere act of being on site translates into a more effective prayer, such a notion may imply that the more distant one is from a locale, the less effective one's prayers may be. For example, if I thought for a moment that merely being there and praying in the region somehow wards off demonic spirits, I would run the risk of thinking that any of my prayers for those living in regions on the other side of the planet might be ineffective. Why think I can pray effectively for the citizens of Budapest, Hungary, or Bratislava, Slovakia if I am over five thousand miles away from them? Proximity is not the right gauge for the effectiveness of one's prayers. Instead, it is the *circumstances* of the one praying. The only thing an on-site visit can accomplish is instilling in us the right kind of focus and persistence in one's prayer life so that our prayers are more sincere and meaningful. Increased focus and clarity are always good things, but nothing about these things is magical.

That an on-site gathering bolsters the resolve and focus of the ones praying is psychologically undeniable. It's also beneficial in other ways since the ones praying can focus in on the area they are praying for with laser precision.[28] Apart from the personal disciplining and the appreciation those praying can experience, prayerwalking has no mystical element in its own right. Could that person have a "divine appointment" that night? Sure; and for that reason, the commission to *go out into the world and make disciples* (Matt 28:19–20) is what should motivate us to go out into our communities.

---

27. Crawford, "Unceasing Intercession," 5. For Crawford, this is not to say that the practice is *anti*-biblical, for there are many practices we do that are not openly endorsed in Scripture (i.e., closing one's eyes to pray). It is merely a contemporary accoutrement to a more effective intercessory prayer. However, "[w]hile prayer walking is not mentioned as such in the Bible, praying on location most clearly is mentioned" (10).

28. Something Hawthorne and Kendrick allude in *Prayer-Walking*, 45–46.

I just worry that prayerwalking might be construed by some to be a way to release God's power into the community and, by virtue of one's presence, to expel resident demons therein. And yet, neither of these things are what spiritual warfare involve. Nevertheless, like anyone else, I would never discourage the Christian from walking about and praying for those in their regions. It seems like a sensible practice for a variety of reasons—not the least of which is that praying *any* time is usually a good idea provided that one isn't doing it while, say, driving.

The saints need to pray. And it needs to be a primary practice for anyone who follows Christ. Since our primary foes are themselves spiritual, we cannot pretend that anything physical is sufficient to combat those forces. *We can't physically interact with demons; so, there is no other recourse.* Thus, a prepared life is a prayerful life. I will have more to say about the biblical contribution of prayer in the next chapter.

DEALING WITH CURSES

Scripture is filled with instances of curses. Sometimes it is ordinary persons who curse others. At other times, it is God himself who curses. These facts are not disputable by any Bible-believing Christian. But according to a wizardry model of spiritual warfare, there are situations where curses are sometimes passively and anonymously imposed. In these particular situations, they tend to be imposed as a consequence for having participated in some kind of demonic activity or malice—even if engaged in innocently or naïvely.[29] According to Bob Larson, one of Christian culture's most visible advocates of wizardry, curses can be arranged into two species: "implicit or unintentional" and "explicit or intentional."[30] Like Larson, others stud their models of spiritual warfare with frequent discussions about curses—usually of the "unbroken" and "generational" kind. They are "unbroken" if they are never identified and dealt with. They are "generational" if they have been

---

29. "Christians do not realize that curses have been placed on their lives" (Brown and Yoder, *Unbroken Curses*, 11). Brown and Yoder go on to discuss how those who participate in sinister activities bring curses upon themselves (e.g., 117–18). John Eckhardt seconds that notion in his *Identifying and Breaking Curses*. Bob Larson also suggests that curses can be anonymous and speaks (oddly) of them as "causeless curses" (*Curse Breaking*, 21). (His nomenclature here is attributed to Prov 26:2.) He also says that Satan himself can "pin" a curse on someone if "some current event in the person's life" obtains (ibid.) and that demons too can facilitate curses (36). Chris Ojigbani agrees and writes that curses can be unilaterally dished out not only by the devil but also "witches, occultists, and others" (*Spiritual Warfare*, 112).

30. Larson, *Curse Breaking*, ch. 1.

knowingly or unknowingly inherited by descendants. These curses can be over individuals and groups of people alike and the consequences for having them involve being supernaturally blocked from achieving some kind of moral, physical, or economic triumph.[31] Unless those curses are broken, one's condition will not change. Therefore, one must focus on breaking that curse in order to find ultimate victory.

The portrait of a curse according to a wizardry model gets even more controversial. It is here that the magical aspects of cursing are evident. For Larson speaks of "the inherent power of the words of a curse."[32] He also speaks of "ancient curses" that can be triggered by present-day circumstances. It would seem that curses are some kind of independent reality in much the same way a mental or physical illness is. If you are under the right circumstances with the right causal pathways, you can inherit a curse. Larson even says that one can receive a curse *through a blood transfusion or a donated organ*![33] This sort of transmigration of curses suggests that curses aren't just maledictions but that they have some kind of positive ontological status in the created order. That is, they're real things that have causal efficacy in the physical world, just like a virus or a bacterium, and seem to conform to law-like principles. That there is an "inherent power" of a curse further suggests if not downright implies that curses are something magical.

Once again there is a sort of blending of the not-so-controversial with the controversial. The relatively uncontroversial notion of a curse as on display here has to do with the fact that some curses are indeed generational and that they do adversely impact lives. But a well-grounded understanding will ultimately depend on a balanced assessment of what a curse is, specifically what a curse is in Scripture. Such an investigation will shave off the unnecessarily mystical elements being attributed to curses. And if we should disregard those more exotic descriptions, then dealing with curses will be less threatening and more practical (though not necessarily *easy*).

A biblical curse, though various in application, is minimally and universally something that is opposed to a blessing. Blessings are not things that enter into this or that family. And they certainly are not magical forces with an "inherent power" to promote wellness of body and soul. Instead, a blessing, in the biblical sense, is a benediction. That is, it is a declaration of something good that will or has fallen upon the one being blessed. They are often associated with the promises of God, whether of immediate and temporary concerns (such as prosperity and honor) or of lasting and ultimate

---

31. E.g., Eckhardt, *Deliverance*, 198ff.
32. Larson, *Curse Breaking*, 21.
33. Larson, *Curse Breaking*, 105–6.

concerns (such as beatitude). By contrast, a curse is a malediction. That is, it is a declaration or promise of something bad that has or will fall upon the one accursed. As James McKeown points out, blessings and curses have to do with the consequences of how one treats certain *relationships* in that they either support them or destroy them.[34] Blessings and curses are associated with covenant language. This is to say that those who violate their covenant with another will find themselves alone to suffer the ill consequences of a willful abandonment. For example, a citizen who violates a criminal law will be "cursed" to lose some of her benefits by the state. The blessed ones are those who will enjoy the promised fruits of maintaining that covenant relationship (e.g., Ps 37:22). Again, a citizen who obeys the law may enjoy certain privileges such as voting or acquiring a driver's license. All this is to say that there isn't anything mystical or magical or enchanting about a curse itself (or a blessing for that matter). And neither is it a standalone reality. Instead, a curse in God's commonwealth is an edict promising harsh consequences to those who find themselves outside of the will of God. There is nothing spellbinding about the edict itself; it is merely that which God declares will, all things being equal, come about.

A generational curse is nothing substantively different either. That someone would defy their covenantal relationship in such a way that would invite the consequences of that defiance onto one's descendants is nothing magical. It is no more magical than having an unsettled debt being passed on to the next of kin, thus burdening those to whom it is passed. As such, being a generational curse is merely a matter of description about the injuries of a contractual relation being passed on to the next generation. Consider the grandest curse of Scripture, where all of humanity and creation are alleged to be cursed due to Adam's original transgression (1 Cor 15:22; Rom 5:12; cf. Gen 3:17–19). This was not the imparting of some *thing* into Adam or creation (for Adam could have died at any time but was kept from doing so as long as he resided in God's company, as represented by the tree of life), it was the promise that, left to our own devices, we would no longer have the protections of God against the ravages of nature. Death would be inevitable.[35] But for those of us who enter into the new covenant under Christ,

---

34. McKeown, "Blessings and Curses," 84–85.

35. We could go on to point out that none of the other curses in Gen 3 were the imparting of new things not otherwise present. That women would have increased sorrow in rearing up children (Gen 3:16) is not due to the new presence of a thing, but the absence of living in harmony in God's fellowship. The same goes for the curse on the serpent, for he is condemned to go about on his belly—something serpents do anyway!—but in a new way that now emphasizes humiliation (v. 14). As for "the ground" (vv. 17–19), the curse has to do with the experience of "pain" in toiling for our food amidst "thorns and thistles"—not that thorns and thistles are something necessarily

we are on a trajectory to a blessed life that will once again be represented by the tree of life as a sign of the promise of immortality in God's company (Rev 22:14). The same can be said of Jesus's cursing of the fig tree (e.g., Mark 11:12–14). Again, he was not necessarily imparting something to the tree anything magical or mystical; he was likely pronouncing something that was inevitable for a fig tree: that, if it failed to produce figs in the spring, it would naturally not produce later in the year.[36] If its subsequent withering in verses 20–21 is indeed related to the curse, it may be nothing more than God's doing on this occasion. So, there was probably no law-like magic that was being tapped into in the cursing of the fig tree. Even if God acted specially on this occasion, this is the exception and not the rule.

Therefore, speculations about curses in a wizardry model of spiritual warfare make it sound like biblical curses are something akin to fabled Egyptian curses as often portrayed in mummy movies. This is to see curses as something like literal bad luck being supernaturally visited on those who would disturb the tombs of pharaohs. But biblical curses are nothing of the sort. As maledictions instead of benedictions, they are pronouncements of ill consequences on those who distance or dissociate themselves from a covenantal relationship. Even worse for wizardry models, curses (generational or otherwise) are not themselves features of spiritual warfare. Nowhere in the key biblical texts dealing directly with spiritual warfare do we find calls to end or break curses.[37] However, we *are* called to virtue over vice and truth over falsehood. We can define a generational curse innocuously as the sins or the consequences of the sins of ancestors being conditioned in and repeated by their descendants. It would be like one's family lineage being cursed with poverty and debt, wherein one generation's woes are bequeathed to the next generation. If the newer generation did not break this curse by surmounting their impoverished status, or by receiving a financial rescue from a benefactor, then the curse may persist. The same goes for the gift of salvation in Christ being given us in the wake of our being cursed

---

added to creation, but that they are something that will now become a *problem* for creation. The maledictions of Gen 3 are more likely promises of certain consequences that will ensue because of disobedience and rebellion.

36. Craig Keener explains: "On the eastern side of the Mount of Olives, fig trees could already have leaves at Passover season (late March or early April). They did not yet, however, have ripe figs; they had only green early figs, which did not taste good. They could ripen in June, but often fell off beforehand, so that only leaves remained. If a tree had leaves but produced no early figs, it would remain fruitless that year" (*NIV Cultural Backgrounds Study Bible*, 1712).

37. Although we could loosely say that one's donning the "helmet of salvation" (Eph 6:17) breaks the curse of death, so to speak. But this is far from what wizardry models mean by their notion of a curse.

with death as a consequence for our sin. Such an understanding of curses accommodates, if it is not implied by, all of the biblical data on the subject without the extravagant baggage of demonic wizardry. If two (or more) explanations are available in how one ought to understand a given concept, the simplicity and familiarity of one explanation should be preferred in the absence of any mitigating reasons to think otherwise. So, if we must otherwise settle for something more extraordinary and less familiar when it comes to understanding curses, we will need an argument for it. Otherwise, as it stands, breaking a generational curse is probably the usual story of us becoming a new creation in Christ and our putting off the old self in the pursuance of virtue (2 Cor 5:17; Eph 4:22–24). This is not an argument resting on some kind of anti-supernaturalist bias,[38] for I have none. Rather, it is an appropriate epistemic approach that imposes a burden of proof on notions that are more complex and less familiar than widely available and simpler alternatives. From what I can tell, breaking the curse of sin in our lives is nothing magical, but it's surely momentous!

TAKING AUTHORITY OVER EVIL SPIRITS[39]

There is one final component to what I have been calling a "wizardry model" of spiritual warfare. It involves the notion of Christians taking authority over evil spirits. Though I must state, out of fairness, that there is once again a germ of truth that is being lost through the wizardry advocate's embellishments and exaggerations. Luke's report, from which much speculation about this is derived, is benign in its own right:

> And [Jesus] called the twelve together and gave them power and authority over all demons and to cure diseases, and he sent them out to proclaim the kingdom of God and to heal. (9:1–2)

Jesus underscores this report in the next chapter:

> Behold, I have given you authority to tread on serpents and scorpions, and over all the power of the enemy, and nothing shall hurt you. Nevertheless, do not rejoice in this, that the

---

38. Construing curses as consequences to covenants set up by God is no less supernatural given that *God* is the architect of those consequences. It is the complexity and unfamiliarity of curses as defined by wizardry models of spiritual warfare that is being challenged in the present criticism.

39. In some quarters it is an extension of a practice known as "taking dominion"—not to be confused with the political ideology of dominion theology.

spirits are subject to you, but rejoice that your names are written in heaven. (10:19–20)

It is evident that the immediate disciples were given the authority in Christ to expel demons and to perform healings. However, they are not to take pride in their authority to expel demons from the afflicted but to take comfort in the fact that they, through no self-saving ritual of their own, belong to Christ and his kingdom, from whom that authority derives. It is a reminder that the endgame for these disciples is not *eminence* but *evangelism* (cf. Matt 18:1–6). As for whether this authority extends to *all* disciples throughout history (cf. Matt 28:18–20 and John 14:12), we will simply table that controversy in the light of focusing our attention on better understanding what that authority is (for if this is not intended for all disciples, then the discussion is moot). Let's just suppose, then, that Jesus's words here apply even to those of us in the twenty-first century. If such a supposition still rules out the feasibility of a wizardry model, then it matters not whether taking authority is in perpetuity today. The real problem besetting wizardry models, as I will argue, is their *interpretation* of such authority for these or any disciples of Christ throughout history.

For starters, there is a hasty equation made between the "authority" of exorcism in Luke 9:1 and the practice of modern-day deliverance exorcism in believers. Larson presses for this when he, without argument, associates "taking authority" with Jesus's expulsion of the "strong man" in Matthew 12:25–29:

> [Y]ou need to *take authority over the strongman* in a concerted way . . . [Y]ou need to locate and go after the strongman who has engineered the unwelcome superstructure inside you. You may have to wear down some of his minions first, but eventually you need to go after the one who is calling the shots. Once you have weakened and dismantled the work of the evil one inside, your spiritual warfare praying will be unbound and powerful.[40]

Ron Phillips echoes a similar notion: "Command the spirit of infirmity to leave. After taking authority, take deep breaths until you feel rest in your body and soul."[41] Kraft adds to "taking authority" the implementation of

---

40. Larson, *Demon-Proofing Prayers*, 166. *Contra* Larson, while it is indeed exorcism that motivates Jesus's analogy of the "strong man" in Matt 12, the analogy is not directly describing a state of affairs within a singular person (refer to our discussion on "Armor" in chapter 11). Indeed, the "strong man's house" does not itself represent a possession victim's body; it represents the *populated world* under Satan's rule.

41. Phillips, *Everyone's Guide*, 130.

territorial exorcisms, the elimination of diseases, and even the controlling of weather:

> [W]e are to exercise our authority in the same areas in which Jesus ministered—in sickness, death, blessing, deliverance from demons, forgiveness (John 20:23) . . . Asserting our authority vocally is easiest with demons. They can answer back. But when we command illness to stop or weather to change, it is much less obvious that our words have been heard, especially when the change we have commanded does not take place immediately.[42]

Apparently, both natural and supernatural forces are subservient to our (aloud) assertions of authority over them. So understood, one appears to have a certain kind of power of words in our "asserting authority" in both the immaterial and material worlds. For Kraft, one literally inherits the powers of Christ over such worlds. In Larson's case, when you take on members of the immaterial world, you engage in the spiritual equivalent of hand-to-hand combat (for you must "wear down" the opponent ahead of any "spiritual warfare praying"). (Cue the theme from *Rocky*.) Like the climactic scene between Harry Potter and Voldemort in *Harry Potter and the Deathly Hallows*, Christians are to wield their Christ-inherited blocking/banishment spells against their foes in the hopes of driving back the devil and his cohorts.

"Oh, but the power is *Christ's* and not *ours!*" someone might object. Nevertheless, the invocation of Christ's power in the ways suggested by Larson and Kraft still has a sort of law-like tendency that mimics that of what allegedly happens when sages mix reagents or witches pronounce hexes. There is an assumption that having done x we should expect y. The Christian crosses her fingers in the hopes that her "good magic" will finally win over the "dark magic" leveled against her. As long as the Christian endures and perseveres to the end in countering such demonic forces through the various ways of implementing Christ's power, her victory is assured. But should the Christian waver, the demons' dark magic will prevail, and it will take more than the kiss of a princess to change you back.

When we turn to Scripture, this is not what biblical spiritual warfare looks like. We do not find any of this either in the practice of the disciples or the teachings given in the Epistles. The extraordinary powers that Christ himself exhibits are understandable since he is God. Human beings are not. Yes, believers do partake of the divine nature (2 Pet 1:4), but not in the unqualified sense that everything God is and does is at our disposal through incantation. That the authority over spirits has been conferred to

---

42. Kraft, *I Give You Authority*, 49 and 52.

his disciples is no indication that any person has God's ability to manipulate physics. The disciples' authority over evil spirits is to be understood as a *legal* matter, not a thaumaturgical (i.e., magical) one. This authority is as the authority of the good servant who had "authority over ten cities" (Luke 19:17). It wasn't a *magical ability* over those cities; it was a *jurisdiction*. Christ is the king and in him the kingdom of God had come to the people. When we enter his dominion, then our status in Christ will far exceed (positionally) that of Satan. We inherit that elevated authority. We, as a kingdom of priests, are then authorized to call upon Christ in the pursuance of having God's will be done on earth as it is in heaven. It is not an authority to say the right thing to causally alter reality.

Even if one thinks that chanting this or that might automatically ward off demons in the area, there remains the problem that demons are purely immaterial beings. Consequently, they would not (apart from appropriating human ears in a possession case) be able to hear what we say anyway. Speaking to an unembodied demon to depart the area would be as meaningful as using sign language to someone who is blind. And, as discussed elsewhere,[43] how unembodied demons could be in any unpopulated area anyway is metaphysically challenging, for only material things can occupy spatial coordinates. It is simpler to suppose that demons do not reside in unpopulated spatial regions but that, if they reside anywhere at all, they only do so in and through the individuals and people groups they attach themselves to. So, even if demons could somehow hear someone, they still could not be in any spatial location that does not already have at least one human being through which to have any contact with the region. Therefore, there are multiple reasons why there is no sensible way "taking authority" means the bewitchment of demons or their (atmospheric) expulsion from unpopulated regions at the hands of Christian enchanters. Properly understood, authority—the kind that one can "take"—is nothing magical.

CONCLUSION

In this chapter, we have taken on what I have called a "wizardry model" of spiritual warfare. While it is not a systematized theological model, the individual practices covered overlap in that they intimate much of the same methodologies found in witchcraft and occultism. We looked at radical notions of prayer along with radical notions of speaking and commanding

---

43. For more on why being immaterial excludes the possibility of being spatially localizable, see our discussion on "God Is Immaterial" (51–53), "Demon Possession Involves neither Places nor Objects" (159–162), and appendix C, "On Territorial Spirits."

certain things aloud in order to bring about spiritual and physical relief. While there are some elements to these practices Christians should take seriously, most of it ends up being a vestige of the kinds of mystical dualism we find in occultic mythologies.

This chapter effectively ends our interaction with models of spiritual warfare that tend to misunderstand what spiritual warfare is really about. In the next chapter, we shall explore a model of spiritual warfare that, I think, is a fair codification of what the Bible has to say. It is my attempt at systematizing everything we have learned up to now, including our understanding of all of the various warfare passages and what those passages do *not* mean when brought together. Accordingly, I am not actually offering a new model as much as I am offering a philosophically informed way to think about spiritual warfare. That the warfare is real seems right. That it involves exorcism and/or acts of wizardry seems wrong. Instead, it may not be a matter of doing something *against our enemies* as much as it is doing something *for ourselves* in actively pursuing living the life of a Jesus-follower.

18

Spiritual Warfare as the Examined Life Worth Defending

WE HAVE THUS FAR addressed some reasons to think that spiritual warfare is not mythology, mostly on the grounds that it does not account for the portions of Scripture that communicate or imply demonic realism. This is important because if demons *do* exist and such a view accords well with the main objectives the mythologists believe is the Christian's role in spiritual warfare, then we should probably turn to a realist model for a better way to implement those objectives. In turning to realist models of spiritual warfare, we encountered a different set of challenges—some theological and some philosophical. We first looked at exorcistic models of spiritual warfare that incorporate strategies of exorcism (i.e., territorial exorcisms and deliverance exorcisms). Their reliance on dubious assumptions and incoherent premises, not to mention that they coopt an exorcistic strategy not otherwise taught in Scripture, make these unlikely candidates for how one should engage the various demonic threats. We then examined wizardry models where, despite the modest psychological benefits for participants, such models traffic in superstition and metaphysical absurdity. Together, among the many reasons already given in objecting to both models, these would unduly burden the Christian to *identify* when demons are empirically present—something that cannot be done outside of clear-cut possession cases or perhaps through harassments internal to oneself. But this leaves us with a vacuum. What *is* a reasonable and biblically sound model of spiritual warfare, if not any of these?

We should expect that whatever ends up being a correct understanding of spiritual warfare, it will not be substantively different than how spiritual warfare would have been carried out during Old Testament times.[1] That is, it would be odd to think that demons act and behave differently in the Old Testament than they do in the New, or that God's people engage in certain practices and remedies in times of spiritual conflict differently between the Testaments. If the Gospels and Epistles provide us new and dramatic ways to stand our ground, why would these instructions come so much later than the Old Testament? Did not demons tempt and assault human beings in the pre-Christian world like they did in the first century? If the New Testament reveals exorcism and wizardry as the right remedies for demonic assaults, one would be remiss to ignore why no such instructions were given in the Old Testament. Instead, what we find are constant calls to knowing and discerning God's word (Deut 4:1–2; 18:18–22; 30:11–16; Ps 85:8) and to living lives of unremitting holiness (Exod 19:6; Lev 11:44–45; Deut 28:9). These are the things that enabled God's elect to stand against the foes—whether earthly or not—of God. It is more reasonable to suppose that any viable model of spiritual warfare will take into consideration the heart of spiritual warfare as hinted at by our pre-Christian predecessors.

In this chapter, we shall thus consider a better way to understand spiritual warfare by integrating both what Scripture has to say and what philosophy can support. For philosophy is among those disciplines that embodies what it means to have a reasonable approach. I will identify this project—a philosophically informed model of spiritual warfare I shall argue for—as *the examined life worth defending*. This designation is based on a famous statement uttered by Socrates near the end of his trial ("the unexamined life is not worth living").[2] For Socrates, a life is otherwise "unexamined" if it is

---

1. This is not to say that there are *no* differences whatsoever. For, clearly some of the external details are different (e.g., certain ceremonial rites are changed or eliminated in the wake of Jesus's fulfillment of the Law). While the *details* of spiritual warfare may have changed with respect to the shift from Law to grace, its *essence* did not. Analogously, the need for atonement remained constant between the Testaments (the essence of salvation) while the details of atonement surely changed (i.e., the sacrifice of unblemished animals was replaced by the sacrifice of Jesus, which amply fulfilled what the animal sacrifices merely anticipated).

2. Socrates lived from 470 to 399 BC and is considered one of Western society's most iconic and influential philosophers. The city in which he lived, Athens, Greece, was posturing itself as the whole package in terms of being both a military giant and the intellectual center of the known world. When the Athenian leaders, as corrupt as they were, failed to conquer their enemies in pursuit of such vainglory, they looked to the rank and file in Athens for someone to blame (after all, no politician was going to blame himself!). Socrates was a known teacher, but he was not known for teaching in a good way. He was a sort of philosophical journalist who would constantly challenge the

a life that is unwilling to submit to philosophical, and therefore reasonable, reflection. And a "life ... not worth living" refers to a life that is otherwise devoid of virtue. Altogether, it is a rebellious life that refuses to be shaped and groomed by wisdom in order to be virtuous and, so, becomes a life that no longer has the right kind of value as its objective. Hence, by incorporating the Socratic language here, I am coopting the phrase "the examined life" as one that considers intellectual reflection and honest study to be at the heart of the Christian vis-à-vis spiritual warfare. My change to the latter part, a "life worth *defending*," is meant to anticipate the notion that the Christian is in a state of war with a spiritual opposition. I am not merely saying that the Christian life is worth *living*, but that such a life is more than that—it is worth *fighting for*. We are fighting the spiritual forces that oppose us. So, what does this mean?

One thing it means is that while Satan and his demons are the *de facto* villains in God's universe, such villains ought not to be the *focus* of one's combat lest we fall prey to the "demon hunting" problem addressed back in chapter 16. This is all to say that the life of a Christian, both individually and collectively, must be intentionally guarded and preserved against demonic opposition. But not directly, for we oppose them by countering their intellectual and moral contrariety—the usual weapons of demonic attack.

To live the life worth defending, we do not even have to be aware of the aggressors involved (or not). We can oppose ideas and falsehoods without needing to know exactly who is perpetrating them just like we can oppose anonymous emails sent to us that keep pushing misinformation. To think that victory can only come when one is *conscious* of such beings is to also dismiss the spiritual victories had by Old Testament prophets and

---

powers that be to defend the intellectual and moral ideals that gave rise to their seemingly corrupt form of government. It would appear that the children in Athens were, in fact, warm to his teachings.

Hence, by the time he reached his seventies, he was arrested and brought to trial. The charges? He was accused of "atheism," "corrupting the youth," and "irritating the masses." A simple examination of the teachings of Socrates easily reveals he was doing neither. (Though, by Socrates's own admission, he might have been guilty of "irritating the masses," it was not a crime to do so but, rather, was an edict of God.) The charges were bogus at worst and trumped up at best. Nevertheless, the Athenian leaders had found their scapegoat, for Socrates had the stench of one who was inciting ideological division and undermining the very moral fabric of what the leaders stood for. After Socrates was judged guilty by a democratic vote, he assures his fellow Athenians that his work in Athens is a higher calling—that he has been sent by the gods to challenge them to foster true knowledge and virtue in the region. This, to Socrates, is a far greater mission than the preservation of one's physical life. Accordingly, he pronounces that by contrast "the unexamined life is not worth living." And, for this reason, Socrates will gladly accept for himself the sentence of execution if this is what the jury ultimately decides.

patriarchs, who had very little to say about demons. Indeed, the focus of spiritual warfare ought to be on one's own growth and endurance in one's reliance upon God. This reflects the paths of Abraham, King David, et al., for they did not overtly engage in magical or physical confrontations with demons. From what we can learn from our scriptural predecessors, our own growth and endurance are what are important, as Jesus himself makes it clear that the straying of even *one* saint is cause for pursuit and rehabilitation (Matt 18:12–14). No nobler cause than one's spiritual preservation can be imagined. As such, every spiritual life devoted to God, whether we are cognizant of demons directly or not, is what is worth defending.

In what follows we will positively explore what it means for the Christian to be involved in spiritual warfare. I submit that this involves focusing on two main pillars of what I consider the life worth defending: knowledge (against falsehood) and virtue (against vice). These pillars are not mere acknowledgements or matters of head knowledge; they are *practices*. Let us take knowledge first. Knowledge is not the sort of thing that is some passive acknowledgement of some doctrine or teaching since "even the demons believe—and shudder" (Jas 2:19; cf. vv. 14–26). By educating a demon, presumably you just get a smarter demon. Rather, the kind of knowledge in mind here is one that, first and foremost, derives from rightly handling the source of that knowledge (2 Tim 2:15). Secondly, it is to be immersive and personal, which is why the teaching process often involved a more ongoing, relational kind of learning: *discipleship*. To be a disciple is not to be a mere pupil but to be a *follower*. And then there is virtue, which is also not the mere passive pursuit of head knowledge about right and wrong. Instead, we must diligently learn about *all* the virtues that serve to inch us closer to godliness. And to know them is to implement them. For merely knowing about the virtues is not to *be* virtuous. No doubt demons know to some extent what is right and wrong, and yet they deliberately choose wickedness. Knowledge and virtue are both active enterprises and matters we must take seriously as comprising the life worth defending.

I will thus explain and defend this model both theologically and philosophically by first considering its calls to knowledge and virtue as key elements to an integrative model of spiritual warfare: the life worth defending. After that, we will take a look at how such a model effectively positions the Christian to respond to and oppose demonic adversity.

KNOWLEDGE: STUDY TO SHOW YOURSELF APPROVED

One can have knowledge without its being in any way conducive to a worthwhile life. For example, one can have extensive knowledge of mathematics or wood carving and these would not themselves be avenues to having a life of value. For a wood-carver or a mathematician could certainly use their newfound knowledge to harass or bully others with their talents. Contrary to what many ancient Greeks thought, knowledge is not itself enough to guarantee the good life. The same is true of Scripture. There, it is not the mere acquisition of knowledge as such that is championed, but it is having knowledge *of Christ* (John 17:3; 1 Cor 1:18–24) and Scripture (2 Tim 2:15; 3:16–17) that is specified. Likewise, we don't want to be so naïve as to imply that a mere *lack* of knowledge (of Christ) is, on the contrary, the source of all ills. In Ephesians 4:18, Paul seems to credit one's hardness of heart as a cause of, or something at least linked to, an ignorance that leads to spiritual alienation from God. Neither ignorance nor head knowledge are in themselves what make for a worthwhile life or the lack thereof.

Nevertheless, knowledge is indeed linked to other properties that, when combined, do co-constitute a worthwhile life. For example, devotion to God is a central feature of the Christian walk. But it is implied in our having knowledge of Christ because such knowledge, particularly according to the chosen Greek term, *ginōskō*, is not mere intellectual assent (Jas 2:19) but a *dedication* and *faithfulness* to the person of Christ. It is a life of devotion and loyalty. And one cannot be dedicated or faithful to someone unless she *knows* about him intimately and carefully, for it would not be knowing someone properly if you believed the person to be something he was not. For example, if you believed that the two people you had thought were your parents were in fact fraudsters (merely hoaxing the role of being your parents, such as what we find Rooster and Lily doing in the musical *Annie*), then you would be less inclined to be dedicated or loyal to them. It would be clear you did not know them after all.

In this sense knowledge is both personal and transformative. So, we might say that it isn't mere knowledge *per se* that is being touted but, more accurately and more fully, *wisdom*. For Jesus is in fact "the wisdom of God" (1 Cor 1:24, 30). When we speak of wisdom, we're doing more than proffering a certain level of knowledge. We're actually imposing an ethical standard on the knowledge in question. That is, when knowledge is utilized appropriately and productively in promoting righteousness, we have wisdom. The wise person who has knowledge is not wise simply because she has amassed a certain amount of informational content from her teacher but because she now knows how to act on and respond to destructive principles and practices that her teacher has overcome. The ancient Greco-Roman world well understood that instruction involved a change of one's previous lifestyle into one that echoed the teacher's. Teaching was always expected to lead to changes in the student's behavior. This much is evident in Ephesians 4:23–24, wherein Paul links being "renewed in the spirit of your minds" with the "put[ting] on the new self." Indeed truth, which is an essential property of knowledge, is what makes possible our unity in Christ (v. 25). Thus, the reason why the wisdom of God is superior to any would-be wisdom of the world (1 Cor 1:18–31) is because the gospel in its countercultural simplicity offers an authentic fulfillment of life in righteousness whereas the knowledge of the world offers only death (or nothing that would avert it) in sin. Knowledge of and communion with Christ fulfills what it means to be in the image of God—beings who strive to be fulfilled in body, mind, and spirit. So, by way of summary thus far, the right kind of knowledge is wisdom. And the wise person ought to choose Christ and to know him more fully.

Now, we needn't speculate about how knowledge as Christian wisdom might be significant in the fight against spiritual forces in the heavenly realms. Scripture's instructions to the body of Christ make this clear enough, especially in the context of spiritual warfare. While we could revisit all of the spiritual warfare passages discussed in Part II of this book, it is sufficient to highlight the more prevalent ones. Consider first Paul's statements in 2 Corinthians 10:3–6:

> For though we walk in the flesh, we are not waging war according to the flesh. For the weapons of our warfare are not of the flesh but have divine power to destroy strongholds. We destroy arguments and every lofty opinion raised against the knowledge of God, and take every thought captive to obey Christ, being ready to punish every disobedience, when your obedience is complete.

A number of Christians are, unfortunately, content to end at verse 4 ("For the weapons of our warfare are not of the flesh but have divine power to destroy strongholds") and prefer, instead, to speculate without context about what these "weapons" are. We might imagine that territorial exorcism or speaking aloud might be enlisted as two of them. However, as verses 5–6 suggest, the "weapons" are to be associated with that which "destroy[s] arguments and every lofty opinion raised against the knowledge of God" and that which "punish[es] every disobedience." Arguments are not destroyed by any mystical or occultic powers one might muster. Arguments are defeated by rebuttals. And rebuttals are only as good as the truths they point to. Arguments are implied by Scripture to be understood in or analogous to a legal context (Job 23:1–7; Prov 25:9; Isa 43:26)—in the sense that one attempts to support a conclusion based on premises (i.e., reasons). This is something Paul teaches elsewhere. For example, he tells the Colossians to "reach all the riches of full assurance of understanding and the knowledge of God's mystery, which is Christ . . . in order that no one may delude you with plausible arguments" (Col 2:2, 4). Two chapters later he says to "[l]et your speech always be gracious, seasoned with salt, so that you may know how you ought to answer each person" (Col 4:6)—a message that is echoed elsewhere by Peter, who insists that readers should "always [be] prepared to make a defense to anyone who asks you for a reason for the hope that is in you; yet do it with gentleness and respect" (1 Pet 3:15). Even in Jude's small contribution he makes sure to push his readers "to contend for the faith that was once for all delivered to the saints" (Jude 3). In short, the weapons of our warfare have to do with our informed responses to challenges and falsehoods.

In the Old Testament, God himself utilizes reason to motivate people to do what is right (Isa 1:18). And God knows that an honest exchange of arguments will indeed reveal the truth (Isa 43:26). In the New Testament, Paul himself modeled what he said in 2 Corinthians 10 when, in Athens, "he reasoned in the synagogue with the Jews and the devout persons, and in the marketplace every day with those who happened to be there" (Acts 17:17). While he was there, he even managed to demolish a pagan argument or two. For "[s]ome of the Epicurean and Stoic philosophers also conversed with him" and accused him of being "a preacher of foreign divinities" (v. 18). When Paul arrived at the Areopagus, his response to their pushback was to cite the resurrection of Jesus as the basis of his "assurance" (v. 31). In fact, it is the resurrection of Jesus that figures predominantly in Paul's apologetic to the Corinthians (1 Cor 15:3–9) in his attempts to convince them that there is a resurrected life after death (vv. 12–14). It is no surprise that Paul's reasoning with his interlocutors was a constant mainstay in his ministry (Acts 17:2, 17; 18:4, 19; 24:25). Arguments give good support and good support leads to positive change.

As such, it isn't just argumentation that is to be extolled in spiritual warfare. It is the *truth* that is being preserved in that argumentation that stands out as the overall way we stand our ground against the forces of darkness. First Timothy 4 makes it very clear that "in later times some will depart from the faith by devoting themselves to deceitful spirits and teachings of demons" (v. 1). Clearly, heresy that leads to deconversion is a serious matter. What is the recommended response to this? It isn't to perform a territorial exorcism or to chant away any demons. Instead, it is the practice of "being trained in the words of the faith and of the good doctrine that you have followed" (v. 6). And, so, the good servant is instructed to "devote yourself to the public reading of Scripture, to exhortation, [and] to teaching" (v. 13). Only then can truth be acquired so as to become useful in combating the "teachings of demons."

To the Ephesians Paul declares that we are "to equip the saints for the work of ministry" (Eph 4:12), an equipping that is clarified in 2 Timothy 3:16–17 to be "Scripture [which] is breathed out by God and profitable for teaching, for reproof, for correction, and for training in righteousness, that the man of God may be complete, equipped for every good work." The Scriptures themselves serve as the way to both equip and complete "the man of God . . . for every good work." Such attention to scriptural content helps believers to not be "tossed to and fro by the waves and carried about by every wind of doctrine, by human cunning, by craftiness in deceitful schemes" (Eph 4:14)—schemes that are, two chapters later, said to be of the devil (6:11). It is no wonder that Scripture reading was one of the essential attributes of church gatherings in that "they devoted themselves to the apostles' teaching and the fellowship, to the breaking of bread and the prayers" (Acts 2:42). Accordingly, failure to care for one's doctrine as well as the teaching platform amounts to one's being a participant in wickedness:

> Everyone who goes on ahead and does not abide in the teaching of Christ, does not have God. Whoever abides in the teaching has both the Father and the Son. If anyone comes to you and does not bring this teaching, do not receive him into your house or give him any greeting, for whoever greets him takes part in his wicked works. (2 John 1:9–11)

Knowledge and truth acquired by faithful and diligent study are indeed "the weapons of our warfare," for they insulate us from one of the primary weapons in the devil's arsenal: falsehoods that promote apostasy and vice.

Charles Haddon Spurgeon sums up beautifully the role knowledge of Scripture has in the life lived in spiritual warfare:

> The only way to repel Satan's subtlety is *by acquiring true wisdom* . . . If you would successfully wrestle with Satan, make the Holy Scriptures your daily commune. Out of this sacred Word continually draw your armor and ammunition. Lay hold upon the glorious doctrines of God's Word; make them your daily meat and drink. So shall you be strong to resist the devil, and you shall be joyful in discovering that he will flee from you.[3]

---

3. Spurgeon, *Spiritual Warfare*, 37.

However, ignorance and falsehood are not the *only* weapons at Satan's disposal. As we are painfully aware, Satan is branded as the tempter (Matt 4:3; 1 Tim 3:5). Accordingly, Scripture calls on the saints to pursue holiness, not just because it is an ideal fulfillment of who we are, but because the more we make holiness a lifestyle, the less likely temptation will overtake us. Indeed, holiness is the other pillar of spiritual warfare and the subject of the next section.

HOLINESS: BE PERFECT AS YOUR FATHER IN HEAVEN IS PERFECT

Abstract virtue is not quite how the New Testament frames Christian living. Rather, it speaks of "holiness" (2 Cor 7:1), "righteousness" (1 John 2:29), "godliness" (2 Pet 1:3), and "sanctification" (1 Thess 4:3). These things impose on us a standard of living that is far loftier than one of mere virtue. (I'll simply use the term "holiness" as involving all of these aspects of Christian virtue.) It is certainly manageable for a member of the human race to exhibit *some* amount of virtue according to the canons of Greek philosophy. But such virtue for the Greek did not necessarily exclude an occasional dip into sensuality. For Plato, it was more important that one was not *ruled* by her passions in observing that rightful hierarchy where the mind ought to be regarded over the body.[4] So, sure, go ahead and indulge a bit, but always temper the appetites so as not to be governed by them. As for Aristotle, virtue was not some lofty standard but, more modestly, a moral state that should conduce to our teleology (a fulfillment of the kind of thing we are designed to be) as rational animals.[5] We are thus courageous, not because it conforms to some supreme, transcendent standard of valor, but because it is the right balance between utter cowardice and unbridled foolhardiness. It is the reasonable position of a prudent person who knows that there is a time to fight and a time to flee.

Christian virtue, on the other hand, is something stronger. The standard for Christians set forth in Scripture, as expressed by Jesus himself, is to "be perfect, as your heavenly Father is perfect" (Matt 5:48). While "perfect" (*teleioi*) may be best translated as "complete," it still communicates a totality of being utterly without blemish (cf. Lev 22:21). Being completely unblemished is, in fact, an aspect of the teleology of the Christian (Eph 1:4). As such, our moral objective is a divine objective. But it is not an objective that anyone can reasonably attain on her own (Isa 64:6–7; Rom 3:10). No one

4. Plato, *Republic*, IX.
5. Aristotle, *Nicomachean Ethics*, II.

can be supremely good but God (Mark 10:18). Thus, it will take no one less than God to guide us in the striving for holiness (Rom 5:19).

Theologians call this striving "sanctification" after the Latin word *sanctus*, which means "holy." Though Christians differ over precisely how this process obtains, all are in agreement that God is fundamentally responsible for the progressive holiness and ultimate perfection they will achieve in Christ (Rom 6:22). Expressed in other ways, Scripture is filled with instructions and admonitions about living a life of virtue and holiness (e.g., Prov 4:14–15; Rom 12:1–2; 1 Pet 1:15–16). But salient to the present conversation is the fact that such a lifestyle specifically helps protect believers from demonic ensnarement. We're speaking, of course, of *reputation* brought on by character (=a virtuous lifestyle). Once the Christian sustains a life of holiness, her good reputation naturally proceeds such that there are fewer falsehoods that can be directed against her that could bring her down. But it begins with genuinely practicing holiness and not faking it (cf. Matt 6:1–4). For example, Paul tells Timothy that one of the requirements to be an overseer involves his being "well thought of by outsiders, so that he may not fall into disgrace, into a snare of the devil" (1 Tim 3:7). And this is brought about by the overseer's genuine commitment to be

> above reproach, the husband of one wife, sober-minded, self-controlled, respectable, hospitable, able to teach, not a drunkard, not violent but gentle, not quarrelsome, not a lover of money. He must manage his own household well, with all dignity keeping his children submissive. (vv. 2–4)

This is what the virtuous overseer does, not as a way to *be* virtuous but that *because* he is virtuous he will do these things. For the overseer is expected to be someone who has mastered the virtues and, so, exhibits the right kind of reputation that immunizes him from public disgrace.[6] Christian leaders today should take note, for it looks like Satan's weapon of choice for many overseers today is this very thing!

Practicing holiness is not an elitist thing as if something only the upper echelon need pay attention to. Parishioners are no less encouraged to

---

6. The best modern example is, unfortunately, that of the late Ravi Zacharias. It is unquestionable that Zacharias had some of the knowledge (but perhaps not the wisdom) part down, but he seems to have fallen prey to moral failures that precipitated and fed his being an alleged sexual predator of all kinds of women around the world. See Barron and Eiselstein, "Report of Independent Investigation." I should note (and it is only fair to do so in the hope that it may be true) that the Zacharias family maintains his innocence despite the seemingly damning allegations (see Nathan Zacharias, "Defending Ravi," https://defendingravi.com).

such strict holiness (e.g., Eph 5:3–5). For example, Paul tells the Galatians unequivocally to avoid the vices of the flesh:

> Now the works of the flesh are evident: sexual immorality, impurity, sensuality, idolatry, sorcery, enmity, strife, jealousy, fits of anger, rivalries, dissensions, divisions, envy, drunkenness, orgies, and things like these. (Gal 5:19–21a)

Is such avoidance to be done on our own steam? Not at all. Paul prefaced this by imploring the Galatians to "walk by the Spirit, and you will not gratify the desires of the flesh" (v. 16). It is one's relationship to Christ accompanied by full immersion in Christian virtue that help one to avoid giving in to temptation. And lest we think that Paul's list here is exhaustive, he ends with the phrase "and things like these" (*kai ta homoia toutois*), which, according to the common theme of the vices, includes all self-serving wrongdoing.

While most Christians fancy themselves upright because they do not engage in overtly vicious behavior (like murder, adultery, theft, etc.), there is the more subtle sin of moral compromise. In Revelation, John reports the contents of a letter to Laodicea wherein God says, "I know your works: you are neither cold nor hot. Would that you were either cold or hot! So, because you are lukewarm, and neither hot nor cold, I will spit you out of my mouth" (Rev 3:16–17). The contrast of "hot" and "cold" is not one of virtue versus vice, as if God were saying that he would rather the Laodiceans be vicious than morally neutral; rather, the phrase "you are neither hot nor cold" is somewhat equivalent to our modern expression "you don't see things as black and white." Morality is unambiguously binary.[7] God is thus condemning the Laodiceans for compromising their values when it comes to making a buck (cf. v. 18). Instead, each church resident needs to "be zealous" (v. 19) and "one who conquers" (v. 21).

While provision is certainly made for Christians who mess up and fall into sin (1 John 1:9), our moral objective is clear: holiness. And it is not a holiness where one merely acts the part (for this was the error of the scribes and Pharisees, e.g., Matt 23:27). Rather, it is true holiness when one allows herself to be transformed by Christ and made into a new creation—a creation that naturally produces virtuous fruits.

But how does holy living serve to fill out what it means to engage in spiritual warfare? The answer, we might say, is Aristotelian. When Aristotle

---

7. This is not to say that there aren't morally neutral (amoral) acts. Instead, in God's eyes, acts that are moral will either be morally good or morally bad. There is no "it is good for you but not for me" and "it is wrong for you but not for me" kind of moral ambiguity.

spoke of the virtues in his *Nicomachean Ethics*, he explained that such virtues must first be learned and then practiced as a habit. This is how one gets educated in virtue. But because doing the right thing is not a guarantor of an enjoyable life (contrary to Plato) and because it is a fulfillment of her human nature to be virtuous, one must do the right thing despite whether or not it contributes to her own contentment. This will make one characteristically virtuous, for we come to be motivated to do the right thing for all the right reasons and not for selfish reasons.[8] Accordingly, virtue will become second nature. Now, the conventional wisdom has been to insist that if you practice doing good, then that is enough to make you become a virtuous person. But virtue ethicists like Aristotle somewhat invert this. They insist that it is by becoming a virtuous person that you will become one who practices doing good, particularly in uncharted waters where the good is not so easily defined. This squares nicely with the fact that spiritual regeneration results in righteous living and that righteous living is not what results in spiritual regeneration (Isa 64:6; Rom 4:4–5; Eph 2:8–9; Galatians 3:1–9).

By becoming a certain kind of person (i.e., one who is virtuous), we make it a lifestyle irrespective of any benefits or damages that may result. We realize that doing the right thing transcends any cost-benefit analysis. And *that* means when confronted with adversity, we will not be primarily motivated by self-preservation and personal happiness—objectives that often lead to personal ruin anyway (cf. Matt 16:25). In the New Testament, a similar portrait is painted. Paul says that "those who live according to the Spirit set their minds on the things of the Spirit" (Rom 8:5). That is, living according to Christian virtues characterizes those who take the Spirit's point of view.[9] Paul writes elsewhere that virtues like "love, joy, peace, patience, kindness, goodness, faithfulness, gentleness, [and] self-control" are not the *causes* of one's being in the Spirit but are the *fruits* of one's being in the Spirit (Gal 5:22–23). And so he can declare to the Ephesians that "we are his workmanship, created in Christ Jesus *for good works*, which God prepared beforehand, that we should walk in them" (Eph 2:10; emphasis added). What one is precedes what one does. In the Sermon on the Mount,

---

8. See Shafer-Landau, *Fundamentals of Ethics*, 258–59.

9. "In contrast to the law-informed mind defeated by the flesh in [Rom] 7:22–23, Paul speaks here of a 'frame of mind' (habitual way of thinking) guided by the Spirit (8:5–7). Philosophers spoke of focusing the mind on divine matters rather than bodily passions; Paul speaks of a new perspective on reality informed by God's Spirit active in one's life rather than dependence or obsession with one's own ways (8:5). For Paul, the mind-frame of the flesh produced death (8:6); that is, the mind dominated by bodily desires (7:23) stood under the body's sentence of death (7:24). But the frame of mind dominated by the Spirit involves life and peace (8:6): both eternal life (5:21; 6:23) and peace with God (5:1) established through Christ" (Keener, *Romans*, 100).

Jesus himself uses "fruit" as indicative of the kind of person you are (Matt 7:15–20; cf. 1 John 2:4). If you happen to be a false prophet, then you are the kind of person who will visibly produce "diseased fruit" since good fruit is not the sort of thing one expects from them. Such fruit is indeed how "you will recognize them." Similarly, it is also why it is false to think that good works produce salvation, for the New Testament makes it clear that it is salvation that produces good works (Rom 3:20–22; Eph 2:8–10).

Righteous living is that by which we live for the sake of what it means to be human beings created in the image of God. Prudentially, righteous living is that by which human beings can be preserved from the evil that so easily entangles us. The Proverbs of Solomon are filled with examples and scenarios where righteousness is seen as the great preserver. For example, Solomon writes that the "righteousness of the blameless keeps his way straight, but the wicked falls by his own wickedness" (Prov 11:5). Why is this so? Because righteousness is not characterized by things like pride (v. 2) and greed (v. 4), which lead to personal destruction. Righteousness "delivers" us and prevents us from being "taken captive by their lust" (v. 6) because it disregards personal benefit.

The pursuer of righteousness is also considered to ultimately bring honor and life (21:21). It isn't that living the virtuous life will guarantee the good life as such (though it ultimately does so in God's consummate kingdom); rather, it is that living a vicious life often brings ruination. This is so because the vicious person is himself overthrown by sin (13:6). Because such a person is self-driven and his desires constantly shift with the changing circumstances of the self, he cannot be firmly "established" (12:3). And whatever gains he makes in his selfish pursuits, they "do not profit" in the relevant way because they cannot ultimately save one from death (10:2). Righteousness is anchored in God and God never changes (Ps 90:2; Mal 3:6). And God, as the ultimate judge and creator, is quite naturally the only one who can guarantee the good life for us. The righteous, therefore, are firmly grounded in the immutable God, who in himself *is* the Good.

When we turn to the New Testament, we see by example that Jesus was confronted by Satan in the wilderness and later in the garden of Gethsemane. In what can only be construed as instances of spiritual warfare, it was his reliance on the Spirit of God as a virtuous person that allowed him to rebuff Satan's temptations. Though Jesus was in fact God in the flesh (John 1:1, 14), he obviously was not the kind of person who would succumb to sin (2 Cor 5:21). And the wilderness temptation proves this. But the accounts reveal that there was a real struggle—one that took effort to overcome. And Jesus chose not to lean on his own divinity but, instead, on his humanity (Matt 26:39; Phil 2:6–8). As such, only a life in the Spirit could preserve him from seeking what he wanted apart from sacrifice. You see, Jesus was not seeking to merely *be* the Messiah and king, as if a credential was all he was after; rather, he was seeking to save and govern those whom he had chosen—something those titles represent. And that was only going to come about if Jesus carried out his mission in full reliance on the Spirit of God since he had foregone doing so as God.

Yes, being righteous takes work—excruciating work! But our pursuit of virtue at least keeps us centered around God and not around the Almighty Self. The Self is foundationless, unanchored, and fleeting. It is the way of destruction. Peter writes that we ought to "make every effort" to integrate various Christian virtues that supplement faith (2 Pet 1:5–8). While such virtues may come *naturally*, they do not come *effortlessly*. And yet, only by upholding the virtues will they "keep you from being ineffective or unfruitful in the knowledge of our Lord Jesus Christ" (v. 8). That is true wisdom.

So, holiness is something we are, by nature, made to become. By being in Christ and by practicing the Christian virtues, we increasingly become the kind of people who will resist Satan and his tempting advances. But holiness is not something that operates alone. It is directly related to Christian wisdom. The virtues, after all, must be taught to us. And being taught implies the right pursuit of knowledge. In the next section, we will turn to see how Scripture merges these two things in offering us a fuller and more integrative picture of what spiritual warfare is all about.

AN INTEGRATIVE APPROACH: THE ARMOR OF GOD

By way of summary, Paul addresses spiritual warfare to his Ephesian readers by first identifying a salient and sobering truth: that the ultimate enemies of Christians are not the embodied individuals of the world but the unembodied spirits that manipulate them. By orienting his readers to the true enemy, the Ephesian readers, and by extension all of us reading the letter, can better appreciate that a correct response to adversity will not be hand-to-hand combat with material forces but spirit-to-spirit combat with immaterial ones. *How* this is to be meted out constitutes the remainder of the Ephesian warfare narrative.

In chapter 6 of Ephesians, we have the most explicit Pauline reference to what spiritual warfare involves. Although we already examined what the passage seems to be saying (see "Armor" in chapter 11), we'll focus here on how it relates to the two pillars (i.e., knowledge and holiness) of spiritual warfare discussed above. As we will see, the philosophical and the theological come together in filling out what it means to engage in spiritual combat. Ephesians 6, then, lays out a list of distinct pieces of military equipment (the *panoplian*) in the following order:

- The belt (of truth)
- The breastplate (of righteousness)
- Covering for your feet (for readiness/preparation of the gospel)
- The shield (of faith)
- The helmet (of salvation)
- The sword of the Spirit (as the Word of God)

It is doubtful that Paul is *prioritizing* such armor as if listing the armor in order of importance.[10] Nor is he, I think, intentionally metaphorizing these properties as a reflection of that importance (i.e., that salvation is crucial is why it is being depicted as a "helmet" since helmets protect the most vital organ of the human body). It seems that this would be to carry the use of his metaphor beyond its intent. The list is likely not serial but parallel, given that the armor is mutually supportive and not stacked, as it were. As was discussed back in chapter 11, Paul probably has in mind a depiction of the forthcoming Messiah as conveyed in Isaiah and the Psalms.[11] As to whether he is here telling the Ephesians to "put on" Christ (Rom 13:14; Gal 3:27) in a roundabout way, that is something we cannot definitively conclude but nevertheless it seems likely given the Old Testament messianic connections. The apparent connection to Ephesians 4:20–24, particularly with its armor talk of "righteousness," "holiness," and "put[ting] away falsehood," further supports this. Nevertheless, throughout all of Ephesians Paul has been telling the Christians about our engagement with these virtues, which are represented, and likely summarized, by the armor.[12]

---

10. Paul's listings do not necessarily imply priority as evidenced by 1 Cor 13:13. There he lists "faith, hope, and love" but immediately follows with "but the greatest of these is love," thus indicating that faith is not the superior of the bunch. Aside from the order of listing, the King James Version of Eph 6:16 might mislead readers to a different prioritizing of the spiritual armor. The verse reads: "Above all, taking the shield of faith, wherewith ye shall be able to quench all the fiery darts of the wicked." This "above all" (*epi pasin*) does not indicate a hierarchy of importance but a distribution over this "all." The "all" refers not to the aggregate of armor having been mentioned, but to the circumstances in which one must stand. This is to say that the shield is to be wielded over all such circumstances and not just a few. It does indicate that the shield is the superior piece of armor.

11. So, Powlison, "Classical Model," 94–6.

12. Most commentators to see Eph 6:10–20 as a *peroratio* (a summary of major themes) of Paul's overall message to the Ephesians.

But this is not the only thing readers are to pick up on. The burden of the Ephesian letter is to clarify their Gentile identity in relation to the Jews and to establish that our salvation is based on the providence of God and not on our own works. As Gentiles united with Jews, we must all behave in a way befitting the body of Christ. It is no wonder that the themes of truth, righteousness, readiness, faith, salvation, and God's Word are discussed at length earlier in leading up to chapter 6. In fact, Ephesians 4 itself has all these elements present. There the Ephesians are instructed to speak "the truth in love" (4:15) and "put away falsehood" (v. 25). They are "to put on the new self, created after the likeness of God in true righteousness and holiness" (v. 24). They must actively "equip the saints for the work of ministry, for building up the body of Christ" (v. 12), which is achieved via sound doctrine (v. 14) and which is something rooted in both the gospel and the Word of God (cf. 2 Tim 3:16–17; cf. Eph 5:26). It is the "one faith" itself (v. 5) that must be guarded in the promotion of "unity of that faith and of the knowledge of the Son of God" (v. 13). And, of course, they must see that their salvation is by "grace [that] was given to each one of us according to the measure of Christ's gift" (v. 7; cf. 2:8–9).

The mixed metaphors of the *panoplian* tell us two things. As anatomical metaphors, they emphasize *what* is being protected, namely, the Christian body (of both Jew and Gentile together). As military metaphors, they emphasize *how* that body is to be protected, namely, through the spiritual virtues. It is thus important for us to focus on what these spiritual virtues are vis-à-vis the armor of God.

Recall that the virtues listed in Ephesians 6 all belong to one of two broader categories that comprise the examined life worth defending: either they promote *knowledge* or they promote *holiness*. Truth, readiness, and the Word of God are obvious instances of the former. Righteousness is an obvious instance of the latter. However, it might be unclear where faith and salvation belong. Likely these are those things God has the most active part in via his grace. If we take our cue from the rest of Ephesians, it is evident that faith involves both its content (Eph 4:5) as well as its act of commitment (1:13; 2:8). This puts it squarely within the category of knowledge as something to be known in an intimate and sincere way. As for salvation, it echoes Isaiah 59:17's divine warrior motif involving a "helmet of salvation." Clearly, God is the one who saves. But in Ephesians the burden of applying it is ours for we are to "take" it. In 1 Thessalonians 5:8, Paul identifies the conqueror as one "having put on the breastplate of faith and love, *and for a helmet the hope of salvation*" (emphasis added). It is something the Thessalonians have yet to obtain (for they are "destined . . . to obtain salvation," v. 9). Quite likely it is this hope of salvation that is in view in Ephesians 6.

As such, it reflects the Ephesians' identity: they are those chosen by God for salvation (cf. 1:11), who thereby hope for it "in the evil day" (6:13).[13] It is probably associated with knowledge—knowledge of a current reality (i.e., our God who saves) that grounds our knowledge of a future reality (i.e., our salvation from climactic judgment). Thus, knowledge and virtue are indeed the overall running themes in Ephesians 6 that preserve us through spiritual adversity. These are not just interesting tidbits of theology; they end up as practical steps to growing in the right kind of knowledge and virtue.

So, the way one is to "put on" Christ is to in effect become what Christ himself is: the one who embodies both knowledge and virtue. Since Christ is one who is truthful, righteous, prepared, faithful, an exhibiter of grace, and a responsible proclaimer of God's Word, we must strive to be likewise. While Christ himself is the embodiment of these virtues, we are the embodiment of Christ (4:15–16). Accordingly, to exhibit these virtues is to be in Christ and to be in Christ is to exhibit these virtues.

But how does the everyday Christian implement these virtues? What does the armor-clad Christian look like in the twenty-first century? Indeed, real people want to know what this all means for them. It turns out that the specific elements of the armor provide quite practical ways for us to "stand against the schemes of the devil" (6:11). For one, we do not engage the devil *directly* but instead oppose that through which the devil *mediates*, i.e., his "schemes." This is what the "flaming arrows" of verse 16 are; they are the mediated attacks of Satan. There is no indication of any literal hand-to-hand combat or any "power encounters" as evinced by deliverance ministers. Our "stand against the schemes of the devil" involves something more along the lines of countering *lies* and *propaganda*. Truth and knowledge oppose lies and propaganda. Similarly, moral virtue and holy living oppose the moral schemes of the devil: temptations and corruption. And through consistent and successful practice, they publicly accredit the one who stands firm in this way. For the one who successfully opposes Satan's schemes is demonstrated to be a mature Christian—being less likely to apostatize.

What about the contribution of prayer and supplication? Aren't these things a part of what it takes to "stand against the schemes of the devil"? It's true that these are not metaphorized in the *panoplian* but they are no less a part of the Christian warrior's repertoire. In fact, verses 18–20 of Ephesians 6, which discuss prayer and supplication, are grammatically tied to the metaphors we've been discussing. Here, Paul concludes that while we

---

13. The "evil day" is likely an eschatological day of judgment, for "Paul uses a definite article to denote one day rather than simply repeat the claim of 5:16. In this respect Paul is probably referring to some point in the future when God will judge the world" (Fowl, *Ephesians*, 205). Cf. 1 Thess 5:2–4.

are equipping ourselves with (the metaphorized portions of) the armor, we should also be

> praying at all times in the Spirit, with all prayer and supplication. To that end, keep alert with all perseverance, making supplication for all the saints, and also for me, that words may be given to me in opening my mouth boldly to proclaim the mystery of the gospel, for which I am an ambassador in chains, that I may declare it boldly, as I ought to speak.

That this passage lacks a main verb suggests to a number of commentators that prayer and supplication are dependent on, if not a continuation of, the spiritual armor.[14] Thus, while prayer and supplication are not to be isolated from the spiritual armor, they are not themselves a part of that armor (which is why they are not metaphorized as the other elements are). Instead, these things are coextensive with the armor. Perhaps this is because prayer is reliance on God as the one who gives the Ephesians the ability to stand in truth, faith, righteousness, etc. And supplication "for all the saints" maintains the Ephesian church's unity as they seek God's support for others within the body. Jesus's ongoing call to "watch and pray" (Mark 14:38; Luke 21:36)[15] suggests that avoiding temptation—temptation to vice and temptation to falsehood—is of the utmost concern here. Prayer supports the armor. Only then can the Ephesians, along with Paul, be equipped for a bold and perspicuous evangelism in the face of the fears of demonic opposition.[16]

SOME INDEPENDENT PHILOSOPHICAL SUPPORT

I think that philosophical reflection can get us to the same properties of a spiritual warrior as those given in Ephesians 6. I will argue here that by virtue of God's existence and who he is, along with the existence of human beings and the prospect of us having a spiritual enemy, the virtues of Ephesians 6:14–18 are both implied and sufficient for the spiritual warrior.

---

14. Lincoln, *Ephesians*, 451; Best, *Critical and Exegetical Commentary*, 604; Fowler, *Ephesians*, 208.

15. Fowler, *Ephesians*, 209.

16. The Lord's Prayer in Matt 6 mirrors the two pillars being discussed here too. For, in that prayer, we are to petition that God "forgive us our debts, as we also have forgiven our debtors. And lead us not into temptation, but deliver us from [the] evil [one]" (vv. 12–13). Here we seek purification from our sins as it is linked with also being further delivered from the evil one. My thanks to Jonathan King for suggesting this.

Let us begin with the fundamental truth that God exists. If God exists, then his existence implies several things. We saw this back in chapter 7 in our discussion on the nature and attributes of God. As a being on whom all contingent things ultimately depend, we can infer that God is a necessarily existing being (lest he depend on something beyond himself resulting in an infinite causal regress). As a person, he would know all true propositions since it is simpler for that being to have infinite knowledge rather than a specifically delimited knowledge (and he certainly will know something). If God knows all truths, then he knows all moral truths, thus implying his all-goodness (for beings always act in accord with what they think/know is best for them and/or for others). Unless God wrongly believes what is good for himself and/or others, which is impossible given his omniscience, then he will always do the good. We may even find that God's existence implies, in his goodness, that he would create embodied, rational life toward the development of moral maturity—beings created to ultimately share in his eternity.[17] But since we as human beings so described do in fact exist, we needn't worry about the merits of that last inference.

But we can add to these implications of God's existence and the existence of human beings further implications that belong to or are imposed on human beings by virtue of the divine nature. Specifically, we can infer the particular Christian virtues espoused in Ephesians 6 (i.e., truth, righteousness, readiness, faith, salvation, God's Word, and prayer). I will argue here that these practices and only these practices which embody spiritual warfare are implied in a universe where God and human beings exist in a creator-creation relation wherein all are concurrently being opposed by spiritual enemy personalities. That is, if God's people indeed are opposed by spiritual enemy personalities (or demons), then just these virtues are what we would expect of those people in their fortifying their spirituality and in resisting such opposition. Other ancillary practices like deliverance exorcisms, territorial exorcisms, and acts of wizardry, in addition to the challenges such practices already face, will be shown to be superfluous here.

Let us commence here with the notion of righteousness. If God exists, then he is either the locus of righteousness (i.e., its source) or an exemplar of it (i.e., a supreme representation of it). This is true because God is the sole creator, thus eliminating other sources for objective moral values, and he is omniscient, thus making what God believes to be good for him and others never wrong. He is, subsequently, good by nature. He is such that his goodness cannot not fail to obtain. And to be such that one's goodness cannot not fail to obtain as a result of one's nature entails that one is therefore righteous.

---

17. Swinburne, *Existence of God*, ch. 6.

So far, however, this amounts to God's being righteous, not to human beings' need to pursue such righteousness, which is the point of Ephesians 6:14c. What can we say about that?

Considering that human beings were created by God, we must have been created for a purpose. Since we are endowed with a rational faculty and a moral conscience, then our purpose is partly fulfilled in our striving toward moral perfection. To act morally is to act reasonably, for human beings can only act morally if we freely (however this is to be understood[18]) and properly adjudicate which actions we ought to do in promotion of the good life. If God is the author and/or enforcer of both reason and morality, then the two must assuredly coincide. It is not surprising, therefore, that our faculty of reason aims (in part) to promote the good life, which involves doing the right thing (for oneself and others) as much as possible. If righteousness is the highest form of the good life, then it follows that our purpose in life is, in part, to pursue righteousness. So, righteousness, being the pinnacle to which the good life aims, is thus an essential virtue that every human being is to pursue.

From the pursuit of righteousness on our part, we can infer two additional virtues that we must likewise pursue: truth and faith. Let's begin with truth. In a desperate attempt to sidestep the various controversies associated with a doctrine of truth, let us simply say that truth means that p, which represents a given proposition, is true if and only if it accurately represents the reality to which p refers. If p is "snow is white," then it is true if and only if snow is in fact white. If p is "all ravens are black," then it is true if and only if every raven is in fact black. With respect to righteousness, if morality entails meaningful propositions like "snow is white" and "all ravens are black," then moral propositions are also either true or not. Moral propositions include propositions like: "murder is wrong," "justice is good," "minimizing harm to others is right," "injustice is bad," etc. If these propositions are true because they propose something that is in fact the case (or not), then truth and righteousness are inextricably bound together. That is, in order for one to pursue righteousness, it is necessary that one knows which moral propositions are true and in promotion of that righteousness. So, in order to pursue moral perfection, one must come to know that murder is in fact wrong, that justice is in fact good, that minimizing harm to others is in fact right, and that injustice is in fact bad. If one does not know these things are true, then if she should end up refraining from murdering and harming others, she is merely acting *in accord* with morality; she is not

---

18. Refer to our brief discussions on pages 12 and 23–24 on two contrary ways to understand human freedom.

acting morally as such. A dog, which does not know truths from falsehoods, that never harms a human being or any other creature is not acting morally; it is only acting in a way that is consistent with that morality and nothing more (perhaps out of self-interest or out of some survival instinct). In fact, a human being who deliberately never murders or harms another but does so only to avoid incarceration and reprimand does not act morally either. He is acting instead out of pure self-interest, which reduces morality to what is relative to individual desires and aversions. It is not an objective morality rooted in truth and/or God's nature. If one knows what is true about which acts are morally good and which are not, and then proceeds to act on that basis, then she is intending righteousness and not something else. Truth, then, becomes a necessary component to pursuing righteousness. And if that is so, then truth is also an essential virtue for the spiritual warrior.

Righteousness also implies faith. Biblical faith is defined in Hebrews 11:1 as "the assurance of things hoped for, the conviction of things not seen." As "assurance" and "conviction," it is evident that faith involves, though not exclusively, belief. A robust faith is one that is accompanied by trust in God and his promises. But belief is an obvious component, for one cannot put her trust in God and his promises unless she *believes* in God and his promises. Accordingly, faith necessarily involves belief even though faith may not sufficiently be defined by mere belief. So, in order to know which propositions of morality are true, it is necessary to at least believe that those propositions about morality that are true. How odd it would be to say, "I know that murder is wrong," but then to add, "I do not believe that murder is wrong." One cannot know that murder is wrong unless she first believes that it is wrong; otherwise it cannot be knowledge. Moreover, the pursuer of righteousness cannot be fully righteous if she does not keep her word and her commitments to doing the right thing. To break one's word, to fail to trust, and to violate one's commitments (all as acts in opposition to righteousness) amount to acts of *in*fidelity. Thus, the pursuit of righteousness requires fidelity, i.e., faith—not just the essential aspect of belief but also those of commitment and trust in the fully biblical sense.

So, faith on our part is implied by our pursuit of righteousness. But faith itself implies something as well: the Word of God. As noted, one must believe all of the propositions that are true of righteousness in order to properly pursue that righteousness. It is evident that natural revelation and our cognitive access to it are limited (some of us live in conditions that prevent us from seeing the full specter of creation, from reflecting on arguments about God's nature, etc.). On the one hand, nature itself reveals only so much. It may ultimately reveal which acts are right and wrong, and good and bad, but it will not tell us that God so loved the world that he gave his only begotten Son in whom to believe so as not to perish. If it were not for the records of the Gospels and the rest of the New Testament or their preservation through any medium, we would not know of Jesus and his offer of salvation. As inherently unrighteous creatures—or perhaps, more accurately, nonrighteous creatures—we will not achieve the lofty goal of being righteous without a transformation by God that will preclude us from wrongdoing. And this transformation is only possible if God bestows it. But we must come to know what it takes to be a recipient of that salvation and glorification since we do not naturally deserve it or achieve it on our own. There must be, then, a certain amount of special revelation to which we have access. That revelation is God's Word and it communicates not only the particulars of righteous living but also the gospel message that enables us to finally achieve that righteousness. Righteousness requires human beings to be transformed, and that can only happen by appropriating salvation. And salvation can only be appropriated by hearing the Word of God (cf. Rom 10:17). Thus, faith—that is, *saving* faith—requires the Word of God, particularly since this is the only way to achieve righteousness.

Of course, in our present natural state our moral pursuit of righteousness will flounder, especially since we are being assaulted by the enemy triumvirate (i.e., the world, the flesh, and Satan). In order for us to continue to hope and expect that righteousness can be realized in us despite our occasional moral missteps and indiscretions, even if prompted by external influences propagated by spiritual enemies, we must have a plumb line to God, from whom we can ask and receive the forgiveness that brings about salvation. If we were unable to communicate (whether verbally or cognitively) with God, then we would have no means of finding forgiveness and redemption. Now, one might say that God knows perfectly well that we *would* ask for such forgiveness (or not) in the wake of a moral failure even without us doing so (perhaps from Matt 6:8), and on this basis he would bring about redemption without our communicating that fact to him. However, this would relegate the ultimate purpose of human life merely to an abstract righteousness that has nothing to do with enjoying God now and forever in fellowship. It is also not to be expected that God made us to become righteous only for us to live in isolation from him or in acquiring his help in a world dominated by a threefold enemy. What kind of fulfillment of human destiny would it be to reside in communicative isolation from God? Is that not in part what makes the punishment of hell so awful? Indeed, fellowship with God is essential to who we are and it is the fullness of that fellowship that only becomes possible once we are made righteous.

As Christians facing spiritual opposition, or at least spiritual obstacles facilitated by that opposition, the fortification of the believer with just these virtues makes a great deal of sense. For Satan and his cohorts act through the agencies of the flesh and the world. Both of these in-world proxies for the enemy are best rebuffed by growing and maintaining one's pursuit of righteousness, being predicated on faith, truth, salvation, God's Word, and our ongoing communion with God himself. The flesh predisposes us to moral failings due to temptations that increasingly virtuous living will mitigate. The world increasingly pushes us to believing falsehoods, which truth and God's Word counter. Our salvation in and fidelity to God, and our ongoing fellowship with him, assure us that we can be victorious. And these things collectively entail that we must be ready or prepared to endure what the enemy triumvirate will hurl at us. And the unwatchful Christian who does not come to avoid what is false and what is vicious will be unwittingly duped into embracing both.

From this, it seems awkward to think that a territorial or deliverance exorcism, even if possible, could effectuate the spiritual fortitude of a believer. How would *per impossibile* ridding a region of a demonic presence increase the Christian's spiritual posture? Such demons would still be no farther from us than if the proximate region had remained occupied. And if territorial possessions are, as Clinton Arnold prefers, "empire spirits" occupying groups of people and leaders and not locations *per se*, how is this any more detrimental to the Christian than the world is with all its turpitude and opposition? One could also ask of supporters of a wizardry model whether their acts of magic and incantation are any more effective against the world and the flesh than the fortifying of the Christian with the virtues of salvation, righteousness, faith, truth, and God's Word. For the world and the flesh remain present no matter how many demons are "driven away" or how much authority is "claimed" over one's oppressors or how many times one speaks aloud. God is no more responsive to clever chants and incantations than he is to those to whom he promises victory if they practice the established virtues. The Christian adept at these virtues is no more vulnerable to the assaults of the enemy through the flesh and/or the world than the spiritual wizard who believes she can insulate herself through her mystical methods. One can be a supremely spiritual wizard and a perfect exorcist and still not be a serious Christian. But one cannot be a serious Christian in following the virtues of Ephesians 6 and fail to be a spiritual conqueror. And if one insists that these virtues must be held *before* engaging in her ancillary acts of wizardry anyway in order to make them more effective, what remains anymore for those acts to accomplish? Having rebuffed the effects of spiritual oppression through the virtues every Christian believes she must effectuate anyways leaves no more work to be done for any subsequent would-be acts of wizardry and exorcism.

Therefore, it seems that God's nature, human existence, and the real threat of a spiritual enemy implies the very virtues Paul espouses in Ephesians 6. That these virtues pertain to knowledge (as wisdom) and virtue (as holiness), both accompanied by constant prayer, ensures and comforts believers that we will be victorious both individually and collectively in the spiritual warfare in which we find ourselves. That various unorthodox exorcisms (both territorial and deliverance) and acts of wizardry are not implied is a testament to the sufficiency of the New Testament's teachings on spiritual warfare.

CONCLUSION

I have sought to propose that the biblical portrait of spiritual warfare involves fundamentally two main pillars: knowledge and holiness. The knowledge we are to have is a sincere knowledge that leads to, and is to be indistinguishable from, intimate knowledge of Christ. This involves a responsible and correct understanding of the doctrines of Christ and his gospel (i.e., wisdom). It is the foundation upon which genuine faith is even possible, and it is the vehicle by which faith can obtain (Rom 10:17).

Holiness, which is God's nature, is the standard by which all believers are to act. Anything less than holiness is imperfection. Because of this, it is a standard that we cannot attain ourselves. We must be transformed by God through regeneration in order to be guided by the Holy Spirit towards a life of virtue. Holiness—the end of human striving—is something we inch toward in the sanctification process. As imagers of God, we are designed to live a life of virtue—virtue that culminates in righteousness. But only God, the one who makes us legally righteous before him, can and will make us finally holy in the life to come. Living such a life conditions us to making the right decisions when faced with sin and temptation. For we become a virtuous kind of person.

When we follow the New Testament's lead and integrate the practice of those virtues in Ephesians 6 and in rightly handling the Word of God, this ends up being the kind of life that can adequately rebuff the assaults of the enemy. Altogether we have truth, righteousness, readiness (i.e., preparedness), faith, salvation, God's Word, and prayer. As our assessment of Ephesians 6 suggests, we must, first, know Christ in faith personally as well as doctrinally. This knowledge will ensure our immunization from falsehood and false proclaimers. Second, we must imitate Christ and his righteousness in rebuffing temptation and sin. As we do these things, and support them with fervent prayer, we loudly proclaim our collective identity in Christ both in church unity and in our evangelism.

We also saw that not only does the New Testament teach this—particularly in the iconic warfare passage of Ephesians 6—but some philosophical reflection on the matter leads us to the same conclusion. That is, because God is who he is, because human beings were created by him, and because there is ultimately a real spiritual enemy, we can infer that the Christian must become increasingly adept at truth, righteousness, readiness (i.e., preparedness), faith, salvation, God's Word, and prayer. What looks to be unnecessary and extraneous are the suggested tactics of exorcistic and wizardry models of spiritual warfare addressed in previous chapters.

It is evident that the much-celebrated armor of God truly recapitulates what the Christian is already supposed to be doing. It is the implementation not of new tactics and practices, but of preexisting virtues that already ennoble the Christian. For Scripture to tell its readers to don "the breastplate of righteousness," "the shield of faith," "the sword of the Spirit," and so on is not to speak about additional special-use weaponry exclusive to demonic assault; it is to remind the Christian that she needs to be diligent and rehearsed in already living that life worth defending. When we send our children off to school, we may remind them to listen to their teachers, avoid bad behavior, and only associate with peers who share your values. To remind them of such things is not to communicate new tactics and novel practices in their curricular lives; it is to reinforce what we hope is a set of values that have already been instilled.

Does this mean that the underdeveloped Christian who has yet to master such knowledge and holiness is hopelessly vulnerable to the assaults of the enemy? No. And this is where reliance on pastors, teachers, and leaders is paramount. Underdeveloped Christians are not to be disconnected from the body precisely because of their susceptibility to falsehood and vice and/or an unawareness of how to discern them. Therefore, Scripture insists that the older generation is to instruct the younger (Titus 2:1–8). They are to disciple them so as to be prepared in the here and now. While they are not *now* equipped as a mature Christian is, they are nevertheless connected to resources on which to rely. The responsibility thus falls on the teacher and overseer. This is also why Scripture reminds us to "not [neglect] to meet together, as is the habit of some, but [to encourage] one another, and all the more as you see the Day drawing near" (Heb 10:25). Mentorship and discipleship prove, then, to be essential, especially for the underdeveloped. And it is that resource that helps the underdeveloped combat the same spiritual foes.

While abiding by Christian virtues will invite indirect demonic opposition (for demons cannot affect the physical world directly), our steadfastness and resolve will inevitably result in victory. Praise be to God for enabling us to stand against the schemes of the devil!

PART IV

Equipping the Saints

If [Christian leaders] do not teach Christian principles to all followers of Christ, we are not equipping them with God's truth that will overcome worldly influence.

—BILLY GRAHAM, *BILLY GRAHAM IN QUOTES*, 141

19

Recruit Training: Studying to Show Yourself Approved

THIS BOOK ON SPIRITUAL warfare would not be complete without some specific guidance about how to acquire and practice the principles contained herein. While most books tend to focus more on the spiritual disciplines (such as praying, Scripture reading, communal worship, etc.) as well as some offbeat practices thrown in, this book aims to emphasize the significant aspects of knowledge and holiness as forming the bedrock of everyday spiritual warfare. As I have argued, spiritual warfare is not about taking on demonic forces directly, but dealing with that through which they mediate. Certainly, we must pray and regularly attend church. But there are other practices that are just as important in equipping the saints to do spiritual warfare.

I argued that knowledge as wisdom is *one* of the two main pillars of the practice of spiritual warfare. We are not only called to live a life of holiness and sanctification but we are to, as Paul tells Timothy, "present yourself to God as one approved, a worker who has no need to be ashamed, rightly handling the word of truth" (2 Tim 2:15). In this chapter, we will focus on this pillar and discuss some ways for Christians to be people "rightly handling the word of truth." As for what that means, recall that such "handling" involves not only the acquisition of doctrinal knowledge (Eph 4:11–14) but also the wherewithal to defend it (Acts 17:11; 2 Cor 10:5; 1 Pet 3:15; Jude 3). Accordingly, Paul tells Titus that in order to be an elder he "must hold firm to the trustworthy word as taught, so that he may be able to give instruction in sound doctrine and also to rebuke those who contradict it" (Titus 1:9).

"Rightly handling the word," then, involves a sound doctrinal education and a means to ward off those who contradict it. And this is evident in the fact that spiritual warfare involves armor and weaponry having to do with standing firm in the faith and in the truths of Scripture (Eph 6:13–17).

Does this mean that the call to defend the faith and to learn sound doctrine is a matter only for those seeking a pastoral or ministerial post? Not at all. It is true that Paul's comments to Titus are in the context of his strengthening the church on the island of Crete, but his point is that such an overseer would be in a position to *teach others* sound doctrine and be able to authoritatively reprimand those who oppose it. But, learning sound doctrine and defending it are to be features of every mature Christian. The author of Hebrews, for example, says that

> for everyone who lives on milk is unskilled in the word of righteousness, since he is a child. But solid food is for the mature, for those who have their powers of discernment trained by constant practice to distinguish good from evil. (Heb 5:13–14)

Indeed, what characterizes the mature is their level of training and reasoning skills. Likewise, Peter is clear that for "all of you" (1 Pet 3:8) they are to be "prepared to make a defense to anyone who asks you for a reason for the hope that is in you" (v. 15). This is not a function of the elite or of some specially gifted aggregate of super-Christians. We must all be equipped in such a way because we must silence the naysayers (v. 16). The teacher-minister is only expected to do *more* with it than the average layperson insofar as such a person is to train the sheep and to authoritatively avert threats to the flock. That's what shepherds do.

But, as a layperson, I don't know quite how to do this. Let us look at a few practical ways that Christians of all kinds can participate in this aspect (i.e., knowledge) of spiritual warfare. None of what follows are lofty strategies. They're everyday things just about anyone can avail themselves of (some more than others, no doubt, depending on one's circumstances).

RESOURCES AT YOUR LOCAL CHURCH

The local church body should be a reservoir of information for you. Not only that, but it should be a safe environment in which to seek out further guidance and knowledge of Scripture. Some churches will have bookstores that will contain commentaries on the meaning and interpretation of passages in the Bible. They may also have a set of classical readings by some of Christianity's great thinkers, including C. S. Lewis, C. H. Spurgeon, A. W. Tozer,

Dietrich Bonhoeffer, J. C. Ryle, Martyn Lloyd-Jones, J. Gresham Machen, and J. I. Packer (to name a few). However, not all churches have the resources to stock a collection of works such as these. But other resources abound.

Most churches tend to either physically stock a collection of archived sermons (as CDs or videos) or house them on a website and make them available for streaming. What makes this resource a good one is that you are able to pass over topics that may not have an emphasis on understanding Scripture. Indeed, many churches tend to offer more day-to-day practical lessons like managing a household or sustaining interpersonal relationships. Those can be set aside in favor of sermons that tend to focus on books of the Bible or theological subjects that are supported by Scripture. It's basically learning on demand from a church—a church that, I hope, you trust!

A third accessible resource involves courses that your church may be conducting on or off site. Adult Sunday school courses, for example, tend to offer straightforward instruction on understanding basic and sometimes intermediate biblical truths. Such courses will, or ought to, minimally focus on the tenets of the Christian faith—the doctrine of creation, the doctrine of man, the doctrine of God, the doctrine of Jesus, and all of the auxiliaries that support the larger network of our articles of faith. Sometimes you may find courses outside of the Sunday school setting that, instead, are offered elsewhere on campus or in another facility on a different day and time. For example, I myself have conducted courses at churches involving specialized subjects like Christian apologetics and comparative religions. Such courses are excellent opportunities for gaining deeper knowledge of the faith—all with the benefit of an instructor with whom to interact and have your questions answered.

A fourth resource from your church is the church body itself. Take the opportunity to fellowship and lunch with other congregants in order to have open and stimulating conversations about what Scripture has to say. So-called small groups can be ideal for these kinds of conversations, though they are usually more structured and regulated (see "Bible Study" below for more on this possibility). You may find others sufficiently knowledgeable and able to offer up some on-the-fly basic understanding of various scriptural positions and teachings. At the very least, engagement in such conversations can expose those areas where you may need to do more private study.

I recognize that many churches will lack some or perhaps all of these resources. If so, that is a shame and something, I trust, the next generation of Christians will be poised to fix. But it's a place to start your quest for guided studies without having to shell out thousands of dollars for a comparable education at a Bible college or some other formal institution of higher learning. Your church's instruction may not be as rigorous as it ought to be, but it is a start—a budget-friendly start.

BIBLE STUDY

There are two ways that a local Bible study can be advantageous in enhancing your knowledge of Scripture. The first one is obvious: by attending a study that is being conducted by someone able to exposit and systematize Scripture in a responsible way. Such private settings have the added advantage of providing the ability to ask questions—even "dumb" questions—you wouldn't otherwise feel comfortable in asking amidst a class full of fellow learners. Bible studies are more intimate and will be a natural environment where people feel less inhibited in being both honest and careful in making sure they have answered your questions to your satisfaction. There are fewer opportunities of being shrugged off for asking difficult questions. Other attendees may just be willing to pick up the slack where the primary facilitator may be ill equipped. That's the beauty of a plurality. It seems to me that Bible studies are, or should be, the nonacademic equivalent of a graduate seminar. A graduate seminar typically involves each participant doing a bit of reading prior to gathering in a classroom of a handful of like-minded people. They read in anticipation of being ready to have a deep and constructive conversation on the subject. Yes, learning takes place in this environment. But it's more than being *talked at*, you are in fact *participating* by advancing the conversation in attempts to solve some kind of problem. Bible studies should be no different. And it is a marvelous opportunity to grow as you engage in interpersonal dialogue with the expectation of learning something you didn't know prior to your gathering. It seems that home-based Bible studies are trending today, so you shouldn't have too much difficulty finding one close to you. And if there isn't one, why not start one?

There is another way a Bible study can help aid you in your understanding of Scripture. It is by saddling you with the task of *teaching* one (or more) of the sessions (with a little bit of guidance, of course). There is nothing like having to teach a subject matter to thrust you into the arms of good old-fashioned research. If you have a clear objective, then getting to that objective will be your guiding light to understanding the subject matter; and if you haven't met that objective after your studies, then you must revisit your content and modify it accordingly. Start with clearly demarcated sections in the Bible. For example, the first chapter of the Gospel of John has five distinct sections beginning with a discussion about the Word becoming flesh—what that means and how it was received by those who experienced it. The Gospel of John opens with one of the most distinctive Christian doctrines of orthodoxy: the incarnation of the Second Person of the Trinity in a world where there is only one God. That will surely keep you busy studying!

As for amassing research aids in conducting Bible studies, fear not. The internet provides a rich pool of options for everyone. For example, one can access two well-known websites that offer multiple translations of Scripture at your fingertips: biblehub.com and biblegateway.com. Both websites also offer additional study aids and (often public-domain) commentaries. For those preferring something closer to sophisticated scholarly software like that offered by Logos without breaking the bank, I recommend the free software with its familiar interface entitled e-Sword. This can be downloaded at esword.net. From its seemingly endless Bible versions to Bible dictionaries, commentaries, lexicons, interlinears, and word-search capabilities, you'll wonder why it doesn't cost a single cent! (However, Rick Meyers, the creator of the software, does ask that you consider a donation for his efforts—a worthy endeavor if you are led to do so.)

READING SUPPORTIVE MATERIALS

For the more introverted Christian, or for the Christian who does not have the good fortune of a flourishing Christian community, there's always reading material that is accessible to every location that has internet access. Though the internet is filled with published writings that have not been peer-reviewed by anyone, it is your window to reliable sources if you know where to look. Christian philosopher Tim McGrew has recently amassed a list of theological works by precontemporary modern authors whose works are completely available online. See his main hub for "The Library of Historical Apologetics" at http://historicalapologetics.org or access a direct link to a listing of books at https://historicalapologetics.org/library/.

In addition to this marvelous resource, there are other ways to access free books either partially or in their entirety by inputting your choice of keywords into a search engine. One of the most thorough is Google Books, which is directly accessible at books.google.com. On this site, simply input what you would like to turn up and Google Books will list the available resources. I recommend specifying things like "commentary on the Gospel of John," "doctrine of the Trinity," or "Easter sermons." If you catch wind of a good book, take a chance and run a Google Books search, for it may be (partly) available to read online. Amazon.com offers a similar feature on the retailer's own website. When you call up a certain book, it will most likely have a "look inside" feature that allows you to read portions of the work—usually the opening chapters. Related to this, and for the more academically oriented, is the Google Scholar search database. This can be accessed at scholar.google.com. Therein your searches will scan for not only books but also journal articles, newspaper stories, and magazine entries—a number of which are readable in their entirety. And if you are a college student, check with your university or college to see about getting around any paywalls for free. Just about all schools of higher education have deals with journal databases and book repositories that allow free access for students.

And, of course, do not forget about your local library. Typically, a library will avail you of e-resources as well as traditional ones through their respective website portals. If you can't find the resource online, they may have it in stock or you may be able to get it at a location near you. While some of the books and resources you're seeking to get may not be available online or in your local library system, many libraries participate in an inter-library loan program that allows you to request works held in other library systems in your region and have them delivered to your local library—all free of charge. The ones that are typically difficult to get your hands on are the brand-new resources hot off the press. But, other than that, resources abound through your local library. And if they don't have it, they can usually get it—and that includes journal and magazine articles too!

READING CONTRARY VIEWPOINTS

Once you're able to tap into a database or two of resources for study, consider not just works that support the Christian worldview but those that do not. I say this with a *caveat* attached. That is, unless you're already grounded to some extent in the fundamentals of the faith and are not easily rattled by critics that often take little care in how they message their objections, consider reading critics and skeptics. These resources will drive you to consider those areas of Christian theology that are the most vulnerable. While I am confident that you will find those vulnerabilities to be far less of a concern than those poised against Christianity, what critics have to say can reveal the kinds of obstacles people have in coming to the faith. And, in the process, it will strengthen your own.

Chances are the objections to the Christian message are manifestations of doubts that may already be lurking within our subconscious. Since one of the primary means of spiritual attack against Christians is *falsehood*, then we cannot be averse to interacting with those falsehoods and why they are in fact false. When I and my colleagues conduct courses in reasoning and critical thinking, we must survey not only good reasoning practices but false and dubious ones as well. We must inevitably cover arguments that fail to support their conclusions in order to model for our students how arguments flounder either in terms of their structure or their content. Exploring ways in which people make mistakes in the reasoning process will enlighten us further to the errors committed not only by anti-Christian critics but also by well-meaning and sometimes misguided fellow believers. Through this, iron can indeed sharpen iron (Prov 27:17). And if our critic's argument amounts to just a *fact* problem, then we do well to make our acquaintance with it in uncovering the truth. Sometimes we're not even sure what to learn except by observing the ways critics get it wrong.

In my budding years as a Christian, I recall doing this very thing. Once I had a foundation regarding the essentials of the Christian faith, I began to read books, magazines, and publications by pseudo-Christian movements such as Mormonism and the Watchtower organization of the Jehovah's Witnesses. It was through their (bad) arguments that I learned how solid the articles of faith are for orthodox Christianity. It not only assured me that I knew who God really is, but it gave me the tools I needed to begin evangelizing Mormons and Jehovah's Witnesses with confidence. And you should have seen how God moved on some of them when I shared with them what I had learned!

THE ONLINE WORLD OF STREAMING

The twenty-first century offers, of course, a wealth of online media that can be streamed and downloaded to one's device(s). Gone are the days where order forms must be filled out in order to purchase cassettes, CDs, and/or videos of prerecorded sessions. Now, such items are by and large free and ubiquitous! Video streaming sites like YouTube and Vimeo, and to a lesser extend Facebook and Instagram, offer content on just about any subject matter one might dream up. Similarly, there are audio streaming services (mostly in the form of podcasts) that provide audio files for on-the-go streaming or download, which can be appreciated while driving to work, to school, or to play.

The only downside of this marvelous technology and the wealth of individuals who have stepped up to offer viewers and listeners various services to all categories of inquiry is that such material is mostly not vetted. That is, in order to publish a podcast, a video, or any media file on the internet, all you need is the ability to record and the ability to upload that file. That's it. There is no peer review or any editorial board through which one's recorded work must be assessed for publication. You can just submit and go. As such, finding reliable sources for learning about God can be a tedious task. But because it is a free and accessible means of acquiring hours, days, months, and even years of content without end, allow me to offer some reliable links to some audio and video productions that offer up decent content on Scripture, theology, and apologetics. Again, this will just be a partial list, but it should be enough to get you started no matter what stage you're at in the learning process. Here are some suggestions by category in no particular order:

The Bible

- Video: The Bible Project (https://www.youtube.com/user/jointhebibleproject)
- Video: BibleTalk.tv (https://www.youtube.com/user/BibleTalkVideo)
- Audio: Various files by Albert Mohler (https://albertmohler.com)

Theology

- Video: The Table (Dallas Theological Seminary) (https://voice.dts.edu/tablepodcast)
- Video: The Master's Seminary (https://www.youtube.com/user/JoshuaCrooch)
- Video: The Gospel Coalition (https://www.youtube.com/user/TheGospelCoalition)
- Video: Alister McGrath Christian Theology Introduction (https://www.youtube.com/channel/UCycpoOuRTa6cGkgzQMpCeGQ)
- Video: Defenders Class (of William Lane Craig)
- (https://www.youtube.com/user/ReasonableFaithOrg/playlists?view=50&sort=dd&shelf_id=9)
- Audio: Defenders Class (of William Lane Craig) (https://www.reasonablefaith.org/podcasts/defenders-podcast-series-3)
- Audio: The Naked Bible (https://nakedbiblepodcast.com)
- Audio: Pints with Aquinas (https://pintswithaquinas.com)

- Audio: Ask NT Wright Anything (https://www.premierchristianradio.com/Shows/Weekday/Ask-NT-Wright-Anything/Podcast)
- Audio: White Horse Inn (https://www.whitehorseinn.org)
- Audio: Ask Pastor John (John Piper) (https://www.desiringgod.org/ask-pastor-john)

Apologetics (Defending the Faith)

- Video: Apologetics Academy (https://www.youtube.com/channel/UCKJ_EeoOeUtCyRT4g8OUlkQ)
- Video: Apologetics 315 (https://www.youtube.com/user/Apologetics315)
- Video: Various videos by Alisa Childers discussing apologetics and critiquing "progressive Christianity" (https://www.youtube.com/user/alisachilders)
- Video: Reasonable Faith (https://www.youtube.com/user/ReasonableFaithOrg)
- Video: Capturing Christianity (https://www.youtube.com/channel/UCux-_Fze3otFuI_5CArwSmg)
- Video: Lectures of William Lane Craig (https://www.reasonablefaith.org/videos/lectures)
- Video: Debates of William Lane Craig (https://www.reasonablefaith.org/videos/debates)
- Video: Various videos by Lydia McGrew defending biblical reliability (https://www.youtube.com/channel/UCSwhBkovUSg_6prKkR82IDQ)
- Audio: Unbelievable? (https://www.premierchristianradio.com/Shows/Saturday/Unbelievable)
- Audio: Reasonable Faith Podcast (https://www.reasonablefaith.org/media/reasonable-faith-podcast)
- Audio: Cold Case Christianity (https://coldcasechristianity.com/category/podcasts)
- Audio: Cross Examined (https://crossexamined.org/category/podcast)
- Audio: Stand to Reason Podcast (https://www.str.org/podcasts)
- Audio: Come Let Us Reason (http://podcast.comereason.org)

Each of the above sources contains a great deal of good information. Not every episode or entry is being personally endorsed, but they are sites and sources that are generally very reliable. Some of the material may be controversial among fellow Christians (some sites, for example, come from the perspective of Reformation/Calvinist theology, which is bound to conflict with those with so-called Arminian, Jesuit, or Catholic sympathies). Aside from these stipulations, Christians can basically acquire an undergraduate college-level education in Bible, theology, and apologetics—all of which contribute to a well-rounded foundation in knowing God better.

TAKING COLLEGE COURSES

Not everyone is designed to pursue a college degree. However, colleges are not just about credential. They are also there to provide extra learning opportunities in a variety of fields of study. Depending on your region, you may have access to courses in reasoning and critical thinking and perhaps even courses specializing in Christian or biblical studies. Tuition can sometimes be minimized if you opt to take such courses for audit. This means that no matter what grade you earn, that grade does not count against you (and neither does it count in your favor if it's good). But you will learn the same material nevertheless! This gives you the flexibility of a learning environment without the normal stresses of student life. And, if you want, you can still partake of the course assessments in determining whether you are learning the material or not. Instructors tend not to know who is auditing a course and who is taking it for credit.

Consider the ideal, well-rounded Christian to be one who takes courses in critical thinking (to learn *how* to think), comparative literature (to see how *others* think), and particularly Christian studies such as those in theology and Bible (to learn *what* to think). For those outside of a college or university setting where such courses are geographically unavailable, or financially or academically too prohibiting, consider checking out courses from colleges and universities outside of your province that offer distance education options such as web-based instruction (one of the few good things to come of COVID-19 is an increase in such distance education). Start with those that accredit their classes (for quality control purposes) and then, after exhausting that avenue, consider unaccredited options (but do your homework as to the academic rigor). You're not likely looking for a degree in the material, so take that position of flexibility as an opportunity to find a decent balance between cost and rigor.

And, by all means, don't just go at it alone. Consider enlisting friends and family members to join you. Such collegiate studies are always best enhanced when you have a support network of like-minded people. It's like stepping up your Christian fellowship circle. Challenge your Bible study group to all take the same course. Or, call on your coworkers or camping buddies or book club to experiment with you. It's a great experience of togetherness. So, if you don't already have a Bible study group, this may be the very thing that facilitates one!

HAVING FRIENDLY CONVERSATIONS

In an age of social media, the proportion of conversations that are friendly is smaller than it used to be in previous generations. It seems that everyone has an opinion these days and few comments, no matter how benign, are posted without vitriolic backlash. What seems like a disheartening trend, however, can be utilized for your good. Consider deliberately joining Christian groups and Christian debate forums. You need not participate in order to take advantage of the conversations that are posted therein. You can simply read the original posts along with what others have to say by way of support and pushback. Once you're feeling particularly up to the interaction, then perhaps post a conversation starter of your own or continue a thread that has already developed.

It is also a good idea to have in-person conversations with family, friends, or coworkers that have something to contribute. Perhaps you have an uncle or niece or a colleague who is particularly knowledgeable about, say, Christian history or doctrine. If so, set up some coffee dates just to chat about these matters. No matter what venue of conversation you choose or with whom, always go in initially with this attitude: "I'm here to ask questions and to learn; I'm not here to win anything." This is important because nobody should have to put their guard up in a conversation that is intended to be a fruitful learning experience. You're not there to test the waters of debate. Debating is a sporting event that is intended for the edification of spectators, not its participants. Instead, you're there to *absorb*. And any critical questions can be safely asked without concern that the conversation will collapse into a debate. If someone says something a bit off, ask for clarification (and withhold the temptation to correct unless it is being welcomed by the other person). If someone is being critical of *you*, then defuse the situation by redirecting the conversation or by asking a follow-up question that takes you both back to a more amicable topic.

Finally, and perhaps most obviously, be sure to plug in to a local church and Bible study group. To uncover these benefits, refer to my comments above. But I say here that personal interactions ought to *begin* with friends and confidants that are warm to Christianity. It is important to build these interpersonal foundations, not only because of the benefit to you, but because there are bound to be others who will benefit *from* you. You're not the only one wishing to know more about God and his Word in your quest to equip yourself against the enemy's doctrinal and moral assaults. As colaborers in Christ, the fruits of your interactions will be bidirectional. That's how the body of Christ works and why, when it is functioning in this way, it threatens the principalities and powers that be (Eph 3:10). Mutual learning brings unity. And unity is a bulwark against Satan's coordinated attacks—not just in terms of doctrine but also in terms of holiness.

Hopefully these suggestions set you off in the right direction to increasing your knowledge in the Lord. In the next chapter, we will take a practical look at that second pillar of spiritual warfare: holiness and the Christian virtues. We will expand a bit more on what those things mean and have a frank, practical conversation about what Christians can do to live sanctifying lives before God.

20

The Warrior Ethos: Holiness in Practical Living

So FAR WE HAVE been considering some practical advice related to knowledge as wisdom as one of the crucial ingredients for the life of a spiritual warrior. Now, we turn to the subject of practical holiness. Since we are an enfleshed people, we are naturally influenced by desires and appetites that often get us into trouble (and why one of our enemies is the flesh). But, as we have pointed out, Scripture nevertheless requires that we pursue righteousness as we live lives of holiness—a holiness that forms the essence of what it means to undergo the spiritual sanctification process. In this chapter, we will focus more precisely and practically on what it means to live a life of holiness. We will then look at some practical ways we Christians can preserve and guard our lives as we seek to conform ourselves to the righteousness of God. If we're going to take holiness as a serious pillar of spiritual warfare, it is a good idea to fill out precisely when behavior is transgressive and to offer up some practical advice on Christian living in order to avoid such transgressions. That is, we're going to examine some ways to know when and why something is wrong so that we can take steps to avoid the fleshly snares of the enemy.

HOLINESS

At the end of Part III, we looked at spiritual warfare as the examined life worth defending. This model suggests that the practice of spiritual warfare is but the practice of responsibly acquiring and maintaining the right kind of knowledge along with the pursuance of holiness, all under the support of our faithful, prayerful reliance on Christ. It is a standard that is our objective and, paradoxically, one that is beyond our reach. But the mercy of Christ is his making us righteous through his transformative power. We can meet this objective if we continue to rely on Christ in body, mind, and spirit. His is a power that will culminate in us becoming holy at the end of the day (or, should I say, at the end of days?). Holiness is what God's moral character is. It is something that we surely are not. That is why the root of the Greek term for "holiness" (*hagiōsynē*) is *hágios*, for it literally means "set apart" or "wholly other." It connotes something completely different—something God is and not anything else. And while none of us are or can become God, his impeccable nature is the standard set before us.

We saw that holiness is, in Scripture, akin to "righteousness" and "sanctification." Holiness as righteousness is a supreme and perfect good—obviously. It is the highest moral property that can be possessed by anyone. As sanctification, it is the present status of every Christian, but it is also an unfinished process of becoming for the Christian. It is *striving* toward the objective of being righteous while under the supervision and power of God. While Christians have been *legally* sanctified already in Christ (Acts 20:32; 26:18; Rom 4:5, 22–25; 15:16; 1 Cor 1:2; 6:11; Heb 2:11; 10:10, 29), our position in this sanctification is to be met with our active, ongoing alignment with that recognition (1 Thess 4:3; Heb 10:14). In other words, while one is appointed as one who is righteous, she must now accord with that new job description. Consider a useful analogy. Rami Malek is an actor who recently portrayed the late singer Freddy Mercury in the biopic *Bohemian Rhapsody* (2018). While Rami was cast as Freddy, and so *was* Freddy for all intents and purposes during rehearsals, he nevertheless had to "become" Freddy in preparation for the film's final production. It is something that every successful actor must undergo in his or her becoming a certain character. They *are* the character from the start, but they are also *becoming* that character in the end. Similarly, our being declared righteous and holy is what the script (the Bible) says about us, so to speak. However, we must strive to become righteous and holy over the course of our lives. And that can only happen under the guidance of the Holy Spirit living in us.

Will we ever achieve it in this life? No. And John reminds us of this fact in 1 John 1:8. But that does not mean that we should give up. That is where each of us is at now. We are designed to be sanctified human beings, not only legally but also in actuality. And while we can never complete it on our own, eventually Christ will finalize that transformation process in us, with our cooperation, so that we will indeed finally and fully become righteous (Rom 5:19; 6:19–22). The point is that at every step of the way we are to work hard but rely fully and completely on the power of Christ. He is the one who enables us to holiness. If we can do that much—rely on Christ—then, warts and all, we will finally be transformed. It is a relief to know and a joyful reminder that Christ has gifted us with the pathway to finally overcome.

Now, becoming holy will ultimately make us happy. And yet, it's true that being good does not always reap an immediate reward. That's evident far too many times. But that isn't what I'm saying here. Instead, I am saying that becoming holy fulfills a deep-seated desire. Our natures, as imagers of God himself, are designed to strive toward and achieve full fellowship with God. When sin ruptured that road to holiness, it became a much more difficult endeavor. With sin ultimately out of the way, we can once again enjoy an unfettered fellowship with God—something we were meant to participate in. We become holy and, as a pleasant consequence, we become happy—happy not in the fleshly sense of unbridled hedonism and whatnot, but in the sense of *fulfilling our nature as beings in God's image*. When a musician learns how to make music and then produce music, she becomes fulfilled and, so, happy. When a humanitarian learns how to help others and implement what she has learned, she feels a sense of accomplishment and completeness. Likewise, as human beings we yearn for unity and closeness with God. And such unity and closeness require holiness as a way to tear down everything that would impede that intimacy. When human beings ultimately and eventually achieve holiness, they achieve happiness by virtue of achieving that supreme fulfillment—just as the musician and the humanitarian do in their respective practices.

Unfortunately, what we were designed to be has been clouded and marred in the twenty-first century. While Christians hear ministers preach about how they are to emulate holiness in doing good for others and for oneself, we do not seem to reckon holiness to be the end of Christian living. That is, we do not work hard at holiness in fulfilling our nature so as to become happy. Instead, we seek a more short-circuited route to the happiness we desire. We seek the carnal route. Since the flesh does not *really* involve doing what it takes to be united with God in Christ, it opts for a less adequate notion of happiness—a happiness that is but a shadow of true contentment. The result is that when things don't go our way, we get easily frustrated. For we fail to distinguish between *doing what it takes to pursue holiness in being united with God* and *enjoying the benefits of a life lived in pursuit of that holiness*. When someone gets angry with God or walks away from the faith altogether because something has gone wrong (perhaps even seriously wrong) with the world in some way, we are confusing the former with that of the latter. While happiness is inconsistent with a life struck by disaster, misery, struggles, failure, etc, holiness is not. But, in the end, holiness is a guarantee of happiness, which is that sublime state of contentment and fulfillment we seek. Ultimate happiness is thus the result of a life having been lived in the pursuit of Christ-centeredness and holiness. This is the good life.

So, all of this is to emphasize that holiness is not to be conflated with happiness in the unqualified sense. Sure, one can do the right thing and end up in a worse state than before. It reminds me of one of the songs ("No Good Deed") from the Broadway production *Wicked*, where the antihero, Elphaba, musically laments:

> No good deed goes unpunished;
> No act of charity goes unresented.
> No good deed goes unpunished;
> That's my new creed.
> My road of good intentions
> led where such roads always lead.
> No good deed goes unpunished . . .

The song echoes what many cynics think is one of nature's cruelest jokes for those who work hard at practicing virtue. But that at best only shows that we are not to *expect* that good things might come our way if we do good even though such *can* happen. (We also shouldn't be surprised if those who do bad tend to benefit from it and lead joyful lives, by carnal standards.) Our ultimate fulfillment and happiness will not come until Christ raises us from the dead at the end of the age. So, as of right now, there are things we will have to do that will not bring us much joy. They will likely not make us popular or important in the eyes of the world. While we are feeling the pressure from the fact that everybody else is doing wrong and benefiting from it, we are not accountable for the shortcomings of others. We have to live a Christlike life, which will look different from the world. It may invite brutal criticism, scoffing, and, unfortunately, even violent retaliation. But we are called to endure in holiness to the end (1 Pet 3:14–18; 4:12–19).

But *how* do we do this? While Scripture is very clear on some things we are not supposed to do (e.g., murder, steal, or commit adultery) and some things we are (e.g., love your neighbor, engage in fellowshipping with one another, and bear one another's burdens), it is not clear on everything—especially matters peculiar to the twenty-first century (e.g., Is sharing passwords for streaming accounts immoral?; Is having church online instead of in person wrong? etc.). In the next section, we will take a look at some behaviors and practices and how we might properly discern and navigate them in our pursuit of holiness in the current climate of blurred lines and fluid boundaries. By getting us to think philosophically about these matters, we will hopefully appreciate not only the *what* but also the *why* of sin and its corruptive nature. God's commands to holy living are not arbitrary. They make sense. And if we can make sense of why sin is what it is (other than because God has so declared it), then it will add that extra motivation in us to "flee youthful passions and pursue righteousness, faith, love, and peace" (2 Tim 2:22).

HOLINESS AND CHRISTIAN LIVING

Deciding which behaviors to engage in life is not always easy, even if it is seemingly spelled out in Scripture. Because, inevitably, one wants to know precisely what a vice is and what makes it so. Adultery may be forbidden obviously enough, but for some it is unclear if that involves flirting and other forms of "fellowship" with those whom we are attracted to. For better or worse, there are areas of gray that permit so much latitude in many people's minds regarding Christian living. For them, the questions are plenty. Is it a sin to listen to secular music? Is it wrong to have a glass of wine? Most likely the answer is "no" to both questions. And yet, Scripture speaks out against things that compromise sobriety (Eph 5:18; 1 Thess 5:6–8) and things that do not bring Godly edification (Phil 4:8). For the ambiguities, we must enlist our ability to reason appropriately over such matters where the lines get a bit blurry. This seems to be what Paul suggests regarding the observances of vegetarianism and holy days:

> One person believes he may eat anything, while the weak person eats only vegetables. Let not the one who eats despise the one who abstains, and let not the one who abstains pass judgment on the one who eats, for God has welcomed him. Who are you to pass judgment on the servant of another? It is before his own master that he stands or falls. And he will be upheld, for the Lord is able to make him stand. One person esteems one day as better than another, while another esteems all days alike. Each one should be fully convinced in his own mind. (Rom 14:2–5)

On these matters, Paul says, "one should be fully convinced in his own mind." This will require taking such matters critically (i.e., reasonably) as well as prayerfully before the Lord.

Of course, the call for Christian freedom and latitude is not a recent development. The apostle Paul himself backed off from some of the rigid ritualistic practices of his Jewish brethren (Gal 5:1–6; Col 2:16). He also spoke on how we are to be tolerant of fellow believers who sometimes cross the line in our own eyes over matters pertaining to holy days and seasons (Rom 14:6–10; Gal 4:8–11). And he did this to the chagrin of some of his fellow Christians (Acts 15). When we consider the climate of today with the advent of the digital age, questions about what we should do and how we should behave become a bit more complicated. For example, is using your DVR to record an HBO movie and later showing it to friends (who don't have HBO) the same as movie pirating? Digital reproduction isn't like conventional stealing where someone might go into a department store and physically shoplift a DVD off the shelf and take it home. There is no shaking the fact that the concept of digital sharing is more complicated because it is more like duplication than object relocation (where the owner herself has not lost the original product).

We're seeing other similar ambiguities in the Christian mainstream. Is listening to worship music followed by a podcast of a church service sufficient to fulfill our obligations to not neglect the assembling of ourselves (Heb 10:25)? (I think not.) Others are even finding ambiguities in the more obvious sins. For example, lust is considered by some to be harmless. For it does not itself involve any *act* of sin allegedly. It is merely a state of mind that, if it does not lead to deviant sexual behavior, is nothing but harmless fantasizing. Even pornographers insist on its therapeutic value for both single and married people alike.

While we cannot address every specific matter pertaining to human behavior, I have selected a few prominent categories of such behaviors with which to interact. Sexuality is certainly one of them. My overall objective, though, is to provide a reasonable means of how to discern whether something is ethically wrong or not. While "because the Bible tells me so" may be enough for some, we would do well to see why Scripture's condemnations are reasonable in its prohibitions so that one can "be fully convinced in his own mind." If the mind can benefit in understanding why sins are indeed sins, then we may take the matter a bit more seriously and be more inclined to avoid such indulgences even if they don't, at first blush, seem wrong to us.

The fact of the matter is that, as fallen people, we have an uncanny ability to reason our way into compromising principles that adversely affect our pursuit of holiness. Consequently, corrupting our thinking on matters of ethics is one of the primary ways Satan schemes to devour both weak and strong Christians. Since moral purity is crucial for the Christian walk, we shall take care to explain what it is about the most significant practices that are wrong. And perhaps by exploring the more prevalent issues we can acquire wisdom in going forth in areas uncharted.

Sexual Behavior

Arguably, the number one takedown of the Christian walk is how we conduct ourselves in sexual matters, specifically regarding the ethical dimension of how we use our bodies in relation to others. Other than hunger and thirst, no drive is as potent as the sex drive—a feature of the human condition readily exploited by Satan and his cohorts. And it is for this reason that our culture at large is fraught with it. While Christians recognize sex to be a gift from God, it is entrusted to us as something to handle appropriately. Of course, we have done a lousy job as a human species, often waffling on what precisely it means to handle the matter *in*appropriately.

It is not necessary to rehearse everything that Scripture has to say about sex. Some of it is quite clear, including the fact that it is to be practiced solely within the confines of marriage (1 Cor 7:36; Heb 13:4). It is no less clear that sex is not to be between two members of the same sex (Lev 18:22; Rom 1:26–27; 1 Cor 6:9; 1 Tim 1:10) or between human and animal (Lev 18:23). But, in our plight for holiness, we, as human beings at war with the desires of the flesh, find technicalities and concessions that allow us to broaden what acceptable sex is in the life of the Christian. Oh sure, some just bite the bullet and already *know* that they're sinning when they engage in it. For them, it's sex first and repentance later; or, worse, they will have indiscriminate sex and forego their Christian walk altogether, telling themselves that God isn't real or that Christianity as a system has been hijacked by the prude.

Our culture today is facilitating clever ways to downplay the force of Scripture's condemnations of these practices or to pretend that they're not really principled condemnations at all. We, through our chronological snobbery, figure that ancient Christians and Jews are too entrapped by their circles of tradition to appreciate sexual liberation. As a means of control by the elite or as a way to subdue the underprivileged (or whatever), we imagine that any such condemnations are just historically, culturally, and geographically conditioned. Time and again we've been led to believe that the New Testament overrides the Old's supposedly more antiquated and pharisaical practices. Since God's commands for his people tend to get updated, we should expect nothing less of any residual condemnations from the ignorant, even if well-intentioned, of the first century.

This cultural debate has left the Christian with a rather confused portrait of what to think when it comes to these kinds of prohibitions. "The Bible also forbids wearing two kinds of material!"[1] they remind us, as if

---

1. Lev 19:19c.

all of God's commands are cut from the same cloth (pun intended!). But this is not so. First, God issues unique nonmoral commands depending on which covenant he is supervising at the time. For example, in the Noahic covenant, God declares almost unrestrictedly: "Every moving thing that lives shall be food for you. And as I gave you the green plants, I give you everything" (Gen 9:3). However, it is not until the Mosaic covenant that God forbids a subset of animals from being used as food (Lev 11:2; Deut 14). The more principled transcovenantal commands—those that are explicitly about *moral* issues not otherwise intended merely for this or that community—are never fundamentally altered. That there might have been *exceptions* is not to say that such original commands have been superseded or replaced but, rather, that a weightier duty was being preserved. Think of the duty to not lie. While such a duty never changes, that does not mean that there are not situations where upholding another, weightier duty does not trump our duty to tell the truth. For example, lying to protect someone from unjust torture may become someone's obligation, for protecting an innocent person from unjust suffering is weightier than the duty to be honest. The point is that God's moral commands are not temporary or culture specific as are his other, covenantal ones. But some of them are temporarily passed up in the name of preserving a greater good *in that specific instance where a moral conflict has arisen.*

So, what about sexual behavior? First off, there is good reason for seeing God's commands about sexuality as a moral issue and not merely as a supervisory one to be conditioned upon a given culture or some defunct covenant. Its moral status transcends any such contingencies. If Joe taps someone on the shoulder with his finger, no one thinks anything unbecoming has taken place. But if he were to do so with his sexual organ, the matter would be altogether something else. It would likely be a form of sexual assault. This is because we intuitively recognize the moral significance and sacredness of sexual organs such that they are not to be used in the same way as morally insignificant ones. Moreover, there is significant power assigned to human sexuality. It is that by which new life is (naturally) made possible. Only the sexual organs have this kind of power. This power is a testament not only to the uniqueness of sexuality but to the gravity of what it does for the human race. Thus, any vulgar use of those organs would be morally significant and, consequently, inappropriate. It is for the same kind of reason that it is morally wrong to use vocal cords, which have the unique power to build up and tear down another, to verbally abuse another. Such deviance is neither minor nor benign.

There is therefore a right way and a wrong way to engage in morally significant behavior. The basis for this must be defined by that (or more accurately *who*) which purposes that behavior for something. In the Christian worldview, God gives purpose to everything he has created. In thinking about the purpose of sexual behavior, its purpose is twofold: it is the natural pinnacle of a romantic union between a man and a woman and it is in service to human procreation. These are not necessarily independent or unrelated purposes since the latter one—procreation—*evidences* the proper use of the organs involved. They are bound up together. And that much shows what counts as either natural or not in service to the union of a man and woman.

That a man and woman are not to engage in premarital sex is thus understandable given that the sexual union is the *ultimate* or *maximum* form of romantic union. One ought not use the ultimate or maximal form of union in a relationship that is still becoming and not yet in its maximal state. It would be like prematurely giving a standing ovation (a maximal form of praise in theater) to a performance that is not yet finished or is less than deserving. It would also be like participating in voting for a candidate in a region in which you are not yet legally a resident. Rights or privileges are reserved for, and only appropriate in, those relevant relationships in which they belong. Christians therefore ought to reserve the maximal practice of human sex until they have achieved a maximal union—a union that is fully mutual and in which one finally promises to forsake all others for the rest of one's natural life. There is no more maximal state of romantic love one can enter into than this. To extend the sexual privilege to those who have not yet achieved the right to exercise it is nothing short of inappropriate, for they are preferring the maximizing of happiness and pleasure over and above teleology and entitlement.

In addition, the marital union is a living representation of our union with God. To invite the romantic company of others who aren't our spouse would be to commit a form of idolatry, one that we readily call, with a (intentional?) phonetic resemblance, "adultery." This imagery is actually used in Scripture both as the consummatory hope of every Christian believer (Rev 19:6–9; 21:2, 9) and as a scathing rebuke of those who religiously intermingle with false gods (Hosea 1). The marital union is thus serious business with God. We Christians therefore ought to do what we can to preserve its sacredness as well as its twofold purpose. This means that we should not overly concern ourselves with certain adolescent questions like: "How much affection can I legally engage in before it's considered wrong?" In its own right, the question is a legitimate one. But sometimes we're just *looking* for an opportunity to indulge; and that needs to be checked. It is proper to elevate our love for God above our love for any human person. As such, perhaps the better question is: "How much do I love God in avoiding behavior that would otherwise compromise that?" It isn't that this is a different question, but that it helps us bear in mind a proper hierarchy of our relationships. By it we will naturally and reasonably weed out practices that might sully our relationship with God. And asking such a question also forces us to center ourselves on what we *really* want rather than what we merely *think* we want while in the heat of passion.

The way we should conduct ourselves in matters of sexual behavior can be summarized as follows: (i) our behavior must be appropriate for the relationship we currently have, and (ii) our behavior must always take into account our love for God first. To avoid impropriety is to "give no opportunity to the devil" (Eph 4:27). If we lapse in this, our sins will snowball into rupturing our courtship with God that will result in the ultimate divorce: death. We can't be naïve. Matters of human sexuality are at the heart of many battles when it comes to spiritual warfare. A proper mindfulness about the proper role of sexuality will only help us win that battle.

Lust

Dubbed in the fourth century as one of the "seven deadly sins" (probably due to its ubiquity as opposed to its spiritual effect), lust is a matter that is sometimes difficult to disentangle from Godly sexual behavior and attitude. Since sexual behavior is a significant moral issue, then any kind of predisposition that would inch us toward compromising the purpose of sex should be carefully guarded. We are all predisposed, to varying degrees, toward sexual behavior since this is our God-given nature in service to marital union and reproduction. But when such a predisposition gets skewed into becoming a certain kind of ungodly desire, then any satisfaction of that skewed desire is bound to be in violation of the teleology—or designated purpose—of human sexual union. Lust fits this notion of a skewed desire—it takes sexual desire and turns it into something else.

Without getting too far ahead of ourselves here, let us first define what lust is with some specificity. In so doing, we will see why indulging in such a desire is something opposed to godly behavior and why God speaks against it. Lust, though a species of sexual desire, must be demarcated from being *mere* sexual desire or even arousal. For sexual arousal can spontaneously obtain even in the absence of a sexual context.[2] The adolescent who becomes spontaneously, biologically aroused in math class is surely not lusting over his predicament. No, sexual desire is something more than mere arousal. More importantly, we want to know when it becomes *lust*. When sexual

---

2. Kingsberg, "Testosterone Treatment."

desire is conjoined with love for and unity with a beloved, it is counterintuitive to think that such occurrences are lust as we might think of it. This much is observable even by disbelievers in God. Atheist philosopher Simon Blackburn, for example, in his lecture-turned-book simply titled *Lust*, writes: "Lust is a psychological state with a goal or aim . . . [an] enthusiastic desire that infuses the body, for sexual activity and its pleasures *for their own sake*."[3] Unity with a beloved is not the objective of lust. Instead, any unity or togetherness that might obtain at the behest of lust is merely *incidental* to that unity. Coming together is merely instrumental to the self's desire for sexual gratification. By contrast, an appropriate sexual desire tends *toward* sexual unity with a beloved. It seeks a maximal, romantic union with another through an erotic encounter. It is a testament to sex's aim and unitive nature. Think about it. When someone sexually desires another, there is a yearning for a certain kind of closeness. The sex act then finalizes and reinforces the bond by breaking down any trepidation and inhibitions, allowing the couple to lose themselves in the union. The two become one (Gen 2:24; cf. 1 Cor 6:16). I don't think we have to ponder very hard about how lust fails to accomplish this.

By way of separating lust from mere sexual desire, it seems to me that lust plausibly bears two essential and indivisible conditions. First, it is a kind of sexual desire that is either intentionally induced or intentionally sustained, at least in part, which is to say that it is within one's power to cease or avoid at will. This alone, of course, does not set it apart from other volitional states of desire—sexual or not. And we're not talking about mere arousal here since, as we've already noted, that is generally something that can't be controlled. Lust is, first and foremost, a certain kind of intentional state. Being this much, we need to add the second condition. This second condition is that lust is something that seeks primarily only a self-indulgence (and any "unity" or "love" that may result is only incidental, even if instrumental, to that self-indulgence). This indicates that lust is contrary to the natural aim of sexual desire (which is romantic and procreative unity). For lust does not care whether the other is genuinely satisfied and/or unified by the experience *except* insofar as it callously aids the sexual experience. Indeed, it deviates from seeking the beloved *as* the beloved and instead as something else making such a deviation an affront to sex's natural and divine purpose. Aside from opposing genuine unity, it most assuredly isn't in the business of intentionally producing children! These two factors—being under our willful control and being contrary to the purpose of sex—set lust apart from a more innocuous sexual desire.

3. Blackburn, *Lust*, 16 and 19; emphasis added.

Now, as we all know, Jesus openly prohibited sexual lust when he said, "You have heard that it was said, 'You shall not commit adultery.' But I say to you that everyone who looks at a woman with lustful intent has already committed adultery with her in his heart" (Matt 5:27–28). Lust, unlike sexual behavior, is not an activity but an intent—an intent to do something against the natural purpose of sex. But, as we have suggested, it is an intent that can be averted. And, so, as Alexander Pruss observes, "the intentional induction of desires for that which is intrinsically wrong is morally bad."[4] Christ's command to avoid lust, then, seals the deal: lust is not only naturally bad but wrong, and doubly so because it is explicitly prohibited. In short, lust is morally wrong because it is explicitly forbidden, and it is forbidden because it facilitates or permits a certain kind of looming desire that perverts the proper goal of sexual desire.

Therefore, we would do well to avoid situations where sexual desire cannot be properly channeled or disregarded. It is especially true if we have struggled with this before in a number of ways. We ought not to be naïve as to think that any future entanglements will be met with different results. This might involve avoiding certain movies and television shows that fall within a certain rating; it may involve the discontinuation of streaming services or of cutting the cord altogether; it may even require one to impose internet filtering systems—some of which are free and universal for all devices, like OpenDNS.[5] If we can do our best to guard our eyes from those things that would incite lust in us, as difficult as this is for many in urban cities, we will be primed to better live the life of holiness. This is the wisdom behind Jesus's hard sayings about gouging one's eyes out or cutting off one's hands (Matt 18:8–9; Mark 9:43–47). The imagery of self-mutilation reveals the significance of lust as an aberration of an otherwise benign sexual desire. And the fruit of this is quite evident, for holiness in matters of sexual purity will shrink any significant opportunities the devil may have in taking us down.

Pride

We now shift away from sexual matters to something else equally destructive of moral character. Like lust, this vice is also prominent in the list of the "seven deadly sins." I am referring to the nonsexual sin of *pride*. That pride is something that is, or can be, wrong is evidenced by its more familiar monikers: "arrogance," "narcissism," "pomposity" "haughtiness," and "megalomania." These are not considered morally neutral descriptors; they

---

4. Pruss, *One Body*, 339.
5. https://www.opendns.com.

refer to real moral *flaws*. On the other hand, there's the sort of acceptable "pride" that involves being proud of one's achievements, say, in academia, in the arts, or in one's place of work. There is also the pride of heritage, community, and patriotism. Certainly it is a mistake to *not* take pride in *anything*. In fact, lacking appropriate self-esteem is often construed as a sure sign of a human weakness. Even Scripture itself features statements of the faithful declaring their pride unequivocally. For example, the apostle Paul celebrates in Romans 15:16 that "In Christ Jesus, then, I have reason to be *proud* of my work for God." Elsewhere he says, "I am acting with great boldness toward you; *I have great pride in you* . . ." (2 Cor 7:4, emphasis added).

But this same Paul who celebrates his pride both in terms of his accomplishments as well as in terms of his relation to other saints unequivocally condemns pride. In Romans 11:20 he implores the Roman Christians to "*not* become proud, but fear." He forbids the neophyte Christian from ascending to the position of overseer lest he "become *puffed up with conceit* [*typhōtheis*] and fall into the condemnation of the devil" (1 Tim 3:6; emphasis added). His compatriots Peter and James likewise cite the Septuagint (the Greek translation of the Old Testament) favorably, wherein it says, "God *opposes the proud* but gives grace to the humble" (Jas 4:6; 1 Pet 5:5; emphasis added). And no less than Jesus himself lists pride alongside of other wrongdoings including wickedness, deceit, and slander (Mark 7:22). This is not just a New Testament thing, either. The Hebrew Old Testament is equally condemnatory of pride. For in Psalm 31:23, for example, it is promised that "The LORD preserves the faithful *but abundantly repays the one who acts in pride*" (emphasis added).

We must conclude that, like sexual behavior, pride can be qualified to be either benign or sinister—the sinister side being something every Christian needs to avoid. As Scripture further warns, "pride comes before disgrace" (Prov 4:4) and "goes before destruction" (16:18). Those are serious consequences. And this forces us to ask about what qualifies pride to be a bad thing. To answer this, we should consider what pride *without qualification* is. What sets it apart from, say, confidence, valor, or courage? Pride is, first and foremost, an apparent recognition of being in a certain, relevant relation—a "mine" relation to some object or action of excellence. That is, in some sense we have or own whatever it is we are proud of. This "mine" relation is one of two things. One, it could be "mine" in the sense that one stands in a possessive relation to what he or she *does*. This is to say that due to a particular accomplishment one has achieved, she feels herself deserving of a certain amount of excellence or approbation. The sculptor, if she sculpts an aesthetically remarkable statue, has done something probably deserving of commendation. But not all pride is predicated on what one does. For, to mention the second of the "mine" relation, it may be a matter of just being proud of your city or of your ethnic heritage. You may even be proud of your physical looks—a notion that introduces to us vanity, which I just take to be a subspecies of this sense of pride. Unlike achievement-based pride, this kind of pride is predicated on what he or she *is* or *has*—i.e., an identity-based pride. That one is proud of her ancestry or of her social group or dashing good looks is quite appropriate given that one is, in some sense, a member or possessor of those things. Incidentally, it is the "mine" relation that demarcates the feelings of excellence or approbation from the feelings of, say, *envy*. (To envy something involves the acknowledgement that the object of excellence is actually *not* one's own.)

What qualifies pride to be a vice, then? Like lust, it becomes a vice when it defies a particular nature or design pattern. In this case, it is a defiance of a proper dignity as laid out by God. But that defiance must always be one of *over*estimating that dignity (where *under*estimating it would not be pride but something more like *shame* or *disgrace*). In the case of a wrongful pride, it has to do with transgressing this nature or design pattern in some excessive way. That is, the wrong kind of pride occurs when a person feels and believes something about one's own excellence that wrongly exceeds the nature and measure of one's actual dignity. Suppose, for example, Bill is appointed the keynote speaker for a local academic conference. If Bill thought that folks should *worship* him because he is a keynote speaker at an academic conference, you would think him mad. For he would, inappropriately, be expecting a form of adulation that exceeds the nature of his appointment. By contrast, it is an *innocuous* pride when one's attitude about one's dignity rightfully does *not* exceed the nature and measure of one's actual dignity. Bill's believing that others should *respect* him seems more like an appropriate expectation in line with his appointment.

Well, this gets us to why pride is wrong but it doesn't yet reveal whether it's a *moral* wrong or some other kind of wrong. To say that something is morally wrong is to say that one *ought not* to do something of moral significance. And oughtness entails that there are obligations and prohibitions. But prohibitions only make sense if issued by a relevant authority. The Christian has an answer for the objective wrongness of actions. For God is a relevant *and superlative* authority who is in charge of, by virtue of creating, the nature and essence of every type of created thing. And he makes them known by divine commands, or some other means, those natures not to be defied. Since God has created human dignity against the backdrop of himself (that we are in the image of God), he therefore imbues our actions with moral significance. To think unnaturally about our dignity in an inordinate way that elevates it above what it really is (a life desperately dependent on God) is to defy the one in whose image we were created. Pride is literally defacing God by replacing him with the magnificence of our own selves. Like adultery, pride is a form of self-worship, which is yet another form of idolatry.

So, as Christian warriors, how can we avoid instances of pride? Perhaps the best thing to do is to consider whether you would still do *x* even if your identity or endeavor would forever be unrecognized by others. That is, if you knew some beneficial action you were to do would be invisible or anonymous to everyone else, would you still do it? Or, would you only do it for the recognition? Such a question may help us to think more carefully about which actions we are doing for the right reasons and which ones we are doing for our own glory. This is the wisdom behind Jesus's call for his followers to give, pray, and fast "in secret" (Matt 6:3–8). Holiness is easily threatened if we seat ourselves in the place where God should be. And if pride invites judgment (1 Tim 3:6), then the consequences could be disastrous for us and those relying on us to be faithful and humble. It is not a private sin; it is, by definition, a public spectacle. And if we care about the extended body of Christ, we must not think ourselves to be better than we are—sinners saved by grace.

"... And Things Like These"

It is possible to continue to address many of the vices that adversely affect the life of a Christian, but space does not permit an exhaustive study of such vices. Needless to say, Scripture makes it clear what sorts of behaviors are forbidden. Paul, for example, offers a list in Galatians 5:19–21 that includes: "sexual immorality, impurity, sensuality, idolatry, sorcery, enmity, strife, jealousy, fits of anger, rivalries, dissensions, divisions, envy, drunkenness, [and] orgies . . ." Of particular interest is the fact that sexual behavior constitutes the first three (though I would not presume to see these as ranked). And although pride does not make the immediate list here, it does appear ("conceited") in verse 26 as well as in another list of his in 2 Timothy 3:2.[6] As such, Paul is not content in creating a full stop in the initial Galatian list of vices. Instead, he ends that list in 5:21 with "... and things like these" (*kai ta homoia toutois*).

This is obviously meant to indicate that the list is not exhaustive. But it does something else. The inclusion of "and things like these" forces us to

---

6. His list includes "lovers of self, lovers of money, proud, arrogant, abusive, disobedient to their parents, ungrateful, unholy . . ." In this list, pride seems to feature in at least three of these (i.e., lovers of self, proud, and arrogant).

reflect on what relates these vices to begin with. For example, suppose a parent tells her child: "Do not write on, paint on, or carve on the walls in your bedroom, or do things like these." In this case, the child is left to consider what would be "like" the others. The common thread here has to do with her preventing the child from defacing the wall, no matter what form that should take. So, the child would not be immune to discipline if she decided to, say, *stamp* images onto the wall—thinking to herself that stamping is neither writing, painting, nor carving anything in violation of the original command. However, the inclusion of "things like these" would obviously entail other unmentioned actions of the same kind. The child whose heart is set on observing the letter of the law, so to speak, is one that is not interested in obedience and respect. She is, instead, only interested in her own desires insofar as she can shield herself from any punitive repercussions.

This is what confronts us in Galatians 5. It appears that the common thread in the list of vices has to do with matters of *indulging in our carnal passions* (e.g., Gal 5:16). This is to say that it is wrong for us to lack restraint in the face of the deviant desires of our nature. To treat the list as a delimited tally of vices is to miss the point. Instead, it serves to exemplify the kinds of gratifications that constitute violations of holiness. Thus, whether it is an action explicitly forbidden here (like sexual immorality) or one that is "like" this (say, heavy petting), the presumption here is that, no matter the *particular* vice, *anything* that involves the unbridled indulging of our carnal passions without consideration as to what it means to be "in the Spirit" is wrong. It is also interesting to note that Paul does not list these vices as a way to tally those actions that Christians should avoid; instead he treats these vices as what it looks like to walk in the flesh as opposed to the Spirit (vv. 17–19). Thus, Paul isn't saying that by avoiding such behaviors one is now made to walk in the Spirit; rather, he is saying that the one who walks in the Spirit is one who avoids such behaviors. The kind of life you live determines whether you are fruitfully virtuous or vicious, not the other way around.

The child who seeks to circumnavigate the list of prohibitions in order to do *something* to the wall is one who does not love or respect or honor (or whatever) her parent enough. But the child who truly wants to please her parent will not even *approximate* defacing the wall. She does not dance around the boundaries of what was explicitly forbidden and what was not. But she *goes the extra mile* in ensuring that her behavior does not even give the appearance of misdeed regarding the wall. Similarly, for the Galatian who walks in the Spirit, he or she will naturally avoid the explicitly listed vices. But he or she will also avoid anything "like these." The moment we ask ourselves "How much can I do before it falls within the Pauline list of prohibitions?" is the moment we reveal that our walk is not in the Spirit but in the flesh. For a lover of God will purpose not to do anything that would even appear unbecoming of a Christ-follower.

It is no wonder that Paul elsewhere places such a heavy emphasis on even avoiding ordinarily benign behaviors like eating meat (Rom 14:1–3[7]), sacralizing one day over another (vv. 5–6), or drinking wine (v. 21) if they should lead to causing a fellow brother (or sister) in the Lord to stumble (vv. 13ff.). If these things would *look* evil insofar as they would promote discord in the body of Christ, then they are to be avoided.[8] And this mentality is quite understandable by analogy: If a husband truly loves his wife, he will not only not cheat on his wife but he will not give his wife the impression that he is cheating. Indeed, he won't even do anything that leads one to suspect that he is cheating on her. It should never occur to a loving spouse to ask the question "How much can I get away with before it becomes wrong?" when it comes to his or her interactions with others.

The ethos of holiness is not to be as the old pharisaical attitude of merely abiding by the letter of the law. Instead, it is to be one that neither flirts with the boundaries of wrongdoing nor will be construed by others as morally problematic. *Wait! Is this to say that the moral opinions of others determine what is right and wrong for us?* In a sense, yes. This is what it means to go the extra mile for the sake of other believers. Of course, such perspective-based restrictions must be reasonable. So, any *un*reasonable demands on what is good (e.g., refraining from lifelong practices like marriage; cf. 1 Tim 4:3a) are not included. As for the more reasonable ones (e.g., temporal, fleeting, and insignificant practices), if we care for the body of Christ, the call for such restraint on our behavior shouldn't offend us. Some people, due to their own shortcomings, tend to be more sensitive to certain practices than others. In this sense, it isn't that the opinions of others are determinative of the morality of this or that action; rather, it is the threat of weakening the faith of another that becomes the higher moral obligation. So, it isn't the practice itself that is taking on this or that vicious moral property; it is the intent to risk the spiritual well-being of another for the

---

7. This would seem to fly in the face of Paul's statement in 1 Tim 4:3, wherein he condemns those who "require abstinence from foods that God created to be received with thanksgiving by those who believe and know the truth." However, Paul's discussion about avoiding eating meat among other things is not about the act itself but about doing such things *in the presence of other Christians*. The presumption is that a mature believer must first mentor or train the "weaker" believer first and not simply engage in such behaviors that would be shocking to a recent convert.

8. One may have in mind 1 Thess 5:22, wherein it says, in the King James Version at least, "Abstain from all appearance of evil." As to why this particular translation ought not to be preferred, despite its being supportive of what I'm arguing for, see Fee, *First and Second Letters*, 223f.

sake of personal preferences that does. In and of itself, it is not considered wrong by most to play football recreationally. But if a brother or sister in the Lord considers the sport to be inappropriate, it would be wrong to engage in it in their presence. This is not necessarily to incriminate the sport, but the obvious negligence you would be promoting in knowingly rattling another's relationship with God.

The overall lesson here is that we should not be teasing ourselves with certain boundary conditions like the disobedient child mentioned above, for it would reveal our lack of honor and seriousness to God and others in our relationships. But we can add to this that while sexual immorality, impurity, and sensuality are explicitly listed, we ought not to engage in gateway behaviors because they may easily entangle us into the more obvious vices, even if those gateways are not themselves wrong. The Christian man who sees himself as pure while cohabitating with his girlfriend in an apartment, and perhaps even remaining physically abstinent, is nevertheless ensconced in a circumstance that gnaws away at that perpetual purity. Lustful thoughts and/or sexual contact become inevitable. If we are implored to "give no opportunity to the devil" (Eph 4:27), then behaviors that (reasonably) incline us to any vices are behaviors to be avoided. If you are unsure about something, seek the advice and counsel of an elder, pastor, minister, or overseer. Let the body of Christ ensure its own health; and let us desire to see the church as a pure bride adorned for her Husband.[9]

CONCLUSION

In this chapter, we have considered what it means to live the life of holiness. We examined some prominent vices like lust and pride and saw how they violate God's holy code of conduct. They are vices precisely because they violate the intended purposes set out by God in creation. We also looked at how we are not just to avoid explicitly listed vices but we are to conduct ourselves as we would toward a spouse whom we love dearly. This moves us to separate ourselves sometimes from things that may not be wrong in

---

9. Someone might well ask, "If we do not know if a brother or sister opposes some innocuous practice, should we not take any chances and thus avoid the practice while in their company?" It seems to me that to do so would put an undue burden on every believer—putting everyone on high alert over potentially every practice. Instead, I would say that if the practice was a known controversy in the wider community (say, that there is at least a 30–40 percent disagreement rate), then I would refrain from that practice in the public eye. Otherwise, given the potential that just about *anything* might be construed as faith-rattling to another, it would be unreasonable to deny oneself of a good without any grounds for doing so (cf. Luke 10:38–42).

and of themselves. For if they give the appearance of impropriety, or could reasonably lead us to ruin, then we should preserve the self and the church body at all costs and avoid those gateway behaviors. This is what it means to live the warrior ethos. For the Christian warrior means to fight against anything that would sully the cause of holiness even if it means avoiding things that the average citizen does not consider wrong. The warrior does not complain about this situation but presses onward until the time comes to lay down arms. That time is not yet.

21

The Front Line: Apologetics

WE HAVE ESTABLISHED THAT an examined life worth defending involves equipping the warrior Christian to be both wise and virtuous—where the former effectively paves a pathway to the latter. Indeed, Christians are called to rightly handle our knowledge of God in all its iterations and must live the kind of life that yearns for righteousness (i.e., one that is sanctifying). We have also been looking at some speculative and practical ways to help Christians mature in these two important areas.

In the current chapter, we will briefly consider how a certain wing of evangelism, known as "apologetics," is entailed by the Christian's quest to know God better through combating world systems that stand in opposition to the gospel. While apologetics is not formally something all believers need with respect to effectively knowing God, it is certainly crucial and essential in enhancing as well as preserving the warrior Christian in her stance against the enemy triumvirate. It is implied if not entailed by the prospect of being a spiritual warrior at all. It also equips the Christian with knowing truth beyond Scripture as well as a means of defending it. And a well-rounded furnishing of the truth (an indispensable feature of knowledge) will put the Christian in an optimal place to combat the falsehoods Satan assaults us with (often through his human proxies).

Apologetics is but a particular use of the knowledge we acquire—a use that is essential for the well-rounded Christian warrior. Formally speaking, apologetics is a branch of theology that involves the justification of a particular worldview, which, in this case, is Christianity. It is primarily implemented for the benefit of the spiritually underdeveloped and/or theologically undecided. Accordingly, apologetics is considered an intellectual aid to evangelism and spiritual growth and has, or should have, the intended goal of bringing one's listeners and readers close(r) to God. And through mastering those strategies in service to that goal, it promises to augment our knowledge of God even further. For example, if one is to defend God's existence by appealing to intelligent design or the origin of the universe, she will come to appreciate how well the secular sciences and philosophical reflections point to God. One then comes to know of God's providence that his "invisible attributes, namely, his eternal power and divine nature, have been clearly perceived, ever since the creation of the world, in the things that have been made" (Rom 1:20). Apologetics supports our knowledge of God, but it also adds to it by revealing how well God has left his fingerprints, so to speak, all over creation. Indeed, the "heavens declare the glory of God" (Ps 19:1a).

Though apologetics is implied by our quest to know God and defend truths about him, I have chosen to relegate this subject to the end of the book. Since apologetics is an extension of the way one comes to know God and defend him, it is an inevitable route for those who seek to increase in their Christian maturity (Heb 5:13–14) and to maximize their spiritual posture as Christian warriors. One cannot fully "stand" (Eph 6:11) against the enemies of truth unless they know it, love it, and seek methods to protect it and blaze pathways for others to participate in it. This chapter, then, is devoted to defining what apologetics is and the important role that apologetics plays in making one's spiritual walk more impervious to satanic resistance.

THE CRUCIAL ROLE OF APOLOGETICS IN SPIRITUAL WARFARE

The term "apologetics" derives from the Greek term *apologia*. The word itself simply means a "defense" despite sharing some incidental semantic similarities with the word "apologize" (*apologoúmai*). Quite frankly, to do apologetics proper is not to apologize for anything. A purely secular illustration is readily available in Plato's account of *The Apology* (of Socrates). It is there that Socrates, who is wrongly accused of "corrupting the youth," "irritating the masses," and even "atheism," defends his self-proclaimed obligation to help his fellow Athenians to be better people through self-examination. His chief concern, he insists, is not personal gain but the collective soul of Athens itself. Despite the uproar his activities have aroused, he is anything but sorry for what he does or why he does what he does. This is why the latter part of *The Apology* reads more as a rebuke of the Athenian leaders and influencers than it does as a legal defense of his innocence. He is more interested in defending his work as a philosopher than he is his life.

Similarly, apologetics should be seen, then, as a kind of defense. It is not merely a legal defense, which is sometimes the case, but a defense of something higher—something missional. It is a defense in much the same way Socrates defended the superiority of ethical living and critical thinking. The Bible uses the term, or one of its cognates, in eight different passages: Acts 22:1; 25:16; 1 Corinthians 9:3; 2 Corinthians 7:11; Philippians 1:7, 16; 2 Timothy 4:16; and the much-celebrated 1 Peter 3:15. In every case a "defense" in the ordinary sense of that word is what is in mind.

As for *Christian* apologetics, 1 Peter 3:15 provides the most insight into what that means for the individual Christian. Amidst his discussion of Christian virtues and the inevitability of Christian suffering he has prefaced in chapter 3, Peter emphasizes that Christians must nevertheless persevere in those virtues. To do so guarantees that one will eventually be blessed. One's practice of the virtues is, of course, rooted in Christ (3:15a). As such, if an evildoer should press you for a reason for this hope of blessedness, the Christian is to offer a calculated and faithful reply: "always [be] prepared to make a defense to anyone who asks you for a reason for the hope that is in you; yet do it with gentleness and respect." As the verses that follow indicate, such a response shames our oppressors and ensures that our suffering is for doing what is truly good.

Three things are evident in the passage. First, the believer is characterized as one who is "always being prepared" (*hetoimoi aei*). This means that one must be in a state of *informational* readiness (cf. Matt 24:44; Luke 12:40; Acts 23:15, 21). She must assemble the relevant data in preparing to make the case for her hope. Second, the preparedness of the believer is to include what it takes "to make a defense." It is methodological. Since this defense is in service to "the hope that is in you," such a defense involves one's publicizing of those reasons for the truth of the gospel message. Thus far, she is to acquire the facts and learn how to wield them in service to her cause. We then come to the third thing, namely, that one is to mount such a defense *with dignity* and is not to defend her positions either indignantly or conceitedly. She is to do so "with gentleness and respect." The emphasis here is for the Christian to be enduringly blameless. The moment she reacts in such a way that is beneath her, she loses all credibility in the eyes of her oppressors. Thus, in 1 Peter 3:15 the tripartite call on the part of the Christian is for substantive preparedness, reasonableness, and tactical congeniality. To be more colloquial, one must comprehend, contend, and be civil.

But what does it mean to be prepared to make a defense in such a way? It means that, as we have learned from other scriptural passages, we are to have a mature and responsible understanding of Christian doctrines. This is not to say that one must become a professional theologian, a scientist, a philosopher, or any kind of academic scholar. Instead, it is (minimally) to be one who submits to sound instruction and who can apply those instructions to one's life in service to one's relationship to God. It is not a unique calling for a pastor or overseer. All instructions about knowing Scripture and utilizing it in bettering one's Christian walk are directed toward all believers in transit to maturity. Overseers are simply called to be in a position where they also "are able to teach" (1 Tim 3:2). However, 1 Peter 3:15 involves something a bit more: we must not only have sufficient knowledge of Scripture, but we must also actively "be prepared" to engage those who query about our "hope." This is a bit more engaging than merely being passively equipped—that is, expecting someone *else* to do the spadework for you.

And Peter's comments here are not unparalleled elsewhere in the New Testament. What Peter says is not unique to Peter's First Epistle. For example, the spirit of the above message was already delivered by Paul in his Epistle to the Colossians. There he writes:

> Walk in wisdom toward outsiders, making the best use of the time. Let your speech always be gracious, seasoned with salt, so that you may know how you ought to answer each person. (Col 4:5–6)

Note the similarities here. Paul implores the Colossians to make sure their speech is "gracious" and that they "know how you ought to answer each person." Now, while Paul does not use *apologia* for "answer," the term he does use, *apokrinesthai*, is no less indicative of the same kind of preparedness of knowledge (*eidenai*). In fact, the imagery Paul adds is that one's speech is to be "seasoned with salt," which is the basis for one's apologetic. What does it mean, then, to have one's speech "seasoned with salt"? Jesus used the metaphor himself to speak about the disciples as being enduring witnesses to nonbelievers (Matt 5:13; Luke 14:34). The Old Testament tends to associate the metaphor of salt with one's covenantal relationship (Num 18:19; 2 Chr 13:5). In other words, to enter into a covenantal relationship with God as his disciple entails being prepared to be an effective witness—a witness that includes making intelligent but respectful responses to outsiders. (Peter may very well have had Paul's epistle in mind when he wrote 1 Peter (see 2 Pet 3:15–16).) Indeed, apologetics by any other name is still apologetics.

Apologetics, then, involves a preparation that enlists the deliverances of all intellectual disciplines in defending one's Christian hope; and it is something that should be done within the confines of the Christian virtues (gentleness, graciousness, etc.). In fact, apologetics is truly an extension of evangelism given how 1 Peter 3 culminates in how the suffering of Christ and the flood of Noah ultimately give rise to transforming the "formerly disobedient" (1 Pet 3:17–22). Likewise, Paul lived this out as one who used apologetics to reach pagan Athenians gathered at the Areopagus (Acts 17:22–34). On that occasion, Paul defended the notion that, based on their own claims to being God's "offspring," God is real, personal, and closer in judgment than they think (vv. 29–31). And this is ultimately assured given Jesus's own proclamations, which were validated by his resurrection from the dead. In fact, even Paul himself was not immune to evidential investigation (vv. 10–11), which moved those in the region to believe in what he preached (v. 12). He fully expected that false arguments, no matter where they come from, are to be refuted and that this procedure is itself an act of spiritual warfare (2 Cor 10:4–5).[1] Apologetics, therefore, is something all of us must do whether it successfully brings forth conversions or not. But there is no question that it is one of the noncarnal weapons of our warfare and is used for our own benefit in addition to the benefit of those who will respond favorably to the Christian message.

APOLOGETICS AND FRIENDLY FIRE

Aristotle once spoke of excess and deficiency as grounds for ruling certain behaviors as vices. The Christian church has a similar position about the move of the Spirit in relation to our intellectualization of the faith. While the ideal Christian should have a healthy balance of both, the more cerebral Christian is perceived to be too intellectual at the expense of his openness to God's communing Spirit. This amounts to having a pharisaical attitude, which involves having an attitude of judgment, self-pride, and a sense of superiority over others. While the cerebral Christian may *say* the right things, she is inordinately focused on the message rather than the transforming power of the Messenger. "This people honors me with their lips, but their heart is far from me" (Mark 7:6).

Aside from this appearance of being disconnected from godly passion, many are concerned that any intellectualizing or defense of the gospel message assumes that God is unable to do so on his own. Apologetics is seen as an industry that is attempting to fix what God could not otherwise accomplish; it is a way to make the gospel more believable while denying that it is the Spirit's role to move persons to believe. And often, so objectors

---

1. See pp. 15–16 and 114–115.

claim, when you intellectualize the faith, you inevitably liberalize it. That is, the only way Christianity has ever had a fair hearing by intellectuals is when its core tenets are reinterpreted to accommodate the sentiments of Enlightenment thinking. It is alleged that one must remove the supernatural elements of the Bible if it is to remain relevant to thinking individuals. And accommodating the pristine gospel message to anything the world does (like intellectualizing) amounts to nothing but an unwelcome compromise.

And, to round off the charge against Christian apologetics, Scripture, objectors will further insist, is overtly opposed to it. For Paul openly condemns "the wisdom of the wise," which is something God will "destroy" (1 Cor 1:19). By contrast, continues Paul, "we preach Christ crucified, a stumbling block to Jews and folly to Gentiles" (v. 23). Philosophers are chiefly among those who question others' beliefs and challenge them. But, as our objectors insist, Paul is also against the use of "philosophy," for it is "according to human tradition, according to the elemental spirits of the world, and not according to Christ" (Col 2:8).

Like all matters of the Christian walk, this area too is a matter of balance. It is clearly wrong to think that any amount of intellectualizing (whatever that signifies) is inherently wrong. As we have seen, Scripture celebrates and mandates that those who love God are to mature in their knowledge of Scripture and of him. Despite the fact that "intellectualizing" is construed as a pejorative in the sense that it is an excess, this is just wrong. To intellectualize is just to make rational sense of something (to be excessive, it would have to be a case of *over*intellectualizing). It is a systematic way to understand something. When Paul talks about the spiritual gifts of speaking in tongues and prophecy, he piously stresses that "I will pray with my spirit, but I will pray with my mind also; I will sing praise with my spirit, but I will sing with my mind also" (1 Cor 14:19). Even when talking about a highly spiritual event such as speaking in tongues, Paul stresses the importance of the mind's understanding. That the mind should come to understand certain content is not itself offensive. It is necessary, in fact. Indeed, it may even be better than any of its purely spiritual advantages (v. 5).

When we study Scripture, we grow and mature. The natural consequence is that we will have intellectualized these aspects of our knowledge of God through his Word. While knowledge alone is not the bedrock of being a Christian, you cannot have a loving relationship with God and be averse to knowing *about* him in a thorough and responsible way. To be intellectual is not itself to be pharisaical. Where the Pharisees went wrong was in their haughtiness and their own selfish agenda for the Jewish people. Jesus was an existential threat to their seat of power and authority, and so they exploited their intellectual ability to challenge him. Sometimes they were rebuffed by the evidence of his miracles; at other times he was able to refute them by providing . . . *wait for it* . . . reasonable arguments (e.g., Matt 12:25–28; John 10:30–38).

Does apologetics imply, as Søren Kierkegaard once thought,[2] an inadequacy on God's part? No more than missionary work does. For we are called to make disciples of all nations (Matt 28:16–20) and to care for the material needs of others (Matt 25:34–40; Luke 18:22; James 2:1–9). Certainly God could do these things without our assistance, but he has expressly chosen to act through his church as an extension of himself (John 17:18; 1 Cor 12:27). This includes evangelism and everything that involves. The success will always be God's, for he is using us to accomplish the mission of discipleship. But we must become equipped in order to do what God has set before us. And this can only be adequately done by relying on him.

Does Scripture really preach against "wisdom" and "philosophy"? Yes, but not unqualifiedly. The "wisdom" decried by Paul in 1 Corinthians is not the responsible handling of knowledge. Rather, it is, in context, "the wisdom of the world" (1:20c; cf. Job 5:13; Ps 49:10). The Corinthians, along with many Greek Christians, were easily impressed with clever rhetoric. Paul is denouncing this intellectual ostentatiousness as a (fool's) gold standard for what is good and true. For the Greeks, the public perception of one's intelligence was everything. For the Christian, even the most "foolish" public perception of God is substantively better than any "wisdom" the world can offer. This is not a polemic against wisdom; it is a polemic against upper-class snobbery.[3] It is why Paul can say one chapter later without self-contradiction that "*we do impart wisdom*, although it is not a wisdom of this age or of the rulers of this age, who are doomed to pass away" (2:6; emphasis added).

As for "philosophy" in Colossians 2:8, the careful reader will note that the *kind* of philosophy under the gun is that which has no good content—being equated with "empty deceit." That is, it is a philosophy of "human tradition, according to the elemental spirits of the world, and not according to Christ." And who can disagree with that? But it is hardly an impugning of the *discipline* of philosophy as if Paul were denouncing a form of knowledge. Quite the contrary; Paul, just one chapter earlier, asks that the Colossians "be filled with the knowledge of his will in all spiritual wisdom and understanding, so as to walk in a manner worthy of the Lord, fully pleasing to him: bearing fruit in every good work and increasing in the knowledge of God" (1:9–10). Indeed, philosophy (which literally means "love of wisdom") is appropriately realized when it is "spiritual wisdom and understanding."

---

2. Kierkegaard, *Sickness Unto Death*, 87.
3. See Fitzmeyer, *First Corinthians*, 154ff.

A number of contemporary churches either incline themselves away from engaging in apologetics or denounce it altogether. This is unfortunate. And, as we have explored, there are no good objections to the employment of apologetics in service to evangelizing the lost. Since spiritual warfare involves standing firm in the fundamental tenets of our faith, then apologetics must be incorporated into the body of Christ in order to protect her from the clever falsehoods of our spiritual adversaries. This doesn't mean everyone must be a vocational or full-time apologist. It only means that we must let those so gifted be enabled and supported in their equipping of the saints. And those of us who are not so gifted should be sure to learn from them how to defend the faith, for, as Peter says, we must *all* be "prepared to make a defense to anyone who asks you for a reason for the hope that is in you."

CONCLUSION

It is evident that we must come to know God and to defend the faith if we are to be a bulwark against the demonic and its propensity for falsehood. However, fellow Christians are skeptical about taking such a "cerebral" approach to our Christian walk. But if the model I laid out earlier about spiritual warfare being the examined life worth defending is on the right track, then we have an obligation to educate ourselves and to intimate apologetics into our quest to increase in our knowledge of God in fortifying it and those who come by it. Since one of the primary weapons of the enemy is falsehood, we have little choice but to learn how to identify it and how to refute it. We need not be professionals at this. The task before us is modest: be equipped enough to defend the hope that lies within us.

As questions are raised, we should not simply shelve them for someone else to handle. *We* must be responsive to challenges and inquiries posed about Christianity so that, if nothing else, folks can see that it is a worthwhile system to explore; that it isn't just a "blind faith" kind of thing to which Christians just mindlessly accede. We need to convey that Christ and his gospel are so important that they are worthy of our time to learn about with sufficient depth and that we know how to respond to the dearth of challenges posed against them. Do not pass up the opportunity to break down intellectual strongholds if it means another soul for Christ can be saved. And in so doing, we will end up strengthening our own faith by coming to see that there are indeed answers to the challenges posed against the Christian faith. By meeting those challenges head-on, we will be effectively combating those "cosmic powers over this present darkness [who are] the spiritual forces of evil in the heavenly places" (Eph 6:12).

22

Concluding Thoughts

THIS BOOK IS FULL of discussions directly related to spiritual warfare. It has been my intention that these discussions serve as a set of exploratory essays in a variety of disciplines including theology, philosophy, apologetics, and evangelism. A proper, systematized view of spiritual warfare can only be fashioned when we have exhausted all means to knowledge on the subject. Far too many authors on the subject have preferred to let whatever emerges from their ministry of spiritual warfare be that which uncritically informs their theology. Others, usually scholars, have attempted to be more careful to let their theology (or Scripture) be what informs their ministry of spiritual warfare. However, even those who rightly elevate Scripture over their interpretations of alleged experiences often have preconceptions, biases, and assumptions that color that theology. We saw that Walter Wink's anti-realism forces him to come up with a doctrine of spiritual warfare where Satan and his demons, as traditionally understood, are not the real enemies. We also saw how those like C. Peter Wagner who have a sort of hyper-permissive realism think that Satan and his demons can do extraordinary things in the physical world. And we saw how those like Neil T. Anderson who claim a more moderate approach nevertheless insist on practices that have dubious support. Accordingly, philosophy and philosophical reasoning are missing in the various attempts at a doctrine of spiritual warfare.

To remedy this problem, I have sought to draw upon all relevant disciplines in addressing everything from the nature of the participants of spiritual warfare—God, angels, devils, human beings, the world, and the flesh—to models of what spiritual warfare is alleged to look like. I then offered a critical analysis of those models as represented by some, specifically what I have designated as "mythological models," "exorcistic models," and "wizardry models." This was done against the backdrop of analyzing a cross section of biblical passages that use warfare terminology in communicating unfiltered spiritual truths. Accordingly, I systematized a spiritual warfare consonant with the biblical data that was covered. Of course, I took care to give special attention to the much-celebrated Ephesians 6 passage as it is often treated wholly apart from its immediate Ephesian context and its broader scriptural background. Along the way, I was sure to philosophically reflect on what we are entitled to believe and not believe about spiritual warfare as given in Scripture. The result is a biblical *and* philosophically informed model I have dubbed "the examined life worth defending."

Since my critical analyses of the various models are backed by both theological and philosophical reflection, this book stands out as the only contemporary book on spiritual warfare to fuse the disciplines of theology and philosophy in making its case. Despite careful attention given to a scholarly approach, I wanted to be equally careful to provide a readable and useful work so that everyone, not just the intelligentsia, can benefit from the material. Thus, I felt a need to end the book with a brief discussion about how Christians can integrate the "examined life" model into their own lives no matter where we are in our walk with the Lord or at what stage—whether as a new believer or a seasoned one or somewhere in between. I doubt many will not agree with all or many of my positions on the matter. But the book's primary objective is not necessarily to convince readers of every opinion offered; instead, among its objectives, it aims to provide a rationale for the reticence I and others have about popularist and even scholarly notions about spiritual warfare that seem to deviate from a faithful reading of the relevant biblical texts. *It's designed to facilitate further—hopefully constructive—conversations.* But I hope we do not lose sight of the book's other objectives, including the offering up of some helpful suggestions about how to think about and increase in the Christian virtues regardless of which model one ultimately adopts. For, everyone should be on board with increasing in wisdom and holiness when it comes to Christian living.

One of the central takeaways from this book is that Christians are not to be transfixed on their personal enemies in the heavenly places (cf. Luke 10:20) such that they end up crafting, not a healthy supernatural outlook, but an unhealthy superstitious one. When we unrestrainedly assign demons more power and abilities than we are entitled to think that they have, we begin to focus on a kind of warfare that actually doesn't ever take place. Since neither Scripture nor reason lead us to think that demons can inhabit and manipulate physical environments on their own, then we needn't focus on extraneous remedies that take away from our positive focus on increasing in godly wisdom and virtue. Demonic threats, though potentially deadly, are no more extravagant than those of governments and political campaign organizations when they dispense propaganda by which they manipulate behavior, entice into wrongdoing, and bury the truth. And the way we are to deal with the demonic is essentially no different than how a citizen ought to rebuff political manipulation: by increasing in wisdom and by holding on to virtue. While we might be overwhelmed on some occasions by the people the powers can manipulate, there is nothing magical about their newfound hostility to all that is godly. For, had they put on Christ and stood in godly wisdom and virtue, they would not have become the physical emissaries of Satan to begin with. The battle must be won where it is waged: in the minds and souls of everyone.

Accordingly, as I have argued, we are to focus on defensive and offensive strategies that are undeniably tied to the Christian lifestyle. Knowledge as wisdom is essential in the fight and we have looked at some ways anyone can pursue such knowledge where he or she is at. Christian virtue is equally essential. Since Christian virtue is, like godly wisdom, a reasonable venture, we can strengthen our resolve by appreciating how much being virtuous makes sense in God's design. We thus looked at some significant issues like pride and lust and discussed what it is that makes these vices. We saw that they are vices because they are deviations from how God has designed true dignity and godly sexual behavior, respectively. Since God's morality makes sense, our minds, as the seats of human conscience, will be emboldened further to stay on the straight and narrow. Being immersed in the knowledge of Christ and the practices of the virtues not only inches us closer to supreme fulfillment as human beings created by God; it also insulates us from the onslaught of the enemy's schemes that impress on us the desire for immediate gratification, which often has deleterious consequences. Satan seeks to take us down through moral failure and deception, not coercion. So, naturally, we must become more adept at countering these things if we are to avoid losing the spiritual battles over our souls.

I pray that this book serves as a blessing for those struggling to overcome the forces of darkness and as a challenge to those who either deny or exaggerate those forces. But in all things, I pray that the book enhances our knowledge of and closeness to God amidst the noise of those arguing for a denial of the demonic and those arguing for an embellishment of the same. I confess that there is something we can learn from the deniers: that there isn't a demon lurking in the atmosphere with aggressive, magical powers with which to manipulate nature. For this I will be branded a liberal. But I think there is also something we can learn from the embellishers: that we must be serious about real demons who interact with human beings and intend us harm. For this I will be branded a fundamentalist. Nevertheless, the present work is a step toward fortifying *every* Christian regardless of our leanings and a step toward taking seriously the contribution knowledge and virtue have in arming the believer in her Christian walk. This, I think, is what it means to follow in the Conqueror's tread. May we not tread lightly.

Appendix A

Why Does God Allow Spiritual Warfare to Befall Us?

IF SPIRITUAL WARFARE REALLY does occur and is inevitable in the lives of believers, then why didn't God just sovereignly arrange things differently to make the Christian walk more manageable? God isn't really threatened by any Satanic power, so why should his beloved creatures be? The questions imply a tension in the Christian worldview: that God *can* make the Christian walk free of seemingly unnecessary demonic assaults and, it would seem, that he would *want* to in order to assure our endurance in Christ. (Those versed in the philosophy of religion will recognize this tension in similar discussions about the problem of evil.) The problem here is particularly acute for Christians because God is, on the one hand, *all-loving* and, on the other, *all-powerful*. That God would seemingly want and would appear to be able to find another, easier route to Christian virtue seems to make spiritual warfare superfluous. Why, then, would such a God allow spiritual warfare to befall his most beloved of all creation?

One way to respond would be to simply punt to mystery. The pious will be satisfied enough to say that Scripture treats spiritual warfare as a reality (e.g., 2 Cor 10:4; Eph 6:12–20; 1 Tim 1:18) and that's all we need to know. While mysteries have and do exist in Christian theology (e.g., Rom 11:25; 1 Cor 15:51; Eph 3:6), punting to mystery really does amount to a non-answer. We must acknowledge that. But, as it turns out, it is not one that need be offered in place of a more reasonable solution. (And by "solution" I don't mean *the* right answer; rather, I mean that there is at least one other possibility that could explain God's permitting of such warfare.) If we can answer the question without ending the query with "it's just a mystery," then we should do so. After all, it is better that the mind should be made to understand even if the spirit has already been satisfied enough to move on (cf., 1 Cor 14:13–15).

In moving on, then, one could take the somewhat novel approach of Gregory Boyd. Boyd argues that God simply doesn't know the future because there is no future to be known.[1] That is, since human beings are in fact free, it is necessary that the future not be a fixed reality with which to make this possible.[2] This means that some actions by demons truly do take God by surprise and, so, he can only implement strategies in the lives of Christians in an effort to "cover all bases." Boyd likens God's foreknowledge to that of a grandmaster chess player: you may not know what strategy and moves your opponent might take, but God certainly knows how to respond to *any* move the opponent ultimately does take. Such foreknowledge is conditional. If God created Satan as a good angel and with free will, God is no less prepared for what Satan might do no matter if he ends up rebelling or not. But the fact that he *does* rebel means that there are genuine consequences that obtain that God will know how to respond to. As such, Boyd's coopted model of divine omniscience (often called "open theism" or the "openness of God") helps answer the question forthrightly: God actually *didn't* know that spiritual warfare would befall us prior to Satan's rebellion. But now that it has because of Satan, God has provided us with the necessary resources, without violating our free will, with which to stand against the enemy's assaults. Remember, God still knows exactly what to do for every move Satan makes.

---

1. Boyd, *Satan and the Problem of Evil*, esp. 85–144.

2. Boyd thinks that if God foreknows the future, then the future is a fixed reality that excludes freedom of the will. Boyd thinks that if God foreknows what is going to happen then his knowing what will happen is incompatible with our freedom to choose otherwise. But I find his objection to be unsuccessful since it gets things backwards. For, God's foreknowledge of x or y is not the cause of our doing x or y. Rather, it is we who are going to do x or y that endup constituting what God foreknows. If God knows that I will eat eggs for breakfast tomorrow, then it is because I will eat eggs for breakfast tomorrow. If I were *not* to eat eggs for breakfast tomorrow, God would have known that instead. And that means that I was not *coerced* or *fated* (or whatever) to eat eggs tomorrow for breakfast. What God's foreknowledge ensures is that he in fact knows, among other things, what we *will* do. And if we do anything *different* or *unexpected*, God would have known that instead (which is just to say that it is actually *false* that we will do some specific action). God's knowledge never fails and is not incompatible with our freely choosing our courses of action. Furthermore, if some strong form of predestination along the lines of an Augustinian-Calvinist view is true, then God's foreknowledge, being due to his determining all (relevant) events, would be principally compatible with human freedom so long as human freedom is not being defined along libertarian lines. Such adherents prefer to call their notion of human freedom *compatibilism*. But, if compatibilism is true, then there is no problem in God's foreknowing the events he has determined and in humans acting to freely bring about those events.

Unfortunately, open theism is too controversial to be a viable solution for the mainstream. And it is actually an unnecessary position for one to hold in answering the question. This is a good thing, because if the price for answering the question is to deny that God has foreknowledge in the way traditional luminaries have believed and taught, which Boyd is willing to do, then believers would have to be committed to what otherwise seems very counterintuitive and ostensibly unscriptural. The knowledge of God seems to be unbounded, extensive, and at face value inclusive of the future (Ps 37:18; Jer 1:5; Matt 24:36; Mark 13:32; Acts 2:23; 1 John 3:20).

So, let's stick with a more traditional orthodoxy here and suppose that God indeed has a fixed foreknowledge. Well, one again can ask why God still decrees this world and not a world where things pan out differently—a world where we are free of any Satanic opposition. The answer is closely related to those reasons he allows *any* evil to oppose us. Yes, the fact that there is evil in the universe God created seems awkward if not outright inconceivable. "Why does he allow it?" one wonders. But once we understand that God may have good reasons for permitting evil, then any concerns about God's character in his permitting the evil of spiritual warfare soon vanish. It is possible that some evils just are necessary to permit in having an optimal world. For example, if Jesus had not suffered and died on the cross, there would be no salvation made available to us. If it had not been for the Babylonian captivity, the Jews might not have been able to return to their homeland under Persian rule. If the man born blind were never blind, his healing would never have testified before others to the wonders of Jesus. The point is that if it weren't for the initial occurrences of evils like these, the future might have been adversely affected and, so, this world would not be an optimal world. If, for example, people could not carry out any abuses (because, say, their fists turn into marshmallows and any verbal assaults suddenly come out as compliments), then there would be no moral responsibility. There would be no consequences to our actions, which means that neither would one have incentive to act morally nor would moral actions make much sense (since no harm could come to others). Since the acts of abuse would be substantively no different than acts of compassion, it is difficult to think that there would be such a thing as moral growth.[3] And if were is no moral growth, then there would be no such thing as repentance. And if there were no repentance, then no one would seek salvation.

The same goes for natural evils like tornadoes, earthquakes, illnesses, and pandemics. If God intervened every time a natural disaster were about to ensue, it would mean that miracles were constantly being performed to

---

3. See Hick, *Philosophy of Religion*, 39–55.

prevent anything bad from happening. While that sounds great in terms of our well-being, it would amount to no growth of knowledge in us (not to mention moral growth regarding virtues like courage, valor, and compassion—all of which imply the existence of real peril). Nothing consistent would happen because God intervenes when harm is about to obtain (depending on whether anyone would be adversely affected or not). If nothing consistent would happen, we couldn't know or anticipate anything. For, if *sometimes* the earth quakes when it releases energy and sometimes it doesn't, then we can no more make a prediction about earthquakes than we can about what combination of numbers make for a lottery winner.

We must understand something up front. While living in a world of inconsistencies where no one gets hurt sounds amazing, it is, quite frankly, one of the worst kinds of worlds we could ask for. Imagine if military boot camps were free of struggles, pain, and injury and were geared more toward making their recruits happy, joyful, and comfortable. No country would have a means of defense. Similarly, in a world of total insulation, nobody matures morally and knowledge becomes impossible; we become nothing notably different than someone's pet animals. That is, life would only be God taking care of his human pets and protecting them from harm. *But is that the kind of life God intends for us here on earth?* Not at all. God has created this life as a preparatory ground for the life to come[4]—a heaven that is the outcome of having risen above the pain, sorrow, and remorse and into a life of God-enabled repentance. Like any other training ground, the challenges are necessary if they are to produce the kinds of results that will adequately equip its participants. This life—one burdened with spiritual warfare—is what will prepare us to be ultimately sanctified by God's Holy Spirit. God can no more unilaterally *make* people be sanctified than he can unilaterally *make* people be profane. It's partly up to us. And in a world with no evils of any sort, there would be nothing to spur us on to such important moral and spiritual growth. Only under the conditions we in fact have—conditions that include living in a state of spiritual war—can heaven be appropriated to the conqueror.

Much more could be said. However, it is enough for us to see that it's at least possible that God might permit certain evils to obtain, including spiritual warfare, even though he foreknew that these things would happen. And such foreknowledge does not compromise human freedom. For it is possible that God permitted Satan and his cohorts to fall from grace in order to preserve the greater goods that perhaps can only obtain in such a world (like salvation and sanctification). Suppose Satan hadn't rebelled. It is

---

4. Hick refers to this as "soul making" (*Philosophy of Religion*, 47).

possible that Adam and Eve would not have fallen from grace either. And if that hadn't happened, it may be that such an alternative world would not be populated with nearly the number of believers as the present world has had (even though a great many nonbelievers also came about). If God wanted x billion believers to ultimately live in this world, it may be that that number would be unachievable in a world where there was no Adamic fall. Why might this be the case? Because it is possible that people would freely choose not to reproduce nearly as much in those circumstances. Or, it could be that Adam and Eve still rebelled, but they quickly died off for other reasons. Or, maybe it ended up being Abel who killed Cain, thus drastically changing the outcome of humankind in the generation immediately succeeding Adam and Eve. The point is, it is possible that only the world that we have—the one where Satan and his cohorts rebel—is the one that has the most acceptable results when it comes to populating the kingdom of God. And that may be only in a world where spiritual warfare is an everyday reality.

Appendix B

Can Satan Read Our Minds?

THERE HAS BEEN AN understandable resistance to the notion that Satan can read people's minds. It is by and large motivated by the desire to not see Satan share such an intimate knowledge said to be had by God (e.g., Luke 16:15). To have such intrusive access to one's intimate and private thoughts seems to encroach upon divine omniscience. But it is unclear how having this kind of access, if indeed Satan has it, would lend itself to Satan being omniscient. It certainly would provide a larger database of knowledge, so to speak. But it would not itself prove a sort of diabolical omniscience. While Scripture seems to be silent on this issue, I can find no independent reason to think that Satan would not have this kind of access.

As for whether it can be shown that such intimate bidirectional communication is not tantamount to divine omniscience, some things can be said. For one, God's omniscience is not necessarily or exclusively based on direct experience. God was omniscient before there even was a material universe to be experienced. His knowledge is more likely due to his knowledge being unbounded by any material or other mediating constraints. He just *knows* directly and immediately. He is, thus, free to know all true propositions. And since there is no reason to suppose that such knowledge is delimited by any other boundary, and if omniscience is accordingly the simplest assumption in the absence of the possibility of not knowing anything, then it follows that God's knowledge is only bounded by the constraints of logic—something that his nature grounds. That is, God is only limited by his own nature. Such is not the case with Satan. Satan's knowledge is mediated, for he relies on cognitive input one thought at a time. If we suppose that Satan can read our minds, Satan's temporality and finitude preclude him from being able to amass the total number (an infinite number?) of thoughts to be known. At best, the only feasible way for a finite agent to come to know every proposition one thought at a time from an initial state of ignorance would be for that agent to endure an infinite timespan. Numbers alone are potentially infinite, and one's coming to have the thought of any n followed by $n+1$ reveals that such an agent could never arrive at $n=\infty$. Thus, no amount of tapping into our thoughts could lead Satan to achieve anything that could approximate omniscience. So, mind-reading or no, Satan would not be *ipso facto* omniscient just because he could read minds. And this means that an argument showing that Satan can read people's minds could still be given without worrying about whether mind reading entails omniscience (for it doesn't).

There may be a probabilistic argument in favor of the notion that Satan can read minds, however. We know that Satan is certainly capable of cognitively interacting with our souls directly in order to incite negative thoughts or temptations in us (e.g., Acts 5:3; 1 Thess 3:5). And, yet, we're supposed to think that Satan cannot *receive* such communication even though he can deliver it. Angelic beings and demons can certainly interact with each other (e.g., Jude 9), which supposes that their communication is on some level a two-way street. One could suppose that this is due to a privileged connection semidivine beings have with each other and that such communicability is off-limits to other species who might enter into the "conversation." But this amounts to an arbitrary limitation, for there is no relevant difference between an angel and a disembodied human soul as far as we know.

As for any scriptural indication that demons can read our minds, I offer two. First, 1 Peter 5:8 reports that Satan "prowls around like a roaring lion, seeking someone to devour." If it is not the case that Satan can receive input from our minds, in what sense could he be seeking someone? For he has no physical eyes or ears or body with which to sense or detect us. We ought to consider his seeking to be a form of cognitive surveillance. But that's just to say that Satan can receive input from another mental source—mind reading, as it were. Secondly, there is the episode of the sons of Sceva who invoke Jesus and Paul in their confrontation with a demoniac. Unfazed by their exorcism, the evil spirit resists them, saying, "Jesus I know, and Paul I recognize, but who are you?" (Acts 19:15). The "know[ledge]" and "recogni[tion]" here do not pertain to something like facial recognition. They pertain to an informational awareness (e.g., their reputations). They're saying, "I recognize who these people are." Again, if the demon lacks physical organs with which to become acquainted with Jesus and Paul, it must have had some other means by which to acquaint itself with Jesus and Paul. Such knowledge must have been cognitively derived. And that just is mind reading.

Appendix C

On Territorial Spirits

A "TERRITORIAL SPIRIT" is thought to be a demon (considered by some to be high-ranking) who resides in and controls a populated region or locale. Sometimes this territorial spirit afflicts the inhabitants of a region with illnesses and/or psychological maladies. Either way, such spirits have a certain amount of ascendancy over the minds and bodies of people groups, always with the intent of bringing about a certain level of spiritual darkness. And such a concept of territorial spirits is nothing new. It was advocated by Jews during the Second Temple Period (543 BC–AD 70)[1] and early Christians certainly picked up on it (e.g., Origen, *Homilies on Luke* 35). Indeed, most of the fathers of the church went on to affirm such a notion.

There are Christians today who enthusiastically believe in territorial spirits and those, likewise, who enthusiastically scoff at the idea. Readers can already avail themselves of the contemporary literature that supports the notion[2] as well as that which opposes it.[3] That such a notion supposes that immaterial spirits can occupy points in space makes it a metaphysically difficult sell.[4] On the traditional view, the roles of territorial spirits are to be understood as something analogous to zone defense and offense in American football—where team members spatially occupy certain regions of the field wherein they are prepared to dominate or control any who might happen upon their field territory. But since demons are immaterial things,

---

1. Heiser, *Demons*, ch. 8.
2. Wagner, *Spiritual Warfare Strategy*; Boyd, *God at War*, esp. 9–22.
3. See, for example, Poythress, "Territorial Spirits"; Lowe, *Territorial Spirits*; Stevens, "Daniel 10"; Arnold, *3 Crucial Questions*, ch. 3; Guntrip, "Pentecostal Study of Daniel's Prince."
4. Refer to my critiques on pages 72–73, 159–162.

they cannot literally be *in* any zone or region (like Babylon or Rome). For spatial coordinates can only be charted on the basis of having spatial boundaries—something demons do not have. That is, in order to be in, say, Babylon, you would have to have at least one essential, material particle in that location. But immaterial things by definition do not have any particles. They are particle-less.

However, it seems to me that this issue is not a binary one, for one can come to think of demons as controlling certain regions in ways that do not commit us to any excessive metaphysical baggage like the possibility of immaterial spirits dwelling in material places. Perhaps they control territories exclusively through the human powers and authorities that immediately preside over them. This would not itself involve spirits being located anywhere, only that they have direct access to the minds of those human powers and authorities. As such, the view can be salvaged. Clinton Arnold suggests that it would be better to call them "empire spirits" instead of "territorial spirits,"[5] for their control is not over the geography of the regimes but over the geopolitical powers that exercise control over their people. Arnold's modification makes better sense of all the data, not the least of which is how demons can rule over nations by proxy without having to be spatially present.

As it turns out, the usual scriptural arguments for territorial spirits (as understood as involving demons residing in geographical provinces) are not all that impressive. So, such accommodation may not have to be made after all. Let us examine the most prominent passages thought to imply the notion of territorial spirits.

There are three Old Testament passages often appealed to in defense of the traditional view of territorial spirits. The first is Deuteronomy 32:8, the second is Daniel 10:13, 20–21, and the third is Psalm 82:1–8.

> When the Most High gave to the nations their inheritance, when he divided mankind, he fixed the borders of the peoples according to the number of the sons of God. (Deut 32:8)

> The prince of the kingdom of Persia withstood me twenty-one days, but Michael, one of the chief princes, came to help me, for I was left there with the kings of Persia . . . Then he said, "Do you know why I have come to you? But now I will return to fight against the prince of Persia; and when I go out, behold, the prince of Greece will come. But I will tell you what is inscribed in the book of truth: there is none who contends by my side against these except Michael, your prince. (Dan 10:13, 20–21)

---

5. Arnold, *3 Crucial Questions*, 153.

> God has taken his place in the divine council; in the midst of the gods he holds judgment: "How long will you judge unjustly and show partiality to the wicked? Selah. Give justice to the weak and the fatherless; maintain the right of the afflicted and the destitute. Rescue the weak and the needy; deliver them from the hand of the wicked." They have neither knowledge nor understanding, they walk about in darkness; all the foundations of the earth are shaken. I said, "You are gods, sons of the Most High, all of you; nevertheless, like men you shall die, and fall like any prince." Arise, O God, judge the earth; for you shall inherit all the nations! (Ps 82:1–8).

According to its advocates, it is of particular importance that these passages be seen as mutually supportive, since, for example, the Daniel passage alone might not be enough to suggest the presence of territorial spirits. The argument goes something like this: Since Deuteronomy 32 allegedly reveals that the "sons of God" (angels and/or demons; cf., vv. 16–17) are distributed and assigned to the various nations ("borders of the peoples," which were about seventy at the time; cf. Gen 10), then we should understand the "prince of . . . Persia," "prince of Greece," and Israel's "prince" in Daniel 10 to be instances of this understanding of Deuteronomy 32. Both Psalm 82 and Daniel 10 thus confirm this understanding of Deuteronomy 32, which itself can be appreciated when looking back from Psalms and Daniel. So, even though there are earlier writings that support the later ones, the later Psalms and Daniel are alleged to illuminate the older Deuteronomy just as the New Testament illuminates the Old Testament messianic passages despite the messianic passages preceding and anticipating the later New Testament. But the elegance of this alleged mutual support between Deuteronomy, the Psalms, and Daniel is only relevant if indeed they all teach or imply a doctrine of territorial spirits.

Let me begin by addressing Deuteronomy and Daniel as mutual support for the doctrine. On this I have three things to say by way of response. First, as mentioned before, the invoking of spiritual agencies, especially in apocalyptically charged contexts, is not to affirm that such beings are indeed present and doing the things ascribed to them.[6] It is possible that these passages are invoking divine beings not because the author(s) wants to say that they are really "out there," but because the invoking of such beings in the present situations provides a conceivable way for the author(s) to punctuate the significance of international conflict. To associate nations with divine beings is to convey to God's people the gravity of enmity they confront. What

---

6. See p. 80.

was written, then, was not meant to be taken as a straightforward, literal description of cosmic conflict. And if not, then even if the passages *mention* territorial spirits, they do not necessarily *endorse* such a reality.

Second, on the supposition that something more literal is meant by the "sons of God" (whoever they are) governing the nations, perhaps the author of Deuteronomy 32 really wants to associate the "sons of God" with the nations. These "sons of God" could very well be territorial spirits. The problem we face here is that it is not a settled issue whether the "sons of God" are angelic (and so also demonic) beings or something else. Even though increased preference is given by scholars for the Septuagint reading ("sons of God") over the Masoretic one ("sons of Israel"), thus attempting to connect the angels that are called "sons of God" in Job 1:6 and 2:1, nevertheless "sons of Israel" (=human beings) may yet reflect one of the earliest but viable understandings of the passage. Consider that even a similar "according" appears in Joshua 4 ("take up each of you a stone upon his shoulder, *according to the number of* the tribes of the people of Israel"; vv. 5, 8; emphasis added). As such, the passage may only mean to correlate the non-Israelite nations with the number of Israelites, for God's nation is the paradigm for what other nations ought to be. Furthermore, just because the numbering of the nations "accords" with the number of the "sons of God," it is unclear how this is supposed to show that such beings *rule* those regions.[7] That verse

---

7. Heiser argues: "Israel is said to be Yahweh's allotted inheritance. This implies that the other nations are 'allotted' to lesser gods [cf., Deut 4:19–20; 29:26]—'sons of God' among Yahweh's heavenly host" (*Demons*, 148). Despite Second Temple Jewish sympathies about believing that angels governed various nations, much of which is predicated on linking Dan 10 (see below), he puts quite a bit of interpretive stock in whether "gods" are allotted in the relevant sense elsewhere. For, 32:8 itself attaches this divine allotment and inheritance not to the "sons of God," but to the nations. Nevertheless, Heiser appeals (as do a number of scholars) to Deut 4 and 29, wherein Yahweh allots the "the sun and the moon and the stars . . . to all the peoples under the whole heaven" (4:19). He thus identifies these celestial bodies as metaphors (cf., 222) for the "sons of God" in 32:8. But 17:2–3 seems to draw a distinction between the luminaries and the "gods": "If there is found among you, within any of your towns that the LORD your God is giving you, a man or woman who does what is evil in the sight of the LORD your God, in transgressing his covenant, and has gone and served other gods and worshiped them, *or* the sun or the moon or any of the host of heaven, which I have forbidden . . ." There is no definitive indication here that the celestial bodies *are* the gods being worshiped as much as the luminaries are being worshiped *in addition to* the gods served. These could just be the luminaries created on day 4, wherein the Pentateuch's author specifies that they should "be for signs and for seasons, and for days and years, and let them be lights in the expanse of the heavens to give light upon the earth" (Gen 1:14–15). It is in this sense that the luminaries were "allotted" to the nations. It is more likely that the teaching of Genesis 1:14–15 is being ignored as it is an implied warning to readers not to worship these created and perfectly ordinary luminaries in the heavens. As for Deut 29:26, it simply refers to "gods whom [Israel] had not known and whom he had not allotted to them." That

17 might mention that demons are behind the foreign nationalistic gods of these other nations does nothing to support a traditional kind of territorial rulership. The point would only be that *at best* false gods often worshiped as nationalistic icons are nothing but demons if there is any reality behind them at all (cf., Ps 96:5, LXX; 1 Cor 10:20).[8]

And third, assuming once again that spiritual beings are not being invoked for literary purposes or imagery, the passage of Daniel 10 still does not warrant a "territorial" reading of demons even though eminent scholars take care to circumvent the metaphysical absurdities involved. As noted already, Arnold opposes the more extravagant notion of territorial spirits. However, he boldly affirms that Daniel indeed gives us "unequivocal support" for something that looks like territorial spirits (="empire spirits").[9] The "prince of Persia" is the prince of Persia insofar as the demon to which that moniker applies is the governing force of its politicians and military leaders. That there is a forthcoming "prince of Greece" with the rise of the Grecian empire is anticipated in verse 20. Taken literally, we could ask whether or not these spirits are demons (could they not be patron deities or good angels instead?) and whether or not they aren't all the *same* spirit. Perhaps each "prince" *just is* Satan, who moves from empire to empire in the never-ending quest to suppress and damage God's elect. Maybe one of these is the case or maybe not. Either way, a supporter might continue to argue, it minimally suggests the notion of *a* territorial spirit.

I mention this because geography may not be sufficient to show which distinct spirit is in play as much as it is to show which regime is or will be under such spiritual influence (thus evading the metaphysical problem that immaterial beings cannot occupy spatial regions). Whether a singular spirit or an aggregate of them (demon or otherwise), there is no reason to commit to the idea that the nations depicted indicate the spirits' location. For,

---

God "had not allotted" the gods "to them" is not to say that he has, nevertheless, allotted them to *other people*. In fact, if the luminaries *are* gods and were simply not allotted to the people of Israel, such an interpretation defies 4:19, which expressly states otherwise: that the luminaries are "things that the LORD your God *has allotted to all the peoples under the whole heaven*." And all of this distracts us from the initial point we started with, namely, that in 32:8 it is the nations that are allotted "their inheritance" and these are not clearly said to be "allotted" to the "sons of God," whoever or whatever these end up being.

8. While it is clear that demons are "behind" the idols, it is not so clear that they are *attached to* or *residing within* those idols. The significance of demons being the true identities of the pagan idols is to say that those pagan cultures and governments that oppress God's people acquire their worldview—their doctrines—from demons (cf., 1 Tim 4:1). National leaders in opposition to God's people are thereby governed by these forces of darkness (which is the point of Eph 6:12).

9. Arnold, *3 Crucial Questions*, 153.

perhaps they inhabit or demonize certain regimes from "afar" in conducting their politics in opposition to God and his people. It is also possible that the "princes" are just cosmic counterparts to the nations they are attached to. In this case it might read along the same lines as how some read Revelation 2–3, where the seven angels of the various churches of Asia Minor might just be representative of the churches themselves. Considering that Daniel is itself an apocalyptic work like Revelation and is the basis for some of Revelation's influence, this is not an unreasonable conjecture. But, then, this would undermine the notion of territorial spirits altogether. For angels (good or bad) are not really governing their respective territories; they are simply cast as cosmic counterparts to the earthly regimes.

Let us now turn to the contribution of the controversial Eighty-Second Psalm. The proponent of territorial spirits will appeal to this psalm to show that (i) there is a plurality of celestial beings, (ii) the celestial beings govern specific nations, and (iii) the celestial beings are sinister in their governance, thus bringing judgment upon themselves.[10] If these propositions are all true, then there is a strong case to be made for territorial spirits so understood. However, there are good reasons to doubt (ii), which serves as the basis for the relevance of (iii). I'll say something about (i) afterwards.

As to whether or not Psalm 82 reveals that celestial beings govern specific nations, this must be one of forced inference and is not directly acquired from the passage. One must assume that the complainant in the psalm is God himself and that he is directing his judgmental ire at the "divine council" (v. 1) for their failure to "give justice to the weak and fatherless" (v. 3), among other abuses of power (vv. 3b–4). However, as John Goldingay has pointed out,[11] there is little reason to think that the complainant is God. Rather, the one who is complaining is more likely *the Psalter*, for he begins his protest with the rhetorical question-making phrase "how long . . . ?," which is significant. When compared to other passages in the Psalms, this phrase occurs numerous times and is *always* the Psalter asking this of God (Ps 6:3; 13:1–2; 35:17; 62:3; 74:10; 79:5; 80:4; 89:46; 90:13; 94:3; and 119:84). Such can also be found outside of the Psalms, especially in Habakkuk 1:2–3, which itself looks quite like what's being leveled in Psalm 82:

> O LORD, how long shall I cry for help, and you will not hear? Or cry to you "Violence!" and you will not save? Why do you make me see iniquity, and why do you idly look at wrong? Destruction and violence are before me; strife and contention arise.

---

10. E.g., Page, *Powers of Evil*, 59; Heiser, *Unseen Realm*, 26–32, 259–60, 322–23; Heiser, *Reversing Hermon*, 101; Heiser, *Demons*, 152–54.

11. Goldingay, *Psalms*, 563–64.

In Habbakuk, the complainant seems to be blaming God (and his "council") for the "violence" and "strife and contention." This is precisely what we have in Psalm 82. And if it is the Psalter laying these charges before God himself amidst his council, then God and his entourage are being held accountable for what happens to the nations. That it is God himself who sets matters in motion that lead to devastating things like the exile explains quite well why the Psalter would subsequently lay such issues at his feet with the hope that he would finally "judge the earth" (v. 8). And this means that it isn't the wider celestial company mentioned in verse 1 that is governing the nations; it is God (with the blessing of his assembly, whoever they are). For he is the one who is due to "inherit all the nations" (v. 8).

As for the identity of the "divine council," it lacks relevance for what is taking place here (except that they are corecipients of the Psalter's complaint). There is a growing consensus that the "divine council" is a congregation of gods and/or angels, but this identity is quite fluid and can refer to a variety of nonhuman beings.[12] Regardless of their identity, however, the point of the reference to this assembly (whether gods, judges, demons, angels, or whatever) is to emphasize that God has been "aroused and stands to make an emphatic statement."[13] That the Psalter is complaining or protesting to God and his council is not to suppose that the members of the council are some aggregate of territorial spirits—possessing authority and direct influence over various earthly regions. It is, at most, a *repurposing* of an antecedent myth in its being used to convey to the Psalter's audience that there is one with supreme regal authority who is listening to the complainant and will act accordingly with authority.

Tethering this council to the concept of territorial spirits likely comes from reading verse 5's use of the implied pronoun "they" (determined by the given verbs) as referring back to the "gods" of verse 1. It reads, "*They* have neither knowledge nor understanding, *they* walk about in darkness; all the foundations of the earth are shaken." The Psalter proceeds to say in the next two verses: "You are gods, sons of the Most High, all of you; nevertheless, like men you shall die, and fall like any prince." The "You are gods" is taken to be a referent for the "gods" of the assembly and that judgment by God is going to be meted out against them. However, the plural "you" and "they" need not refer all the way back to verse 1. They might just refer to "the wicked" of verse 4, which is the most natural reading. In that case, the Psalter could be calling the undisclosed wicked ones "gods" sarcastically or

---

12. Smith, *Origins of Biblical Monotheism*, 6. As for whether the council *qua* "hosts" can be identified with angels, Ps 148:2 would seem to link the two.

13. Goldingay, *Psalms*, 562.

because that is how the people they govern see these individuals (a common understanding in the ancient world). It is also possible that the Psalter *is* referring to the gods of verse 1 and adding that they will "die" and "fall like any prince" is to show not a judgment, but a reality that these gods are powerless and useless to do what only Yahweh can do. That is, it speaks of the gods' natural impotence and inevitable downfall, not to what God is going to do to them. Having circumvented this useless assembly, the Psalter now directly appeals to Yahweh himself to remedy the situation and judge accordingly: "Arise, O God, judge the earth" (v. 8). As someone not already influenced by an angelic-territorial view of Deuteronomy 32, it is a wonder who would think to see Psalm 82 as teaching or inferring such a thing.[14]

By the time we arrive at the New Testament, I acknowledge that some such notion of territorial spirits makes more sense. While most are willing to affirm that the animating forces behind the ungodly regimes are indeed "the rulers, . . . the authorities, . . . the cosmic powers, . . . [and] the spiritual forces of evil in the heavenly places" (Eph 6:12), it is evident that their material effectiveness is in the fact that they directly move and govern the earthly powers. In Revelation, the notion seems to be implied in 2:13a ("I know where you dwell, where Satan's throne is") and 16:14 ("demonic spirits . . . who go abroad to the kings of the whole world, to assemble them for battle on the great day of God the Almighty"). The connections between Satan and demonic spirits with provinces and kings may underscore a sort of behind-the-scenes governing on the part of evil spirits.

This is consistent with Arnold's subtle and less controversial modification (i.e., "empire spirits" instead of "territorial spirits"). It would be analogous to Pontius Pilate's relationship to Tiberius Caesar. While Pilate was the local Roman prefect/governor of Judea, it was said that the region is nevertheless ultimately under the reign of Caesar (Luke 3:1) and that any opposition to the authorities of Judea is, in effect, opposition to the Caesar (John 19:12, 15; cf., Acts 17:7). In the eyes of Rome, any Roman governor is just an extension of the Caesar (who is himself an extension of the late Julius Caesar). And so it is with Satan and his demons. When one fights against earthly powers and authorities, she is fundamentally doing battle with spiritual forces that (are voluntarily permitted to) rule over them.

So, Scripture is not necessarily *against* some notion of territorial spirits, but, at the very least, the way it is traditionally understood (i.e., demons occupying, inhabiting, and possessing regions even apart from human occupancy) as well as defended seems to be defective. But, as noted, one can easily modify their doctrine of territorial spirits along the lines of what

---

14. See Walton and Walton, *Demons and Spirits*, 197–208.

Arnold has done. One could understand territorial spirits to be something like pure, immaterial intelligences that can attach themselves to other intelligences—even embodied ones like human beings. Demons could enter into the physical world in the same way a person enters into another's life by calling them up on the telephone. They could, *mutatis mutandis*, control provinces after all without committing oneself to the notion that immaterial beings can reside in unoccupied geographical provinces.

Let us clarify this further by means of analogy. Consider social media. Nobody is actually "on" social media in the spatio-physical sense of that word. No one is actually *located* at some set of coordinates within the sphere of Facebook or Instagram or in the so-called Twitterverse. Why? Because these outlets are not *here* or *there*. If nobody else were connected to social media, there would be no interaction between the lone user and anyone else. Social media do not depend on regions or locations, they depend on there being other users connected to the system. Accordingly, if no person ever occupied the regions within the Persian or Roman Empires, there would be no demonic presence. But you might say that they were always "online" awaiting a "user" to "log in." It is in this sense that Arnold's "empire spirits" makes better sense. In this way we can maintain the possible biblical understanding that demons do govern and control regimes at this or that location without thinking that they are somehow roaming about on the land masses as a lion does in continental Africa.[15] Indeed, it is more sensible to think that demons roam in a way that is analogous to a child predator who roams the internet seeking a victim.

On the assumption that the authors of Deuteronomy and Daniel are trying to say something along the lines of a traditional doctrine of territorial spirits (which is quite disputable), we can adjust our understanding of the doctrine without abandoning the notion altogether. On the one hand, Scripture could be supporting the notion if by "territorial spirits" we mean something minimal like "empire spirits"—spirits that indirectly (through human political regimes and governing bodies) rule over individual nations and/or people groups. But this is an open-ended question with very little to commend it. But if there really are territorial spirits, then to suppose that demons directly rule areas instead of people or are assigned by God to govern geographies would be to exceed what is reasonable and scriptural to conclude. That Satan and his minions have some measure of governing power over all the people of this world is probably the only thing we can justify.

15. I am aware that 2 Pet 5:8 describes Satan as one who "prowls around like a roaring lion." However, Peter is emphasizing, by use of analogy, the predatory nature of Satan's surveillance. He is not in any way insinuating that Satan is literally roaming around on all fours.

Appendix D

Paranormal Activity and the Occult

So-called occultic practices—practices involving magic and/or anti-Christian supernatural elements—are seen by many Christians as demonic windows into our world. When someone is messing around with a Ouija board, fortune-telling, necromancy, or spell-casting, these Christians become alarmed at the prospect of attracting demonic activity. For, it is argued, such practices are supremely evil and supremely evil practices naturally attract evil spirits. The same goes for unhealthy fascinations with things like ufology and parapsychology (e.g., clairvoyance and telepathy). The rationale is that since such things appear to be real (i.e., the ones that aren't hoaxes or that cannot be passed off as misinterpretations of naturally occurring oddities), they must be in part supernatural.[1] However, since the Christian worldview seems to have no space for supernatural agencies or forces outside of the powers of God, angels, and demons, then putative causes like disembodied spirits, ghosts, magical forces, and magical energies cannot be responsible for the realities and successful effects of occultic practices. And assuredly God and his angels would neither affirmatively engage in such occult practices nor deceive perceivers into thinking that things like disembodied spirits, ghosts, and other phantasms really exist. This leaves the Christian to posit demons as the agents most likely to masquerade as innocuous forces behind such phenomena.[2]

If this is right, then this demon hypothesis entails two things: (i) that demons are capable of interacting with the physical world and (ii) that

---

1. Neil T. Anderson, for example, says outright regarding parapsychology: "I have no question that it works" (*Bondage Breaker*, 115).

2. E.g., Ankerberg and Weldon, *Facts on Psychic Readings*; Ross, Samples, and Clark, *Lights in the Sky*; Rhodes, *Truth behind Ghosts*.

demons are capable of materializing.³ The first entailment here would have to be true if demons are indeed responsible for, say in the case of something like the Ouija, moving the planchette on the board. If they are responsible for poltergeist activity and manufacturing UFOs and flying them about, then they apparently can move upon matter in rather creative ways. The same goes for things like spell-casting and (some forms of) necromancy (e.g., seances). Regarding the kind of paranormal activity that involves alleged apparitions and various forms of metamorphosis, these usually involve the second entailment—that demons can materialize. For in order to be an apparition, transmutation, or a materialization—with accompanying auditory powers in some cases—one must have some physical property with which to be seen and/or heard.⁴ So, if the demon hypothesis is correct, then, at least regarding those occult activities and realities that cannot be dismissed on naturalistic grounds, demons are capable of creatively interacting with the physical world.

However, there are reasons to doubt both of these entailments. Let's start with the first one, that demons are capable of interacting with the physical world. Recall the arguments presented in chapters 4 and 8 about the improbability of demonic and even angelic interaction with the world. I argued that demons in particular, like their angelic kinsmen, are purely immaterial spirits and so have no intrinsic ability to interact with physical things. In fact, there are good reasons to believe that not even the good angels have such power, for God is said to be the agent who grants them power and visibility as the occasion demands (Num 22:31; 2 Kgs 6:17; Rev 7:2). Presumably, demons would not be aided by God in this way. Moreover, demons are never reported to directly interact with physical environments anywhere throughout Scripture; they do so only indirectly, that is, through the manipulation of the minds/souls of human beings (e.g., Judas Iscariot).⁵ It's precisely what we would expect to read in Scripture if demons cannot directly interact with the physical world. If my arguments are successful,

---

3. In some quarters, (i) and (ii) are not independent. One might argue that it is through the mechanism of spirit-matter interaction denoted in (i) that explains the ability to materialize.

4. The exception being that, for some, it is possible that apparitions and materializations, if they occur at all, are mere projections induced in the perceiver's mind and not manipulations of physical reality. This is to say that one might be receiving input from an evil spirit that induces the perceiver to have something akin to a vision or hallucination. It is possible that this is what happened to Jesus in his wilderness temptation (Matt 4:1–11; Luke 4:1–13).

5. There are some passages in Scripture that someone might think implies otherwise. To read my responses to them, see Guthrie, *Gods of This World*, chs. 10–11. I offer an abridged set of responses in my "Christian Demonology."

then demons are likely not be capable of manipulating physical objects or forces with which to carry out their alleged occultic shenanigans.

As for the second entailment—that demons are capable of materializations—much depends on one's understanding of the demons' ontologies (i.e., their natures). Demons cannot visibly masquerade as anything if they lack any physical components with which to cosmetically pull off such a deception.[6] And I have already argued that they likely do not have an intrinsic mystical ability with which to manifest as other beings. The only other way to salvage the demon hypothesis, assuming it to refer to extramental events, is to assert that demons are (quasi-)physical beings after all. But that option seems wrong given that demons are described as "spirits" and that spirits are incorporeal (Luke 24:39), invisible (1 Tim 1:17), and categorically distinct from things that are flesh (1 Pet 3:18) and body (2 Cor 5:1–6). If God, as one also being described as a "spirit" (John 4:24), is purely immaterial, on what basis do we have to suppose otherwise? In those cases where "spirit" is an ontological indicator, the impression is always an ontology that is wholly other than what is flesh—something wholly immaterial. Without any indication to the contrary with which to break that uniform ontological usage of "spirit" with how it is used of God and by Jesus, the prospect of a spirit having any material properties seems very unlikely. This means that the last way to salvage the demon hypothesis as a physical event is now dissolved.[7]

But not all occult activities require these two improbable entailments of demons. In some cases, such as fortune-telling and some elements of parapsychology (e.g., ESP, clairvoyance, and even visions and auditions), one could imagine scenarios where demons merely communicate information to our minds or exploit the relation our minds have to our own bodies (i.e., a psychosomatic relation). Also, it is possible that one can experience demonic apparitions or (seemingly) appearances of deceased people. For demons may have an ability to interact with our minds in such a way so as

---

6. One might have 2 Cor 11:14 in mind as a potential counterpoint: "And no wonder, for even Satan disguises himself as an angel of light." However, the way Satan "disguises himself" here is not physical or cosmetic. It is the disguise of deceit passing itself off as divine. Take a look at the very next verse: "So it is no surprise if his servants, also, *disguise themselves as servants of righteousness* [emphasis added]. Their end will correspond to their deeds." The "servants" here are not his demons but "false apostles, deceitful workmen, *disguising themselves as apostles of Christ*" (v. 13; emphasis added). They weren't disguising themselves *physically*; they were disguising themselves *positionally*—as fake ambassadors of the gospel. This is not a prooftext for demonic apparitions or materializations.

7. For a detailed argument against demonic psychokinesis (=their ability to interact directly with the physical world) and against their being (quasi-)physical (=having any material properties whatsoever), see Guthrie, *Gods of This World*, chs. 7–9.

to project in a person's mind what look to be apparitions coming into one's field of vision (much like an induced hallucination).[8] I have no reason to think such things are not possible for demons to do. And this is enough to entertain the concern that to engage in occult activity is to invite *some kind* of demonic presence into one's life. This is why Paul Thigpen calls the practices of occultism "trojan horses" of demonic activity.[9] For, to wield the tools of the occult is to attract and invite demonic beings into one's life in some aggressive way that must be, so we are told, countered with a kind of extra-special counterstrategy (i.e., a "power encounter" in some quarters) that hopefully mitigates any would-be demonic afflictions that would ensue. This retaliation to an infestation of demons facilitated by the occult is what C. Peter Wagner refers to as *occult-level spiritual warfare*.[10]

The problem of suggesting that the only way to counter demonic forces brought on by occult practices and beliefs is through these extra-special counterstrategies is that they often involve the kinds of remedies found in exorcistic and wizardry models of spiritual warfare. But, just how reasonable is all of this? It certainly isn't scriptural insofar as there is nothing in the Bible that remotely suggests that occultic practices are some special kind of attractor of demonic activity. Rather, they only attract insofar as practitioners are doing what is abominable before the Lord (Deut 18:11–12). And to indulge in the abominable is to become increasingly susceptible to demonic temptation, deception, and manipulation (Eph 4:27; 1 Tim 3:7). Indulging in the occult, then, is no more "magical" than indulging in lust, greed, or pride. It is only a "trojan horse" insofar as *all* sinful and heretical indulgences invite further temptation and deception. But we must not imagine that occult paraphernalia invite some kind of special onslaught of supernatural resistance. Sin is sin, and to indulge in it in any way will naturally spiral us deeper into the throes of demonic control.

Therefore, paranormal activity and the occult are not the results of demons directly interacting with and manipulating the physical world. However, I have no reason to doubt that those who indulge in occultic practices may make themselves susceptible to demonic influence in much the

8. Guthrie, *Gods of This World*, 257–61.

9. Thigpen, *Manual for Spiritual Warfare*, ch. 6.

10. Occult-level spiritual warfare, as roughly defined in Wagner's writings, pertains to our dealing with "demonic forces released through activities related to satanism, witchcraft, Freemasonry, Eastern religions, New Age, shamanism, astrology, and many other forms of structured occultism" (Wagner, *Spiritual Warfare Strategy*, 23). It is not entirely clear what he means by "released" except that it likely involves the summoning and/or increasing the presence of demons near the occult practitioners. One imagines occultic practices to be special attractors of evil spirits and enablers of increased diabolical activity among those involved.

same way that indulging one's lusts or greed does. But neither should our response involve the novel remedies found in exorcistic and wizardry models. For occultic practices and beliefs are fundamentally no different than moral or doctrinal deviations that one might indulge in or practice. And, as argued in chapter 18, appropriating the spiritual armor is itself sufficient for fortifying and protecting the Christian believer. This being the case, the best remedy is, of course, to increase in knowledge and wisdom against such things and to pursue righteousness so that we situate ourselves worlds apart from evil, no matter what form it takes—occult or otherwise.

Bibliography

Allestree, Richard. *The New Whole Duty of Man, Containing the Faith as well as Practice of a Christian.* 29th ed. London: W. Bent, 1810.
Almond, Philip C. *The Devil: A New Biography.* London: I.B. Taurus, 2014.
Alves, Elizabeth. *Becoming a Prayer Warrior.* Bloomington: Chosen Books, 1998.
Anderson, Neil T. *The Bondage Breaker.* Eugene, OR: Harvest House, 1990.
Ankerberg, John, and John Weldon. *The Facts on Psychic Readings: A Modern Deception of Ancient Lies.* Eugene, OR: Harvest House, 1997.
Aquinas, Thomas. *Summa Theologiae.* In *Thomas Aquinas: Selected Writings.* Translated by Ralph McInerny. London: Penguin, 1998.
Aristotle. *The Nicomachean Ethics.* Translated by J. A. K. Thomson. London: Penguin Classics, 1955.
Arnold, Clinton E. *Exegetical Commentary on the New Testament: Ephesians.* Grand Rapids: Zondervan, 2010.
———. *Power and Magic: The Concept of Power in Ephesians.* New York: Cambridge University Press, 1989.
———. *3 Crucial Questions about Spiritual Warfare.* Grand Rapids: Baker, 1997.
Augustine. *The Enchiridion.* In *The Enchiridion on Faith, Hope and Love.* Translated by Thomas Hibbs. Washington, DC: Regnery, 1996.
Bamberger, Bernard J. *Fallen Angels: Soldiers of Satan's Realm.* Philadelphia: Jewish Publication Society, 1952.
Barron, Lynsey M., and William P. Eiselstein. "Report of Independent Investigation into Sexual Misconduct of Ravi Zacharias." https://s3-us-west-2.amazonaws.com/rzimmedia.rzim.org/assets/downloads/Report-of-Investigation.pdf.
Barth, Karl. *Church Dogmatics*, vol. 3, *The Doctrine of Creation Part 3.* Edited by G. W. Bromiley and T. F. Torrance. Translated by G. W. Bromiley and R. J. Ehrlich. Edinburgh: T. & T. Clark, 1960.
Best, Ernest. *A Critical and Exegetical Commentary on Ephesians.* Edinburgh: T. & T. Clark, 2001.
Bignon, Guillaume. *Excusing Sinners and Blaming God: A Calvinist Assessment of Determinism, Moral Responsibility, and Divine Involvement in Evil.* Eugene, OR: Wipf & Stock, 2017.
Blackburn, Simon. *Lust.* New York: Oxford University Press, 2004.
Blomberg, Craig. *The Historical Reliability of the New Testament.* Nashville: B&H Academic, 2016.
Blount, Brian K. *Revelation.* Louisville: Presbyterian, 2009.

Boyd, Gregory. *God at War: The Bible and Spiritual Conflict.* Downers Grove, IL: InterVarsity, 1997.

———. "Response." In *Understanding Spiritual Warfare: Four Views,* edited by James K. Beilby and Paul Rhodes Eddy, 117–22. Grand Rapids: Baker Academic, 2012.

———. *Satan and the Problem of Evil: Constructing a Trinitarian Warfare Theodicy.* Downers Grove, IL: InterVarsity, 2001.

Brown, Rebecca and Daniel Yoder. *Unbroken Curses: Hidden Source of Trouble in the Christian's Life.* Clinton: Whitaker House, 1995.

Burridge, Richard A. *What Are the Gospels?: A Comparison with Graeco-Roman Biography.* Cambridge: Cambridge University Press, 1992.

Cardeña, Etzel, Steven Jay Lynn, and Stanley Krippner. *Varieties of Anomalous Experience: Examining the Scientific Evidence.* Washington, DC: American Psychological Association, 2013.

Carson, D. A., and Douglas J. Moo. *An Introduction to the New Testament.* 2nd ed. Grand Rapids: Zondervan, 2005.

Cook, William F., III, and Chuck Lawless. *Spiritual Warfare in the Storyline of Scripture: A Biblical, Theological, and Practical Approach.* Nashville: B&H Academic, 2019.

Chrysostom, John. "That Demons Do Not Govern the World." In *The Nicene and Post-Nicene Fathers,* ser. 1, vol. 9, edited by Philip Schaff, 177–86. New York: Cosimo, 2007; 1889.

Coleridge, Samuel Taylor. *The Poetical and Dramatic Works of Samuel Taylor Coleridge.* London: Basil Montagu Pickering, 1877.

Collins, C. John. *Genesis 1–4: A Linguistic, Literary, and Theological Commentary.* Phillipsburg: P&R, 2006.

Cook, Christopher C. H. *Hearing Voices, Demonic and Divine: Scientific and Theological Perspectives.* London: Routledge, 2018.

Cook III, William F., and Chuck Lawless. *Spiritual Warfare in the Storyline of Scripture: A Biblical, Theological, and Practical Approach.* Nashville: B&H Academic, 2019.

Crawford, Dan R. "Unceasing Intercession: Prayer Walking as a Method." In *Prayer Walking: A Journey of Faith,* edited by Dan R. Crawford and Calvin Miller, 1–32. Chattanooga, TN: AMG, 2002.

Dawson, John. "Foreword." In *Prayer-Walking: Praying On-Site with Insight,* by Steve Hawthorne and Graham Kendrick, 7–8. Lake Mary: Charisma House, 1993.

De la Torre, Miguel, and Albert Hernández. *The Quest for the Historical Satan.* Minneapolis: Fortress, 2011.

Del Olmo Lete, Gregorio. *Incantations and Anti-Witchcraft Texts from Ugarit.* Boston: Walter de Gruyter, 2014.

Descartes, René. "Meditation I." In *Discourse on Method and Meditations on First Philosophy,* translated by Donald A. Cress, 59–62. 4th ed. Indianapolis: Hackett, 1998.

Douglas, John. *The Criterion: Or, Miracles Examined with a View to Expose the Pretensions of Pagans and Papists..* London: A. Millar, 1754.

Dunnington, Kent. "The Problem with the Satan Hypothesis: Natural Evil and Fallen Angel Theodicies." *Sophia* 57 (2018) 265–74.

Eckhardt, John. *Deliverance and Spiritual Warfare Manual: A Comprehensive Guide to Living Free.* Lake Mary: Charisma House, 2014.

———. *Identifying and Breaking Curses.* New Kensington: Whitaker House, 1999.

Fee, Gordon D. *The First and Second Letters to the Thessalonians*. Grand Rapids: Eerdmans, 2009.
Ferguson, Everett. *Demonology of the Early Christian World*. New York: Edwin Mellen, 1984.
Fitzmyer, Joseph A. *First Corinthians: A New Translation with Introduction and Commentary*. New Haven, CT: Yale University Press, 2007.
———. *The Gospel According to Luke I–IX: Introduction, Translation, and Notes*. New Haven, CT: Yale University Press, 1970.
Forsyth, Neil. *The Old Enemy*. Princeton, NJ: Princeton University Press, 1987.
Fowl, Stephen E. *Ephesians*. Louisville: Westminster John Knox Press, 2012.
Gallagher, Richard. "As a Psychiatrist, I Diagnose Mental Illness. Also, I Help Spot Demonic Possession: How a Scientist Learned to Work with Exorcists." *Washington Post*, July 1, 2016. https://www.washingtonpost.com/posteverything/wp/2016/07/01/as-a-psychiatrist-i-diagnose-mental-illness-and-sometimes-demonic-possession/.
Garrett, Susan R. *The Demise of the Devil: Magic and the Demonic in Luke's Writings*. Minneapolis: Fortress, 1989.
Garrison, Mary. *How to Conduct Spiritual Warfare*. New Kensington: Whitaker House, 2014.
Gilhooly, John R. *40 Questions about Angels, Demons, and Spiritual Warfare*. Grand Rapids: Kregel Academic, 2018.
Goldingay, John. *Psalms 42–89*. Grand Rapids: Baker, 2007.
Graham, Franklin. *Billy Graham in Quotes*. Nashville: Thomas Nelson, 2011.
Guntrip, Elizabeth Dunham. "A Pentecostal Study of Daniel's Prince of Persia (Dan 10:13)." PhD diss., Australian Catholic University Press, 2006.
Guthrie, Shandon L. "Angels, Early Theories." In *The Encyclopedia of Philosophy of Religion*, edited by Stewart Goetz and Charles Taliaferro, vol. 1. Oxford: Wiley-Blackwell, 2021.
———. "Christian Demonology: A New Philosophical Perspective." In *Philosophical Approaches to Demonology*, edited by Benjamin W. McCraw and Robert Arp, 59–74. London: Routledge, 2017.
———. *Gods of This World: A Philosophical Discussion and Defense of Christian Demonology*. Eugene, OR: Pickwick, 2018.
———. "A New Challenge to a Warfare Theodicy." *International Journal of Philosophy and Theology* 5 (December 2017) 35–43.
———. "A New Metaphysics for Christian Demonology: Psychodynamic Immaterialism." PhD diss., Manchester Metropolitan University, 2015.
Hammond, Frank, and Ida Mae Hammond. *Pigs in the Parlor: A Practical Guide to Deliverance*. Kirkwood: Impact, 1973.
Hawthorne, Steve, and Graham Kendrick. *Prayer-Walking: Praying On Site with Insight*. Lake Mary: Charisma House, 1993.
Heiser, Michael S. *Demons: What the Bible Really Says about the Powers of Darkness*. Bellingham: Lexham, 2020.
———. *Reversing Hermon: Enoch, the Watchers & the Forgotten Mission of Jesus Christ*. Crane: Defender, 2017.
———. *The Unseen Realm: Recovering the Supernatural Worldview of the Bible*. Bellingham: Lexham, 2015.

Helm, Paul. "Human Beings, Compatibilist Freedom, and Salvation." In *The Ashgate Research Companion to Theological Anthropology*, edited by Joshua R. Farris and Charles Taliaferro, 245–60. London: Routledge, 2016.
Hesiod. *Works and Days*. In *Works and Days, Theogony and The Shield of Heracles*, translated by Hugh G. Evelyn-White, 1–26. Mineola: Dover, 2006.
Hick, John. *Philosophy of Religion*. 4th ed. Upper Saddle River, NJ: Prentice Hall, 1990.
Hoehner, Harold W. *Ephesians: An Exegetical Commentary*. Grand Rapids: Baker Academic, 2002.
Holvast, Rene. *Spiritual Mapping in the United States and Argentina, 1989–2005: A Geography of Fear*. Leiden: Brill, 2009.
Horsley, Jasun. *Prisoner of Infinity: UFOs, Social Engineering, and the Psychology of Fragmentation*. London: Aeon, 2018.
Ice, Thomas, and Robert Dean Jr. *What the Bible Teaches about Spiritual Warfare*. Grand Rapids: Kregel, 2000.
Josephus, Flavius. *Antiquities of the Jews*. United Kingdom: Library of Alexandria, 2020.
Kaiser, Walter, Jr., Peter H. Davids, F. F. Bruce, and Manfred T. Brauch, eds. *Hard Sayings of the Bible*. Downers Grove, IL: InterVarsity, 1996.
Keener, Craig S. *Christobiography: Memory, History, and the Reliability of the Gospels*. Grand Rapids: Eerdmans, 2019.
———. *The IVP Bible Background Commentary: New Testament*. Downers Grove, IL: InterVarsity, 1993.
———. *Romans: A New Covenant Commentary*. Cambridge: Lutterworth, 2011.
Keener, Craig S., and John H. Walton. *NIV Cultural Backgrounds Study Bible: Bringing to Life the Ancient World of Scripture*. Grand Rapids: Zondervan, 2016.
Kelly, Henry Ansgar. "Reviewed Work: *The Old Enemy: Satan and the Combat Myth* by Neil Forsyth." *Journal of American Folklore* 102 (1989) 107–10.
———. *Satan: A Biography*. New York: Cambridge University Press, 2006.
Kierkegaard, Søren. *The Sickness unto Death, a Christian Psychological Exposition for Upbuilding and Awakening*. Edited and translated by Howard V. Hong and Edna H. Hong. Princeton, NJ: Princeton University Press, 1980.
Kimyai-Asadi, Arash, and Adil Usman. "The Role of Psychological Stress in Skin Disease." *Journal of Cutaneous Medicine and Surgery* 5 (March 2001) 140–45.
Kingsberg, S. "Testosterone Treatment for Hypoactive Sexual Desire Disorder in Postmenopausal Women." *Journal of Sexual Medicine* 4 (2007) 227–34.
Kraft, Charles H. *I Give You Authority: Practicing the Authority Jesus Gave Us*. Rev. ed. Grand Rapids: Chosen Books, 1997.
Larson, Bob. *Curse Breaking: Freedom from the Bondage of Generational Sins*. Shippensburg: Destiny Image, 2013.
———. *Demon-Proofing Prayers: Bob Larson's Guide to Winning Spiritual Warfare*. Shippensburg: Destiny Image, 2011.
Lewis, C. S. *The Screwtape Letters*. New York: HarperCollins, 2001.
Licona, Michael R. *Why Are There Differences in the Gospels?: What We Can Learn from Ancient Biography*. New York: Oxford University Press, 2017.
Lincoln, Andrew T. *Ephesians*. World Biblical Commentary 42. Waco, TX: Word, 1990.
Löfstedt, Torsten. "Establishing Authority in Spiritual Warfare Literature." *HumaNetten* 41 (2018) 4–24.
Lowe, Chuck. *Territorial Spirits and World Evangelisation: A Biblical, Historical and Missiological Critique of Strategic-Level Spiritual Warfare*. Scotland: Mentor, 1998.

Lynch, Jamiel, Konstantin Toropin, and Dianne Gallagher. "Parkland School Shooter Told Detective He Heard a Demon in His Head, Transcript Shows." *CNN*, August 7, 2008. https://www.cnn.com/2018/08/07/us/florida-parkland-nikolas-cruz/index.html.

Lynn, Steven Jay, and Irving I. Kirsch. "Alleged Alien Abductions: False Memories, Hypnosis, and Fantasy Proneness." *Psychological Inquiry* (1996) 150–55.

MacKinnon, Barbara. *American Philosophy: A Historical Anthology*. Albany, NY: SUNY Press, 1985.

MacGregor, Kirk. *Contemporary Theology: An Introduction: Classical, Evangelical, Philosophical, and Global Perspectives*. Rev. ed. Grand Rapids: Zondervan, 2020.

MacNutt, Francis. *Deliverance from Evil Spirits: A Practical Manual*. Grand Rapids: Chosen Books, 2009.

McCloud, Sean. *American Possessions: Fighting Demons in the Contemporary United States*. New York: Oxford, 2015.

McGrew, Lydia. *The Eye of the Beholder: The Gospel of John as Historical Reportage*. Chillicothe: DeWard, 2020.

———. *Hidden in Plain View: Undesigned Coincidences in the Gospels and Acts*. Chillicothe: DeWard, 2017.

———. *The Mirror or the Mask: Liberating the Gospels from Literary Devices*. Chillicothe: DeWard, 2019.

McKeown, James. "Blessings and Curses." In *Dictionary of the Old Testament Pentateuch*, edited by T. Desmond Alexander and David W. Baker, 83–87. Downers Grove, IL: InterVarsity, 2003.

Meade, Scott. *Spiritual Warfare: Fighting Demons*. Createspace, 2010.

Meyer, Joyce. *Battlefield of the Mind: Winning the Battle in Your Mind*. New York: FaithWords, 1995.

Moore, Beth. *Praying God's Word: Breaking Free from Spiritual Strongholds*. Nashville: B&H, 2009.

Moreland, J. P. *The God Question: An Invitation to a Life of Meaning*. Eugene, OR: Harvest House, 2009.

Morris, I. Leon. "Ephesians 6:10–17 and the Full Armor of God: A Christological Fulfillment of Ecclesiological Justice." Unpublished paper presented at the annual meeting of the Evangelical Theological Society, San Diego, November 20, 2019.

Narveson, Jan. "Compatibilism Defended." *Philosophical Studies* 32 (1977) 83–87.

Niebuhr, Reinhold. *Nature and Destiny of Man: A Christian Interpretation*, vol. 1, *Human Nature*. New York: Scribner's Sons, 1941.

Neufeld, Yoder. *Put On the Armour of God: The Divine Warrior from Isaiah to Ephesians*. Sheffield: Sheffield Academic, 1997.

Ojigbani, Chris. *Spiritual Warfare*. Maitland: Xulon, 2009.

Omartian, Stormie. *Prayer Warrior: The Power of Praying Your Way to Victory*. Eugene, OR: Harvest House, 2013.

Origen. *Against Celsus*. In *The Ante-Nicene Fathers: The Writings of the Fathers Down to AD 325*, vol. 4, edited by Alexander Roberts, James Donaldson, and Arthur Cleveland Coxe. New York: Scribner's Sons, 1886.

Otis, Jr., George. *Informed Intercession: Transforming Your Community Through Spiritual Mapping and Strategic Prayer*. Colorado Springs: Gospel Light, 1999.

Page, Sydney H. T. *Powers of Evil: A Biblical Study of Satan and Demons*. Grand Rapids: Baker, 1995.

Pagels, Elaine. *The Origin of Satan: How Christians Demonized Jews, Pagans, and Heretics*. New York: Vintage, 1995.

Payne, William. *Satan Exposed: A Biblical Theology of Spiritual Warfare*. Eugene, OR: Wipf & Stock, 2019.

Phillips, Ron. *Everyone's Guide to Demons & Spiritual Warfare*. Lake Mary: Charisma House, 2010.

Plantinga, Alvin. 1967. *God and Other Minds: A Study of the Rational Justification of Belief in God*. Ithaca, NY: Cornell University Press.

Plato. *The Republic*. In *Plato: Complete Works*, edited by John M. Cooper and translated by G. M. A. Grube and C. D. C. Reeve, 971–1223. Indianapolis: Hackett, 1997.

Plutarch. "Of Superstition." In *Plutarch's Morals*, edited by William W. Goodwin. Boston: Little, Brown, 1874.

Powlison, David. "The Classical Model." In *Understanding Spiritual Warfare*, edited By James K. Beilby and Paul Rhodes Eddy, 89–111. Grand Rapids: Baker Academic, 2012.

———. *Power Encounters: Reclaiming Spiritual Warfare*. Grand Rapids: Baker, 1995.

Poythress, Vern S. "Territorial Spirits: Some Biblical Perspectives." *Urban Mission* 13 (1995) 37–49.

Prince, Derek. *Secrets of a Prayer Warrior*. Grand Rapids: Chosen Books, 2009.

Proctor, John. *First and Second Corinthians*. Louisville: Westminster John Knox, 2015.

Pruss, Alexander. *One Body: An Essay in Christian Sexual Ethics*. Notre Dame, IN: University of Notre Dame Press, 2012.

Rhodes, Ron. *The Truth behind Ghosts, Mediums, and Psychic Phenomena*. Eugene, OR: Harvest House, 2006.

Ross, Hugh, Kenneth R. Samples, and Mark Clark. *Lights in the Sky and Little Green Men: A Rational Christian Look at UFOs and Extraterrestrials*. Colorado Springs: NavPress, 2002.

Shafer-Landau, Russ. *The Fundamentals of Ethics*. 2nd ed. New York: Oxford University Press, 2012.

Schleiermacher, Friedrich. *The Christian Faith*. Edited by Paul T. Nimmo, translated by H. R. Mackintosh. London: Bloomsbury, 2016.

Schnarr, Grant. *The Art of Spiritual Warfare: A Guide to Lasting Inner Peace Based on Sun Tzu's* The Art of War. Wheaton, IL: Quest, 2000.

Sjöberg, Kjell. *Winning the Prayer War: Why and How to Pray for Where You Live*. Chichester: New Wine, 1991.

Smith, Mark S. *The Origins of Biblical Monotheism*. New York: Oxford, 2001.

Spurgeon, Charles H. *Spiritual Warfare in a Believer's Life*. Compiled and edited by Robert Hall. Lynnwood: Emerald, 1993.

Stevens, David E. "Daniel 10 and the Notion of Territorial Spirits." *Bibliotheca Sacra* 157 (2000) 410–31.

Strauss, David Friedrich. *The Life of Jesus, Critically Examined*. Vol. 1. Translated by Marian Evans. New York: Calvin Blanchard, 1856.

Strieber, Whitley. *Breakthrough: The Next Step*. New York: HarperCollins, 1995.

———. *Communion: A True Story*. New York: Avon/Hearst, 1987.

———. "Pain." In *Cutting Edge: Brave New Horror Stories*, edited by Dennis Etchison, 279–301. New York: Doubleday, 1986.

———. *Transformation: The Breakthrough*. New York: Avon/Hearst, 1989.

Swinburne, Richard. *The Existence of God*. 2nd ed. Oxford: Oxford University Press, 2004.

Tate, Marvin E. "Satan in the Old Testament." *Review & Expositor* 89 (1992) 461–74.

Thigpen, Paul. *Manual for Spiritual Warfare*. Charlotte: TAN, 2014.

Thomas, Emily. "The Spatial Location of God and Casper the Friendly Ghost." *Think* 8 (2009) 53–61.

Unger, Merrill F. *Biblical Demonology: A Study of Spiritual Forces at Work Today*. Grand Rapids: Kregel, 1994.

———. *What Demons Can Do to Saints*. Chicago: Moody Bible Institute, 1977.

Wagner, C. Peter. *Breaking Strongholds in Your City*. Shippensburg: Destiny Image, 2015.

———. *Spiritual Warfare Strategy: Confronting Spiritual Powers*. Shippensburg: Destiny Image, 1996.

Walton, John H., and J. Harvey Walton. *Demons and Spirits in Biblical Theology: Reading the Biblical Text in Its Cultural and Literary Context*. Eugene, OR: Cascade, 2019.

Warner, Timothy M. "Dealing with Territorial Spirits." In *Territorial Spirits: Practical Strategies for How to Crush the Enemy through Spiritual Warfare*, edited by C. Peter Wagner, 75–78. Shippensburg: Destiny Image, 2012.

Wiebe, Phillip H. *God and Other Spirits: Intimations of Transcendence in Christian Experience*. New York: Oxford University Press, 2004.

Wierenga, Edward R. *The Nature of God: An Inquiry into Divine Attributes*. Ithaca, NY: Cornell University Press, 1989.

Wink, Walter. *Engaging the Powers: Discernment and Resistance in a World of Domination*. Philadelphia: Fortress, 1992.

———. *Naming the Powers: The Language of Power in the New Testament*. Philadelphia: Fortress, 1984.

———. *Unmasking the Powers: The Invisible Forces that Determine Human Existence*. Philadelphia: Fortress, 1986.

Wray, T. J., and Gregory Mobley. *The Birth of Satan: Tracing the Devil's Biblical Roots*. New York: Palgrave, 2005.

Yong, Amos. *The Spirit of Creation: Modern Science and Divine Action in the Pentecostal-Charismatic Imagination*. Grand Rapids: Eerdmans, 2011.

Subject Index

alien abudctions. *See* paranormal, the: alien abductions
angelology, ix, 5, 61–66. *See also* angels
angels, 60–74, 79–81, 86–87, 98–99, 104–5, 120, 122, 124, 128, 146, 173, 260, 274–78, 281–82
    cherubim, 29, 61–62
    fallen. *See* demons: fallen angels
    finitude of, 63, 65, 66, 70
    immateriality of, 70–73, 81, 159–63, 165
    limited knowledge of, 64–65
    powers of, 66
    seraphim, 62
animism, 150
anthropology (theological), 150
apocalypse, 16, 70, 79–81, 100, 103–5, 110, 116, 128, 129, 134, 274, 277
apologetics, 135, 199, 223, 225, 228–30, 252–59, 260
apostasy, 31, 38, 168, 170, 200, 209
apparitions. *See* paranormal, the: apparitions
Areopagus, 199, 256
argumentation, 198–99
Aristotelianism, 203
Arminianism, 109, 230
armor of God, 88, 95, 206–10, 218
    belt of truth, 94, 106, 207
    breastplate of righteousness, 15, 77, 79, 96, 207, 217
    covering of feet, 207
    helmet of salvation, 96, 187, 207–8
    shield of faith, 79, 207, 217
    sword of the Spirit, 79, 88–90, 94, 154, 207, 217
Artemis, 92–93
atheism, 3, 125, 167, 195, 243, 253
authority (over evil spirits), 86, 188–91

Babylon, 21, 27–29, 63, 79–80, 135, 267, 273
"beast," 16, 20–21, 86–87, 115, 127, 129
binding (and loosing), 148, 154–56

Calvinism, 12, 23, 109, 230, 266
Canaan, 27, 32, 52, 57, 79, 135
cherub (anointed guardian). *See* angels: cherubim.
combat myth, 27, 79–81, 135
compatibilism, 23, 266
concordism, 119
conflict theology. *See* spiritual warfare: as conflict
"conqueror," 1, 87–88, 94, 109–10
conversion disorder, 40
curses, 92–93, 172–73, 184–88

deliverance exorcism, 148, 162–71, 189, 193, 211, 215
deliverance ministry, 147
demoniac, 13, 127, 136
    Capernaum, 128, 129, 166
    convulsing boy, 167
    Gerasene, 13, 127–29, 136, 154, 166
    Syrophoenecian woman's daughter, 129, 136, 166

SUBJECT INDEX

demonology, ix, ,3, 5, 11, 26, 61, 63, 66, 69, 73, 79, 80, 116, 119, 120–37, 163
   anti-realism, 125–26, 139, 146, 260
   realism, 16, 123, 125, 126, 144, 146, 171, 193, 260
demons
   "daimon," 63, 66, 68
   devils, 9, 14, 23, 66, 119, 120, 260
   evil spirits, 34, 40, 67–69, 73–74, 85, 119, 123, 125, 130, 138–39, 142, 143, 158, 164–65, 173, 188–91, 271, 279, 281, 282, 284
   fallen angels, 2, 36, 69–73, 99, 120, 125, 142
   "familiar spirits," 67
   immateriality of, 159–62
   "satyr," 67–68
   "unclean spirits," 71, 128, 160–62
demonization, 73, 148, 164–71, 182, 277
demon possession, 5, 71, 73, 127–29, 138–43, 147–48, 154–55, 157–71, 176, 178, 179, 189, 191, 193, 215, 279. See also demonization
diabolical experiences, 137–39, 142–43
discipleship, 146, 196, 217, 258
divine command theory (of ethics), 33
"divine council," 34, 274, 277–78

Eden, 29, 31, 44, 111
enemy triumvirate, the
   flesh, the, 8, 16, 21–24, 46–49, 55, 99–100, 107, 113–14, 198, 203–4, 215, 233, 235, 239, 248
   world, the, 42–45
   Satan. See Satan
enlightenment, 1, 3, 10, 122, 126, 257
Epic of Gilgamesh, 136
exorcism. See demonization, deliverance exorcism, *and* territorial exorcism
experience (arguments from), 149–53

faith, 213–14
fall (angelic), 30–31
fallacy of division, 166

flesh, the. See enemy triumvirate, the *and* Satan.

Gabriel, 62
ghosts. See paranormal, the: ghosts
God
   as all-good (omnibenevolent), 11, 53–55, 211
   as all-knowing (omniscient), 36, 53, 54, 59, 211, 266, 270
   as all-loving, 53–55, 56, 59
   as all-powerful (omnipotent), 11, 55–58, 59, 96, 179–80, 265
   immateriality of, 33, 34, 51–53
   sovereignty of, 11, 19, 58, 59, 93, 103, 109, 110, 131, 265
   Trinity, 33, 43, 67, 135, 225
godliness, 196, 201. See also holiness
ground-level spiritual warfare. See spiritual warfare: ground-level spiritual warfare

hauntings. See paranormal, the: hauntings
healing, 57, 92, 120, 147, 157, 171, 176, 177, 182–83, 188, 267
"heavenly places," 7, 15, 49, 72–73, 92, 176, 259, 261, 279
hell, 31, 71, 71–72, 81, 85, 214
holiness, 49, 86, 89, 90, 94, 99, 194, 201–8, 216–17, 221, 232, 233–51, 261

image of God, 21, 198, 205, 216, 235, 246
incompatibilism, 23–24

Jehovah's Witnesses, 227
Job (book of), 26, 67, 79, 97, 128

kingdom of God, 9, 44–45, 72, 83, 110, 112, 115–16, 136, 147, 156, 157, 159, 165, 188, 191, 201, 269
kingdom of Satan, 44, 45, 147
knowledge, 8, 16, 51, 96, 108, 114, 138, 162, 163, 195–201, 202, 206, 208–9, 213, 216–18, 221–32, 233–34, 252–59, 260, 262–63. See also wisdom

"Legion," 127, 154
libertarian free will, 12, 266
literary devices, 70, 121, 130, 134
Logos, 79, 89
Lucifer, 28–29
"lukewarm," 203
lust. *See* sexual sins: lust

Manichaeism, 19–20
Michael the archangel, 25, 27, 26, 62, 80–81, 105, 115, 273–74
miracles, 39–41, 57–58, 125, 138, 143, 147, 155, 157, 258, 267
Mithraism, 63
Mormonism, 227

naturalism, 4–5, 143, 174, 188, 282
Natural Law Theory (of ethics), 33
Nephilim. *See* "sons of God"
Nicodemus, 58, 167
Nicomachean Ethics, 201, 204. *See also* Aristotle

occult, the, 165–66, 169, 173, 178, 184, 191–92, 198, 281–85
occult-level spiritual warfare. *See* spiritual warfare: occult-level spiritual warfare
open theism, 36, 266–67
oppression (demonic), 7, 16, 107, 108, 158, 160, 164, 175–76, 180, 182, 215
oracular poetry, 27

panoplian, 92, 207–10. *See also* armor of God
paranormal, the, 73, 141, 145, 281–85
  alien abductions, 139–42
  apparitions, 39, 282–4
  astral projection, 164
  divination, 157
  ghosts, 53, 73, 281
  hauntings, 73, 145, 146, 152
  necromancy, 67, 281–82
  poltergeists, 73, 282
  telepathy, 39, 281
  UFOs, 140–1, 281–82
Pentecostalism, 3
peroratio, 207

phantasm, 53, 123, 281
phantom, 39
philosophy, 4–6, 51, 86, 116, 194, 201, 257–58, 260–261, 265
Pilgrim's Progress, The, 4
Platonism, 33, 79–80
possession. *See* demonization
prayer, 89, 93, 112, 148, 149–50, 157, 200, 209–11, 216, 217, 234, 237. *See also* prayerwalking *and* prayer warrior
prayerwalking, 172, 180–84
prayer warrior, 172, 174–76
pride, 21, 30, 37, 100, 141, 189, 205, 244–47, 250, 256, 262, 284
"Prince of Greece," 80, 273–76
"Prince of Persia," 273–76
problem of evil, the, 265–66
Protestants. *See* Reformers (Protestant),
psychokinesis, 283

Qumran, 77

rationalism, 150
Reformers (Protestant), 12, 230
repossession. *See* demonization *and* "waterless places"
"resist the devil," 100, 177–78, 200
righteousness, 20, 26, 41, 49, 88, 94–95, 99, 106, 108, 154, 162, 197–200, 201, 205–6, 207–17, 233, 252, 285. *See also* holiness *and* sanctification

sanctification, 146, 149, 201–2, 216, 221, 232, 233–35, 252, 268. *See also* holiness *and* righteousness
Satan
  Beelzebul, 32, 91, 112, 136, 160
  devil, the, 7, 23–24, 27, 38, 41, 42, 44–45, 49, 68–9, 71–72, 92, 100, 103, 107–8, 114, 125–26, 165, 177–78, 184, 190, 200, 202, 209, 218, 242, 244, 245, 250
  "god of this world," 22, 32, 44, 125
  immateriality of, 34–35, 39, 47. *See also* demons: immateriality of *and* angels: immateriality of

Satan *(continued)*
  knowledge of, 35–38
  powers of, 38–41. *See also* angels:
    powers of
  "prince," 22
  schemes of, 114, 154, 200, 209, 218,
    238, 262
  serpent. *See* serpent
  "tempter," 32, 201
schemes (of Satan). *See* Satan:
  schemes of
science, 51, 120–21, 142, 253
Septuagint, 25, 66, 68, 108, 245, 275
serpent, 31–32, 44, 186–87
seven sons of Sceva, 166, 179. *See also*
  demonization
sexual behavior, 203, 238, 239–45,
  247, 262
  lust, 21, 48, 70, 205, 238, 242–44
  premarital sex, 241
sola Scriptura, 150
"sons of God," 26, 44, 64, 69–71, 128,
  273–76
spiritual warfare
  as conflict, 10–16, 77–78, 92–93,
    98, 105, 106, 116, 142, 153
  definition of, 6–7, 15
  ground-level spiritual warfare, 149
  occult-level spiritual warfare, 284
  strategic-level spiritual warfare,
    146–47, 153, 155
spiritual mapping, 158
strategic-level spiritual warfare. *See*
  spiritual warfare: strategic-level
  spiritual warfare
Sumer, 135
superstition, 3, 19, 116, 121, 123, 126,
  131, 144, 193
superstitious, 3, 19, 93, 125–26, 132,
  139, 174, 261

Tartarus, 31
"teachings of demons," 68–69, 169,
  199–200
teleology, 201, 241, 242
telepathy. *See* paranormal, the:
  telepathy
territorial exorcism, 147–59, 162, 163,
  190, 193, 198, 199, 211
territorial spirits, 80, 146–57, 160,
  163, 170–71, 182, 272–80. *See
  also* territorial exorcism
theodicy, 5, 11. *See also* problem of
  evil, the
Transcendentalism, 3

Ufology. *See* paranormal, the: UFOs
undesigned coincidences, 136

vanity, 246
vice, 33, 97, 107, 110, 113, 125, 187,
  196, 200, 203, 210, 217, 237, 244,
  246–50, 256, 262
virtues, 4, 11, 38, 54, 79, 90, 94, 97,
  110, 113, 149, 164, 169, 187, 188,
  195, 196, 201–18, 232, 236, 254,
  256, 261–63, 265, 268
visions, 35, 37, 66, 80, 86, 282, 283–84

warfare. *See* spiritual warfare
"waterless places," 160–2
wilderness (motif), 111, 160–61
wilderness (temptation of Jesus), 108,
  154, 205–6, 282
wisdom, 85, 100, 195, 197–201, 206,
  216, 221, 233, 238, 255, 257–58,
  261–62, 285
world, the. *See* enemy triumvirate,
  the: world, the

Zoroastrians, 19–20

Author and Name Index

Allestree, Richard, 24
Almond, Philip C., 125
Alves, Elizabeth, 173, 174
Anderson, Neil T., 147, 160, 164–5, 173–4, 177–8, 260, 281
Ankerberg, John, 281
Aquinas, Thomas, 64–5
Aristotle, 116, 201, 203–4, 256
Arnold, Clinton E., 77, 92–3, 95, 114, 148–9, 166–9, 215, 272, 273, 276, 279–80
Augustine, 11, 12–13

Bamberger, Bernard J., 30, 124–5
Barron, Lynsey M., 202
Barth, Karl, 122
Best, Ernest, 210
Bignon, Guillaume, 23
Blackburn, Simon, 243
Blomberg, Craig, 129, 133
Blount, Brian K., 90
Bonhoeffer, Dietrich, 223
Boyd, Gregory A., 36, 171, 266–7, 272
Brown, Rebecca, 184
Burridge, Richard A., 133

Cardeña, Etzel, 138
Carson, D. A., 133
Chrysostom, John, 13–14
Clark, Mark, 281
Coleridge, Samuel Taylor, 124
Collins, John C., 162
Cook, Christopher C. H., 138
Cook, William F., III, 70–1
Crawford, Dan R., 180, 183
Cruz, Nikolas, 139

Dawson, John, 180
Dean, Robert, Jr., 155
De la Torre, Miguel, 23, 125
Del Olmo Lete, Gregorio, 175
Descartes, René, 55–6
Douglas, John, 140

Eckhardt, John, 184
Eiselstein, William P., 202

Fee, Gordon D., 249
Ferguson, Everett, 63
Fitzmyer, Joseph A., 160, 258
Forsyth, Neil, 27, 63, 79, 124
Fowl, Stephen E., 73, 95, 209, 210

Gallagher, Richard, 138–41
Garrett, Susan R., 155–6
Garrison, Mary, 158
Gilhooly, John R., 167
Goldingay, John, 277–8
Guntrip, Elizabeth Dunham, 272

Hammond, Frank, 163
Hammond, Ida Mae, 163
Hawthorne, Steve, 180–3
Heiser, Michael S., 10, 69–70, 161, 272, 275–7
Helm, Paul, 23
Heraclitus, 79
Hernández, Albert, 23, 125
Hesiod, 63
Hick, John, 11–12, 267–8
Hinn, Benny, 163
Hodge, A. A., 121
Hoehner, Harold W., 73

Holvast, Rene, 158
Horsley, Jasun, 140

Ice, Thomas, 155
Irenaeus, 12

Jones, Martyn-Lloyd, 223
Josephus, Flavius, 136

Kaiser, Walter, Jr., 70
Keener, Craig S., 81, 95, 133, 160, 187, 204
Kelly, Henry Ansgar, 124, 135
Kelsey, Morton, 126
Kendrick, Graham, 180–3
Kierkegaard, Søren, 258
Kimyai-Asadi, Arash, 41
Kingsberg, S., 242
Kraft, Charles H., 151, 177–8, 189–90
Krippner, Stanley, 138

Larson, Bob, 163, 174, 184–5, 189–90
Lawless, Chuck, 70–1
Lewis, C. S., 9, 45, 222
Licona, Michael R., 133
Lincoln, Andrew T., 210
Löfstedt, Torsten, 150
Lowe, Chuck, 272
Lynch, Jamiel, 139
Lynn, Steven Jay, 138, 140

Machen, J. Gresham, 223
MacGregor, Kirk, 3
MacKinnon, Barbara, 3
MacNutt, Francis, 163
McCloud, Sean, 150
McGrew, Lydia, 133, 136, 229
McGrew, Timothy, 225
McKeown, James, 186
Meade, Scott, 158
Meyer, Joyce, 114, 177–8
Meyers, Rick, 225
Mobley, Gregory, 125
Moo, Douglas J., 133
Moore, Beth, 114, 175, 176, 178
Morris, I. Leon, 95

Narveson, Jan, 23
Niebuhr, Reinhold, 124

Neufeld, Yoder, 95

Ojigbani, Chris, 184
Omartian, Stormie, 175
Origen, 27, 63, 272
Otis, George, Jr., 158

Packer, J. I., 223
Page, Sydney H. T., 277
Pagels, Elaine, 125
Payne, William, 69, 146, 149, 151
Phillips, Ron, 189
Philo, 79
Plantinga, Alvin, 56
Plato, 47, 78, 201, 204, 253
Plutarch, 19
Powlison, David, 94, 95, 148, 207
Poythress, Vern S., 272
Prince, Derek, 151, 174, 175
Proctor, John, 99
Pruss, Alexander, 244

Rhodes, Ron, 281
Ross, Hugh, 281
Ryle, J. C., 223

Samples, Kenneth R., 281
Shafer-Landau, Russ, 204
Schleiermacher, Friedrich, 30, 122, 126
Schnarr, Grant, 11
Simon (Magus), 155–6
Sjöberg, Kjell, 158
Smith, Mark S., 278
Socrates, 47, 194–5, 253–4
Spurgeon, Charles H., 200, 222
Stevens, David E., 272
Strauss, David F., 122, 126
Strieber, Whitley, 139–41
Swinburne, Richard, 211

Tate, Marvin E., 27
Thigpen, Paul, 284
Thomas, Emily, 52
Toropin, Konstantin, 139
Tozer, A. W., 222

Unger, Merrill F., 121, 163–4
Usman, Adil, 41

Wagner, C. Peter, 146, 148–58, 164, 180, 260, 272, 284
Walton, J. Harvey, 10–16, 22, 26, 27–8, 34, 68–9, 93–4, 130–4, 137, 142–3, 279
Walton, John H., 10–16, 22, 26, 27–8, 34, 68–9, 81, 93–4, 130–4, 137, 142–3, 279
Warner, Timothy M., 149
Weldon, John, 281
Wiebe, Phillip H., 138

Wierenga, Edward R., 56
Wink, Walter, 43, 72, 85, 122–6, 128–9, 137, 260
Wray, T. J., 125

Yoder, Daniel, 184
Yong, Amos, 122

Zacharias, Nathan, 202
Zacharias, Ravi, 202

www.ingramcontent.com/pod-product-compliance
Lightning Source LLC
Chambersburg PA
CBHW071933240426
43668CB00038B/1423